Lightfoot Guide to the Via Francigena

Edition 9

Canterbury to The Great Saint Bernard Pass

1239 kilometres

www.pilgrimagepublications.com

Copyright 2023 Pilgrimage Publications All rights reserved.
ISBN: 978-2-917183-40-3

The authors have done their best to ensure the accuracy and currency of the information in this Lightfoot Guide to the Via Francigena, however they can accept no responsibility for any loss, injury or inconvenience sustained by any traveller as a result of information contained in the guide. Changes will inevitably occur within the life-span of this edition and the authors welcome notification of such changes and any other feedback that will enable them to enhance the quality of the guide.

The Modern via Francigena of Sigeric

The Lightfoot Guide to the via Francigena, written by Paul Chinn and Babette Gallard presents, in great detail, the official route for walkers from Canterbury Cathedral to Saint Peter's Square in Rome, as endorsed by the European Association of Via Francigena.

The European Association of Via Francigena (AEVF), founded in 2001, is the custodian of the Cultural Route of the via Francigena. In 2006 it became the official body recognised by the Council of Europe for supporting, promoting and developing the route.

However, the route would not exist without the enormous support of the communities along its length and the many associations that have participated in its mapping and signposting and giving encouragement and support to those setting foot on the route.

In France the via Francigena has been adopted by the Fédération Française de la Randonnée Pédestre (FFRP) as the GR°145. GR° is a registered trademark of the FFRP.

About the Authors:

We are two very ordinary people who quit the world of business and stumbled on the St James Way during our search for a more viable, rewarding alternative to our previous lifestyle. Since then we have completed numerous pilgrimages, one of which was particularly tough and finally prompted us to create Pilgrimage Publications and the Lightfoot Guide series in 2006. We have no religious beliefs, but share a 'wanderlust' and need to know about and contribute to the world we occupy.

Pilgrimage Publications has 4 very basic aims:

To enable those who share our 'wanderlust' to follow pilgrim routes all over the world.

To ensure Lightfoot Guides are as current and accurate as possible, using pilgrim feedback as a major source of information.

To use eco-friendly materials and methods for the publication of Lightfoot Guides and travel books.

To promote eco-friendly travel.

Also by Lightfoot Guides:
Lightfoot Guide to the via Francigena:
Canterbury to The Great Saint Bernard Pass
Lightfoot Guide to the via Podiensis
Lightfoot Guide to the Three Saints Way:
Winchester to Mont St Michel
Mont St Michel to St Jean d'Angely
Lightfoot Guide to the via Domitia:
Arles to Vercelli
Lightfoot Companion:
to the via Francigena-Canterbury to The Grand Saint Bernard Pass
to the via Francigena-The Grand Saint Bernard Pass to Saint Peter's Square
to the via Domitia
Lightfoot Guide to Foraging-Wild Foods by the Wayside
A guide to over 130 of the most common edible and medicinal plants in Western Europe
Your Camino
A guide to assist in preparation for a pilgrimage to Santiago de Compostela
Slackpacking the Camino Frances
Taking (some of) the pain out of you pilgrimage to Santiago de Compostela
Camino Lingo
A cheats' guide to speaking Spanish on the Camino English/Spanish and Dutch/Spanish
Cover: L'Abbaye de Mormant - by Jannina Veit Teuten
jannina.net

By offering choices of route, stopping places and accommodation styles the Lightfoot Guides are designed to enable everyone to meet their personal goals and enjoy the best, whilst avoiding the worst, of following the ancient pilgrimage routes.

The authors would like to emphasise that they have made great efforts to use only public footpaths and to respect private property. Historically, pilgrims may not have been so severely restricted by ownership rights and the pressures of expanding populations, but unfortunately this is no longer the case. Today, even the most free-spirited traveller must adhere to commonly accepted routes. Failure to do so will only antagonise local residents, encourage the closure of routes and inhibit pilgrims following on behind.

Please let us know about any changes to the route or inaccuracies within this guide book. Email us at mail@pilgrimagepublications.com

Our special thanks go to:

The many pilgrims who have willing shared information on their journeys.

Sylvia Nilsen, Jonas Ewe and the Confraternity of Pilgrims to Rome for their support of the invaluable facebook group web.facebook.com/groups/19899007360

The late Francis Geere for his tireless dedication to the route and those that pass along it.

Adelaide Trezzini for her contribution to the development and mapping of the via Francigena route www.francigena-international.org

Openstreetmap: The maps in this book are derived from data provided by © OpenStreetMap contributors (www.openstreetmap.org) and the cartography is licensed under the Creative Commons Attribution-ShareAlike 2.0 license (CC BY-SA).

The many contributors to open source software that brings high quality tools to us all.

Wiki Commons for providing photos licensed and attributed under the Creative Commons Attribution-Share Alike 4.0 International license.

The many associations that have cleared and signposted the way.

The families along the route that have willingly opened their homes to countless strangers.

Jannina Veit Teuten for her contribution to reawakening knowledge of the via Francigena in the many communities that straddle the route and for allowing the use of her watercolours in this book - jannina.net

Contents

Introduction   2
The via Francigena Pilgrimage   3
Using Your Lightfoot Guide   4
Finding Your Way   8
The Basics   10
Resources   16
What to Take   18

No.	km	Stage	
1	17.3	Canterbury to Shepherdswell	20
2	15.4	Shepherdswell to Dover	25
3	21.2	Calais to Wissant	29
4	26.0	Wissant to Guînes	37
5	30.7	Guînes to Tournehem-sur-la-Hem	41
6	19.2	Tournehem-sur-la-Hem to Wisques	46
7	23.3	Wisques to Thérouanne	50
8	19.3	Thérouanne to Amettes	55
9	22.0	Amettes to Bruay-la-Buissière	59
10	25.2	Bruay-la-Buissière to Ablain-Saint-Nazaire	64
11	21.5	Ablain-Saint-Nazaire to Arras	69
12	26.9	Arras to Bapaume	74
13	30.7	Bapaume to Péronne	77
14	33.4	Péronne to Saint-Quentin	81
15	35.5	Saint-Quentin to La Fère	85
16	33.0	La Fère to Laon	88
17	29.2	Laon to Corbeny	93
18	23.6	Corbeny to Hertmonville	97
19	16.6	Hermonville to Reims	101
20	17.8	Reims to Verzenay	105
21	23.5	Verzenay to Condé-sur-Marne	108
22	18.7	Condé-sur-Marne to Châlons-en-Champagne	112
23	23.4	Châlons to La-Chaussée-sur-Marne	116
24	22.5	La-Chaussée-sur-Marne to Vitry-le-François	122
25	21.0	Vitry to Saint-Remy-en-Bouzemont	125
26	25.0	Saint-Remy-en-Bouzemont to Lentilles	128
27	33.0	Lentilles to Brienne-le-Château	131
28	27.6	Brienne-le-Château to Dolancourt	135
29	27.1	Dolancourt to Clairvaux	140
30	23.8	Clairvaux to Châteauvillain	147
31	22.4	Châteauvillain to Mormant	151
32	34.9	Mormant to Langres	154
33	24.4	Langres to Torcenay	160
34	35.8	Torcenay to Champlitte	165
35	18.6	Champlitte to Dampierre-sur-Salon	170
36	34.8	Dampierre-sur-Salon to Bucey-lès-Gy	173
37	31.9	Bucey-lès-Gy to Besançon	177
38	37.6	Besançon to Ornans	183
39	38.8	Ornans to Pontarlier	192
40	22.9	Pontarlier to Jougne	196
41	19.3	Jougne to Orbe	202
42	25.9	Orbe to Cossonay	206
43	25.6	Cossonay to Lausanne	215
44	35.0	Lausanne to Villeneuve	220
45	30.7	Villeneuve to Saint-Maurice	225
46	17.6	Saint-Maurice to Martigny	231
47	20.7	Martigny to Orsières	235
48	27.4	Orsières to Col-Grand-St-Bernard	239

Introduction

Traveller, there is no path, paths are made by walking.

Antonio Machado

The via Francigena Pilgrimage

The epitome of the medieval travelling man, the *homo viator*, was the pilgrim who embarked on a journey towards one of Christianity's holy destinations. The practice of peregrination was presented as an example of faith and charity, linked to the metaphor of our journey towards the ultimate spiritual and heavenly goal.
The main destinations were Rome, Jerusalem and Santiago de Compostela, carried out on foot, with the help of nothing more than a *burdon*–a pilgrim staff.
The routes to the holy destinations were of course not a single road but a network connecting many starting points and adapting to avoid both physical and human barriers en route.

The via Francigena, connecting northern Europe to Rome, was also not a single road, but a collection of several possible routes, which changed over the centuries as trade and the pilgrimage culture developed and then waned. Depending on the time of year, political situation, and relative popularity of the shrines of saints along the route, travellers may have used any of three or four crossings over the Alps and the Apennines.
First documented as the Lombard Way and later the Iter Francorum. The via Francigena was only mentioned as such in the Actum Clusi, a parchment produced in 876 in the Abbey of San Salvatore al Monte Amiata (Tuscany).
Then, at the end of the 10th century, Sigeric the Serious, Archbishop of Canterbury, used the via Francigena to travel to Rome for his consecration by Pope John XV. He recorded his return journey, and the places where he stopped, in a document which is now held in the British Library, but nothing in it suggests that the route was new or unique. His itinerary lists the seventy-nine *submansiones*, which have formed the basis of the via Francigena Sigerico as we know it today.
Not surprisingly the *submansiones* typically lie on the vestiges of the Roman road network that was constructed to facilitate trade, conquest and occupation of Britain and Gaul. These roads offer the shortest route from the Channel coast to Rome and even 1100 years after Sigeric's journey they are clearly identifiable features of the landscape.
This book traces the via Francigena from Canterbury to the summit of the Great Saint Bernard Pass - *Col Grand Saint Bernard/ Colle del Gran San Bernardo*. Volume 2 of the series

Using Your Lightfoot Guide

Sigeric's Chronicle

completes the journey to Rome. The Lightfoot Companions provide more information on the culture and history of the places that you will encounter on the way.

Layout

You will find an introductory section followed by 48 chapters, each of which covers a segment or stage of the "Official Route". Each chapter contains:

- A stage summary
- Cultural highlights
- Detailed instructions
- One or more maps
- An altitude profile
- Route alternatives
- Addresses and contact information for accommodation and tourist information points

Accommodation is not only listed for the stage ends but for the entire length of the stage so that is up to you and your body where you decide to stop.

The book charts the "Official Route" for the via Francigena as endorsed by the AEVF. However, over the years this has grown substantially for reasons of safety, tourism and expediency adding as much as 700 kilometres to the route followed by Archbishop Sigeric.

Where available Alternate Routes are also provided that will reduce the length of your journey, take you to places of interest or provide the possibility of travelling more closely in Sigeric's footsteps or more likely hoof-prints. The shorter routes are titled "Direct Route". You will note that stage lengths vary considerably. Many factors influence this, including the availability of accommodation, the difficulty of the stage or perhaps that of prior or subsequent stages.

Using Your Lightfoot Guide

Stages
The stages in this book should not be thought of as definitive, but an initial planning guide. The distances can be covered by an average physically fit walker with a moderately loaded pack in fair weather conditions. They are of course influenced by availability of accommodation and points of interest while also recognising that many readers of this book will be constrained by Schengen visa restrictions. As a result of striving to achieve these goals the stages do not always conform to the stages suggested by the European Association of the via Francigena (AEVF). but you must decide both in the planning stage and when walking just where to break your journey.

Chapter contents:
Summary
The summary provides distance and ascent and descent details as well as overall progress statistics. It will describe the conditions that you can expect to encounter during the stage. In planning your day, 4 km/hour is the usual rate of progress for a hiker over level ground, falling to 3 km/hour or less on steep ascents and descents.

Cultural Highlights
A cultural perspective on the area is provided to prepare the mind as well as the body for the day ahead. More historical and cultural information can be found in the Lightfoot Companion to this guide.

Instructions
The entire route has been GPS traced in detail and every significant intersection logged using GPS co-ordinates and a way point description. Each instruction is identified by its distance from the start of a stage or the alternate route in tenths of kilometres.
Altitudes have been obtained from the best currently available satellite radar data.
It is very likely that you will use a GPS enabled smartphone or sports watch to keep track of your distance. While these devices are very useful their accuracy can be affected by both the environment and the way they are used. In deep valleys and thick woodland satellite signals will be subject to reflections leading to more apparent movement. Military advice is to allow for a 6-7% over estimate of distance travelled under these conditions. When a device is stationary for long periods reflections will again create apparent movement leading to an increased estimate of distance travelled. It is good practice to pause device logging when you are stationary for more than a few minutes.
In addition to the basic instruction, where necessary a visual confirmation is included in [].
The GPS coordinates of each way point can be downloaded from the "GPS Download" tab at the foot the book description page at www.pilgrimagepublications.com
The route signposting has improved dramatically since our first edition and we hope that you will only need the instructions where there are missing signs, doubt over the intended direction or where you choose to use one of the many Alternate Routes.

Maps
The maps provide a north-up visual representation of the route. To reduce clutter on the maps, way points are only shown with a minimum of a 1 km separation. However, all way points and their descriptions are presented in the text. The maps also show the location of each listed accommodation option and information point.
To optimise space within the book the scale varies from map to map but way point distance identifiers and the scale bar allow you to quickly assess your progress and route options.

Altitude Profile
The profiles provide both a rapid visual assessment of the difficulty of each stage with the altitude variations and distance to intermediate towns. Both vertical and horizontal scales are adjusted by stage.
Where alternate routes offer a distance advantage over the "Official Route" then a contrasting profile for the shorter route will also be shown. This may span several stages.
At the end of the book you will find altitude/distance profiles of the entire route from the

Using Your Lightfoot Guide

Canterbury Cathedral to the Col Grand Saint Bernard contrasted with a shorter route taking advantage of the alternate trails that follow more closely the path of Sigeric.

Accommodation Listings

A price banding is used based on the least expensive mid-season option for two people in each establishment–accurate at the time of entry, but of course subject to change. For simplicity, the listing is divided into 4 price bands:

A > (€) 75 B = (€) 40–75 C = (€) 0–40 D = Donation

A range of options is provided where they are available. Prices may or may not include breakfast and some establishments make a supplementary charge for pets. In general, dogs are not welcome in Commercial or Religious Hostels. The general rule for accommodation in Religious Houses is that reservations must be made 24 hours ahead of arrival.

Each listing has been verified before publication of this guide and while in general the accommodation along the route is rarely full, seasonality and increasing popularity of the route mean this cannot be guaranteed. Commercial pressures may also lead to closure or change of ownership between publication and when you travel. We therefore recommend a general rule of where possible booking 48 hours in advance providing enough time for you to find alternatives if your first choice is not available. Longer range planning is possible, but will create pressures to meet a schedule that may prove impossible in the light of weather or injury. In the eBook edition of this guide phone numbers, email and web addresses are presented as active links. There is an inevitable churn in mobile phone numbers, email and web addresses as staff change, technology is updated or cost savings sought. While all the listing data is believed accurate at the time of writing, change will occur and so if you do not receive a response or your messages are rejected then make a web search on the name of the establishment and double check the details.

Donation means just that, you are expected to give what you can and think the accommodation warrants, but remember nothing is free. The hostels require heating, cleaning and maintenance and if you do not pay then someone else must. As a guide 15€ or 20€ per person is normal without an evening meal for which you should expect to pay a similar amount again.

PR-indicates accommodation on which we have received a positive pilgrim recommendation.

Accommodation is classified as:

 Pilgrim Hostel

Hostels that principally accommodate via Francigena pilgrims. Usually with dormitory accommodation, kitchen and shared bathrooms. The hostels may be run by commercial, municipal or religious authorities and may require to see your pilgrim credentials.

 Religious Hostel

A facility with accommodation managed by a religious group which may have space for via Francigena pilgrims. Usually with dormitory accommodation, shared bathrooms and kitchen facilities or the possibility of prepared meals. Credentials will be required. You may find that priority has been given to increasing numbers of homeless refugees.

 Commercial Hostel

Commercial or municipal hostel including youth hostels and gîte d'etape in France. Usually with dormitory accommodation, kitchen facilities and shared bathrooms.

Using Your Lightfoot Guide

 Church or Religious Organisation

Places where limited, basic accommodation or assistance may be offered. Credentials will be required.

 Pilgrim Hosts

Families or secular organisations that wish to support pilgrims by offering limited accommodation in their homes. Credentials will be required.

 Bed and Breakfast

More expensive commercial home accommodation including chambres d'hôtes in France and agriturismos in Italy which may charge by room or by person. There are usually double or family sized rooms with the possibility of a private bathroom. Bed and Breakfasts and agriturismos may be isolated from shops and restaurants. Often dinner can be provided if requested in advance. Kitchen access may also be possible.

 Hotel

Hotels normally are priced by room. Where there is a choice of room types the price band is given for the room type with the lowest price. In some situations there may be seasonal premiums. Many of the hotel chains and booking sites use similar pricing principles to airlines and vary their prices by both time of day of your booking and room availability.

 Room, apartment or whole house rental

Self catering accommodation including *affittacamere*. Multi-room or whole house rentals may have a minimum stay of more than 1 night. Beware of additional costs for cleaning and utilities and tourist taxes.

 Camp-grounds

Generally well equipped camp-sites with showers, laundry facilities and mini-markets. Some will also have a bar/restaurant. In addition to offering sites for tents most offer pre-erected tent, mobile home or chalet rental. They are normally open from early April to late October. While "wild" camping does take place along the route it is illegal in Italy.

 Information Points

Tourist offices and town halls where information can be found on accommodation and services in the community. They may also be willing to assist with making forward bookings. Hours can be erratic, particularly in the low season.

Accommodation booking sites such as booking.com, agoda.com and airbnb.com offer a vast array of options. However, many of the addresses listed in the guide do not have a presence on these sites and the prices offered by direct booking and the booking sites may also differ. It is wise to compare.

Finding Your Way

In England the route follows the established and well sign posted North Downs Way - a long distance footpath leading from Farnham, in the county of Surrey, via Canterbury, to Dover on the Channel coast. The path was fully opened in 1978 following a more scenic route than the prior Pilgrim's Way which was judged to use too many tarmac roads. In Canterbury you will also find a small number of via Francigena signs.

In France, the via Francigena has been adopted as a national footpath in the form of a route Grand Randonée.

The standards for a GR® path are set by the Fédération Française de la Randonnée (FFRP) and require very sparing use of tarmac roads. With echoes of the North Downs Way, in Pas-de-Calais, now a department in Hauts de France, the route has been constructed by largely following the pre-exiting GR®128 while in the Grand Est an existing chemin de St Jacques GR®654 has been adopted. This approach has led to better route maintenance, but at the expense of a loss of some of the historical context e.g. many of the Sigeric *submansiones* are bypassed and it has also led to a substantial increase in distance. The Alternate Routes in this guide endeavour to counter some of these excesses.

The GR® signposting comprises red and white painted or adhesive signs sometimes also showing the number of the GR®. Beware of confusion where two GR® routes intersect it is often unclear to which route the signs refer.

On the GR®145 the red and white signs have been supplemented with bi-directional via Francigena signs on metal or wooden poles. These are normally located at main intersections where access is possible for the installation crews and are typically between 1 and 3 kilometres apart. In populated areas both types of sign are subject to vandalism, while in agricultural areas free standing signs may have been damaged by farm machinery. As a result it is not possible to rely on every junction being clearly signed.

In Bourgogne-Franche-Comté a stencilled yellow and white pilgrim is extensively used in addition to the GR®145 signs or those from the overlapping GR®595 and GR®5 trails.

The book will follow the GR®145, which we term the "Official Route" ,except for the final stage in France where the GR®145 diverts towards Sainte Croix following an earlier and erroneous view that the Sigeric route making a wide and unnecessary diversion to Yverdon-les-Bains.

Finding Your Way

Turn right

Turn Left

Straight on

Wrong Way

In Switzerland the via Francigena has been established as regional walking Route N° 70 by Swissmobility - the national trail mapping and signposting authority. There are good clear signposts at most intersections showing this name and often with time or distance measurements to the next commune. Between these signs yellow diamonds indicate that you are on the route.

Unfortunately part of Route N° 70 follows an earlier interpretation of the historic pilgrim route believing that Sigeric crossed the Swiss border near Sainte Croix and not as now believed near Jougne. Our route will follow this current interpretation. Nonetheless we will describe Route N° 70 as the "Official Route" from Orbe to the Italian border. In common with England and France, the desire for scenic beauty and pathway standards will add considerably to the distances that the long distance pilgrim will need to travel and so we  will continue to propose Alternative Routes which will ease your journey or have greater historical significance.

The Basics

The Basics in Britain

Currency
The pound sterling - £. A few of the big shops will accept Euros, but they are rarely used in Britain. Standard Banking Hours Monday-Friday 09:30 - 15.30. Some branches stay open until 17.30, and a few are open Saturday morning. Most banks will have an ATM (Automated Teller Machine) outside the bank where you can draw out money with a credit or debit card. Many of these are available to use 24 hours a day, but some do still close for a few hours during the night. You may be charged for their use.

Emergencies
999 is the long standing emergency number for the United Kingdom, but calls are also accepted on the European Union emergency number, 112, and from mobile phones, the United States emergency number, 911. All calls are answered by 999 operators. Calls are always free.

Post Offices
Standard Opening Hours 09.00 - 17.30 Monday - Friday. Some open on Saturday morning. Post Offices are increasingly found as counters within other shops. Post Offices are shut on Sundays and Bank Holidays. You can find out if a post office offers a Poste Restante service by emailing customercare@postoffice.co.uk. Once set up, simply send your letter or package to the chosen Post Office. The Post Office will normally retain for up to 14 days and then return it if not recovered and you have included a return address.

Telephones
There are still public telephones in a number of public places. Some of them also give internet access. Illustrations and instructions demonstrate how to use the phone. Mobile phone SIM cards can be purchased from phone and many convenience stores together with prepayment or top up. European legislation has eliminated roaming charges for phones using European SIMs, but beware exceeding you pre-paid data limit when higher charges may be incurred. There are a number of international internet services that will provide top-ups while travelling with on-line payment.

Basic Business Hours
Mondays - Saturdays 09.00 - 17.30, though some shopping centres stay open until 8 pm or later. Sunday - 10.00 - 16.00, though Sunday shopping has become popular in recent years and most large shops in towns are open for 6 hours on Sundays. On public holidays some shops open and some shops do not. Nearly all shops are closed on Christmas and New Year's Day. Most shopping centres are closed on Easter Sunday with reduced shopping hours on Easter Monday. In villages, some rural shops still follow the tradition of an early closing day (usually a Wednesday) when they close at 13.00.

Health Care
Information on accessing healthcare for visitors to the UK from EU countries, Norway, Iceland, Liechtenstein and Switzerland can be found at www.gov.uk/guidance/healthcare-for-eu-and-efta-citizens-visiting-the-uk

The Basics

Food
British food has traditionally been based on beef, lamb, pork, chicken and fish and generally served with potatoes and one other vegetable, but now you can eat any meal from just about every culture - the Indian curry probably being the most popular. You will find that food is served at just about every hour of the day, but rarely cheaply. The traditional English pub now generally offers good food at reasonable prices.

Vegetarian and Vegan options are widely available.

Accommodation
English hotels are graded from zero to five stars and the price more or less corresponds to the number of stars. Bed and Breakfast (B&B) provide guests with accommodation in private houses and are served breakfast by the owner, who often has useful local knowledge. Youth Hostels provide accommodation where guests can rent a bed (sometimes a bunk bed) in a dormitory and share a common bathroom, kitchen, and lounge. As the birthplace of modern camping, England has a large number of places to stay of every kind – from small, quiet spots to big lively parks offering a wide range of facilities and entertainment.

Public Transport
There are a number of train companies in the UK, with Network Rail managing most of the national network. Prices can be high without concessions. You can book and purchase tickets at www.thetrainline.com . Eurostar offers services between London or Ashford, Kent to Paris and Brussels via the Channel tunnel www.eurostar.com .

Intercity bus services are plentiful and often cheaper than trains, while local bus networks can be found in most municipalities although rural communities are not well served.

Taxis are broadly available. However, a ride in an iconic black cab in London will be significantly more expensive than other public transport options. Uber is present in most large towns.

Air transport has become dominated by the budget carriers with Ryanair and easyjet the market leaders.

The Dover - Calais ferry route is currently operated by 2 ferry companies. The DFDS Seaways service runs up to 15 times per day with a sailing duration of around 1 hour 30 minutes ww.dfds.com while the P&O Ferries service runs up to 23 times per day also with a duration from 1 hr 30 minutes www.poferries.com . A choice of meals can be obtained on the ferries. The ferry services are largely targeted at motorists and as a consequence, services for foot-passengers have been substantially reduced or removed from time to time as cost saving measures. At the time of writing P&O offer limited day time only crossings for foot-passengers while DFDS have withdrawn the service completely. Cyclists are generally more welcome but it would be wise for both groups to check before making firm plans.

The Basics

The Basics in France

Currency:
Euro - €. Standard banking Hours: Monday-Friday 09.30-12.00 and 14.00-16.00. Closed on Sundays and usually Monday, with half day opening on Saturday morning . ATM's are available at most banks and post offices and in larger supermarkets.

Emergencies
112 will give you access to: Fire, Police, Ambulance, Coastguard, Mountain Rescue or Cave Rescue. The call is free and can be dialled from any telephone (including mobile phones).

Post Offices (La Poste)
Standard opening hours Mon - Fri - 09.30-12.00 and 14.00-17.00. Half day opening on Saturday morning. You can receive mail at the central post offices of most towns. It should be addressed (preferably with the surname first and in capitals) "Poste Restante, Poste Centrale", followed by the name of the town and its postal code. To collect your mail you will need a passport or other convincing ID, and there may be a charge of around a euro. You should ask for all your names to be checked, as filing systems are not brilliant. Stamps may also be purchased from a *tabac*.

Telephones
You can make domestic and international phone calls from any public telephone box and can receive calls where there is a logo of a ringing bell.

There are 4 major mobile phone providers in France and all of them are offering prepaid SIM cards for tourists:- Orange, SFR, Free Mobile, Bouygues Telecom

Orange is the largest operator and has perhaps the best coverage. There are long sections of the route where there is no coverage. You can buy a pre-paid SIM directly from the operator's stores that can be found in most cities. However, be aware that some of the tourist packages are restrictive.

Basic Business Hours
08.00-12.00 and 14.00-18.00. Almost everything in France - shops, museums, tourist offices etc. - close for two hours at midday. Food shops often don't reopen until half way through the afternoon, but close at 19.30 or 20.00. The standard closing days are Sunday and Monday in small towns, but you will find that many large supermarkets are now staying open throughout the day.

Boulangeries will open from 06.00 or 07.00 to 12.00 and then reopen at 16.00 to 19.00.

Health Care
All EU citizens are eligible for free health care if they have the correct documentation. Non-EU citizens must arrange personal health insurance.

The Basics

Food
In France, the best way of eating breakfast is in a bar or café, at a fraction of the cost charged by most hotels. Expect a croissant or some bread with coffee or hot chocolate.

At lunchtime and sometimes in the evenings you'll find most cafés and restaurants offering a plat du jour, which is by far the cheapest alternative if you don't fancy cooking yourself.

Evening meals will be more expensive, although a *formule* may offer a small discount if you take 2 or 3 courses. Outside large towns, vegetarian options are rarely displayed, but will normally be provided if requested. Very few restaurants offer a pilgrim menu.

Accommodation
In country areas, in addition to standard hotels, you will come across chambre d'hôtes and ferme auberge, bed and breakfast accommodation in someone's house or farm. These are rarely an especially cheap option, usually costing the equivalent of a two star hotel and are progressively moving up market.

Youth hostels (auberges de jeunesse) are great for travellers on a budget. They are often beautifully sited and they allow you to cut costs by preparing your own food in their kitchens or eating in cheap canteens.

A feature of following pilgrim trails in France is that many private homes will offer to pilgrims accommodation, an with an evening meal and breakfast *en famille* either for a donation or a price substantially less than commercial alternatives - in this book these are described as "pilgrim hosts" 🏠 . An extended list may be obtained from the Confraternity of Pilgrims to Rome or the Fédération Française Via Francigena

Gîte d'étape are community facilities and provide bunk beds with kitchen and washing facilities at a reasonable price.

Gîte and Gîte rural tend to be larger apartments or entire houses and are normally let for more than one night. However when they are available owners are frequently willing to make an exception.

Campsites in France are nearly always clean and have plenty of hot water. On the coast there are superior categories of campsite where you will pay prices similar to those of a hotel for access to facilities such as bars, restaurants and usually elaborate swimming pools.

AirBnB is active in the major cities and tourist zones, but less so in rural communities.

Public Transport
The French railway network is operated by the state-run SNCF, and is managed as a public service. The network includes suburban, regional and national and international lines. SNCF also operates a high speed train (TGV) service linking most French regions and is a cheaper alternative to the plane. International TGV services also link Paris with London (by Eurostar) and Brussels and Amsterdam (by Thalys). Book tickets at www.oui.sncf.fr .

The Basics

Intercity bus services are cheaper than rail but less frequent than in the UK. Eurolines offer national and international services www.eurolines.fr while FLixbus is growing rapidly throughout Europe www.flix.com .

Local buses and trams are again operated as a public service and are excellent in large cities. However rural services are poor often compounded by borders between administrative authorities. Where rural services exist they will largely be timed to serve school hours.

Sharing of cars with a contribution to fuel and toll charges *covoiturage* is increasingly popular. Bookings can be made at www.blablacar.fr .

Taxis are highly regulated in France with restrictions on where they can operate and what they can charge. In the cities they can be expensive and have resisted the entry of Uber although this is beginning to happen. in major cities. Most small towns or large villages will have a taxi operator to provide essential services for the population that do not have a car. You may see taxi and ambulance are almost interchangeable. These can be booked by telephone with number obtained from the internet, a local bar or Mairie.

Air France operates between a number of the country's main airports such as Paris, Bordeaux, Nice and Lyon, although services to and from smaller regional airports tend to centre on Paris. Budget airlines are increasing the number of internal flights and as a result Air France prices are falling.

In periods of social and economic change transport strikes - *les greves* - are a favourite weapon of resistance and can occur without warning. If your journey timing is vital then give yourself some slack or have a fall back plan.

The Basics in Switzerland

Currency:
Swiss Franc CHF. Standard banking Hours: 08:30–16:30 (Mon–Fri). Closed on Saturdays and Sundays

Emergencies
Dial the police on 117 who will tell you where to call or directly connect you. If you need an ambulance, dial 144.

Post Offices
Post offices opening times vary but are typically Monday to Friday 8.30 to 12.00 and 13.30 to 18.30 with Saturday 8.30 to 12.00. Stamps can be bought in Post Offices and tobacconists' shops. Poste Restante is available at any post office: all you need to know is that town's four figure postal code. Swiss phonebooks and www.post.ch list them. The correct format is, for example: Your Name, Poste Restante, CH-3920 Zermatt ("CH" is the standard postal designation for Switzerland).To minimize confusion at pickup, you should ask anyone writing to you to print your surname in underlined capitals, and include only one initial. If you want to receive mail at a smaller countryside office in the German-speaking part of the country (where the term "Poste Restante" may be less understood), you should get your correspondents to add the German equivalent – Postlagernde Briefe – to the address. You

The Basics

need your passport to pick up your mail, and the service is always free. Uncollected mail is returned to sender after 30 days.

Basic Business Hours
Monday, Tuesday, Wednesday, Friday 09.00 to 18.00. Shops in smaller towns and villages may close on Monday (either morning or all day). Thursday 09.00 to 20.00 or 21.00 (mainly in larger cities and towns). Saturday 09.00 to 16.00. Sunday and holidays closed (except for bakeries, which may be open in the morning).

Health Care
Switzerland has agreements with the EU states as well as the EFTA states Iceland and Norway, which provide for a so-called mutual benefits assistance. Citizens living outside these countries must arrange personal health insurance.

Food
Swiss cuisine draws heavily on its influences from its French, Italian and German neighbours and also from the climatic and geographic conditions of the area. Alpine food features soup and heavier kinds of food. Cheese is ever present.

There are also some good wines worth investigating, but watch out - nothing in Switzerland is cheap.

Accommodation
Swiss hotels are very similar to the French, in terms of the types available. In addition to standard hotels, you will also find chambre d'hotes, ferme auberge and bed and breakfast accommodation in someone's house or farm. Youth hostels are a good, cheaper option, but unfortunately there are not many on the Via Francigena route. As you would probably expect, Swiss campsites are well equipped and provide just about everything the average camper will need. Price and location are the only possible drawbacks. AirBnB is active in cities and larger towns.

Public Transport
Switzerland claims one of the world's most reliable public transport services, which makes reaching even the most remote parts of the country relatively easy, but this comes at a price. Without a discount card trains can be prohibitively expensive www.sbb.ch .

Cities boast efficient public transportation. Trams and buses form the core of the urban network with a choice of a one hour ticket, one day or one month pass or a prepaid discount card.

Almost all villages in Switzerland can be reach by regional buses, many of which depart several times throughout the day. PostBus Switzerland operates regional and rural services with a timetable integrated with the rail network www.postauto.ch .

Taxis are available in cities, but are expensive with prices sometimes doubling at night. Be sure to agree a price at the beginning of your journey. Uber is currently only available in the larger cities.

Resources

Useful Links

www.viefrancigene.org - the official website of the European Association of the via Francigena (AEVF) and source for pilgrim credentials.

www.pilgrimstorome.org.uk - the Confraternity of Pilgrims to Rome provide practical information and sell credentials, guides and souvenirs.

www.francigena-international.org - International Association for the via Francigena - publishes maps of the route in walking stages as well as route instructions and accommodation lists .

www.viefrancigene.com - an Italian site providing information and credentials.

www.ffvf.fr – French language site containing: news of the via Francigena in France,. Also sells credentials and an accommodation list for the route in France.

www.tourisme-champagne-ardenne.com/voir-faire/randonnees-pedestres/chemins-de-grande-randonnee-en-champagne-ardenne – multilingual site containing: information on the route in the Champagne-Ardenne region of France

www.tourisme-langres.com/fr/GRANDE-RANDONNEE-GR145_viafrancigena-gr145 – multilingualsite with information on the route in the south of the Grand Est

gronze.com - maps and accommodation lists

pelgrimswegen.nl - pilgrims association in the Netherlands

www.eurovia.tv - a German language site with information on European pilgrim trails

www.camminideuropageie.com - an Italian, Spanish, French collaboration to promote cultural tourism in Europe

www.csj.org.uk - the Confraternity of Saint James UK chapter - providing a wealth of information about the many pilgrim routes to Santiago de Compostela in Spain as well as general guidance and advice to pilgrims and an online bookstore. It is well worth visiting if this is your first pilgrimage.

www.caminoways.com - provides fully organised tours of the via Francigena and the Camino

www.sloways.eu - provides organised tours on foot or bike

www.pilgrimstales.com - Pilgrims Tales Publishing is passionate about inspiring others with the possibility of discovery, understanding and peace through travel.

www.visitbritain.com - nationwide tourism website

www.france.fr - French Tourist Board

www.myswitzerland.com - Swiss national tourist board

osmaps.ordnancesurvey.co.uk - purchase or view maps of the UK

www.ign.fr - purchase or view maps of France

www.schweizmobil.ch - online mapping resources for Switzerland

Facebook:

web.facebook.com/groups/1532376317014068 - large Italian group

web.facebook.com/groups/19899007360 – multilingual group for all with a valid interest in the route

web.facebook.com/groups/251274001687610 – Spanish language group

web.facebook.com/francigenatoscana - the via Francigena in Tuscany

Resources

Recommended Reading

The Art of Pilgrimage	Phil Cousineau
The Essential Walker's Journal	Leslie Sansone
The Pilgrim's France - A Travel Guide to the Saints	Jonathan Sumption
Along the Templar Trail	Brandon Wilson
Rome: A Pilgrim's Companion	David Baldwin
The Age of Pilgrimage: The Medieval Journey to God	Jonathan Sumption
In Search of a Way: two journeys of spiritual discovery	Gerard Hughes
Traveling Souls: Contemporary Pilgrimage Stories	Brian Bouldrey (Editor)

What to Take

It is said that your backpack should weigh no more than 10% of your body weight. If you weigh 75 kg (165 pounds), your backpack should not weigh more than 7.5 kg (16.5 pounds). You will also have to allow for the weight of water (up to 2 litres or 2 kg.)

Mental preparation for your trip begins when reflecting on what is truly essential to take. The more weight, the tougher the walk. You might want to follow this tried and tested maxim:

1. Make a list of only essential items
2. Tear the list in half.
3. Pack your bag
4. Throw half of its contents away

It is wiser to have to buy something en route than carry an unnecessary item. You are never so far from a shop that this is not possible.

Packing Checklist

Backpack (35-40 litres): Your backpack should be suited to your morphology and have a rain cover.

Sleeping bag liner or super thin sleeping bag: Many hostels provide blankets so that a liner is generally sufficient.

Foot wear: (1) Light-weight hiking shoes that are water resistant, but breathable. No need to take hiking boots, which are too heavy and ill-suited for long distance walking and (2) flip flops or sandals, for the evening

Walking poles (optional)

Water bottles (at least 2 litres) or CamelBak (optional)

Documents: Identity Card/Passport, Insurance Card, credit cards, Pilgrim Passport/Credential, and a waterproof bag to put them in.

Miscellaneous: Safety pins (to hang clothes to dry), knife, headlamp, basic sewing kit, mobile phone and charger with international socket adapter, camera (optional), guide book.

Clothing: Invest in clothes that are specifically adapted to hiking or sport, and are breathable, lightweight and quick-dry:
- 2 quick dry T-shirts
- 1 long sleeved shirt
- 1 fleece or sweater for cool evenings
- 1-2 pairs shorts (quick-dry)
- 1 hiking pants
- 1 rain paints
- 1 ultra-light rain coat
- 3 underwear
- 3 pairs of hiking or running socks, which allow for ventilation and reduce friction
- Swim wear
- Pyjamas
- In winter add wind and rain resistant jacket, hat and gloves

Accessories and toiletries:
- Sun: hat, sunglasses, sun screen
- Toiletries: Quick-dry towel, shower gel/shampoo, toothbrush and tooth paste, moisturizer, nail clippers, comb/brush
- Earplugs (snoring protection)
- Soap/detergent for washing clothes.
- Health: First aid kit, blister prevention foot cream (applied before walking to reduce friction), 2nd skin blister patches
- Other medicines, as needed

Canterbury to the Great Saint Bernard Pass
1239 Kilometres

Omnes viae Romam ducunt
All roads lead to Rome

stage 1 — Canterbury to Shepherdswell

Length:	17.3km
Ascent:	319m
Descent:	215m
Canterbury	0km
Col Grand Saint Bernard:	1239km

Canterbury Cathedral

Route: the journey to Dover offers the choice of 2 short days giving ample time for the ferry crossing on the second day or a long first day (33 km) before over-nighting in Dover and perhaps taking an early ferry on your second day.

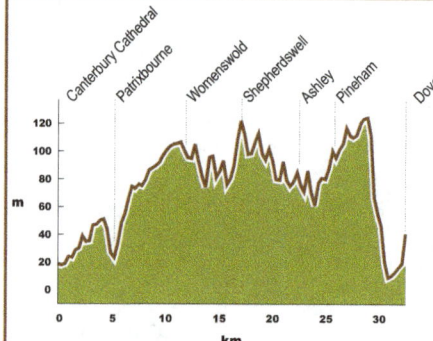

Accommodation in the Shepherdswell area is limited and so be sure to book ahead. The terrain on both stages comprises gentle rolling hills, passing through small Kentish villages. Shepherdswell has a pub that offers both food and drink and even makes space for campers if you buy your dinner there. However there are few other possibilities for refreshment between Canterbury and the outskirts of Dover.

After leaving Canterbury the route from Canterbury to Shepherdswell uses mainly pathways and some minor roads following the signposted North Downs Way (NDW). For the most part the NDW offers easy going for mountain bikers. However, there are sections prohibited to cyclists and there are stiles and kissing gates to be negotiated. The well signed National Cycle Route N° 16 also connects Canterbury to Dover.

There is a choice of Channel ferry companies. However, not all will allow bikes and there have been restrictions on foot passengers in the height of the pandemic. In the day-time, ferries depart hourly but allow time to check in, normally 60 minutes before departure. Allow 90 minutes for the crossing but beware changes in time zone that may add another hour to your schedule. Only online booking was possible at times during the pandemic, please verify the current situation with the company web-sites. In the event of difficulties bus (eurolines) and train services (Eurostar) connect London with destinations in

Canterbury to Shepherdswell — stage 1

France, although it is probable that you would need to back-track by bus or train to Calais.

The Canterbury area has been inhabited since prehistoric times. In the first century AD, the Romans captured the settlement and rebuilt the town with new streets in a grid pattern, with a theatre, temple, forum, public baths and later a wall, enclosing an area of 130 acres (53 hectares), with 7 gates. St Augustine arrived on the coast of Kent as a missionary to England in 597 AD. He was given a church in Canterbury by King Ethelbert whose Queen, Bertha, was already a Christian. Augustine established his seat within the Roman city walls (cathedra – Latin word for seat) and built the first cathedral there, becoming the first Archbishop of Canterbury.

(0.1) On leaving **Canterbury Cathedral** grounds through Christchurch gate turn left onto Burgate Street[Pass the market cross on your right]**(0.3)** Continue straight ahead[Pass church of St Thomas on your right]**(0.4)** Cross over Lower Bridge Street onto Church Street[Magistrates Court on right]**(0.5)** Turn right and then immediately left onto Longport[The grounds of St Augustine's Abbey are behind the buildings on your left]**(0.6)** At the roundabout, bear left[Direction Littlebourne, A257]**(1.0)** Straight ahead on North Holmes Rd[St Martins Church on left]**(1.1)** Turn right onto Spring Lane**(1.2)** Turn right to follow the NDW**(1.3)** Turn left onto footpath[Iron railings on left] **(1.5)** At the T-junction, turn left onto Pilgrim's Way[Sports field on the left] **(1.7)** At the T-junction, turn right to cross the railway bridge**(2.2)** Continue straight ahead on small tarmac road **(2.7)** At the crossroads, continue straight ahead on the track[Towards a line of trees ahead]**(3.2)** Fork left **(4.9)** At the T-junction, bear left[Cycle Route n° 16]**(5.0)** At mini roundabout, bear right direction Patrix-

The North Downs Way

stage 1 — Canterbury to Shepherdswell

bourne**(5.4)**In the centre of **Patrixbourne**, turn right on Patrixbourne Road, towards St Mary's church[Cycle Route N°16 leaves to the left]**(5.6)**Immediately after the last house on the left, turn left onto the path and diagonally cross the field**(5.7)**Turn right, keep the woods close on the left **(6.6)**At the end of the field, bear left through the trees[Highway parallel on the right]**(7.1)**Cross over small road[Road bridge on right]**(7.2)**Bear left and cross field

towards trees**(7.4)**Bear right[Keep the edge of the wood on the left] **(7.6)**Continue along the edge of the field, trees to left[Telephone mast ahead]**(7.7)**Cross Coldharbour Lane and continue straight ahead down the middle of the field **(8.9)**Go through the small wicket gate and continue straight ahead[Telephone mast on left]**(9.4)**Cross the small road and continue straight ahead into the field **(9.9)**At the junction in the tracks bear right[Towards the farmhouse on the ridge]**(10.7)**Continue straight ahead[Upper Digges farmhouse on left]**(10.8)**Turn left onto a track between a line of trees and fence and go through the metal gate **(10.9)**Turn right onto the gravel track**(11.2)**Bear left across the field, towards the road**(11.5)**Cross the road and continue straight ahead on the track[Electricity post to the left] **(12.0)**Fork left**(12.1)**At the junction in **Womenswold** centre, turn left and then immediately right onto a gravelled track[Brick wall and house on the left]**(12.2)**Continue straight ahead along the edge of the field[Line of trees directly on the right]**(12.9)**Cross the road and continue into the wood**(12.9)**At the next road, turn right[Towards Woolage] **(13.0)**Turn left just before entering village and follow the edge of the field[Pass a playground on the right]**(13.2)**Sign indicates cutting across children's playground, but we recommend continuing straight ahead[Around the edge of the field]**(13.3)**Turn right[Towards the road]**(13.3)**Turn left just before reaching the road[Keep hedge to your right]**(13.8)**Turn right through a gap in the hedge and turn left on the road[Farm buildings on the ridge to

Canterbury to Shepherdswell — stage 1

the right]**(13.9)**At the bend in the road, turn right to continue on the track between the trees on the left and the hedge on the right **(15.2)**Turn right towards road**(15.3)**Turn left onto the road[Cross over the railway bridge]**(15.3)**Turn right along Long Lane**(16.1)**Walkers turn right onto the track. Note:- to avoid a stile, cyclists are advised to remain on the road and take the Alternate Route V**16.4)**Turn right on the road and then right again in the direction of Shepherdswell. Note:- Shepherdswell is also known as Sibertswold[Meadow Bank cottage on left]**(16.5)**Immediately after the railway level crossing, turn left through the kissing gate**(16.5)**Pass through the small gate and turn left on the gravel road and then right**(16.6)**Continue straight ahead over the stile**(16.8)**Cross over stile and continue across the field in the direction of the houses**(17.0)**Bear right after going through a 5-bar gate**(17.0)**Continue straight ahead between two fences[Equestrian Centre on the right]**(17.1)**Continue ahead on the narrow path[Wooden fence on the right, high hedge on the left]**(17.2)**At the T-junction with the road, turn right on Mill Lane[Towards the village green] **(17.3)**Arrive at **Shepherdswell** village green with the Bell public house ahead[Church on the left]

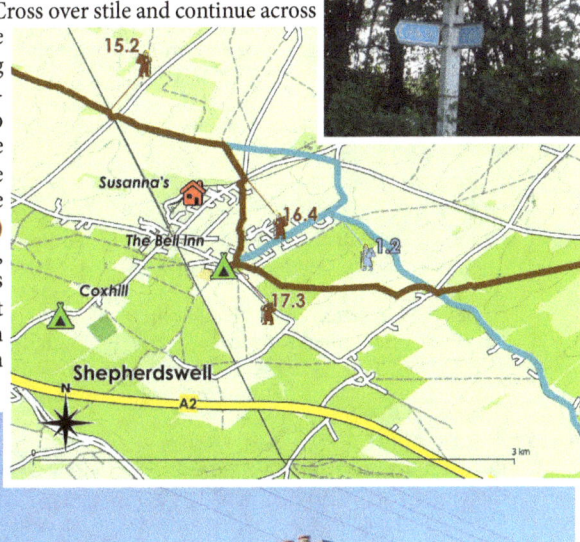

The Bell Inn - Shepherdswell

stage 1 — Canterbury to Shepherdswell

Cyclist's Diversion

Route: this short diversion will enable cyclists to avoid a series of obstacles on the approach to Sherperdswell.

Length:	2.0km
Ascent:	58m
Descent:	11m

(0.0) Continue straight ahead on the road[Long Lane] (0.2) At the crossroads, continue straight ahead[Remain on Long Lane] (0.6) At the next crossroads again continue straight ahead[Pass Eythorne Road on your right] (0.7) At the third crossroads, turn right onto Mill Lane[Follow Cycle Route N° 16 sign] (1.2) At the road junction on the edge of Shepherdswell, continue straight ahead. If you wish to bypass the village, then turn left and follow the Alternate Route from the next section[Cycle Route N° 16, turns left] (2.0) The "Official Route" emerges from the right and continues on the Mill Lane towards the village green[White house "The Old Bakery" on the right]

Accommodation and Tourist Information

Canterbury

YHA, 54 New Dover Road, Canterbury, CT1 3DT, United Kingdom; Tel:+44(0)8453 719010; Email:canterbury@yha.org.uk; www.yha.org.uk; Price:B

B&B - Hornbeams, Jesse's Hill, Canterbury, CT4 6JD, United Kingdom; Tel:+44(0)1227 830119; +44(0)7798601016; Email:hornbeamsbandb@btinternet.com; www.hornbeams.co.uk; Price:A

B&B - The Four Seasons, 77 Sturry Road, Canterbury, CT1 1BU, United Kingdom; Tel:+44(0)1227 787078; Email:bookingenquiries@aol.com; www.bedandbreakfast.eu/; Price:B

Pilgrims Hotel, 18 The Friars, Canterbury, CT1 2AS, United Kingdom; Tel:+44(0)1227 464531; Email:info@thepilgrimshotel.co.uk; www.pilgrimshotel.com; Price:A

Greyfriars Lodge, 6 Stour St.,, Canterbury, CT1 2NR, United Kingdom; Tel:+44(0)1227788455; Email:enquiries@greyfriarslodgecanterbury.co.uk; www.greyfriarslodgecanterbury.com; Price:B; Convenient location free breakfast

Canterbury Cathedral Lodge, The Precincts, Canterbury, CT1 2EH, United Kingdom; Tel:+44(0)1227 865350; Email:stay@canterbury-cathedral.org; canterburycathedrallodge.org; Price:A

Abode Canterbury, 30 High Street, Canterbury, CT1 2RX, United Kingdom; Tel:+44(0)1227 766266; Email:info@abodecanterbury.co.uk; www.abodehotels.co.uk/canterbury; Price:A

Canterbury Camping and Caravanning Club Site[Helen Stewart], Bekesbourne Lane, Canterbury, CT3 4AB, United Kingdom; Tel:+44(0)1227 463216; www.campingandcaravanningclub.co.uk/campsites/uk/kent/canterbury/canterbury; Price:C

Canterbury Visitor Information Centre, 18 High Saint, Canterbury, CT1 2RA, United Kingdom; Tel:+44(0)1227 862162; Email:canterburyinformation@canterbury.gov.uk; canterburymuseums.co.uk/the-beaney/visitor-information/

Shepherdswell

B&B - Susanna's [Susanna Rogers], 20 The Glen, Shepherdswell, CT15 7PF, United Kingdom; Tel:+44(0)7856 297007; +44(0)1304 830367; Email:susanna2705@hotmail.com; Price:B; *This is a family home with 2 dogs a cat and teenage child*

Coxhill Camping, Cox Hill, Shepherdswell, CT15 7ND, United Kingdom; Tel:+44(0)7869 375034; Email:coxhillcamping@gmail.com; www.coxhillcamping.co.uk; Price:C; *Campsite on a working farm*

The Bell Inn, 22 Church Hill, Shepherdswell, CT15 7LG, United Kingdom; Tel:+44(0)1304 830661; web.facebook.com/TheBellInnShepherdswell; Price:C; *Space for 2 small tents in the pub garden limited outdoor facilities please call ahead may be possible to arrange snacks with prior warning*

Shepherdswell to Dover

stage 2

Length:	15.4km
Ascent:	347m
Descent:	432m
Canterbury	17km
Col Grand Saint Bernard:	1222km

Dover Castle

Route: the journey from Shepherdswell to Dover continues on the pleasant North Downs Way, including a section of Roman road that connects the initial landing place for the Roman legions at Richborough (*Rutupiae*) with Dover (*Dubrae*), before skirting and then crossing the busy A2 highway.

A slightly shorter Alternative Route is suggested for cyclists to bypass further obstacles on the NDW. This road route may also be preferred by walkers in muddy conditions.

Dover offers a wide range of facilities and accommodation choices.

Ferry tickets can normally be purchased at the ferry terminal or online. However, during the period of the pandemic only online booking was possible and further restrictions were imposed on foot passengers. Please verify with the company websites before travelling.

The White Cliffs

Looming high above the dark waters of the channel, the seven white chalk cliffs of Dover are one of the most recognisable British sights. For many hundreds of years, the Straits of Dover have been both Britain's frontline and gateway. Dover controls the English Channel and is known as the Lock and Key of England. Julius Caesar tried to land here during the Roman Invasion of 55 BC and it was the prime objective of the invasion plans of William the Conqueror, Napoleon and Hitler.

stage 2 — Shepherdswell to Dover

(0.0) From the village green in Shepherdswell, return along Mill Lane [Public House directly behind] **(0.0)** From Mill Lane turn right and pass through the kissing gate onto the North Downs Way. Note:- to avoid more obstacles, cyclists should continue on Mill Lane and follow the Alternate Route **(0.2)** Straight ahead into the large open field [Keep hedgerow close on the right] **(0.4)** Cross a second open field after passing through a line of trees **(1.0)** Proceed through narrow gap in the fence between two posts **(1.1)** Straight ahead across the next field [Towards the stile] **(1.2)** Turn left after crossing the stile into the grounds of Coldred Court Farm [Fence on left, large **(1.4)** Cross over the stile and continue through a sm road **(1.4)** At the crossroads continue straight ahead ont right] **(1.5)** Immediately turn left onto the track **(1.5)** Cro 3rd stile cross the field towards the corner of an area of w on the right] **(2.5)** From the corner of the woods, cross the stile and continue straight ahead towards the road junc House on the right] **(3.1)** On reaching the road turn righ Waldershare House] **(3.3)** Pass through white gates mar on the left] **(3.6)** At the fork, take the track betweer across the field and skirt the copse of trees on your left (3 the churchyard] **(3.9)** Turn right after passing through the ered gate] **(4.0)** Turn right on Sandwich Road **(4.1)** Turn

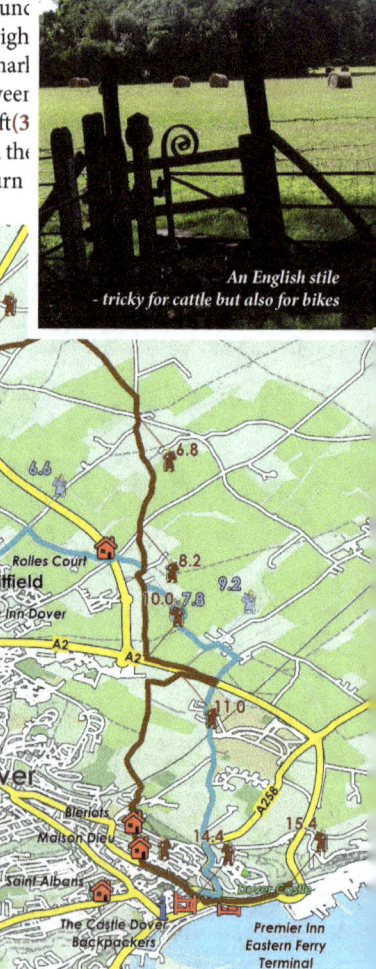

An English stile - tricky for cattle but also for bikes

Shepherdswell to Dover   stage 2

cross the road bridge**(4.3)**Turn left on a concrete road (4.6)Before entering the farm turn right. The road leads to a track, cross over a stile and through a field[Minacre farmhouse on left]**(4.7)**Leave the main track and turn left over a stile and diagonally cross the field**(5.0)** Cross the stile and turn left on the road**(5.4)**Turn right at junction in the village of **Ashley**[Waldershare Road sign]**(5.6)**Turn right into North Downs Close (5.6)Turn left down narrow track[Houses on the right]**(6.5)**Leave the field and turn right on Roman Road (6.8)At the crossroads continue straight ahead[Direction Whitfield]**(6.9)**Bear left on the track at the top of the hill**(7.7)**Continue straight ahead on the track[Milestone "5 kilometres to Dover"] **(8.2)**Cross straight over the road and continue on the track ahead. Note:- continue to follow the Roman road**(8.7)**At the road junction, turn left and then immediately right and pass through the village of **Pineham(8.9)**Bear left on the road**(9.0)** Turn right onto the track - Roman road **(10.0)**Turn left and continue following the track[Parallel to the main road on the right]**(10.6)**At the T-junction with Dover Road, turn right and cross the bridge over the A2 highway[Village of Guston to the left]**(10.7)**Immediately after crossing the bridge, turn right onto the footpath[Continue parallel to the highway] **(11.0)**Bear left on the path across the open field[Metal gate to your right]**(11.2)** Bear right on the path between the trees**(11.3)** Turn left[Remain between the trees]**(12.0)** Continue straight ahead to join the narrow tarmac road[Pass a house on your right] **(13.0)**At the complex road junction, beside the churchyard entrance, take the pedestrian ramp[Metal balustrade on your right]**(13.3)** Cross Connaught Road and continue on Park Avenue**(13.8)**At the traffic light, bear left on Maison Dieu Road[Towards Ferries] **(14.4)** Continue straight ahead towards the sea. Note: Alternate cycle route joins from the left**(14.5)**At the crossroads, turn left to join the hiking route[Woolcomber St.]**(14.5)**At the traffic lights, turn left on the A20, Townwall Street[Direction Ferries] **(15.4)**Arrive at **Dover** Eastern Docks ferry terminal[Ticket office to the right]

stage 2 — Shepherdswell to Dover

Cyclist's Direct Route

Length:	12.9km
Ascent:	210m
Descent:	318m

Route: follows quiet tarmac country lanes avoiding the stiles and gates of the North Downs Way and passing close to Dover Castle. The route saves 1.5 km of the overall distance and could be considered by hikers in muddy conditions or those on a tight ferry schedule. (0.0)Continue straight ahead on Mill Lane(0.8) Turn right[Follow Cycle Route n°16] (1.8)At the crossroads, continue straight ahead onto Singledge Lane[Cycle Route n° 16, Coldred to the right] (5.1)Turn left onto Nursery Lane[Cycle Route n° 16] (5.8)At the crossroads in the centre of Whitfield, continue straight ahead onto Napchester Road[Cycle Route n° 16] (6.6)At the crossroads, turn right in the direction of Dover[Cycle Route n° 16] (7.4)Turn left towards West and East Langdon[Cycle Route n° 16, cross the road bridge] (7.5)Immediately after crossing the bridge, turn right[Direction Pineham] (7.8)Turn right rejoining North Downs Way[Pass through the hamlet of Pineham] (7.9)Bear left remaining on the North Downs Way[Cycle Route n° 16] (8.0)Bear left remaining on the road and leaving the NDW (9.2)Turn right on The Street[Cycle Route n° 16, direction Dover] (9.5)At the T-junction in Guston, turn right on Dover Road[Cycle Route n° 16, towards the public house] (11.4) Continue straight ahead on Dover Road[Connaught Barracks to the left](11.9)At the T-junction turn right onto the A258, direction Dover[Castle directly ahead] (12.9)Turn left and left again into St. James Street and rejoin the "Official Route" at the traffic lights[Pass the ruins of St James the Apostle church on the left]

Accommodation and Tourist Information

Dover

The Castle - Dover Backpackers,Russell Street, Dover, CT16 1PY, United Kingdom; Tel:+44(0)7776 127592; Email:thecastleinndover@gmail.com ; doverbackpackers.wordpress.com; Price:C

B&B - Maison Dieu Guest House,89 Maison Dieu Road, Dover, CT16 1RE, United Kingdom; Tel:+44(0)1304 204033; Email:info@maisondieu.co.uk; www.maisondieu.co.uk; Price:B; **PR**

B&B - Saint Albans,71 Folkestone Road, Dover, CT17 9RZ, United Kingdom; Tel:+44(0)1304 206308; booking.com; Price:B

B&B - Bleriots Guest House,47 Park Ave, Dover, CT16 1HE, United Kingdom; Tel:+44(0)1304 211394; Email:info@bleriotsguesthouse.co.uk; www.bleriotsguesthouse.co.uk; Price:B

B&B - Rolles Court[Jill or Ian],Church Whitfield, Dover, CT163HY, United Kingdom; Tel:+44(0)1304 827487; Email:enquiries@rollescourt.co.uk; www.rollescourt.co.uk; Price:A

Hotel - Premier Inn - Eastern Ferry Terminal,Marine Parade, Dover, CT16 1LW, United Kingdom; Tel:+44(0)3337774649; www.premierinn.com; Price:A; *Price group B in low season*

Visitor Information Centre,Dover Museum - Market Square, Dover, CT16 1PH, United Kingdom; Tel:+44(0)1304 201066

Whitfield

Holiday Inn Dover,Singledge Lane, Whitfield, CT16 3EL, United Kingdom; Tel:+44(0)1304 821230; Email:reservations@leafhoteldover.co.uk; www.holidayinn.com/dover; Price:B

Calais to Wissant

stage 3

Length:	21.2km
Ascent:	658m
Descent:	654m
Canterbury	33km
Col Grand Saint Bernard:	1206km

Town Hall - Calais

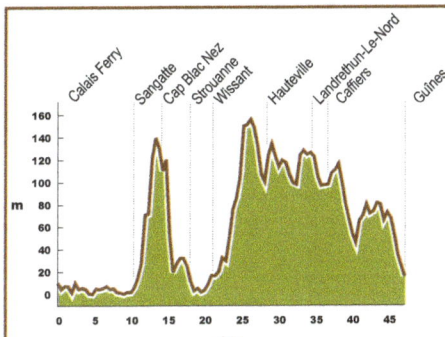

Route: the "Official Route" in France has now been merged with the *Grande Randonnée/ GR®* network of long distance hiking trails and has been designated as the GR®145. As many sections also form parts of other routes you will often see multiple trail names on signposts. The stage from Calais to Wissant follows the GR®145 and GR®120 - *Sentier du Littoral*. To avoid the coastal road the route will use sections of beach, which may be difficult for heavily packed walkers and cyclists; paths through the sand dunes and along the cliff tops and will briefly turn inland and climb les Noires Mottes above Cap Blanc Nez. It is believed that Sigeric's journey used the port of Sombre, perhaps modern day Wissant. Alternate Routes are possible for cyclists using the coast road and also for those walkers that are pressed for time and may wish to bypass the dog leg to Wissant and head straight for Guînes (LXXVII).

Cafés and shops can be found in Sangatte but there are no further facilities directly on the route until you reach Wissant. In July and August the coast is a popular destination and accommodation may be fully occupied.

The closest French town to England, Calais overlooks the Straits of Dover, the narrowest point in the English Channel, which is only 34 kilometres wide at this point.
Virtually the entire town was destroyed by heavy bombardments during World War II, so little in Calais pre-dates this, and for most visitors the town is simply a place to pass through on their way to other destinations. The town centre is dominated by its distinctive city hall, built in the Flemish Renaissance style, with the statue **Les Bourgeois de Calais**, by Auguste Rodin, directly in front.

stage 3 Calais to Wissant

🚶 **(0.0)** On leaving the Ferry control area turn right and take the foot bridge[Cyclists need to take the feed road and then turn sharp right towards Centre Ville] **(0.2)** At the foot of the pedestrian ramp, turn right on Avenue du Commandant Cousteau and take the second exit from the roundabout[Direction - Centre Ville, towards the lighthouse] **(0.6)** At the end of

the fencing surrounding the ferry terminal, continue straight ahead[Cross the bridge beside the lock] **(0.7)** Turn right, direction Plage[Pass the lighthouse on your left] 🚶 **(1.2)** At the road junction beside the Chamber of Commerce, turn left on rue Jean Noël Dubout. Note:- the "Official Route" will pass by the church and make a loop returning to the junction beside the apartment building that spans the road ahead. 500m may be saved by remaining on boulevard des Alliés[Direction Eglise Notre Dame] **(1.5)** Pass through the archway under the apartment block and turn right at the junction. Note:- this is the official start to the

Les Bourgeois de Calais

Calais to Wissant
stage 3

GR©145[Eglise Notre Dame ahead at the junction]**(1.7)**At the crossroads beside Tour du Guet, turn right on rue de la Mer. Note:- to dramatically reduce the distance to Guînes by bypassing Wissant, take the Alternate Route to the left**(1.9)**At the crossroads with the apartment building that spans the road on your right, continue straight ahead[Direction la Plage and Fort Risban] **(2.3)**Continue straight ahead at the roundabout on avenue Raymond Poincaré[Direction la Plage and Centre Européen de Séjour]**(2.7)**At the roundabout take the second exit[Beach and Poste de Secours on the right] **(3.6)**As the road turns inland, turn right into the car park and take the paved footpath beside the beach[House n° 1167 on the left]**(3.9)**At the circle at the end of the paved footpath, turn right towards the beach. Note:- the "Official Route" crosses stretches of sand and involves wooden stairways over the dunes. The path is prohibited for cyclists and may be difficult for heavily packed walkers, who should bear left on the tarmac to take the Alternate Route by road to Wissant**(4.0)**After passing the beach huts turn left and proceed parallel to the sea**(4.9)**Approximately 50m after the line of wooden posts following the last bunker on the left, turn left and take the path between wire fences into the dunes**(5.1)**At the foot of the flight of wooden steps, before reaching the wooden kissing gate, turn right on the gravel track[Keep the

Le Cap Blanc Nez

dunes to your right]**(5.3)**Take the left fork on the gravel track[Between bushes]**(5.4)**Take the right fork on the gravel track **(6.0)**Continue straight ahead, avoiding the track to your left. At the foot of a flight of wooden steps, take right fork on the less well defined track[Close beside the fencing on your right and behind the buildings with the triangular features on the roofs]**(6.8)**Shortly after reaching a concrete section of track, continue straight ahead at the crossroads[Dunes on your right and the main road on the left] **(7.1)**Take the left fork on the broader track[Pass remnants of a concrete bunker on your right]**(8.0)**With the car park on your left, bear right, pass through a kissing gate and then turn right on the broad gravel track to join the sandy path towards the sea[Pass the radar beacon on your left] **(8.1)**After descending the steps, turn left on the sea wall **(9.5)**The GR®145 and the "Official Route" briefly diverge, with the GR®145 turning left and then right on the D940 to pass through the length of Sangatte. The Official route continues straight ahead on the path.**(10.4)**Shortly before reaching the end of the concrete path, turn left up the steps and then turn right on the D940[Church beside the road junction in **Sangatte**] **(10.8)**On

stage 3 — Calais to Wissant

the exit from Sangatte, turn left towards the cemetery**(10.9)**At the entrance to the cemetery, turn right on the track parallel to the main road**(11.2)**At the crossroads, with a tarmac road, continue straight ahead on the gravel track uphill. Note:- the road to the left leads to the ancient route from the Sangatte, la Leulene[Calvaire to the right at the junctions] **(12.5)**After passing through the gate, with a view of the lake and Calais on your left, take the right fork[Uphill, towards radio tower]**(13.0)**At the crossroads in the track, turn right and pass through the gate[Uphill] **(13.8)**At the junction with the tarmac road, turn right

Plaque from Eglise Saint-Nicolas - Wissant

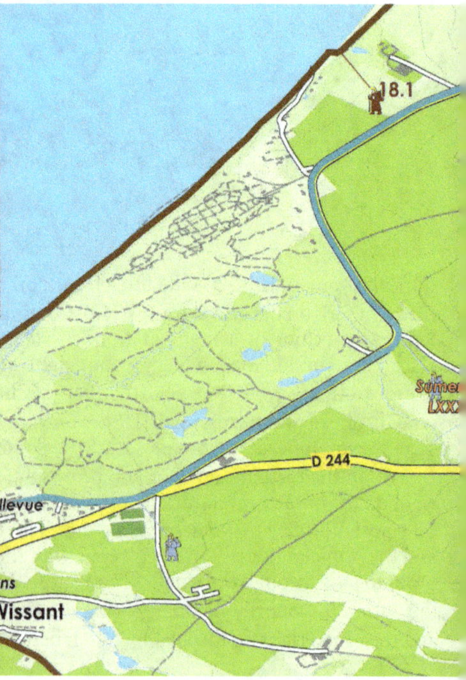

Calais to Wissant — stage 3

and continue downhill[Radio tower to the left, view of the Dover Patrol monument on the right]**(14.2)**Carefully cross the main road and follow the tarmac road straight ahead[Towards the **Cap Blac Nez** car park]**(14.5)**At the end of the car park pass through the barrier and continue straight ahead[Towards the monument]**(14.5)**Take take the gravel path to the left[Keep the monument on your right] **(15.8)**At the foot of the hill turn left in the car park[**Cran d'Escalles**]**(15.8)**At the end of the car park, turn sharp right and take the cliff top path on the other side **(18.1)**Take the wooden steps to the beach and turn left[Hamlet of **Strouanne** ahead] **(20.8)**Shortly before reaching the sea wall in Wissant, turn left to leave the beach on the tarmac road[Wooden chalets overlooking the sea on your left]**(20.8)**At the junction, continue straight ahead up the hill**(21.0)**At the T-junction, turn right, direction Hôtel de la Plage[House n° 6 directly ahead]**(21.0)**At the T-junction turn right[Towards the church]**(21.2)**Arrive at**Wissant** centre, place de la Mairie[Tourist Office to your right]

The White Cliffs seen from Wissant

stage 3 — Calais to Wissant

Cyclist's Route

Route: after leaving Calais the route follows the coastal road - D940. While the road is normally quiet, in the high season and at weekends it attracts more traffic including high speed motor bikers. There is a surprisingly stiff climb over Cap Blanc Nez, before an easy descent into Wissant.

Length:	16.3km
Ascent:	306m
Descent:	296m

(0.0) Turn left on avenue de la Plage [Towards cemetery] (0.2) At the crossroads turn right on rue Vigier [Keep cemetery to the right] (1.1) Turn sharp left on rue du Fort Lapin [Path from the beach on the right] (1.3) Turn right onto the D940, road runs parallel to the beach [After Sangatte look to the right for the white cliffs of Dover] (10.5) At the crossroads in Escalles turn right onto rue de la Mer, remain on D940 [Keep hotel to the left] (14.2) Beside the junction to your left, continue straight ahead on the D940 [Direction Wissant, the main road bears right] (15.3) Fork right on rue Paul Crampel [Towards Wissant Centre] (16.2) In place Edouard Houssin turn left [Towards Hôtel de la Plage] (16.3) Rejoin the "Official Route" at the end of the stage in Wissant centre

Hubert Latham - first man to cross the English Channel by aeroplane - Cap Blanc Nez

Calais to Wissant — stage 3

Direct Route to Guînes

Route: a gentle section beside the "Calais à St. Omer" and "Calais à Guînes" canals, saving 34 km and avoiding the sandy sections and stiff climbs of the coastal route. (0.0)From the junction of rue Royale and rue de la Paix, head south on rue Royale[Towards Office de Tourisme](0.7)At the roundabout in front of the Hotel de Ville turn left[Pass the tower of the Hotel de Ville on your right](0.9)Just

Length:	11.6km
Ascent:	62m
Descent:	60m

before the bridge over the canal turn right[Keep trees and canal close on the left] (1.6)Continue straight ahead on Quai du Commerce[Pass a footbridge and mobile bridge on the left](2.1)Continue straight ahead on Quai Gustave Lamarle[Pass a bridge on the left, keep the canal on your left] (2.8)Continue straight ahead on Quai Gustave Lamarle[Pass a further footbridge and mobile bridge on the left](3.1)Continue straight ahead on Quai d'Amérique[Pass under the railway and motorway bridges] (4.4)Beside **Pont de Coulogne** continue straight ahead onto the chemin de Halage[Mobile bridge on the left and bar on the right](4.9)With the railway bridge over the canal on the right, cross the bridge over the joining canal, pass under the railway and turn right and then immediately left to follow the **Voie Verte Coulogne-Guînes** (6.2)Cross the road and continue straight ahead[Remain on the Voie Verte](6.9)At the junction with rue de l'Ecluse Carrée cross straight over and take the wooden bridgelt[Continue on the Voie Verte] (8.2)Bear left away from the canal[Chemin de Halte, houses on the right](9.0)Continue straight ahead on the track (11.0)On entering Guînes, at the T-junction with rue Léo Lagrange, turn right(11.2)At the roundabout turn right[Towards the Office de Tourisme](11.5)At the crossroads turn left[Rue Massenet](11.6)Arrive in the centre of Guînes[Beside clock tower]

35

stage 3 — Calais to Wissant

Accommodation and Tourist Information

Calais

🏠 **Centre Européen de Séjour**,116 rue du Marechal de Lattre de Tassigny, 62100 Calais, France; Tel:+33(0)3 21 34 70 20; Email:reservation@cescalais.com; www.auberge-jeunesse-calais.com; Price:B

🛏 **Hôtel Restaurant - de la Plage**,693 Digue Gaston Berthe, 62100 Calais, France; Tel:+33(0)3 21 34 64 64; plagecalais.com; Price:B

🛏 **Hôtel - Première Classe**,3 Quai du Danube, 62100 Calais, France; Tel:+33(0)8 92 23 20 55; +33(0)3 21961010; Email:premiereclassecalais@orange.fr; calais-centre-gare.premiereclasse.com; Price:B

🛏 **Brit Hotel**,2 rue des Soupirants, 62100 Calais, France; Tel:+33(0)3 21 46 14 00; Email:calais@brithotel.fr; hotel-calais.brithotel.fr; Price:B

⛺ **Camping le Grand Gravelot**,275 rue d'Asfeld, 62100 Calais, France; Tel:+33(0)3 91 91 52 34; Email:camping@mairie-calais.fr; www.camping.calais.fr; Price:A

ℹ **Office du Tourisme**,12 Boulevard Clémenceau, 62100 Calais, France; Tel:+33(0)3 21 96 62 40; www.calais-cote-dopale.com

Coquelles

🛏 **Hôtel - F1 - Calais Coquelles**,Chemin de Bernieulles, 62231 Coquelles, France; Tel:+33(0)8 91 70 52 06; Email:H2454@accor.com; all.accor.com; Price:C

Escalles

🏠 **Chambre d'Hôtes - Ferme de l'Église**,3 Place de la Mairie, 62179 Escalles, France; Tel:+33(0)6 07 74 24 16; www.chambres-hotes-blanc-nez.com; Price:A; *Closed mid-November to early March SMS dates for reservation*

🛏 **Hôtel - l'Escale**,4 rue de la Mer, 62179 Escalles, France; Tel:+33(0)3 21 85 25 00; Email:reservation@lescale.online; hotel-lescale.com; Price:A; *Closed mid-December to early Febnruary*

⛺ **Camping Côte d'Opale-le Blanc Nez**,18 rue Mer, 62179 Escalles, France; Tel:+33(0)3 21 85 27 38; Email:camping.leblancnez@gmail.com; camping-blancnez.fr; Price:C; *Chalets mobile homes and rooms also available to rent*

Sangatte

⛺ **Camping du Fort Lapin**,21 D940, 62231 Sangatte, France; Tel:+33(0)3 21 97 67 77; Email:campingdufortlapin@sfr.fr; camping-du-fort-lapin.fr; Price:C

Wissant

🏠 **Chambres d'Hôtes - Chez Edwige**,9 rue Gambetta, 62179 Wissant, France; Tel:+33(0)3 21 35 95 84; Email:chezedwige@wanadoo.fr; www.chezedwige.com; Price:B

🏠 **B&B - Les Moussaillons**,12 rue Gambetta, 62179 Wissant, France; Tel:+33(0)3 21 85 54 03; +33(0)6 07 10 02 70; Email:lesmoussaillons.wanadoo.fr; lesmoussaillonswissant.com; Price:B

🛏 **Hôtel - Bellevue**,10 rue Paul Crampel, 62179 Wissant, France; Tel:+33(0)3 21 35 91 07; Email:hlebellevue@wanadoo.fr; www.wissant-hotel-bellevue.com; Price:B

🛏 **Hôtel - Le Normandy**,Place de Verdun, 62179 Wissant, France; Tel:+33(0)3 21 35 90 11; +33(0)3 21 82 19 08; Email:hnormandy@wanadoo.fr; www.lenormandy-wissant.com; Price:A

🛏 **Hôtel - le Vivier**,3 rue Gambetta, 62179 Wissant, France; Tel:+33(0)6 03 38 17 67; Email:levivierwissant@gmail.com; www.levivier.com; Price:B

🛏 **Hôtel de la Plage**,1 place Édouard Houssin, 62179 Wissant, France; Tel:+33(0)3 21 35 91 87; Email:hotelplage.wissant@orange.fr; www.hotelplage-wissant.com; Price:A

ℹ **Office du Tourisme**,Place Mairie, 62179 Wissant, France; Tel:+33(0)3 21 82 48 00; Email:tourisme@terredes2caps.com; www.terredes2capstourisme.fr

Wissant to Guînes

stage 4

Length:	26.0km
Ascent:	520m
Descent:	519m
Canterbury	54km
Col Grand Saint Bernard:	1185km

German Bunker - Wissant Beach

Route: the route from Wissant to Guînes follows the GR®145/128 on farm and forest tracks and climbs Mont de Couple, before entering la Forêt Domaniale de Guînes. In common with many of the forest paths, you will encounter muddy conditions in all but the driest periods and with the risk of the GR® signs being obscured by new tree growth. It is advisable to follow the guide instructions with care.

The "Official Route" bypasses Guînes (LXXVII) but offers a circuitous route '"variante" to reach the facilities of the town. At 19.0 km an Alternate Route provides more direct access to the town - passing close to the recommended "Camping la Bien Assise"

On your journey the many of the relics of war that you will see may lead you to contemplate man's inhumanity to his fellow man. Today, at Mimoyecques near Landrethun-le-Nord, you will pass beside the site of the planned 130m long V3 canon, one of Hitler's secret weapons of mass destruction. With its 25 barrels it was intended to bombard London, 165 km away, raining one enormous shell every 12 seconds.

Guînes (LXXVIII) is the first town you will pass through, directly mentioned in the chronicle of Sigeric. Today it is a pretty, but otherwise unremarkable town.

The clock tower - Tour de l'Horloge - stands on man made hill which was the site of a former Viking watch tower. The clock tower, built in 1763, today also serves as the town museum.

stage 4 — Wissant to Guînes

(0.0) From place de la Mairie (beside the church) take rue du Lieutenant André Baude[Entrance to the Mairie directly behind]**(0.1)** At the foot of the short hill, fork right on rue Ferdinand Buisson**(0.2)** At the junction with the main road (D940), beside the traffic lights, take the pedestrian crossing and continue straight ahead[Towards Herlen]**(0.4)** At the junction continue straight ahead on chemin d'Herlen[Direction Herlen, no through road] **(1.1)** At the crossroads with the track, continue straight ahead on the road**(1.7)** Immediately after passing the stone farm buildings on your left, turn left on the gravel track **(2.9)** At the T-junction in the tracks, turn right[Direction Mont de Couple]**(3.4)** At the T-junction with a tarmac road, turn right[View of Wissant and the coast on your right]**(3.6)** Turn left, uphill on the track **(4.0)** Continue straight ahead up the steep incline[Concrete bunker on your right]**(4.1)** At the T-junction at the top of the hill turn left[Pass the monument on the summit to your right,] **(5.3)** At the crossroads in the track, turn left on the gravel track[The bell tower of the Calais Mairie is visible on the left] **(6.7)** At the T-junction at the foot of the hill, turn right on the tarmac road**(7.3)** At the junction in the centre of **Hauteville**, turn left[Pass a sign for rue du Moulin on your right]**(7.4)** At the T-junction with the main road in Hauteville turn right and continue beside the road[Towards the tabac]**(7.7)** Just before the brow of the hill, turn left onto a gravel track[House n°114 on your right at the junction] **(8.5)** At the junction, continue straight ahead on the partially tarmacked track[Motorway close on your right]**(8.7)** At the T-junction with the tarmac road,

turn right and pass under the motorway**(9.4)** Shortly after the road bends to the left, turn left onto the gravel track between the fields. Note:- the "Official Route" makes a tour of the fields and woods to your left and returns to this road 1300m ahead. By remaining on the road you can reduce your journey by 1500m **(9.8)** At the T-junction, turn right[Towards wind-generators in the distance]**(10.8)** At the T-junction in the tracks, turn right on the broad track **(11.7)** At the T-junction, bear left to rejoin the tarmac road**(11.8)** Just before the brow of the hill turn left on the track between the fields[Towards the wind generators and mobile phone tower]**(12.4)** At the crossroads in the tracks, continue straight ahead[Towards the church steeple] **(12.7)** At the next crossroads, again continue straight ahead[Towards the church steeple]**(13.4)** At the T-junction with the road, turn left beside the road into **Landrethun-le-Nord(13.5)** At the roundabout beside the church, continue straight ahead[Direction Guînes]**(13.7)** Turn right on the gravel track[Beside the calvaire]

38

Wissant to Guînes stage 4

(13.8) At the crossroads with a main road, continue straight ahead on the track between the fields[Towards distant church spire] **(15.0)** At the junction beside the tunnel under the railway, continue straight ahead on the broad track[Keep the railway on your right] **(15.5)** At the T-junction with the D250, turn right beside the road and cross the railway[Village of **Caffiers**] **(15.8)** Beside the bar, turn left[Pass the church on your right] **(16.2)** At the junction immediately after passing the château, bear left towards the large pylons **(16.6)** At the T-junction, turn right[Pass under the electricity lines] **(17.1)** Under the electricity lines, turn left onto a gravel track **(17.8)** At the junction, continue straight ahead towards the woods. Avoid the farm track on the left[Electricity line parallel to track ahead] **(18.8)** At the T-junction, with the woods directly ahead, turn left **(19.4)** Approaching the bend to the left, turn right into the woods and quickly right again. Note:- the "Official Route" and "variante" to Guînes follow a dog-leg route through the sometimes difficult forest tracks. The distance to Guînes can be reduced by 3km by following the Alternate Route **(19.7)** Bear left **(20.3)** At the T-junction in the tracks, turn right[Broad track] **(20.4)** Turn left into the woods **(20.9)** At the T-junction with the very busy road, turn left beside the road **(21.1)** Immediately before reaching the crash barriers, turn sharp right into the forest **(21.7)** At the crossroads with a broad forest track, continue straight ahead on the narrow track which bears slightly to the left **(22.0)** At the crossroads in the track, continue straight ahead **(22.1)** At the T-junction with the broader track, turn right on the stony track[Metal barrier and centre equestre to your left at the junction] **(22.2)** At the crossroads in the tracks, continue straight ahead on the small track **(22.8)** At the T-junction with the road, turn left to follow the "Official Route" – "variante" to the centre of Guînes **(23.4)** After descending from the railway bridge, turn sharp left on the small tarmac road **(23.5)** At the end of the track, facing the fencing beside the railway, turn right on the very narrow track[Keep the fencing immediately on your left] **(24.1)** Bear right on the broad track between the fields[Towards the white house] **(24.6)** Bear left to remain on the broad track[Pass the white house on your right] **(25.6)** At the T-junction with the main road, turn right towards the centre of Guînes **(26.1)** Arrive at **Guînes (LXXVIII)** beside the crossroads[Bar at the junction]

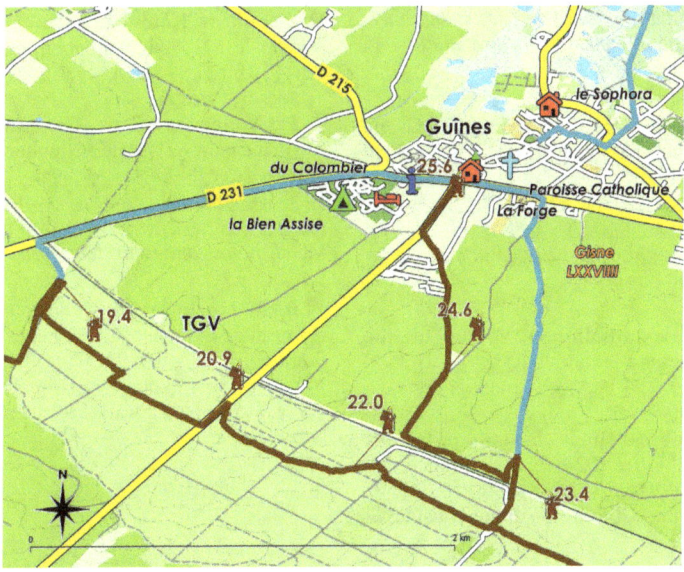

stage 4 — Wissant to Guînes

Direct Approach to Guînes

Route: shorter approach to Guînes centre by the D231 avoiding the dog leg through the forest. (0.0)Continue straight ahead towards the railway track and then bear left[Forest initially on your right] (0.3)Descend the embankment towards the main road and then turn right and proceed with care beside the road[Pass under the railway] (2.0)At the roundabout take the second exit towards Guînes centre[Pass la Bien Assise on your right] (2.3)Arrive in Guînes (LXXVIII) at the end of the stage beside the crossroads[Bar at the junction]

Length:	2.3km
Ascent:	17m
Descent:	46m

Accommodation and Tourist Information

Audembert
⌂ **Chambre d'Hotes – la Ferme du Dizacre**[Chantal & Gérald Leleu],4 la Baronnerie, 62250 Audembert, France; Tel:+33(0)3 21 33 70 76; Email:contact@ledizacre.fr; ledizacre.fr; Price:A

🔑 **Gîte Rural- les Santolines**[Chantal and Paul Delliaux],301 rue de la Vallée, 62250 Audembert, France; Tel:+33(0)3 21 91 70 01; +33(0)6 70 82 37 94; Email:les.santolines@free.fr; www.les.santolines.free.fr

Bouquehault
⌂ **Chambre d'Hôtes - La Forge** ,32 rue de Guizelin, 62340 Bouquehault, France; Tel:+33(0)3 21 34 70 14; +33(0)6 62 99 44 50; +33(0)6 61 86 44 50; Email:la_forge_2@hotmail.fr; la-forge.voyagefrancais.top; Price:B; *A pilgrim has reported that hygene was not up to standard and access was only possible after 18.00. Others have made positive reports*

Fiennes
🛏 **Chambre d'Hôtes - La Ferme du Grand Air**[Rachel],132 rue Henry Hamy, 62132 Fiennes, France; Tel:+33(0)3 21 35 01 60; +33(0)6 80 9310 34; +33(0)7 89 25 15 88; Email:contact@lafermedugrandair.fr; www.lafermedugrandair.fr; Price:B; *Bar and restaurant on site*

Guînes
✝ **Paroisse Catholique**,12 rue de Guizelin, 62340 Guînes, France; Tel:+33(0)3 21 35 21 43; +33(0)6 99 11 22 92; Email:david.godefroit@arras.catholique.fr

⌂ **Chambre d'Hôtes - le Sophora**,16 rue du Maréchal Joffre, 62340 Guînes, France; Tel:+33(0)9 81 26 13 35; +33(0)6 89 29 60 02; chambres-dhotes-le-sophora.business.site; Price:A

🛏 **Auberge - du Colombier**,Bien Assise avenue Verdun, 62340 Guînes, France; Tel:+33(0)3 21 36 93 00; Email:la.ferme.gourmande@orange.fr; www.aubergeducolombier.com; Price:A; *Price Group B in low season closed mid-December to mid-January*

⚠ **Camping la Bien Assise**,Avenue de la Libération, 62340 Guînes, France; Tel:+33(0)3 21 35 20 77; www.camping-la-bien-assise.com; Price:C; *Can also provide rooms with advanced booking and presentation of credentials. Open early February to end September* ; **PR**

ℹ **Office du Tourisme**,9 avenue de la Libération, 62340 Guînes, France; Tel:+33(0)3 21 35 73 73; www.paysdopale-tourisme.fr

Hervelinghen
⌂ **Chambre d'Hôtes - a Leulène**,708 rue Principale, 62179 Hervelinghen, France; Tel:+33(0)3 21 97 98 70; www.france-balades.fr; Price:A

⚠ **Les Voiles des 2 Caps - Camping**,901 rue Principale, 62179 Hervelinghen, France; Tel:+33(0)3 21 36 73 96; +33(0)6 19 45 34 30; Email:contact@lesvoiles-des2caps.fr; lesvoilesdes2caps.fr; Price:C; *Mobile homes and safari tents also available*

Leubringhen
⌂ **B&B - Opale des Caps**[Didier],207 Hameau de Bainghen, 62250 Leubringhen, France; Tel: +33 (0) 6 99 30 06 40; +33 (0) 7 66 83 79 40; Email:contact@opal-edescaps.fr; opaledescaps.fr; Price:A; *No evening meal*; **PR**

Guînes to Tournehem-sur-la-Hem — stage 5

Licques Abbey

Length:	30.7km
Ascent:	665m
Descent:	650m
Canterbury	80km
Col Grand Saint Bernard:	1159km

Route: the "Official Route" from Guînes to Tournehem-sur-la-Hem retraces its path towards the TGV track and re-enters the Forêt Dominiale de Guînes and then continues generally on broad farm tracks following the GR®145/128 initially to the small town of Licques where you may choose to break your journey at one of the camp sites that also offer chalets and caravans to rent.

The entire stage may be shortened by approximately 1 hour and 2 steep climbs avoided by taking the short-cut at 19.8 km.

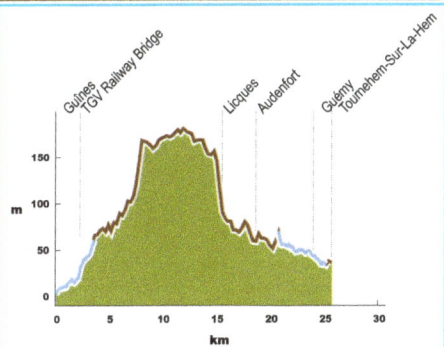

The stage will pass close to the location of one of the earliest and, perhaps, most famous Summit Meetings - Camp du Drap d'Or - the Field of the Cloth of Gold. After seeing his kingdom divided by the French royal family and royal marriages, which latterly put Flanders under Spanish rule, the new King of France, François I persuaded Henry VIII to attend a meeting, at a place within easy travelling distance of the port of Calais where the traditional enemies could agree a bond of friendship. The place earned its name from competition between the kings to outshine each other with tents and clothes made of golden cloth.

stage 5   Guînes to Tournehem-sur-la-Hem

(0.0) From the crossroads of Boulevard Delannoy and Avenue de Verdun, take the D127. Note:- to avoid the very narrow track beside the TGV line cyclists should take the Alternate Route using the tarmac chemin de Bois de Guînes[Direction Hardinghen]**(0.4)** Bear left on chemin du Moulin aux Corneilles[Calvaire and wooden footpath sign] **(1.9)** On reaching the TGV track, turn left[Proceed close by the railway]**(2.5)** Turn left on the track[Keep road parallel on the right]**(2.7)** Turn sharp right and join the road. Note:- Alternate Route for cyclists joins from the left[Cross the **TGV railway bridge**] **(3.2)** Beside the picnic area, turn left onto the track, follow the long straight track through the woods[Pass red and white metal barrier] **(4.3)** At the T-junction at the end of the track, turn right on the broad track**(4.8)** At the T-junction, turn left, slightly uphill on the gravel track **(5.3)** At the crossroads with a tarmac road, continue straight ahead**(5.5)** At the bottom of the short descent, turn right on the narrow path into the woods. Note:- caution this path is easily missed[Sentier de l'Epinette, cycle route n° 11]**(6.0)** At the junction with a broad stony track, turn left up the hill on the stony track**(6.3)** Shortly before the top of the rise, following

the dip, turn right on a smaller forest track **(6.9)** At the crossroads with a broad grass track, continue straight ahead on the clear, but narrower track**(7.4)** At the crossroads in the track, turn left[Parallel to the edge of the forest]**(7.6)** Exit from the forest under power lines and beside a metal barrier. Continue on the broad farm track between the fields**(7.8)** At the T-junction, turn right onto a minor road towards the farmhouse **(8.2)** At the T-junction, after the farm buildings - Puits de Sars, turn left, slightly uphill[Wind generators to the right]**(8.4)** Bear right on road[Modern house on left]**(9.0)** Immediately after passing Gîte du

Guînes to Tournehem-sur-la-Hem — stage 5

Mât take the first turning to the left **(9.9)** Turn left onto a deeply rutted track and continue along the edge of woods **(10.1)** At the T-junction, turn left beside the D248 **(10.2)** Just before the road bends to the left, turn sharp right onto a track **(10.7)** At the T-junction at the foot of the slope, turn right and then immediately left [Towards the houses] **(10.9)** Just after passing house n° 467, turn left on the broad gravel track [Pass a conifer hedge on your right] **(11.4)** At the junction, continue straight ahead, avoid sentier du Vontus on the left **(11.7)** At the T-junction, turn left beside the broader tarmac road [Leave chemin d'Eseries] **(12.1)** Continue straight ahead on the broad stony track [Pass house n° 765] **(12.2)** Bear left on the broad gravel track **(12.6)** At the junction, continue straight ahead direction Vallée Madame **(13.0)** Fork right on the track [Remain on the ridge] **(14.7)** At the foot of the hill, turn left [View of Abbaye Notre-Dame de Licques ahead] **(14.9)** At the junction with the tarmac road, bear left [Keep the Abbaye to your right] **(15.2)** At the junction with the main road, just after passing the déchetterie, continue straight ahead **(15.5)** Turn right on impasse du Courgain **(15.9)** At the T-junction, turn left **(16.0)** In **Licques** at the T-junction beside the ivy covered building take the D191 [Direction St Omer] **(16.8)** At the crossroads, shortly after the top of the hill, turn left on rue de la Commune [Keep the calvaire on the right and the sports ground on the left] **(17.0)** With the children's playground on your left, take the right fork on the track [Impasse des Noisetiers] **(17.6)** At the T-junction with the tarmac road, turn right beside the road [House n° 561 ahead] **(17.6)** At the junction, continue

straight ahead beside the road [Avoid rue de Canchy on the right] **(18.0)** Where the road, bends to the left, turn right onto a broad stony track [Pass farm building on the left] **(18.1)** Take the right fork **(18.4)** Continue straight ahead avoiding the track on the right **(18.9)** At the T-junction with road, turn right down the hill towards the hamlet of Audenfort. Note:- at the time of writing a section of track ahead was overgrown and impassable. To avoid this risk, turn left up the hill and then right at the T-junction and rejoin the "Official Route" by turning left at the next junction on route du Val **(19.1)** At the T-junction at the foot of the hill in **Audenfort**, turn left [Towards the Gîte St. Thérèse] **(19.4)** With house n° 49 on your left, fork left on rue du Calvaire **(19.5)** On the crown of the bend to the right, leave the road and take the track directly ahead uphill. Note:- at the time of writing the track was totally overgrown. It is possible to bypass the track by remaining on the road to the T-junction and then turn left to reach the next waypoint at the end of the track where you should turn right on route du Val **(19.8)** At the crossroads with the main road, continue straight ahead on

stage 5 — Guînes to Tournehem-sur-la-Hem

route du Val, and climb the hill. Note:- approximately 3.5km and a stiff climb can be avoided by turning right on the road, passing through Clerques and continuing straight to the village of Guémy **(21.2)** At the top of the hill, continue straight ahead beside the road. Note:- the GR®128 leaves to the left and rejoins the road at the next waypoint[Ferme du Mont on your right] **(22.3)** In **Le Val** continue straight ahead on the road **(23.5)** At the junction in West Yeuse, turn right on rue de la Chapelle[House n° 642 on your left]**(23.9)** At the junction at the entry to Yeuse bear right into the centre of the village[Rue de la Chapelle]**(24.1)** In the centre of **Yeuse** fork left, pass the chapel on your right**(24.3)** At the road junction, bear left[Keep house n° 790 on your right] **(24.8)** Turn left remaining on the road and avoid the 2 tracks to the right**(25.2)** Shortly before reaching the bridge over the TGV track, turn right on the broad stony track[Towards the woods] **(26.2)** Bear right on the broad gravel track, avoid the turning to the left[Keep the large woods close on the right] **(26.6)** Turn left on the broad track, avoid the tracks into the woods **(27.5)** Continue straight ahead on the track[Pass **la Chapelle St Louis** on your right]**(27.9)** At the foot of the hill, bear left and then turn right on to the road[D225 downhill towards Guémy] **(29.0)** In **Guémy** take first road to the left[Route de Guémy]**(29.4)** After passing the attractive farm buildings on your right, leave the road and take the track to the right[Beside a line of mature trees] **(30.4)** At the T-junction at the end of rue des Prés du Roi in Tournehem-sur-la-Hem turn right[Towards the bridge]**(30.7)** At the T-junction, after crossing the river Hem, turn left[Direction St Omer]**(30.7)** Arrive at **Tournehem-sur-la-Hem** centre in place de la Comtesse Mahaut d'Artois[Café and Mairie beside the place]

The solitary Chapelle Saint-Louis de Guémy - approaching Tournehem-sur-la-Hem

Guînes to Tournehem-sur-la-Hem — stage 5

Direct Route from Guînes to the TGV Bridge

Route: alternative for cyclists or others wishing to avoid the narrow path beside the TGV line. After leaving Guînes the route follows a small, quiet tarmac road to the edge of the forest.

Length:	2.3km
Ascent:	56m
Descent:	7m

(0.0) From the crossroads of Boulevard Delannoy and Avenue de Verdun, take the D231[Towards St Omer](0.4) Shortly after the junction towards the Auberge de Trois Pays, turn right on the small road[Industrial buildings on the right, embankment on your left](0.7) Keep left on the road (2.3) Continue straight ahead to rejoin the "Official Route"[Towards bridge over the TGV line]

Accommodation and Tourist Information

Clerques

Auberge - du Moulin d'Audenfort,16 Impasse du Gué, 62890 Clerques, France; Tel:+33(0)6 07 49 83 10; Email:marion.pillot@live.fr; lemoulindaudenfort.fr; Price:A

Gîte - Sainte Thérèse,54 rue d'Audenfort, 62890 Clerques, France; Tel:+33(0)6 22 26 38 08; +33(0)3 65 98 03 62; Email:gitesaintetherese62@gmail.com; www.gites-de-france-nord-pas-de-calais.fr; Price:A; *3 bedrooms*

Licques

Camping les Pommiers des Trois Pays,273 rue du Breuil, 62850 Licques, France; Tel:+33(0)3 21 35 02 02; www.pommiers-3pays.com; Price:C; *Also offers accommodation in 4-8 berth chalets and mobile homes with restaurant on site Higher prices at weekend and public holidays*

Camping le Canchy,830 rue du Canchy, 62850 Licques, France; Tel:+33(0)3 21 82 63 41; +33(0)6 88 70 66 79; Email:campinglecanchylicques@orange.fr; www.camping-lecanchy.com; Price:C; *4 person dormitory.Caravans may also be rented*

Mairie,54 Parvis de l'Abbaye, 62850 Licques, France; Tel:+33(0)3 21 35 00 19; ; *Open Monday to Friday mornings*

Nort-Leulinghem

Chambre d'Hôtes - Ferme du Pre Vert,8 rue de la Mairie, 62890 Nort-Leulinghem, France; Tel:+33(0)9 50 98 24 56; +33(0)782898497; Email:pat62890@outlook.fr; www.lafermeduprevert.fr; Price:A

Tournehem-sur-la-Hem

Chambres d'Hôtes - Lysensoone,30 rue de Valenciennes, 62890 Tournehem-sur-la-Hem, France; Tel:+33(0)3 21 35 60 56; Email:henri.lysensoone@orange.fr; www.tourisme-saintomer.com/annuaire/mme-lysensoone/; Price:B; *Contact by phone during the eveniing*; **PR**

Hôtel - Bal,500 rue du Vieux Château, 62890 Tournehem-sur-la-Hem, France; Tel:+33(0)3 21 35 65 90; Email:contact@hotel-camping-bal.fr; www.hotel-camping-bal.fr; Price:B

Bal Parc Camping,291 rue du Vieux Château, 62890 Tournehem-sur-la-Hem, France; Tel:+33(0)3 21 35 65 90; Email:contact@hotel-camping-bal.fr; www.hotel-camping-bal.fr; Price:C; *Mobile homes also be available. Open April to end October*

Le Fond d'Ecambre Camping,Guémy, 62890 Tournehem-sur-la-Hem, France; Tel:+33(0)3 21 85 19 03; www.campingdefrance.com/fr/camping/10200/fond-d-ecambre; Price:C; *Open April to end October*

Mairie,4 place Comtesse Mahaut d'Artois, 62890 Tournehem-sur-la-Hem, France; Tel:+33(0)3 21 35 61 34; Email:mairie-de-tournehem@wanadoo.fr; www.mairie-tournehem.fr

stage 6 — Tournehem-sur-la-Hem to Wisques

Length:	19.2km
Ascent:	415m
Descent:	345m
Canterbury	111km
Col Grand Saint Bernard:	1128km

Abbey of Saint Paul

Route: from Tournehem-sur-la-Hem to Wisques the route continues on small country roads and farm tracks over rolling countryside which offers easy going for all groups. The route briefly intersects with la Leulene – the ancient road and pilgrim trail from the Roman port of Sangatte.

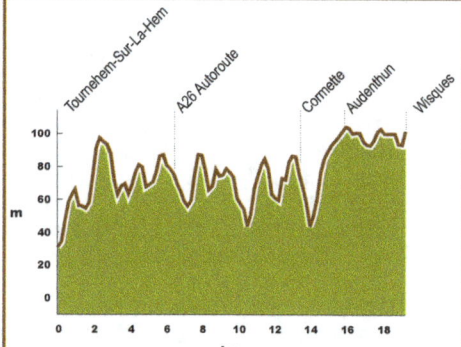

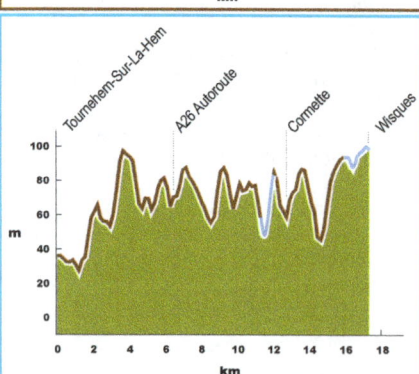

The route bypasses the small villages of Pas-de-Calais and so offers few opportunities to buy food or drink except perhaps for the bakery in Zudausques.

Wisques is dominated by the abbeys of St Paul and Notre Dame, but has few shops. The large town of St Omer lies 5 km to the north-east.

Saint Paul's Abbey was built at the end of the 15th century by the Saint-Aldegonde family, but has undergone many changes over the centuries. First housed in the Petit Château, a fine 18th century mansion situated opposite the present-day cemetery, the monks later moved to the Grand Château which they still occupy today. The most noteworthy parts of the buildings are the bell-tower, the keep (built at the end of the Middle Ages) and parts renovated by Dom Bellot.

Notre Dame, founded in 1889 by the nuns of Saint Cécile of Solesmes, was originally lodged in part of the Grand Château, but relocated when the Abbey of Notre Dame was built in 1891. The building layout was created by Lille architect Paul Vilain, who was considered to be the most eminent representative of the neo-gothic school in the north of France. Although a cloistered order, the chapel is open to the public and there is a shop selling monastic products.

Tournehem-sur-la-Hem to Wisques — stage 6

(0.0) From the Mairie in the place turn right and take the second road on the right[Rue de Broukerque]**(0.2)** At the T-junction, beside the bus shelter, turn left[Keep the church on your left]**(0.3)** As the main road turns to the right, turn left and then immediately right. Note:- the GR°128 and GR°145 separate at this point, we will continue on the GR°145[Direction Nort-Leulinghem]**(0.6)** Take the left fork, chemin de St Omer**(1.0)** As the road begins to turn right, turn left on the stony track downhill. Note:- your distance can be reduced by 600m and a stiff climb avoided by remaining on the road and keeping left at the next junction. The "Official Route" will rejoin the road from the left in 800m[Towards the caravan park] **(1.6)** At the T-junction in the tracks, turn right, uphill**(2.3)** At the T-junction with the small road turn left **(2.6)** Turn right onto a grass track[Towards the woods and the former windmill in the valley]**(3.0)** Beside the woods bear left[Parallel to the motorway]**(3.1)** At the junction with the small tarmac road, continue straight ahead on the stony track[Towards the windmill] **(3.7)** At the crossroads in the tracks, shortly after passing the windmill, bear slightly right on the minor track between the hedges[Village of Nort-Leulinghem to the left]**(3.9)** At the crossroads with a tarmac road on the edge of Nort-Leulinghem continue straight ahead on the broad stony track**(4.6)** At the crossroads with

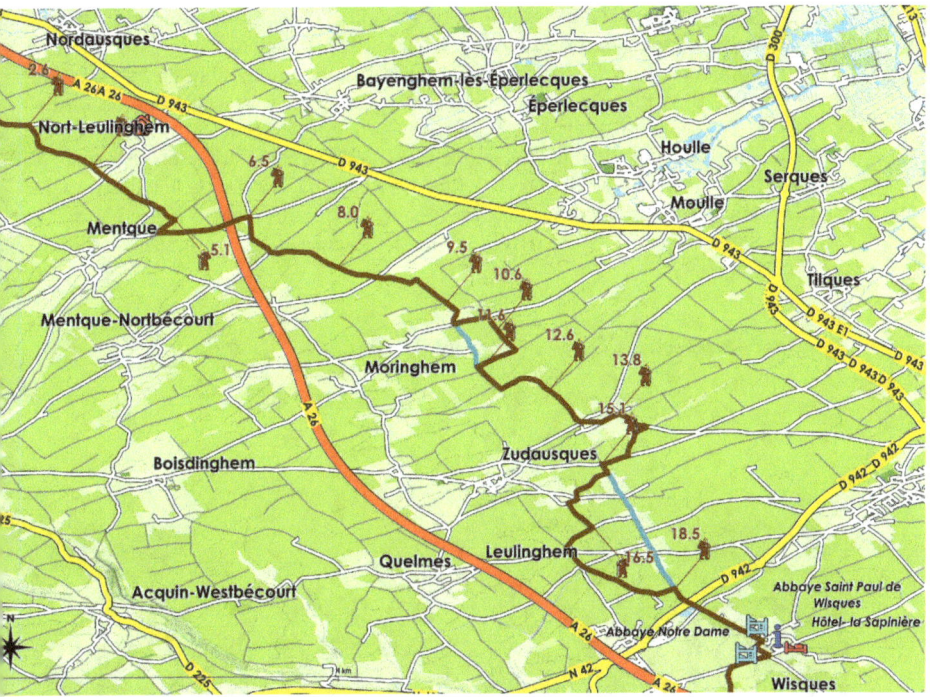

D221, cross straight over and continue on the gravel track[Motorway visible on the brow to the left] **(5.1)** At the T-junction at the top of the hill, turn right**(5.4)** At the T-junction, turn sharp left on the D222, uphill **(6.5)** After crossing the **A26 Autoroute** turn right at the first crossroads, downhill[Direction Culem, pass a quarry on your left]**(7.1)** At the bottom of the hill, where the road turns right, take the second track on the left uphill[Woods on your right] **(8.0)** At the junction in the tracks, continue straight ahead downhill on the stony track[Towards the road]**(8.5)** At road junction, cross straight over and continue on the stony track uphill **(9.5)** At the junction in the tracks, continue straight ahead. Note:- there

stage 6   Tournehem-sur-la-Hem to Wisques

are some confusing GR® signs that should be ignored at this point[Uphill]**(9.9)**At the crossroads with the D207 turn left beside the road. Note:- 800m may be saved by continuing straight ahead on the road, the "Official Route" will rejoin from the left 300m after the church[Village of Moringhem to the right]**(10.3)**Turn right, downhill on the stony track[La Leulene milestone on your right] **(10.6)**Continue straight ahead[Uphill]**(11.0)**At the T-junction at the top of the hill, turn right**(11.5)**At the T-junction, turn left **(11.6)**At the junction in the tracks, continue straight ahead downhill[Avoid the track leading to the windmill]**(12.0)**At the end of the track, turn left**(12.2)**Bear right onto the more defined track, uphill[Woods initially on your left] **(12.6)**Continue straight ahead, uphill on the tarmac track[Direction St Omer]**(13.3)**At the crossroads with rue de Cormette, continue straight ahead on rue Saint Lambert[Direction Cormette]**(13.7)**In **Cormette** with the church on your left, bear left **(13.8)**Bear right on the road downhill, between the trees**(14.2)**Turn right onto the grass track**(14.8)**At the T-junction with the road turn right **(15.1)**Turn left on the D212E2[Direction Leulinghem]**(15.2)**Turn right on chemin des Marronniers. Note:- approximately 1.5km may be saved by remaining on the D212e2 - route de Leuline, until the "Official Route" rejoins from the right prior to crossing the D942 and entering Wisques**(15.9)**At the crossroads in **Audenthun**, continue straight ahead[Chambres d'hôtes and boulangerie on your left]**(16.0)**With house n° 45 on your left, turn left on the road **(16.5)**At the T-junction, with a radio mast visible ahead, turn right on the road**(17.0)**At the crossroads with a major road, continue straight ahead on the D212[Direction Leulinghem]**(17.3)**At the crossroads beside the church in Leulinhem, continue straight ahead and climb the hill on the D212[Pass the church close on your right] **(18.5)**At the T-junction with the D212e2, turn right. Note:- direct route rejoins from the left[Direction Wisques]**(19.0)**At the crossroads, continue straight ahead on the D212[Direction Wisques]**(19.3)**Arrive at **Wisques**[Entrance to Abbaye St. Paul on the left]

V-2 Rocket Launch Complex - La Coupole, Wizernes, Pas de Calais

Tournehem-sur-la-Hem to Wisques — stage 6

Accommodation and Tourist Information

Saint-Omer
Hôtel - Ibis Budget Saint Omer Centre, Avenue Charles de Gaulle, 62500 Saint-Omer, France; Tel:+33(0)8 92 68 13 42; Email:H5919@accor.com; www.accorhotels.com; Price:B
Office du Tourisme, 7 place Victor Hugo, 62500 Saint-Omer, France; Tel:+33(0)3 21 98 08 51; www.tourisme-saintomer.com

Wisques
Abbaye Saint Paul de Wisques, 31 rue de l'Ecole, 62219 Wisques, France; Tel:+33(0)3 21 12 28 50; +33(0)3 21 12 28 55; Email:stpaulwisques@gmail.com; arras.catholique.fr/stpaulwisques; Price:D; *Men only*
Abbaye Notre Dame, 24 rue Fontaine, 62219 Wisques, France; Tel:+33(0)3 21 95 57 30; +33(0)3 21 95 12 26; Email:hotellerie@ndwisques.fr; arras.catholique.fr/faire-sejour-hotellerie.html; Price:D; *Outstanding*;
PR

Hôtel- la Sapinière, 12 route de Setques, 62219 Wisques, France; Tel:+33(0)3 21 38 94 00; Email:contact@sapiniere.net; sapiniere.net; Price:A
Mairie, Rue Ecole, 62219 Wisques, France; Tel:+33(0)3 21 93 39 10; Email:maire.wisques@nordnet.fr; mairie-wisques.com

Wizernes
Paroisse Catholique - Résidence Marie Curie, Rue Bernard Chochoy, 62570 Wizernes, France; Tel:+33(0)3 21 93 81 41; Email:paroisse.valaa@orange.fr

Abbey of Notre Dame

stage 7   Wisques to Thérouanne

Length:	23.3km
Ascent:	461m
Descent:	525m
Canterbury	130km
Col Grand Saint Bernard:	1109km

La Leulene

Route: after an initial section following a tarmac road through the Bois de Wisques the "Official Route" from Wisques to Thérouanne zig-zags on farm tracks making a broad loop before following a long minor road to the once vital crossroads town of Thérouanne. The route skirts the villages along the way providing little opportunity to buy food or drink except potentially at the Café du Centre on the route in Delettes. The Alternate Route substantially shortens your journey by following a section of la Leulene.

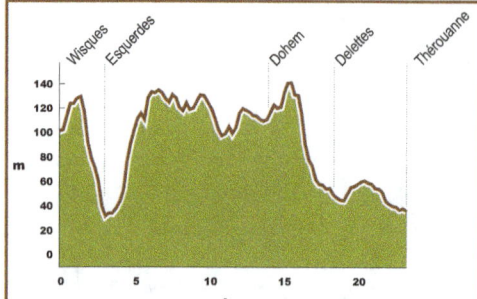

Nestling in the Lys valley, Thérouanne used to be the capital of Morini before it became the seat of one of the wealthiest bishoprics in the North of France in 638. Thérouanne was a favourite stopping place for many pilgrims following the Via Francigena.

Thérouanne was reputed to be a French stronghold and while at war with François I, Charles V ordered that the town be destroyed, along with all of its civic and religious buildings.

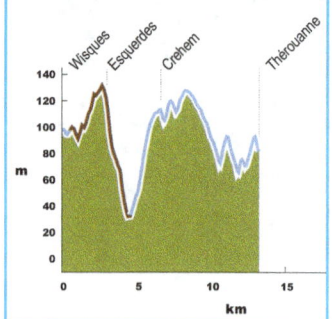

Thérouanne fell on August 22nd, 1513 and soldiers were set to work demolishing the walls of the town and three large bastions, which were pushed into the deep defensive ditches. The Milanese ambassador to Maximilian, heard that it was planned to burn the town after demolition was completed and he approved.

Siege of Thérouanne - British Museum

Wisques to Thérouanne

stage 7

(0.0) From the gates of the Abbaye de St Paul turn left to follow the D212 [Towards the village centre] **(0.4)** As road, bends to the left and with a cemetery on your right, continue straight ahead on the pathway [Grounds of the Abbaye de Notre-Dame on your right] **(0.6)** At the T-junction with the road, turn right uphill [Towards the entrance to the Abbaye] **(0.7)** Bear left on the road [Entrance to the Abbaye de Notre-Dame on your right] **(1.0)** At the crossroads, beside the water tower, turn right and follow the major road with great care [Routes de Setques] 🚶 **(1.4)** Shortly after the brow of the hill, turn left on the road into the woods [Pass red and white metal barrier] 🚶 **(3.0)** At the T-junction with a major road in **Esquerdes**, turn left and then bear right [House n° 765 ahead] **(3.2)** At the crossroads, turn right on rue de la Poste. Note:- to reduce your distance by 10km continue straight ahead on the more direct Alternate Route **(3.7)** In the place Jean Jaurès in front of the church, turn left

stage 7 — Wisques to Thérouanne

up the hill[Keep the church on your left]**(3.8)**At the T-junction at the top of the hill, turn right and cross the railway 🚶 **(4.0)**Immediately after crossing the railway, turn left on the tarmac[Towards the cemetery]**(4.1)**Immediately after passing the cemetery, turn right uphill on the gravel and tarmac road 🚶 **(5.7)**At the T-junction in the heart of the forest, turn left, uphill on the stony track**(6.4)**At the crossroads continue straight ahead with the woods on your left and open fields on your right[Towards the wind generator] 🚶 **(7.2)**At the junction with the tarmac road, keep left and continue on the unmade road between the wind-generators**(7.6)**At the T-junction, turn left on the gravel track 🚶 **(8.2)**Follow the track to the right**(9.1)**At the T-junction with the main road, in the village of Crehem, turn right beside the road[Pass a bus shelter on your right] 🚶 **(9.2)**With the farmhouse n°1 on your right, turn left between the 2 brick buildings**(9.7)**At the junction with the access road towards the wind generators, continue straight ahead[Towards the tree-lined main road]**(9.9)**At the crossroads with the major road, continue straight ahead on the farm track between the fields 🚶 **(10.4)**At the junction in the tracks, turn right, downhill on the gravel track[Towards the woods]**(11.3)**At the T-junction in the tracks, turn left[Hedgerow on the left of the track] 🚶 **(11.6)**At the crossroads in the tracks, turn right[Towards the hamlet]**(12.2)**At the T-junction in front of the house with the circular window, turn left[Keep the small park on your left]**(12.4)**At the road junction, continue straight ahead[Rue d'Herbelles] 🚶 **(12.6)**As the road bends to the left at the exit from Cléty, turn right on the partially obscured path[Between hedges]**(12.9)**At the junction in the tracks, continue straight ahead on the narrow track[Between hedges]**(13.3)**At the end of the track, turn left beside the road[Direction St Omer] 🚶 **(13.8)**At the crossroads with the major road (D341), continue

Bois de Wisques

Wisques to Thérouanne — stage 7

straight ahead on the small road[Towards the radio tower]**(14.0)**At the crossroads just before the entry to **Dohem**, turn left on the track[Pass the building with the radio antenna on your right] **(15.3)**At the T-junction at the end of rue de la Froide Orielle, turn right beside the road**(15.5)**As the road bends to the right, take the left fork on the small road downhill - la Roullette[Pass the chapel on your left]**(15.7)**At the crossroads, turn left**(16.1)**Take the right fork steeply downhill between the trees **(16.9)**At the junction in the tracks, continue straight ahead on the grass track continuing downhill towards the wind generators[Hedgerow on your left and open fields on your right]**(17.3)**At the T-junction in the tracks, turn left[Steep embankments on both side of the track] **(18.4)**At the T-junction with the main road, turn right[Enter the village of **Delettes**]**(18.6)**At the crossroads with a major road with the bridge on your right, cross the major road and continue straight ahead**(18.6)**Turn right over the small wooden bridge, follow the cinder track and then turn left**(18.7)**Continue straight ahead[Over the metal and concrete bridge]**(18.9)**At the end of the riverside path, continue straight ahead beside the red and white barriers[Towards the tennis courts] **(19.1)**At the T-junction with the road, turn left[Towards the bar]**(19.2)**Beside the bar, turn right[Rue Haute] **(19.4)**At the road junction at the top of the hill, continue straight ahead[Rue de Nielles] **(20.9)**At the road junction continue straight ahead[Pumping station on your left] **(22.2)**At the road junction in Nielles, continue straight ahead[Pass the church on your left]**(22.9)**At the T-junction, with house n° 2 directly ahead, turn left **(23.3)**Arrive at **Thérouanne (LXXVII)** centre at the T-junction facing the petrol station[Mairie and Tourist Office to the left on the main road]

Direct Route to Thérouanne

Length:	10.0km
Ascent:	177m
Descent:	175m

Route: follows the direction of la Leulene, now small tarmac roads and routes departmentales, before entering Thérouanne on a more major road while saving 10 km. **(0.0)**Continue straight ahead on the road, uphill[Pass small field on your right]**(0.1)**Bear left and then right, uphill on the road[Towards railway crossing]**(0.3)**Bear left remaining on the D192e1[Pass house n° 530 on your right] **(3.3)**On the outskirts of **Crehem**, continue straight ahead on the D192, avoid the turning to the right to Lumbres[Direction Herlen, no through road]**(3.6)**At the crossroads with the major road, continue straight ahead[Rue de Thérouanne]**(3.9)**Continue straight ahead on the D192, avoid the turning on the left to Pihem[Direction Therouanne] **(6.1)**Take the left fork towards the crossroads and then continue straight ahead on the small road, rue Brocquoise[No Entry sign, pass metal calvaire on the right] **(8.2)**At the T-junction with the major road, turn left beside the road. Note:- you are joining the historic Chaussée Brunehaut[Towards the brow of the hill]**(8.6)**At the roundabout take the second exit[Direction Thèrouanne] **(9.6)**At the junction in Thèrouanne, beside the bar and tabac, bear left and then right on Grand Rue[Pass the Mairie on your right]**(10.0)**End of the stage in Thérouanne (LXXVII) centre[Junction beside the petrol station]

stage 7 — Wisques to Thérouanne

Accommodation and Tourist Information

Delettes

🏠 **Chambre d'Hôtes - les Dornes**[Jacqueline and Gilles Blondel],520 rue des Deux Upen, 62129 Delettes, France; Tel:+33(0)3 21 95 87 09; +33(0)6 88 82 55 96; Email:lesdornes@lesdornes.com; lesdornes.com; Price:A

Mametz

⛺ **Camping Domaine le Chateau de Mametz**,32 rue du Moulin, 62120 Mametz, France; Tel:+33(0)6 83 96 19 85; Email:vandaele.manon@hotmail.fr; web.facebook.com/Camping-du-Château-295799897495716/; Price:C; *Mobile homes available*

Rebecques

⛺ **Camping du Lac de Rebecques**,121 Chemin des Etiais, 62120 Rebecques, France; Tel:+33(0)6 23 55 79 85; +33(0)6 27 05 23 26; Email:dcampingdulac@hotmail.fr; www.tourisme-saintomer.com/annuaire/camp-de-loisirs-du-lac-de-rebecques/; Price:C; *Mobile homes and Safari tents available*

Thérouanne

🏠 **Eden Lodge Gîte**[Alain & Patricia Millamon],30 Grand rue, 62129 Thérouanne, France; Tel:+33(0)3 21 93 23 13; +33(0)6 80 10 79 07; Email:lamaisonpresdumoulin@laposte.net; Price:C; *Great host immaculate*; **PR**

ℹ **Mairie**,5 place de l'Église, 62129 Thérouanne, France; Tel:+33(0)3 21 95 51 87; Email:therouanne.mairie@wanadoo.fr

Thérouanne to Amettes — stage 8

Length:	19.3km
Ascent:	308m
Descent:	265m
Canterbury	153km
Col Grand Saint Bernard:	1086km

Saint Sulpice - Amettes

Route: this gentle stage from Thérouanne to Amettes largely follows farm tracks that parallel the ancient Chaussée Brunehaut.

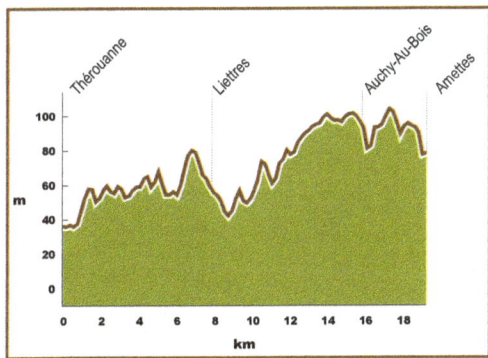

There is the opportunity for refreshment and accommodation in Auchy-au-Bois.

Amettes is a small farming town with very limited facilities, but is best known as being the birth place of Saint Benedict Joseph Labre (1748-1783).

A French mendicant, and latterly a Roman Catholic saint, Jospeh Labre was the eldest of fifteen children of a prosperous shopkeeper, and religious from a very early age. He was noted for performing public acts of penance for his sins, even minor sins. At the age of sixteen, he attempted to join the Trappists, Carthusians and Cistercians, but each order rejected him as being unsuitable for communal life. The abbots of these orders suspected some form of mental illness, which would make Labre unable to fulfil the vow of obedience necessary for any cloistered religious life. Labre took this as a sign that it was God's will that he should abandon his country and his parents to lead "A life most painful, most penitential, not in a wilderness nor in a cloister, but in the midst of the world, devoutly visiting as a pilgrim"

Saint Benedict first travelled to Rome on foot, subsisting on what he could receive by begging. He then travelled to most of the major shrines of Europe, often multiple times. He visited Loreto, Assisi, Naples and Bari in Italy, Einsiedeln in Switzerland, Paray-le-Monial in France and Compostela in Spain. During these trips he would always travel on foot, sleep in the open or in a corner of a room, with his clothes muddy and ragged. He lived on what little he was given and often shared the little he did receive with others.

Saint Benedict Joseph Labre

stage 8 — Thérouanne to Amettes

(0.0) Take the D341 Grand Rue[Keep the petrol station and bank on your left]**(0.3)** At the junction, bear left on the D157[Direction Aire sur la Lys]**(0.9)** Immediately before leaving Thérouanne, take the right fork, tarmac road, uphill[Pass house n° 27 on the corner, chemin du Blanc Mont] **(1.8)** Take the right fork, uphill[Towards the wind generators]**(2.3)** At the junction, continue straight ahead, avoid the turning to the left[Towards the wind generators]**(2.5)** At the junction, continue straight ahead, avoid the turning to the right **(3.9)** At the crossroads with the D130, continue straight ahead on the partially made road[Water tower visible above the trees on the left]**(4.2)** Avoid the turnings first on the right and then on the left and continue straight ahead, uphill[Pass a copse on your right, towards the the wind generators] **(5.0)** At the junction, continue straight ahead, downhill[Towards the quarry]**(5.2)** At the bottom of the slope, turn left and begin to skirt the quarry[Towards the prominent church on the horizon]**(6.0)** At the T-junction with the D159, turn right, slightly uphill[Pass a conifer hedge on your right] **(6.2)** Shortly after leaving Blessy, turn left on the track, uphill **(7.8)** At the crossroads with a main road, turn right[Church visible in the valley]**(7.9)** Turn left, downhill into the village of **Liettres**(8.0)** Halfway down the hill, with a parking area on your left, turn right**(8.3)** Beside the football pitch bear left and take the grassy track downhill**(8.7)** At the T-junction with the D186 in Longhem, turn right[House n° 21 ahead] **(9.0)** Turn left onto the small road[Pass large metal barn on your right]**(9.5)** At the T-junction with the major road – Chaussée Brunehaut, turn left, cross the road with care and immediately turn right beside the stream[Rue du Transvaal] **(10.3)** Immediately after passing the patterned brick house n° 4, turn left**(11.0)** Shortly before the T-junction with the road, fork left, uphill on the grass track. Note:- there are barriers on the track, which may prove difficult for cyclists. To avoid these, cyclists should bear right and then left on the road to the centre of La Tirmande. Then turn left beside the calvaire and then right immediately before the old railway bridge. The "Official Route" will join the road from the left 400m after

Maison Saint Benedict - Amettes

Thérouanne to Amettes — stage 8

the bridge (**12.5**) Emerge from the former railway track onto a small road, bear left, uphill (**13.1**) At the crossroads with the D90, continue straight ahead onto the track [Small chapel to the left of the junction] (**14.0**) At the crossroads in the tracks, turn sharp right (**14.8**) At the T-junction with the road, turn left [Towards the water tower] (**15.0**) At the crossroads beneath the water tower, turn left [D94] (**15.3**) Shortly after passing under the power lines, turn right and leave the main road, route de Heslan (**15.8**) At the T-junction facing house n° 7, turn right (**15.9**) In la Place, in the centre of **Auchy-au-Bois**, continue straight ahead, towards the church spire [Chambres d'Hôtes to the left] (**16.1**) Take left fork on rue Louis Part, downhill [Pass church on your right] (**16.8**) At the crossroads at the foot of the hill, go straight ahead on the stony track [Between open fields] (**18.3**) At the crossroads continue straight ahead on the tarmac road [Towards the water tower on the horizon]

(**18.6**) At the crossroads, continue straight ahead, slightly uphill [Towards the village] (**19.0**) Bear left and at the T-junction with a main road (D69) turn left. Note:- both the GR®145 and GR®127 pass through Amettes. They join briefly before separating beside the church. Cyclists should turn right at the T-junction and then take the first left, rue de l'Egliset to rejoin the "Official Route" beside the church [Pass the Amettes bus stop on your right, GR®127 sign] (**19.1**) Turn right on the track between houses n°s 19 and 20, pass through the wooden gate and climb the steps towards the church [Pass la maison St Benoit on your right] (**19.3**) Arrive at **Amettes** centre [Beside the church of St Sulpice]

stage 8

Thérouanne to Amettes

Accommodation and Tourist Information

Amettes

🏠 **Gite d'Etape - la Ferme des Deux Tilleuls**[Jean-Baptiste Gevas],2 rue Eglise, 62260 Amettes, France; Tel:+33(0)3 21 27 15 02; +33(0)6 38 81 34 15; Email:fermedes2tilleuls@wanadoo.fr; gite-pelerin.e-monsite.com; Price:C; *Evening meal available* ; **PR**

🏠 **Chambre d'Hôtes - la Ferme des Deux Tilleuls**[Jean-Baptiste Gevas],2 rue Eglise, 62260 Amettes, France; Tel:+33(0)3 21 27 15 02; +33(0)6 38 81 34 15; Email:fermedes2tilleuls@wanadoo.fr; gite-pelerin.e-monsite.com; Price:B; *Evening meal available*

ℹ **Mairie**,Place Mairie, 62260 Amettes, France; Tel:+33(0)3 21 27 06 60; Email:mairie.amettes@orange.fr

Auchy-au-Bois

🏠 **Chambre d'Hôtes - la Ferme de la Vallée**[Brigitte de Saint Laurent],13 rue Neuve, 62190 Auchy-au-Bois, France; Tel:+33(0)3 21 25 80 09; Email:brigitte.de-saint-laurent@wanadoo.fr; www.lafermedelavallee.com; Price:B; *Dinner possible* ; **PR**

Enquin-Lez-Guinegatte

🏠 **Chambre d'Hôtes - La Ferme des Templiers**,2 rue des Templiers, 62145 Enquin-Lez-Guinegatte, France; Tel:+33(0)3 21 39 74 21; +33(0)6 11 64 75 57; Email:fdt-maes@sfr.fr; ferme-des-templiers.fr; Price:A; *Price Group B in a dormitory an Airstream caravan also available*

Liettres

🏠 **Chambre d'Hôtes - les Chambres du Relais**,4 rue du Moulin, 62145 Liettres, France; Tel:+33(0)7 72 66 27 98; +33(0)6 84 49 49 03; Email:chambresdurelais@gmail.com; leschambresdurelais.webnode.fr; Price:B; *Dinner bed and breakfast at discounted price for pilgrims with credentials*

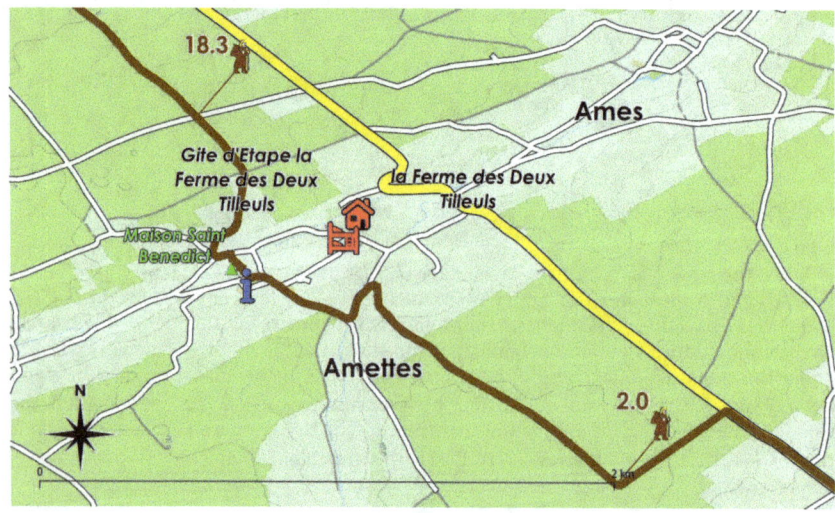

Amettes to Bruay-la-Buissière

stage 9

Pit N° 2 Marles-les-Mines

Length:	22.0km
Ascent:	420m
Descent:	457m
Canterbury	172km
Col Grand Saint Bernard:	1067km

Route: the "Official Route" from Amettes to Bruay-la-Buissière crosses the Chaussée Brunehaut and meanders on country and woodland tracks before finding its way through former mining villages and parkland to reach Bruay-la-Buissière (LXXVI). While signposting is generally good, there are some challenges to locate the signs in the woodland and evidence of some vandalism to the signs. A more direct Alternate Route is also described. Bruay offers accommodation and a full range of facilities. The route in Bruay bypasses the town centre with much of the accommodation a further 2-3 km to the east and so allow time to locate where you will stay.

Brunehaut or Brunhilde, was raised as an Arian Christian, but converted to Roman Catholicism after her marriage to Sigebert. From here she took a keen personal interest in the bishoprics and monasteries within her dominion, and incidentally commissioned the building of several churches and the abbey of St. Vincent in Laon (580).

The death of Brunhilde

Unfortunately, the rest of her history is less positive and it appears she became embroiled in a number of assassinations. Ultimately this behaviour led to her own death, when, according to the Liber Historiae Francorum:

"The army of Franks and Burgundians joined into one, agreeing all together that death would be most fitting for the very wicked Brunhilda. King Clotaire ordered that she be

stage 9 Amettes to Bruay-la-Buissière

lifted on to a camel and led through the entire army. Then she was tied to the feet of wild horses and torn apart limb from limb. Finally she died. Her final grave was the fire. Her bones were burnt.

(0.0) At the top of the steps and facing the church, turn left and bear right on the road [Church on your right, downhill] **(0.1)** At the road junction, continue straight ahead [Rue des Berceaux] **(0.4)** At the foot of the hill, turn left on the tarmac road [Beside the calvaire] **(0.6)** Turn right and leave the road, continue uphill **(2.0)** Follow the stony track as it turns left [Towards the main road, Chaussée Brunehaut] **(2.6)** At the T-junction, turn right beside main road D341. Note:- the road can be very busy and the grass verges are very narrow **(3.4)** In the village of **Ferfay**, take the second turning on the left [Pass between the auberge and boulangerie, sentier de Burbure] **(3.8)** At the T-junction, after passing the cemetery, turn right on the tarmac road **(4.2)** At the crossroads, continue straight ahead. Note:- to avoid the difficult navigation through the woods ahead, turn left at the junction and continue straight ahead then at the next crossroads turn right. The "Official Route" will join from the right in a further 500 m **(4.4)** At the road junction, continue straight ahead, downhill [Follow the turn to the left] **(4.6)** At the end of the concrete road, continue straight ahead on the

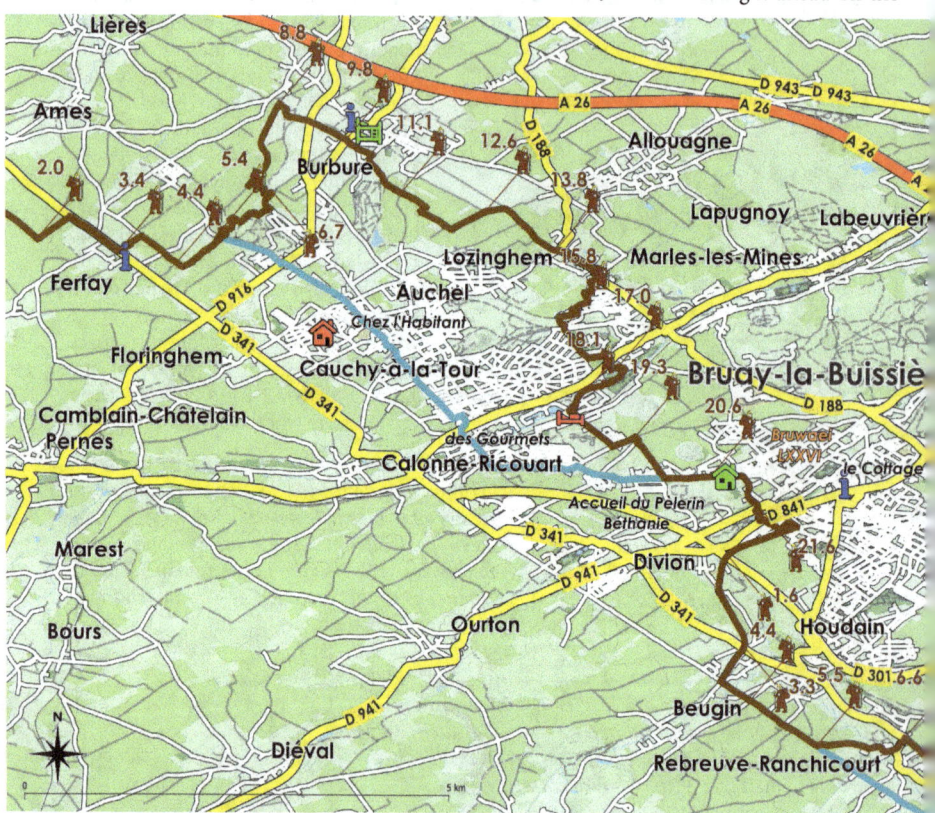

grass track **(5.2)** Take the left fork **(5.4)** At the crossroads with the main road, continue straight ahead, re-enter the woods and bear right on the broad track. Note:- to reduce the

Amettes to Bruay-la-Buissière   stage 9

distance to Bruay by 8km, avoid some difficult navigation and possible hunting in the woods ahead, turn right on the road and follow the Alternate Route**(5.3)**At the crossroads in the woods, turn left[Follow sentier de la Scyrendale, mountain bike route]**(5.4)**Take the right fork 🚶 **(5.4)**At the T-junction, turn right**(5.6)**Take the right and lower fork**(5.7)**At the T-junction in the tracks, bear left, uphill**(5.7)**At the T-junction after a short, but steep climb, turn right on the broad track[Between the pine trees]**(5.9)**At the crossroads in the tracks, turn left on the broader track and then continue straight ahead at the crossroads[Follow the sign for sentier de la Scyrendale]**(6.0)**Continue straight ahead on the main track, avoid the turnings to the right and left**(6.1)**At the T-junction in the track, turn right on the broad track[Hollow in the ground to your left]**(6.2)**At the T-junction with a broad track, turn left[House visible ahead]**(6.4)**At the T-junction with a pasture ahead, turn left 🚶 **(6.7)**At the junction turn sharp left, downhill**(6.9)**Take the left fork, uphill**(7.1)** At the top of the hill, turn left [Keep the trees close on your right]**(7.1)**At the T-junction with the broad level track, turn right 🚶 **(8.8)**Turn sharp right onto a partially obscured track, downhill and bearing right**(8.9)**At the T-junction, turn right. Note:- the stone memorial marks the place where the bodies of the murdered Irish Saints Lugle and Luglien where discovered in 696AD**(9.0)**Turn left onto a narrow track, pass wooden barrier**(9.2)**At the T-junction with a broad gravel track, turn left towards the main road**(9.3)**At the crossroads with the D916, carefully cross the main road and continue straight ahead on the small tarmac road[Towards the cemetery] 🚶 **(9.8)**In **Burbure** at the crossroads with the main road, continue straight ahead[Rue du 11 Novembre]**(10.3)**At the T-junction,with a pasture directly ahead, turn right[Rue Bois Rimbert]**(10.3)**Take the left fork towards the grassy track[House n° 26b on your right]**(10.4)**Continue straight ahead on the track[Pass the barrier]**(10.8)**At the crossroads in the tracks, approaching the top of the hill, continue straight ahead. At the end of the fence bear left towards the road signs on the skyline ahead[Wire fence on your right] 🚶 **(11.1)**At the crossroads with the tarmac road, continue straight ahead on the stony track[Towards the television tower on the horizon]**(11.5)**At the T-junction, turn right on the stony track[Keep the large industrial buildings on your right] **(12.1)**With the water tower and industrial buildings on your right, turn left downhill on the broad stony track [Towards the church spire in Allouagne] 🚶 **(12.6)**At the junction at the foot of the hill, bear right[Towards the church spire]**(12.8)**At the junction, turn right and right again[Towards a prominent church]**(13.5)**At the junction, continue straight ahead[Towards the church] 🚶 **(13.8)**At the end of rue Achille Hibon, bear left towards the Stop sign and then continue straight ahead over the pedestrian crossing and pass through **Lozinghem**[Direction Marles les M. on the D188, towards the church]**(14.5)**Turn right onto rue des Champs Dorés[Small parking area on the left of the junction] 🚶 **(14.8)**At the end of the road, bear right on the track, uphill[Pass the church on your left]**(14.9)**At the end of the hedgerow, turn left and pass through the metal barriers into the playing fields**(15.0)**On reaching the road turn right and then quickly turn right again on the footpath at the rear of the houses**(15.3)**At the end of path turn left on the road[Pass house n° 14 on your right]**(15.4)**At the crossroads, turn right beside the road[Towards

Monument to the first miners

stage 9 — Amettes to Bruay-la-Buissière

the spoil heap]**(15.6)**Turn left through a gap in the crash barriers onto the pathway into the woods 🚶 **(15.8)**At the T-junction with the rue de Cracovie, turn right[Follow the sign for Centre Ville]**(16.4)**At the crossroads with the archway and post office directly ahead, turn left[Direction Centre Ville]**(16.6)**In **Marles-les-Mines**, turn right and pass directly in front of the Mairie**(16.8)**At the junction with the road, turn right and then immediately left downhill[Rue de l'Egalité] 🚶 **(17.0)**Shortly before reaching the church, turn right on the small road[Pass through the barriers into the park]**(17.1)**At the top of the short rise, turn right on the tarmac path[Pass through the park parallel to the river on your left]**(17.4)**At the T-junction with the road, turn left over the bridge and then immediately right on the track 🚶 **(18.1)**At the T-junction with the road, turn left beside the road, uphill[Lake to the right at the junction]**(18.3)**At the crossroads after crossing the railway tracks, continue straight ahead up the hill[Centre Equestre to the right]**(19.0)**At the T-junction at the top of the hill, turn left[Pass bus stop on your left] 🚶 **(19.3)**Turn right and remain on the road, uphill[Large spoil heap on your left at the junction]**(19.4)**Bear left initially on a track and then joining a tarmac road behind the crash barriers[Towards the twin spoil heaps]**(20.1)**At the T-junction with the road, turn left. Note:- the Alternate Route rejoins from the right[Continue with the hedge on your right] 🚶 **(20.6)**At the No-Entry sign, continue straight ahead with caution[Pass grass area on your left]**(21.0)**At the crossroads, turn right on rue Gaston Blot[Pass a boulangerie on your left] 🚶 **(21.6)**At the junction at the foot of the long descent, carefully cross the D302 and take the pathway into the parc de la Lawe and bear left over the wooden bridge[Allée Martin Luther King]**(21.7)**At the top of the steps turn left on the cinder path[Skirt the lake on your right]**(21.9)**Turn left on the uphill path towards the main road[Pass hippo sculpture on your right]**(22.0)**At the road junction, take the pedestrian crossing and turn left[Towards the petrol station]**(22.0)**Arrive at **Bruay-la-Buissière (LXXVI)** at the junction between rue de la République and rue Chopin. Note:- the town centre is straight ahead[Petrol station ahead]

Direct Route to Bruay-la-Buissière

Route: largely undertaken on suburban roads, again parallel to the Chaussée Brunehaut, passing through the former mining towns that have merged with the conurbation of Bruay. The route will reduce your distance by 8 km, but unfortunately bypasses the pilgrim hostel in Burbure.

Length:	7.7km
Ascent:	129m
Descent:	138m

(0.0) Turn right and proceed on the grass beside the main road**(0.9)**At the T-junction with the main road, turn left[Pass small park on your left]**(0.9)**Turn right[Pass second park on your right] 🚶 **(2.0)**At the crossroads, continue straight ahead[Boulevard Emile Basly]**(2.4)**At the traffic lights in **Auchel**, continue straight ahead[Pass the Lycée on your right]**(2.7)**At the roundabout, bear right into place Jules Guesde[Pass between the church and la Poste]**(2.9)**Leave the car park and turn left on rue Roger Salengro[Road immediately bears right] 🚶 **(4.4)**At the T-junction, turn left[Rue de Colmar]**(4.5)**At the T-junction, turn right[School ahead at the junction] **(4.7)**Keep right on the small road[Pass under the main road]**(5.0)**At the T-junction, turn left[Leave rue de la Cavée]**(5.1)**At the Stop sign turn right[Direction Centre Ville - **Calonne-Ricouart**]**(5.3)**At the roundabout continue straight ahead, up the hill[Pass under railway bridge] 🚶 **(5.6)**Bear left on the road, rue de Katowice[Embankment on the right] 🚶 **(6.6)**At the crossroads turn right on rue du Bois Rietz[Turn just before the supermarket] **(6.9)**At the crossroads go straight ahead on rue Paul Langevin[Water tower behind houses to the right]**(7.4)**At the crossroads go straight ahead on rue du Maréchal Léclerc[Pass bus stop on the right] 🚶 **(7.7)**At the junction, continue straight ahead and rejoin the "Official Route"[Field on your right]

Amettes to Bruay-la-Buissière — stage 9

Accommodation and Tourist Information

Béthune
🛏 **Béthune Bruay Tourisme**,3 rue Aristide Briand, 62400 Béthune, France; Tel:+33(0)3 21 52 50 00; tourisme-bethune-bruay.fr

Bruay-la-Buissière
🏠 **Accueil du Pèlerin - Béthanie**,215 Rue Paul Eluard, 62700 Bruay-la-Buissière, France; Tel:+33(0)675979919; +33(0)675333141; Email:annie.bureau@numericable.fr; Price:B; *1 bedroom 40€ pp including dinner and breakfast*

🛏 **Hôtel - B&B Hotel**,350 rue Eric Tabarly Parc de la Porte Nord, 62700 Bruay-la-Buissière, France; Tel:+33(0)2 98 33 75 29; www.hotel-bb.com; Price:B

🛏 **Hôtel Restaurant - Dolce Vita**,2049 rue de la Libération, 62700 Bruay-la-Buissière, France; Tel:+33(0)3 21 62 00 22; +33(0)6 81 10 21 99; dolcevita-bruay.com; Price:B

🛏 **Hôtel - Ibis Styles**,Parc de la Porte Nord, rue des Frères Lumière, 62700 Bruay-la-Buissière, France; Tel:+33(0)3 21 01 11 11; Email:H9188@accor.com; all.accor.com; Price:B

🛏 **Hôtel - le Cottage**,292 avenue Libération, 62700 Bruay-la-Buissière, France; Tel:+33(0)3 21 53 14 14; Email:lecottagehotel@wanadoo.fr; lecottage-hotel.com; Price:B; *A pilgrim commented on the lack of hospitality*

🛏 **Mairie de Bruay-la-Buissière**,23 place Henri Cadot, 62700 Bruay-la-Buissière, France; Tel:+33(0)3 21 64 56 00; bruaylabuissiere.fr

Burbure
✉ **Gîte d'Etape du Presbytère**,Place de l'Église, 62151 Burbure, France; Tel:+33(0)3 21 61 02 00; Email:mairie.burbure@wanadoo.fr; burbureviagite.wordpress.com; Price:C; *Contact the Mairie for reservationa nd access. 7 beds washing machine shower and kitchen*

🛏 **Mairie du Burbure**,22 rue Noémie Delobelle, 62151 Burbure, France; Tel:+33(0)972283871; Email:contact@burbure.fr; burbure.fr

Calonne-Ricouart
🛏 **Auberge - des Gourmets**,Rue du Mont Saint Éloi, 62470 Calonne-Ricouart, France; Tel:+33(0)3 21 62 26 58; Email:lesgourmetscalonnix@free.fr; lesgourmetscalonnix.free.fr; Price:B

Cauchy-À-la-Tour
🏠 **Chambre d'Hôtes - Chez l'Habitant**,35 rue Jules Devy, 62260 Cauchy-À-la-Tour, France; Tel:+33(0)6 11 44 78 43; Email:delphine.lioneldeclerck@gmail.com; Price:B

Ferfay
🛏 **Mairie**,41 Chaussée Brunehaut, 62260 Ferfay, France; Tel:+33(0)3 21 52 77 10; Email:ferfay.mairie@ferfay.fr; ferfay.com

stage 10   Bruay-la-Buissière to Ablain-Saint-Nazaire

Length:	26.1km
Ascent:	621m
Descent:	559m
Canterbury	194km
Col Grand Saint Bernard:	1045km

Notre Dame de Lorette

Route: initially the route from Bruay-la-Buissière to Ablain-Saint-Nazaire follows a disused railway and then briefly following a quiet section of the Chaussée Brunehaut the "Official Route" follows the path of the established GR°127, climbing the wooded ridge to the north of Sigeric's probable route. The route passes the cemetery of Notre Dame de Lorette before beginning the descent to return to the Douai plain.

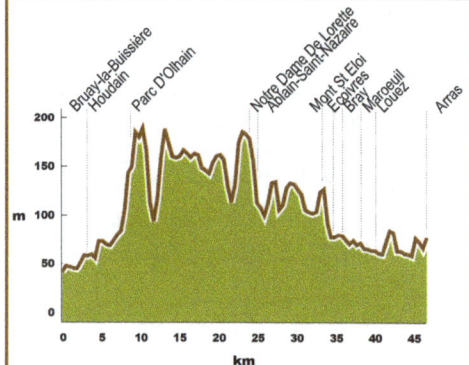

Opportunities to buy food and drink are again very limited after leaving the conurbation of Bruay.

The Alternate Route remains close to the Chaussée Brunehaut and reduces the distance to Arras by 12 km.

At the start of World War I, the Battle of Lorette lasted from October 1914 to October 1915, resulting in high casualties on both sides: 100,000 killed and as many wounded. A French national cemetery was built on thirteen hectares nearby and comprises 20,000 graves, laid out irrespective of rank or military training. In eight ossuaries, around the base of the lantern tower, are the remains of 22,970 unidentified soldiers. A portion of the cemetery has also been reserved for Muslim soldiers.

(0.0) From the junction between rue de la République and rue Chopin take rue Chopin, uphill [Leave the parc de la Lawe directly behind you] **(0.2)** At the top of the hill, turn left [Pass a row of miner's cottages on your right] **(0.4)** At the end of the road, go down the flight of steps and continue on the road **(0.4)** Turn right on rue Rossini **(0.6)** At the end of

Bruay-la-Buissière to Ablain-Saint-Nazaire — stage 10

rue Rossini, climb the embankment and turn right on the track**(0.6)**At the T-junction, turn right on the grit track that follows the former railway[Pass a petrol station on your left] **(1.6)**Continue straight ahead under the road bridge**(2.2)**At the crossroads with a tarmac road, continue straight ahead[Pass beside the barriers] **(3.3)**Take the pedestrian crossing over the busy D341 and continue straight ahead on the old railway[Beside the former **Houdain** railway station]**(3.9)**At the road crossing turn left and leave the railway[Beside the rue Ville Juif bus stop]**(3.9)**At the crossroads, continue straight ahead, uphill[Chaussée Brunehaut] **(4.4)**At the roundabout, just before the top of the hill, continue straight ahead[Rue du Bon Val]**(4.7)**At the crossroads with the track, continue straight ahead on the tarmac, towards the brow of the hill**(5.0)**At the crossroads in the hollow, continue straight ahead on the road **(5.5)**Turn left onto the small tarmac road. Note:- the "Official Route" makes a major loop climbing to the ridge top on your left and then meandering on woodland and farm tracks before returning to the historic route near the ruins of the Abbaye de Mont St Eloi. The "Official Route" involves some steep climbs and can be treacherous in wet conditions. The Alternate Route proceeds more directly and saves 12km**(6.2)**At the T-junction, turn left and follow the road as it skirts the château on the left[Pass large metal building on your right] **(6.6)**At the T-junction with the main road, turn left on the gravel path beside the road**(6.8)**At the mini-roundabout take the first exit, slightly uphill[Rue d'Olhain]**(7.3)** As the road narrows at the top of the hill, continue straight ahead[Basketball court on your left] **(7.7)**At the crossroads in the tracks directly under the power line, turn left towards the forest**(8.4)**At the entry to the woods, take the left fork **(8.7)**At the top of the hill continue straight ahead on the path[Pass a camp site on your right]**(8.9)**At the T-junction with the road, turn right, uphill[Entrance to **Parc d'Olhain**]**(9.1)**Beside the camping reception, continue straight ahead on the road[Towards parcours Aventure, passing a red and white metal barrier] **(9.9)**Bear left in front of the central reception building**(10.0)**After passing the reception area, bear right on the tarmac[Towards the Salle Polyvalente]**(10.2)**At the end of the tarmac, continue straight ahead across the grass with the trees immediately on your left, towards the gap in the trees in the corner**(10.3)**Immediately after entering the woods, turn right and remain close to the grassy area**(10.5)**Turn left and continue through the field with the edge of the woods on your left**(10.8)**Continue straight ahead and briefly renter the woods **(10.9)**Shortly before again leaving the woods turn right, down hill[Follow the path through the trees separating the open fields on your left and right]**(11.0)**Take the left fork[Golf course on your left]**(11.4)**At the T-junction with the tarmac road, turn left[Car park on your left] **(12.7)**At the entrance to the Forêt Domaniale d'Olhain, turn right on the track[Continue with the woods on your left and a field on your right] **(13.3)**At the junction in the tracks, turn right in the edge of the woods**(13.6)**In the corner of the field, continue straight ahead on the forest track **(14.2)**At the T-junction with the road, turn left and immediately take the turning to the right on the tarmac[Pass modern bungalow on your left]**(14.5)**At the first crossroads, turn left on the gravel track**(14.9)**Bear left and then right on the track[Keep the tall transmitter mast on your left] **(15.0)**Enter the village of Servains and keep right**(15.4)**Pass a small stone chapel on your left and continue straight ahead **(16.3)** Turn left towards the football fields**(16.6)**At the T-junction, continue straight ahead on the gravel track[Pass metal barrier] **(17.6)**At the road junction turn right and keep

Notre Dame de Lorette
Lantern Tower

stage 10   Bruay-la-Buissière to Ablain-Saint-Nazaire

right[Military cemetery to the left]**(18.3)**Bear left and pass between the roundabout and the car park[Direction Ablain St. N.]**(18.4)**Pass the Mairie on your left and then take the next left[Narrowing tarmac road] **(18.8)**At the crown of the bend to the left, turn right on the gravel track**(19.6)**Take the left fork and keep left[Initially remain between the trees] **(19.7)**At the crossroads, turn right on the partially made road[Chemin de la Chapelle] **(20.3)**At the junction, continue straight ahead on the track[The track will turn right then left]**(20.4)**Turn right in the clearing with the woods directly ahead[Downhill]**(20.6)**Bear left keeping the woods to your left and an open field on your right**(20.9)**As you approach the village turn sharp left on the broad track. Note:- At the expense of bypassing the French military cemetery of Notre Dame de Lorette 3 km may be saved by continuing straight ahead into the village of Ablain-Saint-Nazaire. The "Official Route" will cross from the left 700m ahead[Pass through a valley as you reclimb the hill] **(23.7)**At the junction in the tracks turn right**(24.3)**At the junction in the tracks, continue straight ahead in the edge of

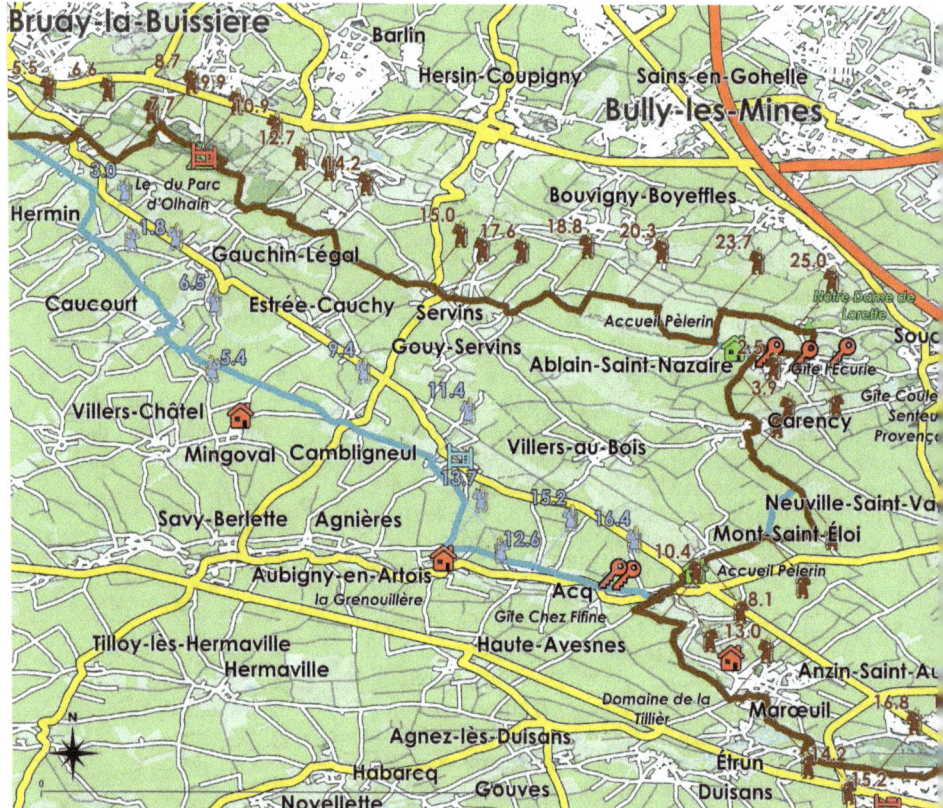

the woods **(25.0)**At the T-junction with the road beside the cemetery of **Notre Dame de Lorette**, turn right on the pathway that skirts the cemetery**(25.0)**At the road junction, bear left remaining beside the cemetery. Note:- at the time of writing the pathway ahead was closed because of the discovery of unexploded ordnance. To avoid this path, bear right on the road, down the hill in the direction of Ablain St Nazaire. The "Official Route" will join

Bruay-la-Buissière to Ablain-Saint-Nazaire stage 10

from the left in 500m**(25.3)**Shortly before reaching the main entrance to the cemetery, turn right down the steep wooded track**(25.7)**At the T-junction with the road, turn left and continue downhill**(25.9)**As the road turns to the left, turn right on the unmade track into the trees[Ruins of the old church of Ablain-Saint-Nazaire below] **(26.1)**Arrive at **Ablain-Saint-Nazaire** outskirts. Note:- the most direct route to the village centre is to leave the "Official Route" and turn left down the hill on rue Ponthiers and then right at the subsequent T-junction, cyclists are advised to follow this route to avoid barriers ahead on the "Official Route"[T-junction with road, sports field directly ahead]

Direct Route Towards Mont St Éloi

Route: will remain close to the now unfortunately busy Chaussée Brunehaut - the probable historic route - but will use broad gravel tracks and minor roads to cross the Douai plain and avoid the infamous Vimy Ridge. The route will bypass the accommodation options in Ablain-Saint-Nazaire but will make it possible to stay	**Length:** 17.2km **Ascent:** 232m **Descent:** 228m

with the very pilgrim oriented family at the Château de Villers-Châtel or for stronger walkers to reach Arras in a single day. **(0.0)**Continue straight ahead[Chaussée Brunehaut]**(0.6)**At the crossroads go straight ahead[Modern houses on both side of the road]**(0.9)**At the crossroads at the bottom of the hill, continue straight ahead[Uphill between the trees] **(1.8)**At the Stop sign turn right[D72, direction Hermin]**(2.2)**On the crown of the bend to the left, bear right onto track towards the water tower[Beside semi-buried building]**(2.7)**At the road junction beside the water tower turn left on the road towards Hermin[Pass cemetery on the left] **(3.0)**In the centre of **Hermin** bear left and immediately turn right onto a smaller road[Pass the church on your left and Mairie on your right]**(3.3)**At fork in the road bear left[Rue du Calvaire]**(3.5)**At the junction, continue straight ahead[Towards the brow of the hill] **(4.4)**s[D73, direction Caucourt]**(5.1)**On the entry to **Caucourt** fork left on rue du Parc[Calvaire to the left] **(5.4)**At the T-junction after crossing a small bridge turn right[Stream on your right]**(5.9)**At the T-junction with the main road, turn sharp left on the D73[Uphill, embankment on the right] **(6.5)**After leaving the village take the first road to the left[Towards the transmission mast on the horizon]**(6.6)**Bear right on the road

stage 10 — Bruay-la-Buissière to Ablain-Saint-Nazaire

(9.4) At the junction with the D73e2 turn left[Enter Cambligneul] (9.8) At the crossroads with the D75 continue straight ahead[Direction Camblain-l'Abbé] (11.4) At the T-junction in **Camblain-l'Abbé** bear right on rue de l'Eglise and then left on rue Cojon[Follow sign for Cycle Route] (11.7) Take the left fork[Direction Acq] (12.6) At the junction, bear right[Between open fields] (13.7) At the crossroads, shortly before entering Frévin-Capelle turn left[Chemin de Mont Saint Éloi] (14.2) At the crossroads continue straight ahead[Uphill] (14.6) Take the left fork[Chemin d'Aubigny] (15.2) At the crossroads in **Acq**, go straight ahead on rue de l'Egalité[Public toilet to the left] (15.5) Continue straight ahead on farm track[Large farm buildings on the right] (16.0) At the road junction go straight ahead on the main road, D49[The ruins of Mont St Éloi visible on the left] (16.4) On the outskirts of **Écoivres**, take the left fork, rue de Douai[Pass wooden sign on the left] (16.9) Take the right fork[Rue Oboeuf] (17.0) At the T-junction turn right[Towards church] (17.1) Continue straight ahead on rue Oboeuf[Pass a stone wall and church on the right] (17.2) Turn right into place d' Eglise. Note:- the "Official Route" rejoins from the left[Church on right]

Accommodation and Tourist Information

Ablain-Saint-Nazaire
🏠 **Accueil Pèlerin**[Claire Dubocage],8a rue de Lens, 62153 Ablain-Saint-Nazaire, France; Tel:+33(0)3 21 29 24 62; +33(0)6 82 38 00 06; Email:gite-lescheminsdelorette@orange.fr; Price:B; *Only Friday Saturday and Sunday*
🔑 **Gîte - l'Écurie**,6 rue des Scieurs, 62153 Ablain-Saint-Nazaire, France; Tel:+33(0)3 21 45 13 62; +33(0)6 85 10 60 45; Email:decoupigny.serge@wanadoo.fr; decoupignyserge.wixsite.com/gitedelecurie; Price:B
🔑 **Gîte - les Chemins de Lorette**,51 rue Marcel Lancino, 62153 Ablain-Saint-Nazaire, France; Tel:+33(0)3 21 29 24 62; +33(0)6 82 38 00 06; Email:gite-lescheminsdelorette@orange.fr; web.facebook.com/giteleschemin-sdelorette; Price:A
🔑 **Gîte - Couleurs et Senteurs Provençales**[Sylviane Labenne],9E rue Marcel Lancino, 62153 Ablain-Saint-Nazaire, France; Tel: +33(0) 670 30 70 84; Email:pierre.lebenne@orange.fr; tourisme-lenslievin.fr/?s=couleurs+et+senteurs; Price:B

Camblain-l'Abbé
🍴 **Collège St-jean Baptiste**[Frère Jean Bosco],5 Rue du Perroy, 62690 Camblain-l'Abbé, France; Tel: +33 (0) 622 868 601; Email:michelherve6206@gmail.com; Price:C

Frévin-Capelle
🏠 **Chambre d'Hôtes - la Grenouillère**[Olivier Demoulin],15 rue Marechal Léclerc, 62690 Frévin-Capelle, France; Tel:+33(0)6 33 27 94 00; Email:contactlagrenouillere@gmail.com; web.facebook.com/lagrenouillere62; Price:A

Houdain
🏠 **Résidence de Séjour Ethic Étapes - Parc d'Olhain**,Parc de Loisirs d'Olhain, 62150 Houdain, France; Tel:+33(0)3 21 27 91 79; Email:reservation@parcdolhain.fr; www.parcdolhain.fr/la-residence-daccueil-et-de-sejour-ethic-etapes; Price:B; *Open all year*

Maisnil-les-Ruitz
⛺ **Le Camping du Parc d'Olhain**,Rue de Rebreuve, 62620 Maisnil-les-Ruitz, France; Tel:+33(0)3 21 27 91 79; Email:contact@parcdolhain.fr; www.parcdolhain.fr/le-camping-du-parc-dolhain; Price:C; *Chalets also available*

Villers-Châtel
🏠 **Chambre d'Hôtes - Château de Villers-Châtel**,92 rue Émile Delaire, 62690 Villers-Châtel, France; Tel:+33(0)6 35 16 01 06; +33(0)3 21 59 02 52; Email:jeandefranssu@hotmail.fr; www.arraspaysdartois.com/en/accommodation/en-chateau-de-villers-chatel/; Price:D; *Special rates for pilgrims with credentials that book ahead* ; **PR**

Ablain-Saint-Nazaire to Arras

stage 11

Length:	21.5km
Ascent:	310m
Descent:	338m
Canterbury	220km
Col Grand Saint Bernard:	1019km

The towers of Mont-Saint-Éloi abbey

Route: the route from Ablain-Saint-Nazaire to Arras continues on farm tracks and minor roads, crossing a further ridge before climbing to pass the ruins of the Abbey of Mont Saint Éloi and then returning to the Douai plain. The entry to the large and historic town of Arras initially uses cycle tracks beside the main roads and then pathways through the park of les Grandes Prairies before following the busy roads through the town centre to the Place des Héros.

For many centuries, Arras was on the border between France and the Low Countries, and frequently changed hands before firmly becoming French, in the late 17th century, the fortifications upgraded by Vauban helping to keep it in French hands. The town was closely linked to the trade of Flanders and later became an important centre for sugar beet farming and processing, as well as a prosperous market centre. In the 14th and 15th centuries, Arras was a thriving textile town, specialising in fine wool tapestries that were sold to decorate palaces and castles all over Europe. Few of these tapestries survived the French Revolution, when hundreds were burnt to recover the gold thread that was often woven into them. Nevertheless, the term arras is still used to refer to a rich tapestry, no matter where it was woven.

During the First World War, Arras was near the front, and the long series of battles fought nearby are known as the Battle of Arras. A network of medieval tunnels beneath the city, unknown to the Germans, became a decisive factor in the British forces holding of Arras (guided tours available). Nevertheless, the city was heavily damaged and had to be rebuilt after the war. In the World War II, 240 suspected French Resistance members were executed in the Arras citadel.

Today, Arras has thoroughly absorbed its historical past as a pilgrim thoroughfare, and as you are walking you can look down and see signs on the pavement for both the via Francigena and St James Way.

stage 11 — Ablain-Saint-Nazaire to Arras

(0.0) At the T-junction with the road, turn right on the road which quickly becomes a stony track. Note:- if leaving from the centre of the village the most direct route is to briefly follow the D57, with the church on your left, and then rejoin the "Official Route" by turning left on rue des Vauxchaux[Wire fencing on the left]**(0.1)** At an oblique crossroads, continue straight ahead with the open field on your left[Church steeple on the left at the junction] **(0.3)** As the main track bears right, continue straight ahead through the wooden barriers[GR®127 sign]**(0.7)** Turn left over the small bridge and continue with the fence on your left**(0.8)** Continue straight ahead on the tarmac road[Pass house n°10 on your left] **(0.9)** At the crossroads with the D57, continue straight ahead on rue des Vauxchaux **(1.4)** Keep left on the smaller road**(1.9)** At the top of the hill, continue straight ahead avoid the turning to the left[Mont St Éloi visible ahead] **(2.5)** At the T-junction with a tarmac road, turn left and enter the village of Carency**(2.7)** At the road junction, bear left continuing downhill[Rue du Moulin]**(2.9)** At the T-junction at the top of the hill, turn right and then immediately left[Direction Mont St Éloi, GR®127 sign]**(3.1)** At the crossroads with a church on your left, turn right[Rue Jules Ferry]**(3.3)** At the road junction, turn left on rue du Général Barbot **(3.9)** Take the left fork towards the woods[Mont St Éloi ahead] **(4.9)** At the junction in the track, continue straight ahead and then turn right and right again to circle the field. Note:- 800m may be saved by turning right and rejoining the "Official Route" immediately after passing the farm [Woods on your left at the junction] **(7.0)** At theT-junction with the road, turn left **(8.1)** At the top of the hill, continue straight ahead[Ruins of **Mont St Éloi** on your left]**(8.2)** With the entrance to the ruins immediately on your left, turn right[Rue des Tours]**(8.4)** At the T-junction at the foot of the hill, turn left**(8.7)** At the junction with the main road, Chaussée Brunehaut, carefully cross the road and continue straight ahead on the pathway between the houses**(8.9)** At the T-junction with the tarmac road, turn right, downhill [Towards the church spire] **(9.1)** At the T-junction turn right

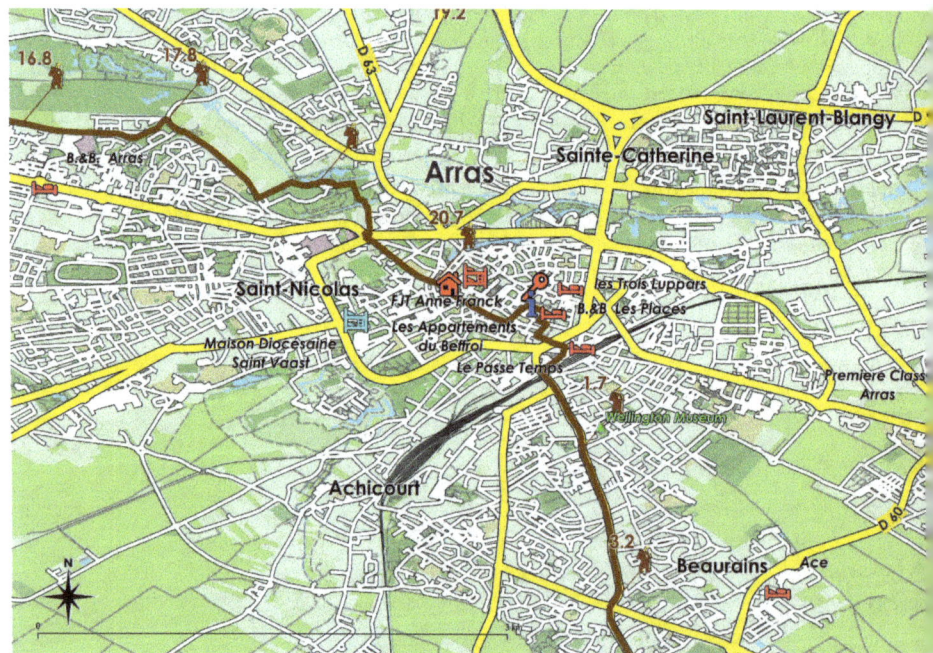

Ablain-Saint-Nazaire to Arras — stage 11

towards Acq[Stone calvaire at the junction]**(9.5)**At the road junction beside the church in **Écoivres**, bear left and then right. Note:- the Alternate Route rejoins from the right[Rue de l'Eglise]**(10.0)**Turn left on the tarmac road immediately after going under the railway bridge 🚶 **(10.4)**Turn left over the bridge**(10.8)**On entering the village of **Bray**, turn right on

rue de l'Ecole**(11.3)**Immediately after re-crossing the railway, turn left on the stony track[Initially parallel to railway] 🚶 **(13.0)**At the T-junction turn left over the level-crossing**(13.1)** Bear right on D56, towards Maroeuil Centre**(13.2)**Bear left on D56 again towards **Maroeuil**(13.4)At the road junction, turn right on rue du Vert Bocage[Keep the iron railings on your left]**(13.5)**At the Stop sign, turn left[Cross the river la Scarpe]**(13.5)** Turn right on rue de la Marlière[Parallel to river on the right]**(13.7)**Turn right on rue de la Source 🚶 **(14.2)**Shortly after passing La Source de Sainte Bertille, turn right[Pass through the car park]**(14.3)**Turn left on a narrow grass path to continue beside river - do not cross the bridge[River on the right]**(15.1)**At the T-junction with the road, turn right[Enter **Louez**] 🚶 **(15.2)**Turn right towards Louez military cemetery[Direction Aubigny en A.]**(15.6)**As the road bears right, turn left on rue des Maçons (marked No Through Road) - road becomes track**(16.1)**Proceed straight ahead under the road bridge 🚶 **(16.8)**Continue straight ahead on the track[Golf course in the valley to the left, commercial area to the right]**(17.5)**At the T-junction, bear left on the gravel path[New houses immediately on your left]**(17.7)**Continue straight ahead[Down the steps]**(17.8)**Pass through metal turnstile gate and then bear right[Towards the main road] 🚶 **(17.8)**At the T-junction with the main road, turn right on the footpath and bike track[D64, rue du 8 Mai 1945]**(17.9)**At the traffic lights, continue straight ahead and take the pedestrian crossing[Continue to follow the bike track] **(18.8)**At the end of the soccer pitch turn left into the park. Note:- a number of GR° routes pass through the park and as a result the GR° markings can be confusing 🚶 **(19.2)**Bear left on the path[Keep the stream close on your left] **(19.4)**At the crossroads after the car park turn left**(19.5)**At the end of the road, turn right[Towards large building]**(19.6)**Turn left and then right[Cross the bridge]**(19.7)**After the second bridge, continue straight[Climb steps]

Le Beffroi

stage 11 — Ablain-Saint-Nazaire to Arras

(20.0) At the complex junction at end of chemin de la Baudimont, take the pedestrian crossings to follow the road towards Centre Ville[Rue Baudimont] **(20.7)** At the traffic lights, continue straight ahead towards Centre Ville[Rue Saint Aubert] **(21.0)** At the crossroads, continue straight ahead[Direction Les Places] **(21.3)** Turn left on rue Désiré Delansorne[Direction Les Places, bell tower ahead] **(21.4)** At the traffic lights, continue straight ahead[Towards bell tower] **(21.5)** Arrive at **Arras (LXXV)** place des Héros[Beside bell tower]

Place des Héros - Arras

Ablain-Saint-Nazaire to Arras — stage 11

Accommodation and Tourist Information

Arras

🏠 **FJT - Anne Franck**,21 Rue du Bloc, 62000 Arras, France; Tel:+33 (0) 3 21 71 92 97; Email:plateformelogementjeunes@4aj.fr; plateformelogement.wixsite.com/jeunesarras; Price:C; *Hostel for young workers convenient location*

🛏**Maison Diocésaine Saint Vaast**,103 rue Amiens, 62000 Arras, France; Tel:+33(0)3 21 21 40 38; Email:aison.diocesaine@arras.catholique.fr; arras.catholique.fr/accueil-hotellerie; Price:C; **PR**

🏠 **B&B - Au Carré Saint Éloi**,3 place du Wetz d'Amain, 62000 Arras, France; Tel:+33(0)3 21 51 00 98; +33(0)6 84 85 61 68; aucarresainteloi.com; Price:B; *Reduced price for back-packer's room* ; **PR**

🛏**Hôtel - Le Passe Temps**,1 place Mar Foch, 62000 Arras, France; Tel:+33(0)3 21 50 04 04; Email:le-passe-temps-62@orange.fr; www.arraspaysdartois.com/en/accommodation/en-le-passe-temps; Price:B

🛏**Hôtel - les Trois Luppars**,49 Grand'place, 62000 Arras, France; Tel:+33(0)3 21 60 02 03; www.hotel-les3luppars.com; Price:A

🛏**Hôtel - B&B Hôtel Les Places**,Place Ipswich, 11 rue de Justice, 62000 Arras, France; Tel:+33 (0)2 98 337 529; www.hotel-bb.com/en/hotel/arras-centre-les-places; Price:A

🛏**Hôtel - B&B Hôtel Arras**,Rue de la Symphorine, 62000 Arras, France; Tel:+33(0)2 98 33 75 29; www.hotel-bb.com/en/hotel/arras; Price:B

🔑 **Apartment - Les Appartements du Beffroi**,3 place Héros, 62000 Arras, France; Tel:+33(0)6 16 56 43 50; Email:info@arras-appartement-diamant.com; arras-appartement-diamant.com; Price:A; *Will accommodate 4 to 6 people*

ℹ **Office de Tourisme**,Place des Héros, 62000 Arras, France; Tel:+33(0)3 21 51 26 95; www.arraspaysdartois.com

Beaurains

🛏**Hôtel - Ace**,11 avenue des Coquelicots, 62217 Beaurains, France; Tel:+33(0)3 21 60 50 00; www.ace-hotel.com; Price:B; *In the south of the city 1.5 km from the official route*

Maroeuil

🏠 **Chambre d'Hôtes - Domaine de la Tillièr**,113 Chemin de Bray, 62161 Maroeuil, France; Tel:+33(0)3 21 58 79 30; +33(0)6 71 27 97 74; Email:contact@domainedelatilliere.com; domainedelatilliere.com; Price:B; *Hunting centre*

Mont-Saint-Éloi

🏠 **Accueil Pèlerin**,9 rue du Général Barbot, 62144 Mont-Saint-Éloi, France; Tel:+33(0)6 76 92 56 51; Email:jpcdegouge@gmail.com; Price:C; *Breakfast incuded 1 bedroom*

🔑 **Gîte - Chez Fifine**,21 rue de Douai Hameau d'Écoivres, 62144 Mont-Saint-Éloi, France; Tel:+33(0)6 89 72 04 65; Email:contact@chez-fifine.fr; chez-fifine.fr/; Price:A; *Room able to accommodate 6 people*

🔑 **Gîte - des Menhirs**,33 rue de Douai Hameau d'Écoivres, 62144 Mont-Saint-Éloi, France; Tel:+33(0)7 82 17 74 24; +33(0)3 21 55 84 62; Email:contact@legitedesmenhirs.fr; www.legitedesmenhirs.fr; Price:A; *Room able to accommodate 7 people*

Tilloy-Lès-Mofflaines

🛏**Hôtel - Premiere Classe Arras**,27 avenue d'Immercourt, 62217 Tilloy-Lès-Mofflaines, France; Tel:+33(0)3 91 20 32 03; Email:arras.tilloy@premiereclasse.fr; www.premiereclasse.com; Price:C

stage 12 — Arras to Bapaume

Length:	26.9km
Ascent:	295m
Descent:	248m
Canterbury	241km
Col Grand Saint Bernard:	998km

Chapelle Notre-Dame de La Salette - Boisleux-Saint-Marc

Route: progress on the route from Arras to Bapaume is relatively easy using straight and generally level minor roads and tracks across farmland and first world war battlefields.

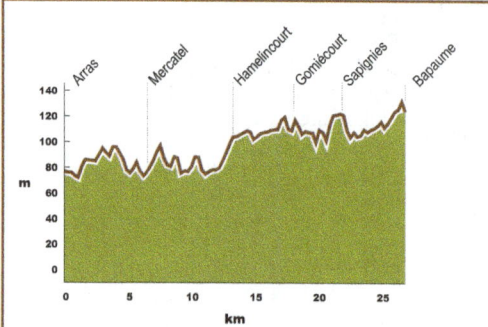

Sadly, in common with much of rural France, there are few intermediate facilities on this stage.

Bapaume is a small town but has all necessary facilities.

It is on a crossing point between Artois and the plains of Flanders on the one hand, and the valley of the Somme and the Paris basin on the other - a position that made it the focal point for wars throughout its history. In 1335, Bapaume was fortified outside the castle walls, but unfortunately the fortifications were ineffective and the city was repeatedly taken. In 1540, Charles V ordered a fortified palace to be built, with thick walls and bastions, including defensive systems such as tunnels and galleries. These fortifications were later reinforced by Vauban.

By the 19th century, Bapaume was no longer regarded as a fortified town, with the result that the walls and bastions were blown-up and the moats filled in. Only the tower and part of the bastion of Dauphin are still visible. Work has been done recently to restore and make accessible the underground galleries used as shelters during both world wars.

Bapaume Bastion

Arras to Bapaume
stage 12

(0.0) From Arras centre with the bell tower behind, follow the right hand side of the place des Héros[Car park on the left]**(0.1)** Turn right to leave the place[Rue des Balances]**(0.2)** At the T-junction, turn left[Rue Emile Legrelle]**(0.2)** Take the first turning to the right[Narrow street, rue Briquet Tailliander]**(0.4)** At the T-junction, turn left[No-Entry sign, rue Gambetta]**(0.5)** At the traffic lights continue straight ahead[Towards the railway station]**(0.6)** Turn right in place du Maréchal Foch[Station ahead]**(0.7)** Bear right into rue du Dr Brassart[Pass the hotel on your right and railway on your left]**(0.9)** At the T-junction, turn left on the avenue du Maréchal Léclerc[Cross over the railway] **(1.7)** Continue straight ahead at the crossroads[D917 (former N17) direction Beaurains] **(3.2)** At the traffic lights, continue straight ahead[Direction Bapaume]**(4.0)** Turn right onto rue Robespierre, towards the water tower[Restaurant La Nouvelle Auberge on the corner] **(4.4)** Continue straight ahead on the tarmac, pass under the highway bridge **(6.0)** Take the right fork and remain on the tarmac[Keep the church and trees on your left]**(6.6)** At the crossroads in **Mercatel** continue straight ahead on rue de l'Abbiette[Small chapel to the left of the junction] **(7.5)** Continue straight ahead on the road[Pass under the TGV track] **(8.8)** Continue straight ahead and avoid the path to the right[Pass Montaigu Chapelle on your right]**(9.3)** Cross the road and bear right then left onto the track[Cutting the corner]**(9.4)** Briefly rejoin the road and turn left onto a pathway into the woods **(10.0)** At the junction with a tarmac road, continue straight ahead on the grassy track between the trees[Cemetery on your right]**(10.2)** At the crossroads with a further tarmac road, continue straight ahead on the disused railway track[Brick built house on your right] **(10.4)** Continue straight ahead on the old railway track, avoid turning to the right[Radio tower visible on your right] **(11.3)** At the crossroads with the tarmac road, turn right on the road**(11.5)** At the junction in the tracks, continue straight ahead on the grassy track[Towards the wind generators and church steeple on the horizon]**(12.2)** At the junction with the broader track, turn left and continue slightly uphill[Towards the church] **(13.2)** At the junction in the tracks, continue straight ahead on the tarmac[Pass small chapel on your right]**(13.3)** At the crossroads with the D12, continue straight ahead on the track[Pass the village of **Hamelincourt** on your right]**(14.0)** At the T-junction in the tracks, turn right **(14.3)** At the crossroads with the D12, continue straight ahead on the tarmac road and then immediately turn left on the track **(16.4)** At the T-junction with the road, turn right on the road towards the village of Courcelles-le-Comte[Chapelle Saint Sulpice ahead]**(16.8)** At the road junction, turn sharp left and pass beside the Chapelle Saint Sulpice[Direction Gomiécourt, C9] **(18.1)** At the T-junction in **Gomiécourt** turn right,

stage 12   Arras to Bapaume

C'est clair. Oui? All roads lead to Rome

direction Achiet-le-Grand and then immediately turn left[Direction Gomiécourt South Cemetery]**(19.0)**At the T-junction, turn left[Towards Gomiécourt South Cemetery] **(19.2)**Just before reaching the cemetery, turn right on the tarmac road[Slightly uphill, between embankments]**(19.9)**At the junction, continue straight ahead on the tarmac [Hedgerow on your left] **(20.8)**Just before the brow of the hill, continue straight ahead on the tarmac[Pass large barns on your right]**(21.2)**At the crossroads, continue straight ahead on the track[Towards Bapaume on the horizon]**(21.4)**At the crossroads with the tarmac road, turn left[Towards the church spire] **(21.9)**At the crossroads beside the church in **Sapignies**, turn right[Towards the German military cemetery] **(23.5)**At the crossroads with a tarmac road, continue straight ahead on the track **(25.0)**At the T-junction with a road and with an ivy covered house ahead, turn left and immediately right**(25.3)**At the T-junction with a tarmac road, turn left**(25.6)**At the T-junction with D929 turn right, cross the disused railway and then turn left[Pass Mr Bricolage on your right] **(26.1)**At the crossroads, turn left towards the green spire**(26.2)**At the crossroads, turn right[Rue Oribus] **(26.3)**At the T-junction, turn right and then bear left and follow the path as it circles inside the park**(26.7)**At the T-junction, turn right and then bear left[Pass the church on your left] **(26.9)**Arrive at **Bapaume** centre[Beside war memorial]

Accommodation and Tourist Information

Bapaume

Paroisse Notre Dame Pitie,3 rue Eglise, 62450 Bapaume, France; Tel:+33(0)9 60 51 20 69; +33(0)3 21 07 13 37; Email:paroissend.depitie@wanadoo.fr; Price:D; *Minimal facilities but kind can be difficult to contact*
Hôtel Restaurant - le Gourmet,10 rue Gare, 62450 Bapaume, France; Tel:+33(0)3 21 07 20 00; Email:contact@le-gourmet.fr; www.le-gourmet.fr; Price:B

Hôtel - de la Paix,11 avenue Abel Guidet, 62450 Bapaume, France; Tel:+33(0)3 21 22 28 28; +33(0)6 01 68 51 84; Email:contact@hoteldelapaix-bapaume.fr; hotel-de-la-paix-bapaume.com; Price:A

Mairie - Bapaume,36 place Faidherbe, 62450 Bapaume, France; Tel:+33(0)3 32 15 05 88 0; Email:accueil@bapaume.fr; bapaume.fr

Bapaume to Péronne

stage 13

Length:	30.7km
Ascent:	338m
Descent:	408m
Canterbury	268km
Col Grand Saint Bernard:	971km

Museum of the Great War

Route: the route from Bapaume to Péronne parallels the Roman road, which is now a very busy *route departmentale*. Although this is a potentially long stage, approximately 5 km may be saved by using the 2 short Alternate Routes over minor roads in place of wide loops through farmland. Care may be needed with navigation in the stretches of open farmland as signs are infrequent and often damaged by farm machinery.

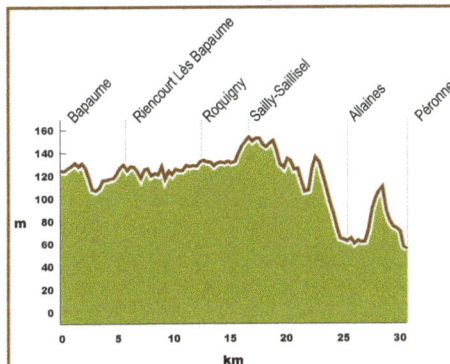

Péronne offers a broad choice of accommodation and eating places. There is a café in the village of Rocquigny.

Péronne is located at the confluence of the rivers Somme and Cologne. Its geographical situation being extremely important throughout its history.

Few towns have been destroyed so often. Burned and pillaged in the time of the Normans, gravely damaged during the Spanish occupation, devastated by the Germans in 1870, totally destroyed in 1917 and finally bombarded and burned by the German airforce in May 1940.

In tune with this rather sad history, Péronne is also equally well known for its Monument to the Fallen, the work of the architect Louis Faille, representing a Picardy woman with clenched fist raised above the body of her son or husband killed by the war.

stage 13   Bapaume to Péronne

(0.0)With the war memorial to your right take the D917[Direction Saint Quentin](0.4) Turn right on rue de Lesboeufs. Note:- 2.5km may be saved by continuing straight ahead on the more direct Alternate Route(0.8)At the stone calvaire, take the left fork on the track (2.8)At the T-junction with the road, turn left on the road towards the church spire[Military cemeteries on your left and right] (4.6)After crossing the TGV track and the motorway, turn left at the T-junction with the D11e2(4.7)At the crossroads with the D917, turn left and immediately right onto a small tarmac road(5.3)At the junction in tracks, continue straight ahead(5.5)Take the right fork on the stony track[Towards the farmhouse] (5.8)At the T-junction beside the farmhouse on the edge of **Riencourt lès Bapaume**, turn right on the road. The Alternate Route joins from the left[Rue Principale] (6.4)Shortly after passing the Manchester Military Cemetery, turn left on the track. Note:- 2.2km may be saved by continuing straight ahead and following the Alternate Route (7.1)Turn right on the grass track between open fields[Sign "Turn right in 300m on the VF"](7.5)At the T-junction in the tracks, turn right[Large farm building on the right of the track ahead](8.1) Take the left fork (8.5) Turn left on rue du Calvaire[Calvaire ahead] (8.7)At the crossroads beside the calvaire, continue straight ahead on the track[Towards the trees] (10.0)At the T-junction with the road, turn left[Towards the copse of trees](10.1)At the crossroads, turn right on the stony track(10.5) At the junction with a small tarmac road, continue straight ahead[Church spire on your left] (11.0)At the T-junction with the road, turn right and then immediately right again[Pass a calvaire on your right](11.9)At the T-junction with a gravel track, turn left. Note:- Alternate Route joins from the right[Towards the modern church tow-

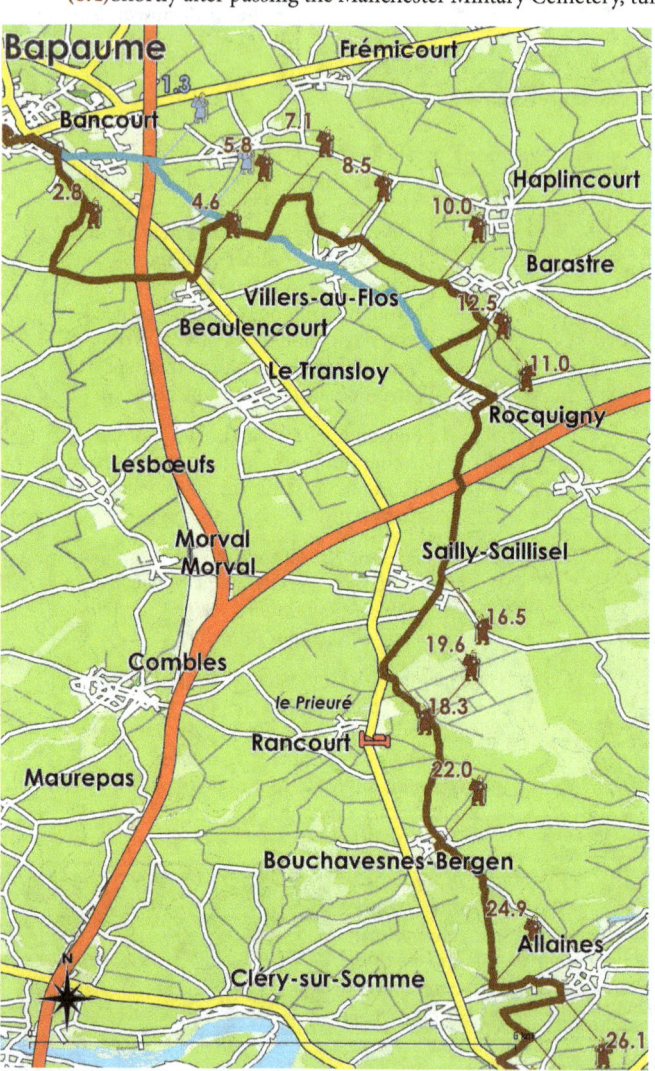

Bapaume to Péronne

stage 13

er] (12.5)The track joins a tarmac road in front of cemetery, continue straight ahead at the junction[Village of **Roquigny**](12.8)Beside the bell tower, continue straight ahead, direction Betancourt, D19, rue du Calviere[Café on the left](13.0)Turn right on rue de Sailly(13.4)At the junction bear left on the road[Leave the village] (16.5)At the junction with the D172, continue straight ahead[Towards the village](16.8)At the crossroads in **Sailly-Saillisel** continue straight ahead[Pass conifers on your left](17.2)Take the left fork[Pass close to crucifix on your left] (18.3)At the T-junction, turn left[Towards the water tower] (18.5)Turn left on the track [Towards the woods](18.7)Turn right in front of gates[Keep

the woods close on your left] (19.6)Bear right on the track between the fields[Roughly parallel to the main road](20.3) At the junction with the tarmac road, continue straight[Slight downhill] (22.0)At the T-junction beside the church, turn left then immediately right[Towards the phone mast] (22.9)Turn right on the track[Downhill, pass embankment on your right] (24.9)At the T-junction, turn left[Follow tree lined canal on your right](25.4)Cross the bridge over the canal[Enter the village of **Allaines**](25.9)At the small roundabout, turn right[Towards the small bridge. Spire on your left at the junction] (26.1)At the T-junction, turn right on rue du Mont Saint Quentin[Pass a garage with a "stork" on the roof](26.2)As the road turns left, continue straight ahead on the track and then take the first track to the left[600m may be saved by remaining on the road] (27.5)At the T-junction, turn right on the road[Pass an embankment on your left](28.1)Just before reaching the main road, turn left[Pass a barn on your right] (28.6)At the T-junction, turn right and continue straight ahead at a series of roundabouts (29.9)Take the left fork[Pass a small park on your right](30.0)Turn right on the road[Direction Centre Hospitalier](30.3)At the mini-roundabout continue straight ahead[Avenue de la République](30.7)Arrive at **Péronne** centre[Beside Musée de la Grande Guerre]

stage 13 — Bapaume to Péronne

Direct Route to Riencourt lès Bapaume

Route: follows a normally quiet country road, saving 2.5 km. (0.0)Continue straight ahead[D917](0.1)Turn left[Direction Bancourt, D7] (1.3)After crossing over the **autoroute**, turn sharp right onto a minor road[No-Entry sign] (2.6)On reaching **Riencourt-lès-Bapaume** bear left[Direction Villers au Flos, D11e3](2.8)Continue straight ahead on the road. Note:- the "Official Route" rejoins from the right[Rue Principale]

Length:	2.8km
Ascent:	25m
Descent:	20m

Direct Route via Villers au Flos

Route: follows normally quiet country roads and farm tracks, passing through the village centre. of Villers-au-Flos. (0.0)Continue straight ahead on the road[Towards the village] (0.9)At the crossroads, beside the Mairie in **Villers-au-Flos**, bear left[Direction Bancourt, D11](1.0)In the centre of the village, turn right[Rue du Transloy] (1.2)Beside the cemetery take the left fork[Pass the cemetery on the right](2.2)After left and right bends, leave the road to take the track ahead[Leave at the next bend to the left] (3.2)Continue straight ahead on the stony track. Note:- the "Official Route" rejoins from the left

Length:	3.2km
Ascent:	24m
Descent:	22m

Accommodation and Tourist Information

Péronne

Paroisse - Saint Jean Baptiste de Péronne,16 rue Saint-Jean, 80200 Péronne, France; Tel:+33(0)3 22 84 16 90; Email:paroisse.de.peronne@wanadoo.fr; https://paroissedeperonne.wixsite.com/monsite; Price:D

Chambre d'Hôtes - Noir Lion,16 rue du Noir Lion, 80200 Péronne, France; Tel:+33(0)6 87 22 18 33; Email:sophie.legros@yahoo.fr; www.noirlionperonne80.fr; Price:B

Hôtel Restaurant - La Picardière,7 Faubourg de Bretagne, 80200 Péronne, France; Tel:+33(0)3 22 84 02 36; Email:lapicardiere80@orange.fr; web.facebook.com/lapicardiere.peronne; Price:B

Auberge - des Remparts,17 rue Beaubois, 80200 Péronne, France; Tel:+33(0)3 22 88 41 10; +33(0)6 89 79 28 96; Email:resa@aubergedesremparts.net; www.aubergedesremparts.fr; Price:B; *Dormitory available for larger groups*

Hôtel - le Saint-Claude,42 Pace du Commandant Louis Daudre, 80200 Péronne, France; Tel:+33(0)3 22 79 49 49; Email:contact@hotelsaintclaude.com; www.hotelsaintclaude.com; Price:B

Hôtel - Kyriad Péronne,142 route de Paris, 80200 Péronne, France; Tel:+33(0)3 22 84 22 22; Email:manager.peronne@kyriad.fr; www.kyriad.fr; Price:B

Camping Municipal Etang du Brochet,Rue Georges Clemenceau, 80200 Péronne, France; Tel:+33(0)6 36 12 10 72; Email:campinglebrochet@gmail.com; campinglebrochet.fr; Price:C; *Mobile homes also available*; **PR**

Camping du Port de Plaisance,Route de Paris, 80200 Péronne, France; Tel:+33(0)3 22 84 19 31; Email:contact@camping-plaisance.com; camping-plaisance.com; Price:C; *Chalets also available Open March to end October*

Office du Tourisme,1 rue Louis Xi, 80200 Péronne, France; Tel:+33(0)3 22 84 42 38; Email:accueil@hautesomme-tourisme.com; www.hautesomme-tourisme.com

Rancourt

Hôtel - le Prieuré,24 route Nationale, 80360 Rancourt, France; Tel:+33(0)3 22 85 04 43; Email:contact@hotel-le-prieure.fr; www.hotel-le-prieure.fr; Price:A

Péronne to Saint-Quentin — stage 14

Length:	33.4km
Ascent:	404m
Descent:	370m
Canterbury	299km
Col Grand Saint Bernard:	940km

The Somme

Route: the stage from Péronne to Saint-Quentin combines primarily farm tracks and generally minor roads over level ground. Saint-Quentin has a wide range of facilities. However, it is possible to shorten the stage by overnighting in Trefcon.

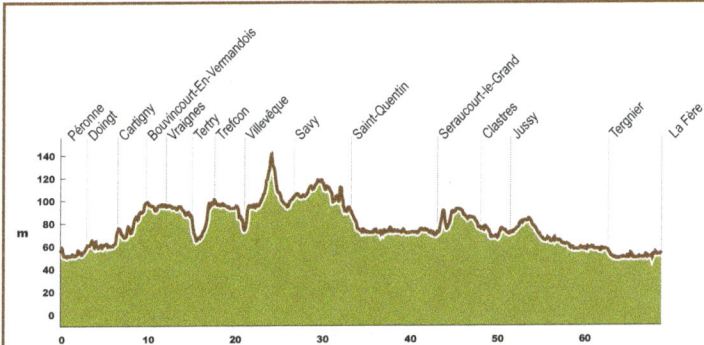

While the "Official Route" passes through Saint-Quentin it is possible to save considerable distance by following the Alternate Route directly to Seraucourt-le-Grande (LXXIII).

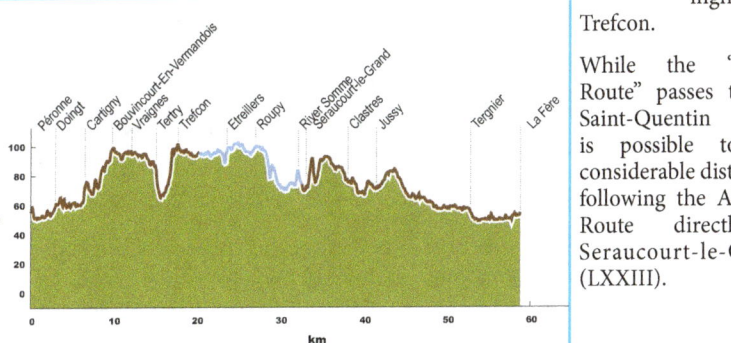

The Somme department is named after the Somme river and Amiens is its capital. The many cemeteries that cover the Somme region serve as poignant reminders of the mass slaughter that took place on the Western Front in World War 1. Between July 1 and November 21, 1916, the Allied forces lost more than 600,000 men and the Germans at least 465,000. The Battle of

stage 14 — Péronne to Saint-Quentin

the Somme, a series of campaigns conducted by British and French armies, against fortified positions held by the Germans, relieved the hard-pressed French at Verdun, but the Allies only managed to advance sixteen kilometres. By the end of the battle, the British had learned many lessons in modern warfare, while the Germans had suffered irreplaceable losses. British historian Sir James Edmonds stated, "It is not too much to claim that the foundations of the final victory on the Western Front were laid by the Somme offensive of 1916."

(0.0) Starting from the entrance to the château, Musée de la Grande Guerre, go straight ahead through the car park[Main gate behind]**(0.1)**Turn left into rue du Gladimont, uphill[Pedestrian zone, pass Hotel St Cloud on your left]**(0.1)**Turn right and cross the square, place du Commandant Louis Daudré and continue into rue Saint Jean[Pass the church of St Jean on your left]**(0.4)**At the end of the road, turn left on the Boulevard des Anglais[Pass vegetable gardens on your right]**(0.6)**At the T-junction, turn right[Memorial ahead at the junction] **(1.1)**Immediately after the road bends to the right, turn left onto the gravel track. Note:- cyclists wishing to avoid the obstacles on the track should remain on rue Joliot-Curie until reaching Doingt[Pass house n° 45 on your right]**(1.4)**Continue straight ahead[Former railway track] **(2.5)**Continue straight ahead with the old railway crossing house on your right[Track passes under the main road]**(3.0)**At the crossroads following the **Doingt (LXXIV)** railway station, continue straight ahead[Remain on the old railway track] **(3.8)**At the crossroads with a tarmac road, continue straight ahead on the old railway track[Crash barriers to your left] **(6.2)**Continue straight ahead on meeting

the tarmac and then turn right after the second house and follow rue Galopins into Cartigny**(6.6)**In **Cartigny**, at the T-junction beside a high wall, turn right**(6.7)**At the T-junction, turn left[Direction Hancourt] **(7.3)**Continue straight ahead at crossroads[Direction Hancourt]**(7.6)**Just before the Cartigny exit sign, continue straight ahead and pass the chapel on the hill to your left[Ivy covered brick wall on right]**(7.9)**After passing the chapel, bear right on the initially tarmac track between the fields[Water tower visible on the skyline to the left at the junction] **(9.9)**At the top of the hill, bear left at the fork and immediately turn right at the crossroads[Village of **Bouvincourt-en-Vermandois**, rue de Beaumetz]**(10.2)**In the village centre, with house n° 1 on your right, turn left on the road[Pass the war memorial on your left] **(11.9)**At the junction with the D15, turn right into the

Péronne to Saint-Quentin stage 14

village of Vraignes-en-Vermandois[Signpost for Bouvincourt on the right]**(12.2)**Beside the church in **Vraignes**, turn left on rue Base and keep right**(12.6)**As the road bends to the left, bear right on the track[Pass house n°32 on your left] **(13.3)**Cross the busy road with care and continue straight ahead on the track[Factory on the brow on your right]**(13.8)**Take the left fork[Towards the trees] **(15.2)**Pass terrain des boules on your right and continue straight ahead at the crossroads[Enter **Tertry**]**(15.9)**As the road turns hard to the right, turn left and left again on the track[No-Entry sign] **(17.1)**Turn left and continue with an open field on your right**(17.4)**Continue straight on the tarmac[Enter Trefcon]**(17.8)**In

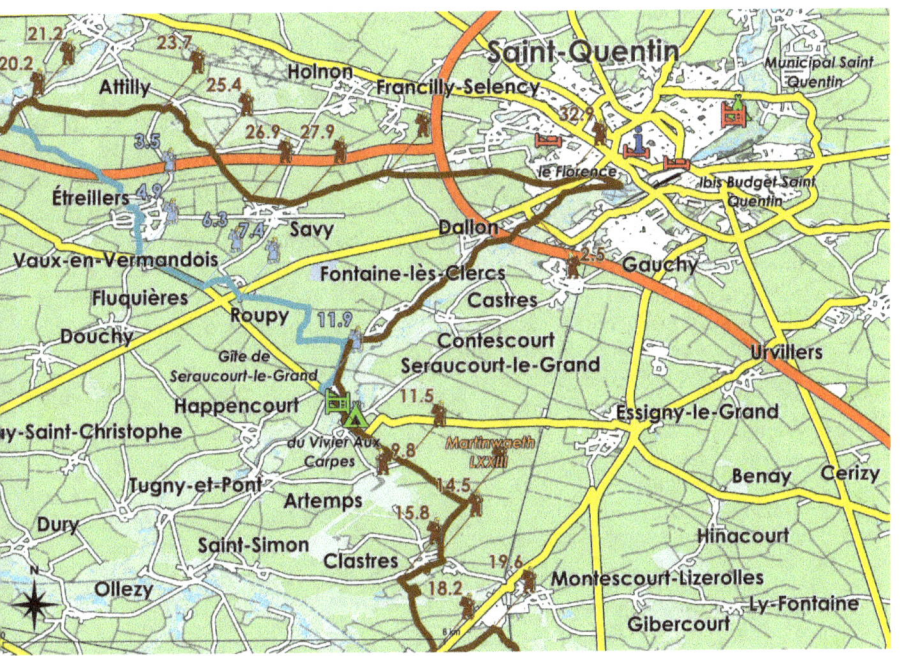

Trefcon centre and turn left at the crossroads and follow the D345 **(18.7)**At the crossroads, proceed straight ahead on a part made road[Sign for the Trefcon British cemetery on the left] **(20.2)**At the T-junction, turn left[Direction Villevêque, D73]**(20.3)**Continue straight ahead on the D73. Note:- the Alternate Route to Seraucourt-le-Grand leaves on the track to the right **(21.2)**In **Villevêque**, turn right beside the house with eagle gate posts **(23.7)**At the T-junction in Attilly, turn left and take the next road to the right[Towards the church]**(24.2)**On the sharp left-hand corner, continue straight ahead on the gravel path and then bear right **(25.4)**At the T-junction with the road, turn left and then right[Continue over the autoroute bridge] **(26.9)**On the edge of the village of **Savy**, bear left on the grass track[Keep the fields on your left]**(27.3)**Cross the road and continue on the grass track[Beside the cemetery] **(27.9)**Bear left on the grass track beside the road[Pass a crucifix on your right] **(29.6)**Turn right across a gravel area and follow the grass track[No Entry sign]**(29.9)**Cross the road and continue on the former railway[Path will pass under the autoroute] **(32.9)**Descend the steps, cross the road and continue up the steps to rejoin the old railway**(33.4)**Arrive at **Saint-Quentin** at the intersection between the old railway and rue de Paris. Note:- the town centre can be found to the left.

stage 14 — Péronne to Saint-Quentin

Direct Route to Seraucourt-le-Grande(LXXIII)

Length:	12.4km
Ascent:	88m
Descent:	111m

Route: the direct route follows broad farm tracks and minor roads except for 2 short sections beside the busy D32. The route will pass a bar and shops in the village of Étreillers. (0.0) Turn right on the track(0.5)At the T-junction with the road, turn right[Follow the road as it crosses the autoroute] (3.7) Bear right on rue Maurice Dallongeville[Village of **Etreillers**](3.7)At the crossroads, continue straight ahead[Rue des Docteurs](3.8)At the T-junction turn right on Avenue du Général de Gaulle and then take the first turning to the left[Direction Seraucourt-le-Grand] (4.9)At the crossroads, shortly after passing under a bridge, turn left with great care beside the busy road[D32, towards Roupy] (6.3)Turn left on the small road towards the village. Note:- the D32 can be very busy, but if you are content to continue on the road to Seraucourt-le-Grand you will reduce your distance by 2km[Rue du Moulin](6.8)At the crossroads, turn right into the village of **Roupy**[Walled garden on the right](7.3)At crossroads in Roupy, continue straight ahead on rue Barette[Church on the left of the junction] (7.4)On the edge of Roupy turn left onto rue de Fontaine[Pass a large barn on your right] (8.7)While climbing the hill on the stony track, turn right and continue beside a line of trees on your right(9.7)Track bends to the left[Towards the woods] (10.5)At the T-junction turn right onto the road[Towards the water tower] (11.9)At the crossroads, turn left in the direction of Seraucourt-le-Grand, D32[Road crosses the **river Somme**](12.4)Continue straight ahead to rejoin the "Official Route"

Accommodation and Tourist Information

Saint-Quentin

🏠 **Auberge de Jeunesse - Saint Quentin**,Boulevard Jean Bouin, 02100 Saint-Quentin, France; Tel:+33(0)3 23 06 92 61; +33(0)3 23 06 94 05; www.saint-quentin.fr; Price:C

🛏 **Hôtel - Ibis Budget - Saint Quentin**,84 rue Michelet, 02100 Saint-Quentin, France; Tel:+33(0)8 92 70 12 79; Email:h7410@accor.com; all.accor.com; Price:B

🛏 **Hôtel - Première Classe Saint Quentin**,ZAC de la Vallee, rue Antoine Parmentier, 02100 Saint-Quentin, France; Tel:+33(0)3 23 64 21 72; Email:stquentin@premiereclasse.fr; www.premiereclasse.com; Price:B

🛏 **Hôtel - le Florence**,42 rue Emile Zola, 02100 Saint-Quentin, France; Tel:+33(0)3 23 64 22 22; Email:leflorence@orange.fr; www.hotel-le-florence.fr; Price:B

⛺ **Camping Municipal - Saint Quentin**,Boulevard Jean Bouin, 02100 Saint-Quentin, France; Tel:+33(0)3 23 06 92 61; +33(0)3 23 06 94 05; www.saint-quentin.fr; Price:C

ℹ **Office de Tourisme**,3 rue Emile Zola, 02100 Saint-Quentin, France; Tel:+33(0)3 23 67 05 00; Email:tourisme@saint-quentin.fr; www.destination-saintquentin.fr/

Trefcon

🏠 **Chambres d'Hôtes - le Val d'Omignon**[M. Hubert Wynands],3 rue Principale, 02490 Trefcon, France; Tel:+33(0)3 23 66 58 64; +33(0)6 99 19 95 47; Email:le.val-domignon@wanadoo.fr; www.picardie-val-domignon.com; Price:C; *Will accept horses. Dormitory at 20 €/person/night*

Vraignes-en-Vermandois

⛺ **Camping des Hortensias**[Nicolas and Gaelle Plaquet],22 rue Basse, 80240 Vraignes-en-Vermandois, France; Tel:+33(0)3 22 85 64 68; +33(0)605343091; Email:campingdeshortensias@gmail.com; www.campinghortensias.com; Price:C; *Mobile homes also available*

Saint-Quentin to La Fère

stage 15

Length:	35.5km
Ascent:	372m
Descent:	399m
Canterbury	332km
Col Grand Saint Bernard:	907km

Saint Quentin canal

Route: the stage from Saint-Quentin to La Fère incorporates 2 long but pleasant sections on water-side paths, first beside the river Somme and later beside the canal de Saint Quentin. These are linked by minor roads and farm tracks. It is possible to break your journey at Seraucourt-le-Grand.

Tergnier is a former railway town which is slowly being redeveloped, but with still a limited choice of facilities. If necessary there are regular trains from Tergnier to Saint Quentin, or Laon and beyond.

There is a slightly greater choice of accommodation in La Fère which also has the advantage of reducing the long following stage to Laon.

The Aisne landscape is dominated by masses of rock with steep flanks. These rocks appear all over the region, but the most impressive examples are at Laon and the Chemin des Dames ridge, so make sure you look out for them.

Agriculture dominates the economy, especially cereal crops, with the result that vast tracts of the area are featureless, and all too reminiscent of the dust bowl prairies. Nevertheless, silk, and wool weaving still flourish in Saint-Quentin and other towns.

Les Roches

stage 15 Saint-Quentin to La Fère

(0.0) From the intersection between the old railway and rue de Paris, continue east on the old railway **(0.6)** Just before the bridge over the river, turn right down the steps, turn right again and continue with the river on your left ♦ **(2.5)** Climb the ramp and turn left to cross the bridge, immediately turn right onto the tarmac road. Continue on the path beside the river to Seraultcourt-le-Grand[Keep the river close on your right] ♦ **(8.7)** Bear left on the tarmac path[Pass a dismantled bridge on your right] **(9.3)** At the T-junction with the road

turn left into Seraultcourt-le-Grand[Gîte d'Etape on your right and bar on your left] ♦ **(9.8)** In **Seraucourt-le-Grand (LXXIII)** bear right direction Artemps, D32[Church on your left] **(10.0)** At the crossroads beside the Madonna continue straight ahead on the D72. Note:- the GR®655 crosses our route[Direction Essigny-le-Grand] **(10.5)** Where the road turns sharply to the left, continue straight ahead on the stony track ♦ **(11.5)** At the T-junction with the road, turn left and follow the road. Note:- the GR®655 turns right at this point and leaves the via Francigena [Towards church spire on the horizon] **(12.3)** At the crossroads continue straight ahead ♦ **(13.1)** Bear right[Remain on the road] **(13.9)** As the road bears right, fork left on the left most track[Grassy track, towards the church] ♦ **(14.5)** At the junction with the tarmac road, continue straight ahead[Towards the church] **(14.6)** At the junction keep left[Pass the church on your right] **(14.7)** In **Clastres**, at the T-junction, turn right[Beside the church] **(15.0)** Turn left onto ruelle Bequemin **(15.2)** At the T-junction, turn right, then bear left on rue de la Longue Ruelle[Uphill] ♦ **(15.8)** At the end of the road turn left **(16.1)** With the farm buildings on your right, turn left on the track and then right and right again to skirt the field **(16.5)** Turn left through the trees and follow the long straight track to the village of Jussy ♦ **(18.2)** At the road junction in **Jussy**, turn left and then immediately right on chemin de Remigny. Note:- 2 km may be saved by bearing right on the alternate route and joining the canal path. However, the canal path has been sometimes reported as overgrown. However, the pa[Mairie to your right at thr junction] **(18.4)** Fork left on the gravel road[Beside garden fence] ♦ **(19.6)** Shortly before reaching the water tower turn sharp right **(20.2)** Cross over the railway bridge and bear right[Parallel to the railway track] ♦ **(20.9)** At the crossroads with the tarmac road continue straight ahead **(21.6)** Bear

Saint-Quentin to La Fère — stage 15

left and join the canal-side track[Canal on your ight, towards lock] **(23.9)**Follow the tow path under the highway**(24.8)**Continue along the tow-path under the bridge[Beside lock] **(28.1)**Continue on the path under the road bridge **(29.4)**Keep right and continue on the canal-side path under the road bridge. Note:- **Tergnier** facilities can be accessed from the main road over the bridge[Beside the lock] **(31.0)**Turn left and then right to cross the canal bridge, then turn left to follow the canal on the other bank **(34.7)**After the arched concrete bridge, turn right and then left to follow the road to the east[Pass a supermarket on your left]**(35.2)**Bear right at the roundabout[Rue de Bourget] **(35.5)**Arrive at **La Fère** centre at the junction of rue Paul Doumer and rue de la République[No-Entry sign]

Accommodation and Tourist Information

Danizy

Chambre d'Hôtes - Domaine le Parc[Jedy and Damien],Rue du Quesny, 02800 Danizy, France; Tel:+33(0)3 23 56 55 23; +33(0)6 82 68 64 61; Email:contact@domaineleparc.fr; www.domaineleparc.fr; Price:A

La Fère

Apartment - London City[Bruno],1 Rue de la Foulerie, 2800 La Fère, France; Tel: www.gites.fr/gites_london-city_la-fere_h4623530.htm; Price:B; *Great host also listed on* booking.com; **PR**

Apartment - Cosy Place[Remy Dasse],4 Rue de la Libération, 2800 La Fère, France; Tel: booking.com; Price:B

Seraucourt-le-Grand

Le Camping du Vivier Aux Carpes[Alexandra & Sébastien],4 rue Charles Voyeux, 02790 Seraucourt-le-Grand, France; Tel:+33(0)3 23 60 50 10; Email:contact@camping-picardie.com; www.camping-picardie.com; Price:C; *Caravan also available for rent. Open April to end September*

Tergnier

Notre-Dame de Thérigny – Paroisse de Tergnier[Curé Frédéric Da Silva],17 Av. du Général de Gaulle, 02700 Tergnier, France; Tel:+33(0)3 23 40 27 16; Email:Lnfo@soissons.catholique.fr; www.soissons.catholique.fr/zone-pastorale-de-chauny/paroisse-dame-de-therigny/

Apartment - Harmonie,21 Boulevard Gambetta, 2700 Tergnier, France; Tel:+33(0)3 23 57 27 63; Email:olucie13@gmail.com; www.booking.com; Price:B; *Apartment with shared kitchen no wifi. A pilgrim noted not properly cleaned*

Le Camping de la Frette,Rue de la Prairie, 02700 Tergnier, France; Tel:+33(0)3 23 40 21 21; Email:camping.lafrette@ville-tergnier.fr; campinglafrette.tergnier.fr; Price:C; *Mobile homes and large pre-erected tents are also available*

Mairie,Place Paul Doumer, 02700 Tergnier, France; Tel:+33(0)3 23 57 11 27; www.ville-tergnier.fr

Musée de la Résistance et de la Déportation Tergnier

stage 16 — La Fère to Laon

Length:	33.0km
Ascent:	857m
Descent:	732m
Canterbury	368km
Col Grand Saint Bernard:	871km

Cathédrale de Notre-Dame - Laon

Route: this long stage from La Fère to Laon crosses the huge forest of St Gobain. Some distance may be saved by following the quiet road through Saint-Nicolas-aux-Bois where you can find a restaurant. There are few other opportunities for a meal break en route. There is a stiff climb near the Abbaye St Nicolas and on the final approach to the medieval centre of Laon.

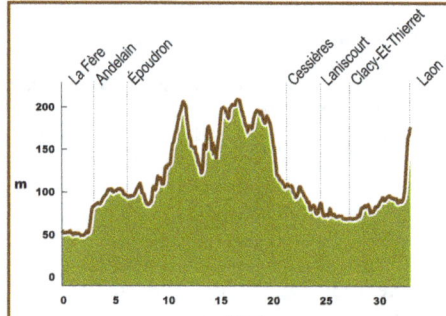

Laon has a full range of facilities. There is a frequent train service between Tergnier and Laon, but no public transport directly on the route.

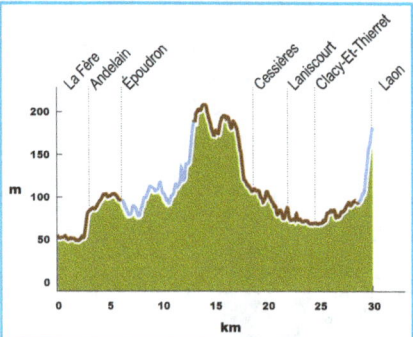

The first sign of Laon as you approach will be the towers of the cathedral, giving one a sense of how awestruck the Medieval travellers must have felt after days of walking or riding through woodland and open countryside. If today's pilgrims feel in need of a break, this is an endlessly fascinating place to take it. Laon occupies a dramatic site on top of a long ridge surrounded by wide plains. At the end of the 5th century, Remigius, Archbishop of Reims, instituted the bishopric of Laon. As a result, Laon became a principal town in the kingdom of the Franks, though possession of it was often disputed. Cathédrale de Notre-Dame was completed in 1235, and was one of France's first major Gothic buildings, even predating the Notre Dame in Paris. Unfortunately, it lost two of its original seven towers during the Revolution. The use of local white stone for the interior of the nave renders the space even more luminous. Look out for the 12th-century font, the painted relief of the Passion from the 14th century and a Serbian icon donated to the cathedral by Pope Urban IV in the 13th century. The Alms Hospital is the oldest of its kind remaining in Northern France. The Knights Templar chapel is particularly special because they are relatively rare finds in France, and even rarer to see one in such good condition.

La Fère to Laon　　stage 16

(0.0) From the centre of La Fère, head east and take the left fork on rue Paul Doumer [Pass No-Entry sign] **(0.2)** Bear right on rue Général de Gaulle[Keep the large parking area on your left] **(0.5)** At the roundabout, continue straight ahead on rue Maréchal Foch[Cross the bridge] **(0.6)** Turn right onto Square Foch[Park on your right] **(0.8)** Turn right on the path[Pass under the railway tunnel] **(1.1)** Turn right onto rue des Petit Charmes **(2.3)** Bear left to go underneath road and then turn right **(2.5)** Turn left[Towards the farm buildings] **(2.8)** Continue straight ahead with the farm buildings on the right **(3.1)** At the crossroads in **Andelain** continue straight ahead on rue de Bertaucourt **(3.5)** At the T-junction turn left[Leave the village of Andelain] **(4.2)** Turn left onto the track[Pylons on the right of the junction] **(4.9)** Bear left to stay on the track **(5.2)** Turn right onto the tarmac road[Pass a row of poplars on your left] **(5.5)** At the complex road junction continue straight ahead[Direction Missancourt,D55] **(6.2)** In **Époudron**, shortly after the crossroads, turn right onto the track. Note:- 2.5km may be saved by remaining on the road through Missancourt and Saint-Nicolas-aux-Bois to the crossroads at the top of the ridge[White house on the left] **(6.5)** Turn right onto the grass track between the church on the right and the barn on the left **(6.6)** At the T-junction, turn left and then bear left just after the the bend to the right[Long track between open fields] **(8.8)** Cross the tarmac road, turn right onto

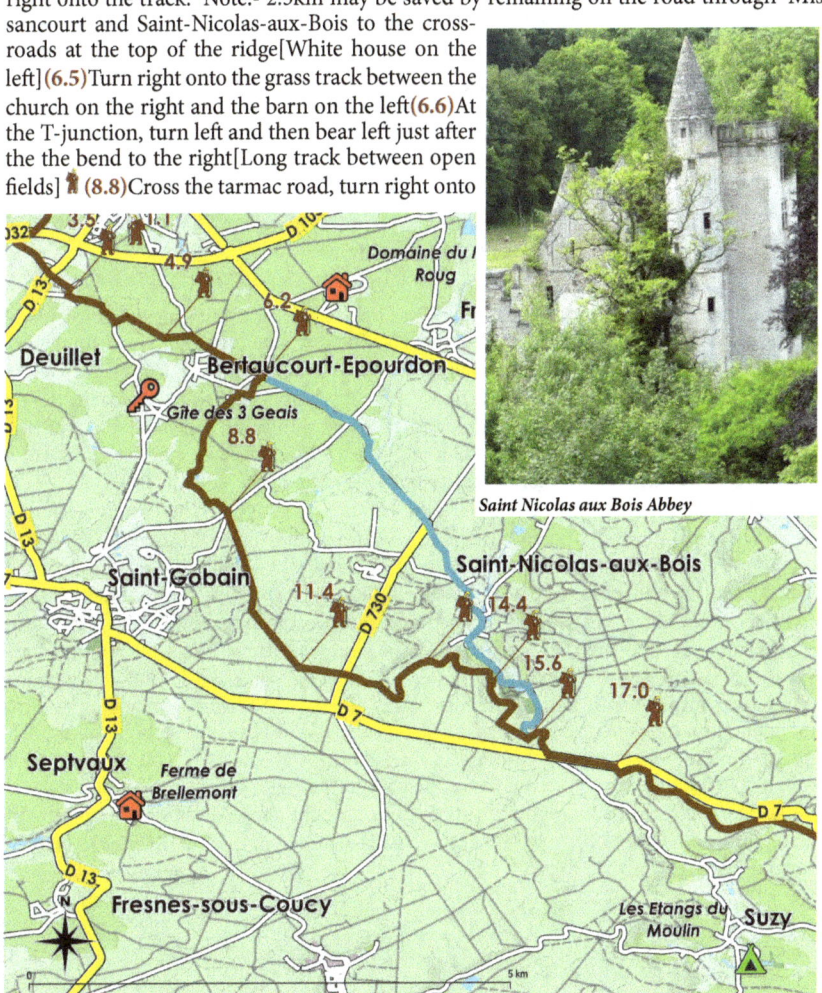

Saint Nicolas aux Bois Abbey

stage 16 — La Fère to Laon

the leftmost fork and then bear left on the forest track[Barrier across track] **(11.4)**At the crossroads in the tracks, turn left**(11.9)**Cross over the road and continue straight ahead on the track **(13.2)**Take the right fork, uphill[Pass an open field on your left] **(14.4)**As you approach the main road, take the right fork[Keep the field and abbey on your left]**(15.3)**At the T-junction, turn left **(15.6)**Turn left and then turn right on the main road**(16.3)**At the crossroads, at the top of the hill, turn left[Direction Cessières, D7] **(17.0)**Turn right to leave the road and then bear right[Laie du Rendezvous]**(17.1)**In front of the house, turn left on the broad track and continue through the woods roughly parallel to the main road **(20.2)**Briefly approach the main road and then bear right on the track across the field**(20.9)**

Continue straight ahead onto the tarmac[Pass beside the farm buildings] **(21.4)**At the end of rue Gerrienne in **Cessières**, take the left fork and then turn right[Chemin de Calvaire]**(21.7)**Bear left on the track and continue across the road ahead **(23.2)**Bear right at the junction**(23.5)**Take the left fork**(23.8)**Take the right fork[Returning briefly to the woods]**(24.2)**At the T-junction with the road, turn right[Towards Laniscourt] **(24.6)**Approaching **Laniscourt** turn left onto the track[Pass a white house on right as you turn] **(25.7)**Cross over the road to continue straight[Direction Clacy-et-Thierret] **(26.8)**Turn right[Direction Clacy et Thierret]**(27.2)**At the entrance to **Clacy-et-Thierret** turn left onto the track[Pass camper vans on your left] **(28.0)**Turn right to enter the forest **(29.4)**With the railway close on your right, turn left and cross the railway bridge and then immediately take the road to the left[Towards the factory buildings] **(30.6)**At the roundabout, bear left[Direction Centre Ville]**(31.1)**At the roundabout, continue straight ahead[Direction Centre Ville]**(31.3)**At the traffic lights, continue straight ahead. Note:- for a more gentle and shorter approach to the high town turn right on the Alternate Route **(32.3)**At the roundabout turn right on avenue Carnot. Note:- after a long stage you may wish to avoid the final climb by using the funicular railway[Railway and funicular stations on the left] **(32.5)**Climb the steps, escalier Municipal, towards the high town**(32.7)**At the road junction, turn left and then immediately take the path to the right[Towards the ramparts, with the funicular close on your right]**(32.9)**Continue straight ahead on the road with the funicular on your right**(33.0)**Arrive at **Laon (LXXII)** old town in front of the Mairie[Place du Général Léclerc]

La Fère to Laon

stage 16

Ascent to the Laon Medieval Centre

Route: this short diversion saves a little distance and allows a more progressive climb to the high medieval centre of Laon and the cathedral. (0.0)Turn right and right again[Rue Général de Lattre Tassigny, towards the high cathedral](0.4)At the T-junction, bear right[Uphill, Rampe Saint Marcel](0.8)Bear right on the steep road[Rue de l'Eperon](1.0)At the T-junction with the main road, turn right[Pass funicular (POMA) station on your left] (1.1)Take the left fork, rue Franklin Roosevelt[Pass a hotel on your right, No-Entry](1.2)At the T-junction, turn left and left again[Direction Hôtel de Ville](1.3)End of stage at Laon (LXXII) old town in front of the Mairie[Place du Général Léclerc]

Length:	6.9km
Ascent:	214m
Descent:	120m

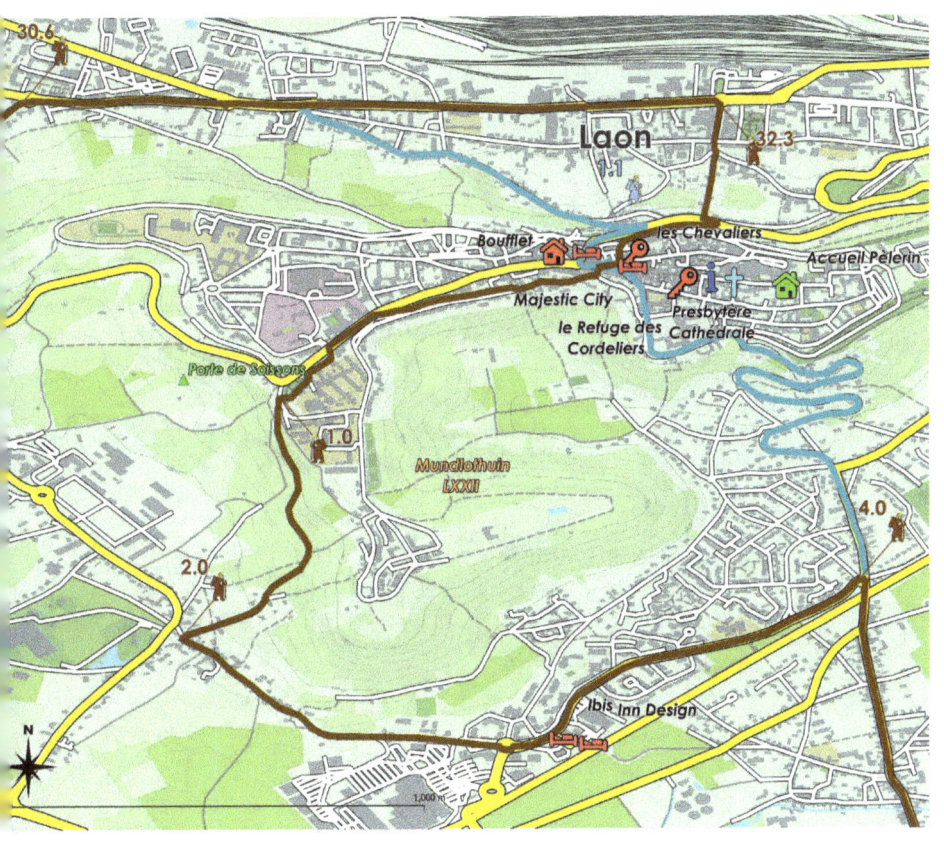

stage 16 — La Fère to Laon

Accommodation and Tourist Information

Bertaucourt-Epourdon
🔑 **Gîte - des 3 Geais**,9 rue Georges Domissy, 02800 Bertaucourt-Epourdon, France; Tel:+33(0)6 12 32 81 90; gitedes3geais.e-monsite.com; Price:B; *Moderrn well equipped gite*

Cessières
ℹ **Mairie**,1 Ruelle Buet, 02320 Cessières, France; Tel:+33(0)3 23 24 14 49; www.cessieres.fr

Laon
⛪ **Presbytère Cathédrale**,8 rue du Cloître, 02000 Laon, France; Tel:+33(0)3 23 20 26 54
🏠 **Accueil Pèlerin**[Mme Tordeux-Bernard],22 rue du Cloître, 02000 Laon, France; Tel:+33(0)6 81 19 53 56; Price:D; **PR**
🏠 **Chambre d'Hôtes - Boufflet**,22 Rue Saint-Jean, 2000 Laon, France; Tel:+33 (0)7 82 84 50 60; chambres-boufflet.com.es; Price:B; *Excellent location a little tired but clean*
🏨 **Hôtel - Kyriad**,111 avenue Charles de Gaulle, 02000 Laon, France; Tel:+33(0)3 23 23 42 43; Email:laon@kyriad.fr; laon.kyriad.com]]>; Price:B
🏨 **Hôtel - les Chevaliers**,3 rue Sérurier, 02000 Laon, France; Tel:+33(0)3 23 27 17 50; Email:hotelchevaliers@aol.com; www.meilleurhotel.top/hotel-les-chevaliers; Price:A
🏨 **Hôtel - Inn Design**,1115 avenue Georges Pompidou, 02000 Laon, France; Tel:+33(0)3 23 20 36 37; Email:hid.laon@gmail.com; hotel-inn-laon.fr; Price:B
🏨 **Hôtel - Ibis**,1134 avenue Georges Pompidou, 02000 Laon, France; Tel:+33(0)3 23 20 18 11; Email:H2059@accor.com; all.accor.com; Price:A
🏨 **Hôtel - de la Banniere de France**,11 rue Franklin Roosevelt, 02000 Laon, France; Tel:+33(0)3 23 23 21 44; Email:hotel.banniere.de.france@wanadoo.fr; hoteldelabannieredefrance.com; Price:A
🔑 **Apartment - le Refuge des Cordeliers**,12 rue des Cordeliers, 02000 Laon, France; Tel:+33(0)6 76 28 11 19; www.hotelmania.net/hotel/laon/le-refuge-des-cordeliers; Price:B
🔑 **Apartment - Majestic City**[Bruno],19 Rue Châtelaine, 2000 Laon, France; Tel: www.gites.fr/gites_majestic-city_laon_h4617524.htm; Price:B; *Good location also listed on* Booking.com
⛺ **Camping la Chênaie**,Allée de la Chênaie, 02000 Laon, France; Tel:+33(0)3 23 23 38 63; Email:contact.camping.laon@gmail.com; camping-aisne.fr; Price:C; *Open April until end September*
ℹ **Office du Tourisme**,Place du Parvis G.de Mortagne, 02000 Laon, France; Tel:+33(0)3 23 20 28 62; Email:info@tourisme-paysdelaon.com; www.tourisme-paysdelaon.com

Mons-en-Laonnois
🏠 **Chambre d'Hôtes - Domaine de l'Etang**[Patrick Woillez],2 rue Saint-Martin, 02000 Mons-en-Laonnois, France; Tel:+33(0)3 23 24 44 52; +33(0)6 26 62 36 41; Email:gitemons@sfr.fr; www.domaine-deletang.fr; Price:B

Rogécourt
🏠 **Chambre d'Hôtes - Domaine du Mont Roug**[Delphine and Jean-Pierre],Route Départementale 1044, 02800 Rogécourt, France; Tel:+33(0)6 83 14 19 36; +33(0)7 83 14 80 73; Email:domainedumontrouge@gmail.com; domaine-mont-rouge.com; Price:A

Septvaux
🏠 **Chambre d'Hôtes - Ferme de Brellemont**,4 route de Brellemont, 02410 Septvaux, France; Tel:+33(0)3 23 52 57 45; Email:daniel.steichen@orange.fr; giteaisne.pagesperso-orange.fr; Price:C; *Pension for horses possible Open all year*

Suzy
⛺ **Les Etangs du Moulin**,7 Bis rue de l'Arbre Rond, 02320 Suzy, France; Tel:+33(0)3 23 80 92 86; Email:contact@etangsdumoulin.fr; www.etangsdumoulin.fr; Price:C; *Tipis gipsy caravans and chalets also available*

Laon to Corbeny

stage 17

Length:	29.2km
Ascent:	508m
Descent:	596m
Canterbury	401km
Col Grand Saint Bernard:	838km

Abbaye de Vauclair

Route: the stage from Laon to Corbeny will continue on farm tracks and minor roads passing beside the ruins of the Abbaye de Vauclair. The woodland sections can be very muddy and difficult for cyclists.

You will find cafés and grocery stores in Bruyères-et-Montbérault, but elsewhere the route will bypass the larger villages.

Abbaye de Vauclair was formerly a Cistercian abbey, founded in 1134 by Saint Bernard of Clairvaux. Its east-west orientation led Bernard to name it Vauclair (Vallis clara), reversing the name of the mother abbey (Clara vallis). Supported by gifts from rich families, the abbey quickly prospered and was given several estates and farms. Fighting during Hundred Years' War heavily damaged the structure, though it managed to survive until the French Revolution in 1789, when it was finally demolished and sold to the French state as national property. Only ruins now remain, but the grounds include an arboretum of apple and pear trees and a medicinal herb garden.

Corbeny is a small town straddling the Chemin des Dames (Ladies' Way), which is 30 kilometres long and runs along a ridge between the valleys of the rivers Aisne and Ailette. The name dates back to the 18th century when Louis XV's daughters, Adelaide and Victoire, travelled to Château de La Bove, near Bouconville-Vauclair, on the far side of the Ailette. The ridge's strategic importance first became evident in 1814, when Napoleon beat an army of Prussians and Russians at the Battle of Craonne. Then, during World War I, the Chemin Des Dames lay in the part of the Western Front held by French armies, a position that led to several bloody battles.

stage 17　　　　　　　　　　　Laon to Corbeny

Porte de Soissons - Laon

(0.0) From the Mairie in the place du Général Léclerc turn to the right on rue du Bourg and then turn left into the narrow passge. Note:- approximately 1km may be saved by following the Toutes Directions signs on rue Châtellaine and bearing right on the winding rue Paul Doumer to rejoin the "Official Route" as it passes under the highway bridge[Passage opposite la Poste]**(0.1)**At the foot of the steps, turn right[Rue des Chenizelles]**(0.3)**Bear right up the steps and continue ahead on the road above the city walls**(0.7)**Keep right[Towards the abbey]**(0.8)**After passing l'Abbaye de Saint Martin on your right, take the left fork**(0.9)**Where the road turns left, take the pathway to the right[Towards the Porte de Soissons] **(1.0)**Cross the road and turn left, downhill on the cobblestones[Rue de la Vieille Montagne] **(2.0)**At the crossroads at the foot of the hill, turn left[Rue Romanette]**(2.3)**Immediately after passing house n°17 on the left, keep left[Towards the commercial centre]**(2.9)** At the roundabout, continue straight ahead on avenue Georges Pompidou **(4.0)**At the crossroads, turn right under the highway bridge[Direction Reims] **(5.0)**Turn left[Rue Sainte Salaberge] **(6.1)**Cross the road and continue on the track slightly to your left **(7.5)**Take the right fork[Shortly after entering the woods]**(8.3)**Continue straight

Laon to Corbeny stage 17

ahead[Football pitch on your right] **(9.0)** At the road junction, bear left[Towards the church] **(9.3)** At the crossroads in the centre of **Bruyères-et-Montbérault**, continue straight ahead[Pass the church on your right] **(9.7)** At the mini roundabout, continue straight ahead[High wall on your right] **(9.8)** At the next roundabout, take the right fork[Direction chemin des Dames] **(10.3)** Take the right fork on the small road up the hill **(11.6)** Cross the road and continue on the track ahead **(12.2)** At the next road junction, again continue straight ahead[Direction Martigny-Courpierre] **(13.2)** Immediately before entering **Martigny-Courpierre**, turn right on the track and then bear right when you rejoin the road **(13.7)** At the road junction after passing the church, turn right on the track. Note:- the "Official Route" makes a loop around the field to the right before returning to the road. 1km can be saved by remaining on the road **(14.2)** Turn left[Trees on initially on your right] **(14.8)** At the T-junction turn left[Back towards the road] **(15.7)** At the junction with the road, turn right[Down the hill on the tarmac road] **(16.2)** Turn left at the T-junction[Towards the lake] **(16.4)** Bear right towards the lakeside track, then turn left and follow the walkway as it passes under the road bridge. Skirt the car park and continue on the track parallel to the main road **(17.3)** Keep to the left side of the next car park and continue parallel to the road on the grass track **(17.8)** Continue straight ahead beside the road. Note:- an earlier version of the route turned left at this point and made an unnecessary climb and tour of the fields on the left **(18.1)** Cross the road and continue on the track on the other side **(18.3)** Immediately before entering **Neuville-sur-Ailette** turn right[Follow Voie Verte] **(18.6)** Cross the road and continue on the Voie Verte[Direction Abbaye de Vauxclair] **(21.0)** At the road junction, turn right and then left[Continue on chemin du Roi] **(22.6)** Turn right and skirt the lake on your left side **(22.8)** At the T-junc-

stage 17 — Laon to Corbeny

tion with the road, turn left[Pass the ruins of **Abbaye de Vauclair** on your right]**(23.2)**Turn right on the forest track[Chemin du Roi]**(23.5)**At the crossroads, continue straight ahead[Remaining on chemin du Roi] **(26.3)**At the T-junction with the road, turn right and then bear left[Direction Corbeny, D62] **(28.5)**At the T-junction, bear left on the D18 towards Corbeny centre[Place Saint Marcoul]**(29.2)**Arrive at **Corbeny (LXXI)** centre[Beside the church]

Accommodation and Tourist Information

Chamouille
🏠 **Chambre d'Hôtes -Le Castailette**,16 rue Henri d'Ersu, 02860 Chamouille, France; Tel:+33(0)3 23 21 20 11; Email:lecastailette@orange.fr; Price:A

🛏 **Hôtel - du Golf de l'Ailette**,23 Rue du Chemin des Dames, 2860 Chamouille, France; Tel:+33 (0)3 23 24 84 85; Email:hotelrestaurant@ailette.fr; www.ailette.fr; Price:A

Corbeny
🛏 **Hôtel - du Chemin des Dames**,4 rue Pierre Curtil, 02820 Corbeny, France; Tel:+33(0)3 23 23 95 70; +33(0)6 22 57 32 24; Email:hotelchemindesdames02@gmail.com; www.hotelchemindesdames.com; Price:B

⛺ **Aire de Camping - Corbeny**,12 rue Marc Lavetti, 02820 Corbeny, France; Tel: Price:C

ℹ **Mairie**,10 rue Pierre Curtil, 02820 Corbeny, France; Tel:+33(0)3 23 22 41 40; Email:mairie.corbeny@wanadoo.fr; corbeny.fr

Pontavert
🏠 **Mme Nadine Dumon and M Portet**,10 Rue du Château, 02160 Pontavert, France; Tel:+39 (0)3 23 25 88 19; +33(0)9 51 59 35 68; +33(0)616457618; Price:D; *6 km from the official route but situated on a direct route from abbaye de Vauclair to Cormicy;*
PR

🛏 **Hôtel - Relais de Fleurette** ,5 route de Craonnelle, 02160 Pontavert, France; Tel:+33(0)3 23 20 53 05; relais-de-fleurette.fr; Price:B; *6 km from the official route but situated on a direct route from abbaye de Vauclair to Cormicy*

Sainte-Croix
🏠 **Chambre d' Hôtes - la Besace**,21 rue Haute, 02820 Sainte-Croix, France; Tel:+33(0)6 42 07 11 15; la-besace.fr; Price:B; *Dinner possible*

Lac de Ailette *Poudou99*

Corbeny to Hertmonville — stage 18

Length:	23.6km
Ascent:	326m
Descent:	311m
Canterbury	430km
Col Grand Saint Bernard:	809km

Champagne vineyards above Cormicy

Route: the stage from Corbeny to Hertmonville will continue to track the Roman road,

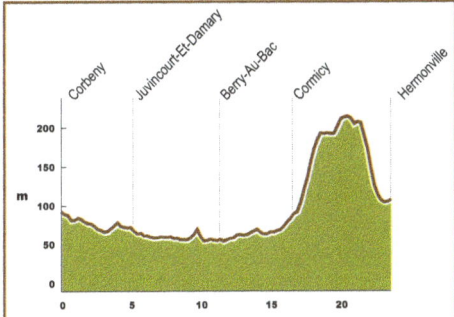

crossing to the east by small roads and farm tracks, before returning to the west at Berry-au-Bac and then beginning the first ascent of the champagne hills - les Monts de Reims.

Berry-au-Bac has a restaurant and you will encounter the first champagne houses in Cormicy.

Hermonville has a small number of food stores and cafés. The price for accommodation is of course affected by the exclusivity of the champagne brands.

As your route meanders through the vineyards of the department of Champagne, it is worth remembering that these grapes will be producing an elite French wine – the exceptional nature of the soil determining their unique flavour. Most vineyards are situated halfway up the hillside, and the roots of the vine grow deep down into chalky depths.

The climate of the Champagne area also plays a major role. The young vines must adapt to the dangers of frost in springtime, and poor weather during the flowering period. Grape picking begins towards the end of September, about 100 days after the flowering of the vine, and involves a wealth of special precautionary measures found only in this area. Picking is by hand, the grape bunches examined one by one and the green or damaged ones discarded. The initial two or three rapid pressings of the grapes produce the cuvée juice, subsequent pressings give the premier taille and then the deuxieme taille. After this any further juice is of insufficient quality to become Champagne. To produce its characteristic bubbles, Champagne has to undergo a process of double fermentation.

stage 18   Corbeny to Hertmonville

(0.0) From the crossroads of the D18 and D1044, beside the church in the centre of Corbeny, take the pavement beside the very busy D1044 and head south-east[Direction Reims, pass the church on your right]**(0.2)** Turn left and immediately bear right[Direction Juvincourt-et-Damary, D62] **(4.5)** Approaching Jouvincourt, turn right on the track and then take the first turning to the left. Note:- the "Official Route" skirts the field ahead at the cost of a few hundred meters of extra distance. You may continue on the road and turn right and immediately left in the village to save the extra distance**(5.2)** At the junction with the road, turn left[Towards the church and **Juvincourt-et-Damary** centre]**(5.4)** Turn right onto[Rue de l'Abreuvoir] **(5.9)** After passing the agricultural machinery store, bear left[Pass a large barn on right]**(6.3)** Fork left and cross the bridge[Cross the river, la Miette] **(6.5)** Turn right after the bridge[Woodland on your right, large open field on the left] **(7.6)** At the junction, continue straight ahead on the track[Wood and marshland on right] **(8.8)** Continue straight ahead[Pass a strip of uncultivated ground on your left]**(8.9)** Follow the grassy track as it turns left and climbs the hill[Pass the monument on the summit to your right]**(9.6)** Cross straight over the D925 and continue on the road in the direction of the village[Large grain silo in the distance. No-Entry signs] **(10.2)** At the crossroads, continue straight ahead on the tarmac[Metal fence on your right]**(10.9)** At the crossroads continue straight ahead[Follow rue Dorigny]**(11.2)** At the T-junction, turn left and then bear right **(11.4)** At the junction with the main road in **Berry-au-Bac**, avenue Général de Gaulle, turn left[Restaurant de la Mairie to the right]**(11.8)** Cross the 3 bridges and continue straight ahead beside the road[Pass grain silos on your left]**(12.2)** Turn right on rue de Cormicy, D530**(12.3)** At the crossroads, turn right and then bear left on the stony track. Note:-

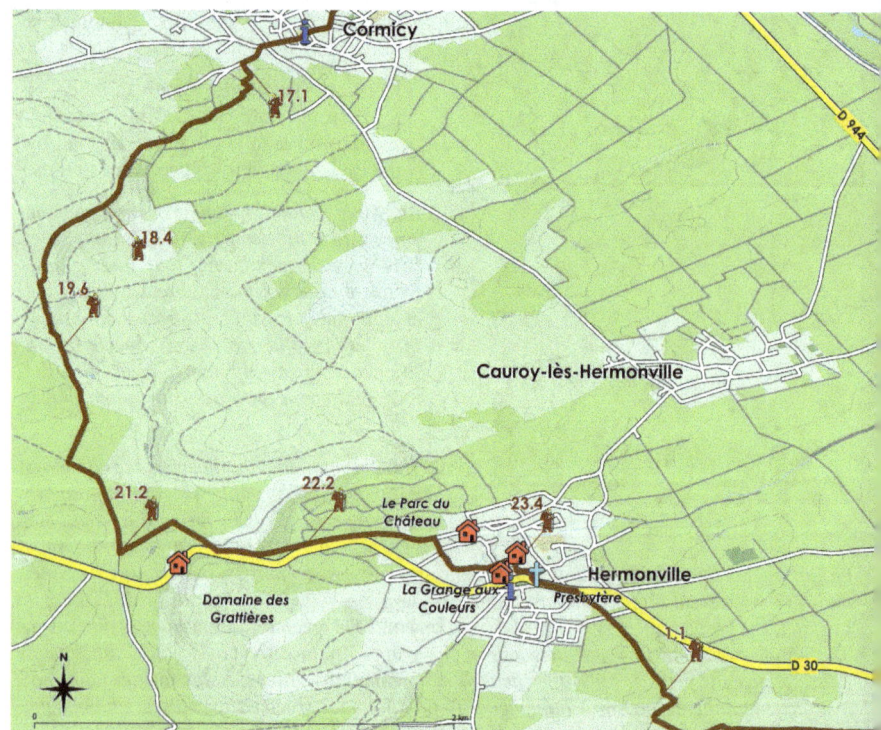

Corbeny to Hertmonville stage 18

the "Official Route" makes a dog leg through the fields before returning to this road. 1.5km may be saved by remaining on the D530 to the crossroads at the entrance to Cormicy[Between the fields] **(14.2)**At the crossroads in the tracks, turn left on the grass track[Towards the church spire]**(15.0)**At the crossroads in the track, continue straight ahead[Towards the village] **(16.0)**At the crossroads with the tarmac road, continue straight ahead[Pass the sign "Bienvenue à Cormicy" on your right]**(16.2)**At the junction take the second turning to the right[Wall to the cemetery on your left]**(16.4)**At the crossroads, continue straight ahead towards the church[Direction "Maison des Jeunes"]**(16.5)**At the crossroads with the D32, in **Cormicy**, turn right[Church on your right]**(16.9)**Shortly after passing the pharmacy, turn left on rue du Bois de Pré **(17.1)**Beside house n° 1, turn left on the concrete track, uphill**(17.2)**At the T-junction, turn left and immediately bear right on the concrete track**(17.5)**Approaching the top of the hill, at the end of the concrete track, bear left on the stony track[Towards the trees]**(17.9)**At the crossroads in the tracks, continue straight ahead on the grass track between the woods and the vines**(18.0)**At the fork in the track, continue straight ahead on the main track[Into the woods] **(18.4)**At the crossroads in the woods continue straight ahead**(19.1)**At the T-junction in the track, turn left on the broad track **(19.6)**At the crossroads in the tracks, continue straight ahead, slightly uphill**(19.8)**Avoid the track on the left and continue straight ahead[Towards the field on your right]**(20.5)**At the T-junction, turn left, initially towards the corner of the forest[Continue on the track between the fields as it bears right] **(21.2)**Turn left on the grass track between the fields[Direction le Mont Chatte]**(21.5)**Bear right, downhill[Towards the trees]**(21.7)**At the junction with the broad gravel track, continue straight ahead. Downhill, into the trees**(22.0)**Emerge from the trees and continue straight ahead on the track between the vines[Parallel to the road, below] **(22.2)**At the crossroads in the tracks, continue straight ahead[Towards the silos]**(22.7)**At the junction in the tracks, continue straight ahead[Pass a reservoir on your right]**(22.9)**At the the junction with the tarmac road, turn right[Keep the hedgerow on your left and the field on your right]**(23.0)**At the junction with house n° 12 on your left, continue straight ahead**(23.2)**At the end of rue de la Bonne Fontaine, bear left on rue du Temple[Keep the trees on your right] **(23.4)**At the T-junction with rue de l'Eglise, turn right**(23.5)**With the church on your left, turn left[Place de l'Eglise]**(23.5)**At the T-junction, turn right and then right again[Rue Thomas Picotin]**(23.6)**Arrive at **Hermonville** centre[Place de la Mairie]

French National Tank monument - Berry-au-Bac

stage 18 — Corbeny to Hertmonville

Accommodation and Tourist Information

Berry-au-Bac
🏠 **Emmaus Community - Homeless shelter**,3 Avenue du Général de Gaulle, 2190 Berry-au-Bac, France; Tel:+33(0)3 23 79 95 88; facebook.com/emmausReims.Berryofficiel; Price:C; *To book call Tuesday - Saturday 08.00-12.00 or 14.00-17.00 2 beds shared kitchen*

Cormicy
ℹ️ **Mairie**,1 place Armes, 51220 Cormicy, France; Tel:+33(0)3 26 61 30 30; Email:mairie.cormicy@wanadoo.fr; www.cormicy.fr

Guignicourt
⚠️ **Camping Guignicourt**,14 Bis rue Godins, 02190 Guignicourt, France; Tel:+33(0)3 23 79 74 58; Email:campingguignicourt@orange.fr; www.camping-aisne-picardie.fr; Price:C; *Mobile homes available with reservation Open April to end October*

Hermonville
⛪ **Presbytère**,6 rue Thomas Picotin, 51220 Hermonville, France; Tel:+33(0)3 26 61 58 36
🏠 **B&B - Domaine des Grattières**,Route de Fismes, 51220 Hermonville, France; Tel:+33(0)6 22 69 49 52; Email: chris.elle74@orange.fr; www.domainedesgrattieres.com; Price:A
🏠 **Chambre d'Hôtes - Le Parc du Château**,7 Ter rue Visin, 51220 Hermonville, France; Tel:+33(0)662 082 003; Email: sebtrax@orange.fr; www.le-parc-du-chateau.com; Price:A

🏠 **Chambre d'Hôtes - Artelier dans ma cour** ,8 bis Rue de Fismes , 51220 Hermonville, France; Tel:+33 (0) 6 85 56 08 21; artelier-dans-ma-cour.fr; Price:A
ℹ️ **Mairie - Hermonville**,4 place Truchon, 51220 Hermonville, France; Tel:+33(0)3 26 61 51 23; Email:hermonville51@gmail.com; www.hermonville.fr

Saint-Thierry
📧 **Monastère des Bénédictines**,2 place Abbaye, 51220 Saint-Thierry, France; Tel:+33(0)3 26 03 99 37; +33(0)6 71 39 40 25; Email:hotellerie.st-thierry1@orange.fr; www.benedictines-ste-bathilde.fr/les-monasteres/monastere-de-saint-thierry; Price:C

Thil
🏠 **Chambre d'Hôtes - La Grange aux Couleurs**,6 rue de l'Église, 51220 Thil, France; Tel:+33(0)6 16 67 15 64; Email:7menno@free.fr; la-grange-aux-couleurs.eatbu.com; Price:A

Villers-Franqueux
🏠 **Chambre d'Hôtes - Gîte di Massif**,7 rue Pouillon, 51220 Villers-Franqueux, France; Tel:+33(0)3 51 24 65 23; +33(0)6 12 65 49 05; Email:beatrice.fauchereau@gmail.com; gitedumassif.wordpress.com; Price:B

Hermonville to Reims

stage 19

Length:	16.6km
Ascent:	237m
Descent:	255m
Canterbury	454km
Col Grand Saint Bernard:	785km

Notre-Dame Cathedral - Reims

Route: this short stage from Hermonville to Reims follows woodland tracks over the Massif de Saint Thierry before descending towards the city of Reims.

Merfy has a bar and boulangerie.

The final approach to Reims is on a pleasant path beside the canal de l'Aisne à la Marne, where the GR®145 and GR®654 Chemin de Saint Jacques merge. Naturally the city has a rich choice of facilities and excellent access to transport connections. The stage will continue to the doors of the magnificent cathedral of Notre-Dame.

Excavations have shown that the present Notre-Dame Cathedral occupies roughly the same site as the original one founded under the episcopacy of St Nicaise. This church was rebuilt during the Carolingian period and further extended in the 12th century. In 1210, the cathedral was damaged by fire and reconstruction started shortly after. In 1233 a long-running dispute between the cathedral chapter and the townsfolk (regarding issues of taxation and legal jurisdiction) boiled over into open revolt. Several clerics were killed or injured during the resulting violence and the entire cathedral chapter fled the city, leaving it under an interdict which effectively banned all public worship and sacraments. Work on the new cathedral was suspended for three years, only resuming in 1236. Construction then continued more slowly. The upper parts of the facade were finally completed in the 14th century, but apparently following 13th century designs, giving Reims an unusual unity of style. Look out for the Great Rose window, best seen at sunset. The 13th century window depicts the virgin surrounded by apostles and angel musicians. The Smiling Angel, the most celebrated of the many that adorn the building. The Gallery of the Kings, a harmonious west façade is decorated with over 2,300 statues, including fifty-six stone effigies of the French kings.

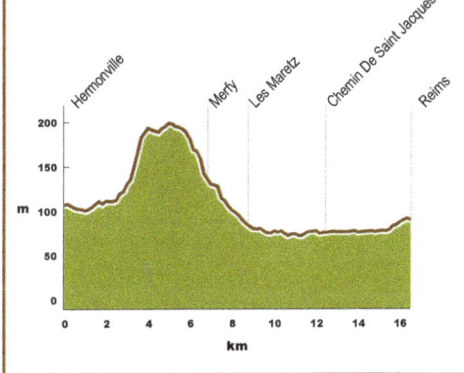

stage 19   Hermonville to Reims

(0.0) From the centre of Hermonville, take the D30 rue de Reims[Pass la Poste on your left] **(0.2)** In front of the bank, turn right and then keep left on rue de Toussicourt **(0.5)** At the crossroads with the tarmac road, continue straight on the track 🚶 **(1.1)** Take the left fork into the trees **(1.2)** With the field straight ahead, turn right[Keep the woods close on your right] **(1.3)** In the corner of the field, bear left on the track[Keep the field on your left and the woods on your right] **(1.8)** Shortly after turning right, take the left fork[Into the woods] 🚶 **(2.5)** At intersection of tracks cross over and then bear right[Forest close on left and field on right] **(3.1)** At the T-junction turn left, slightly uphill[House, Toussicourt, on your left] 🚶 **(3.7)** At the T-junction at the top of hill, turn right on the stony track **(4.4)** At the crossroads in the track, continue straight ahead on the broad track 🚶 **(4.9)** At the junction in the tracks, continue straight ahead on the broad track[Ignore the track to the left] **(5.2)** Bear left onto a small track and immediately bear right parallel to the main track 🚶 **(6.1)** At the T-junction with a small track, turn left **(6.2)** At the T-junction with a broad track, turn right, downhill **(6.7)** At the T-junction with the road, turn right onto the road, downhill **(6.9)** At the crossroads, continue straight ahead into the village of **Merfy** [Remain on rue de Pouillon] 🚶 **(7.1)** At the crossroads, continue straight ahead[No-Entry sign, rue de Pouillon] **(7.2)** At the crossroads with the D26, continue straight ahead[Pass

Saint Peter and Saint Paul meet Saint James

102

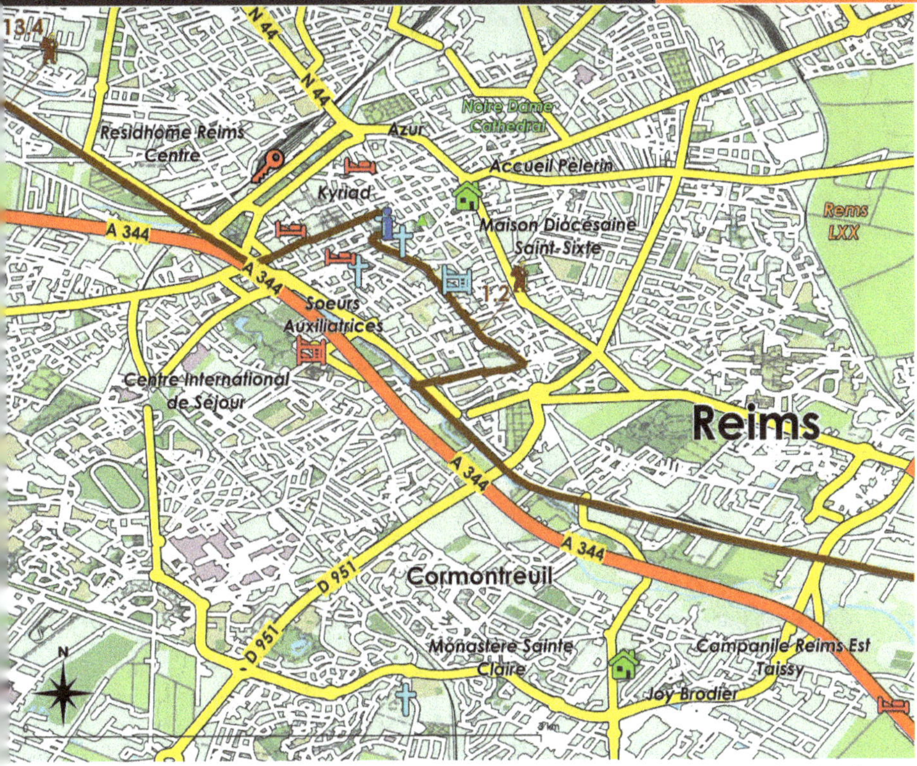

Hermonville to Reims

stage 19

a school on your right](**7.3**)At the next crossroads, again continue straight ahead downhill[Between walled gardens, chemin des Jardins](**7.6**)At the crossroads with the track, continue straight ahead on the tarmac road, downhill[Yellow VF sign – Reims 5.5km] (**8.8**)At the T-junction, in the hamlet of **Les Maretz**, turn left (**10.0**)Continue straight over autoroute bridge[Crash barriers on both sides](**10.3**)Turn right under the power lines[Yellow VF sign - Port Colbert 3km](**10.5**) Pass through the metal gates and continue straight ahead on the track (**11.1**)Turn left with the water treatment plant on your left(**11.2**) Pass through a metal barrier and continue straight ahead(**12.0**)At the crossroads in the tracks, turn left on the small track[Towards the radio tower] (**12.1**)At the T-junction with the road in the industrial zone, turn right on the pavement[Continue towards the radio tower] (**12.2**)At the crossroads with the road, continue straight ahead on the tarmac path[Pass metal barriers](**12.5**)At the T-junction, turn right on the path beside the canal l'Aisene à la Marne. Nore:- the GR654 **Chemin de Saint Jacques** joins from the left (**13.4**)Continue straight

Descending from Les Monts de Reims

stage 19 — Hermonville to Reims

ahead[Under the road bridge] 🕯(15.4)To reach the cathedral and the centre of Reims, climb the steps on the right and cross the bridge over the canal. Note:- the "Official Route" will return to the canal-side after passing the city centre and cathedral[Continue beside the tramway](15.6)At the junction continue straight ahead into the pedestrian zone[Pass 3 black obelisks on your right](16.4)After passing the Tribunal, immediately turn right and continue towards the cathedral[Rue du Trésor] 🕯(16.5)Arrive at **Reims (LXX)** centre[Beside Cathédral doors]

Accommodation and Tourist Information

Cormontreuil

🕯**Monastère Sainte Claire**[Soeur Cécile],2 Bis rue Pierre Bérégovoy, 51350 Cormontreuil, France; Tel:+33(0)3 26 86 95 12; Email:clarissescormontreuil @ orange.fr; clarisses-cormontreuil-catholique.fr; Price:C

🏠 **Joy Brodier**,5 rue Paul Gauguin, 51350 Cormontreuil, France; Tel:+33(0)3 26 35 41 86; +33(0)6 23 21 30 12; Email:joy.brodier@gmail.com; Price:C; *Evening meal 5€ English spoken*

Reims

🏠 **Centre International de Séjour**,Parc Léo Lagrange - 21 Chaussée Bocquaine, 51100 Reims, France; Tel:+33(0)3 26 40 52 60; Email:info@cis-reims.com; www.cis-reims.com; Price:B

⛪**Maison Diocésaine Saint-Sixte**,16 rue du Barbatre, 51100 Reims, France; Tel:+33(0)3 26 82 72 50; Email:secretariat@maisonsaintsixte.fr; maisonsaintsixte.fr; Price:C

🕯**Paroisse Notre Dame et Saint Jacques** ,1 rue Guillaume de Machault, 51100 Reims, France; Tel:+33(0)3 26 47 55 34; Email:cathedrale.reims@orange.fr; www.cathedrale-reims.com

🕯**Vicariat Général de l'Archevêché**,1 rue d'Anjou, 51100 Reims, France; Tel:+33(0)3 26 47 69 55

🕯**Soeurs Auxiliatrices**,46 rue des Capucins, 51100 Reims, France; Tel:+33(0)3 26 47 65 80; Email:contact@auxiliatrices.fr; auxiliatrices.fr

🏠**Accueil Pèlerin**[Marie-Josée Van Den Borre],51 rue Eugène Desteuque, 51100 Reims, France; Tel:+33 (0) 619 897 476; Email:mj.vandenborre@orange.fr; Price:B; *Includes dinner and breakfast*

🏨**Hôtel - Azur**,9 rue des Ecrevées , 51100 Reims, France; Tel:+33(0)3 26 47 43 39; Email:contact@hotel-azur-reims.com ; www.hotel-azur-reims.com; Price:B

🏨**Hôtel - Kyriad**,29 rue Buirette, 51100 Reims, France; Tel:+33(0)3 26 47 39 39; +33(0) 1 73 21 98 00; Email:reims.centre@kyriad.fr; reims-centre.kyriad.com; Price:B

🏨**Hôtel - de la Cathédrale**,20 rue Libergier, 51100 Reims, France; Tel:+33(0)3 26 47 28 46; Email:contact@hotel-cathedrale-reims.fr; www.hotel-cathedrale-reims.fr; Price:B

🔑**Residhome Reims Centre**,6 rue de Courcelles, 51100 Reims, France; Tel:+33(0)326781781; myresidhome.com; Price:A; *Apartment hotel central location*

ℹ️ **Office du Tourisme**,6 rue Rockefeller, 51100 Reims, France; Tel:+33(0)3 26 77 45 00; Email:accueil@reims-tourisme.com; www.reims-tourisme.com

Taissy

🏨**Hôtel - Campanile Reims Est - Taissy**,Rue Édouard Branly, 51500 Taissy, France; Tel:+33(0)3 26 49 06 10; Email:reims.taissy@campanile.fr; reims-est-taissy.campanile.com; Price:B

Tinqueux

🏨**Hôtel - Première Classe - Reims West**,7 rue Louis Breguet, 51430 Tinqueux, France; Tel:+33(0)3 26 04 53 51; Email:Reims.ouest.tinqueux@premiereclasse.fr; www.premiereclasse.com; Price:B

Reims to Verzenay

stage 20

Length:	17.8km
Ascent:	354m
Descent:	251m
Canterbury	470km
Col Grand Saint Bernard:	769km

Moulin de Verzenay   *Dguendel*

Route: the stage from Reims to Verzenay continues to share the route with the Chemin de Saint Jacques - GR®654. The route passes the Basilica of Saint Rémi before returning to the canal-side and then climbing the hills through the champagne vineyards and passing through the woods of the Parc Naturel de la Montagne de Reims. Expect some steep climbs with muddy woodland tracks in wet conditions.

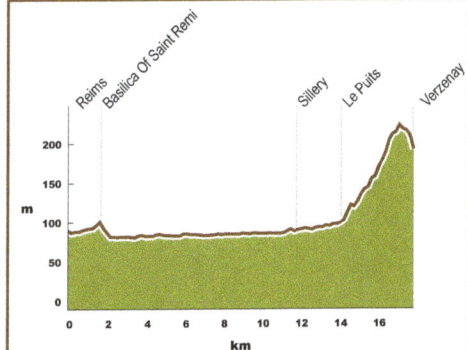

It is possible to take a meal or drink break at Saint-Léonard.

Basilica of Saint Rémi

Accommodation may be expensive in Verzenay and Verzy. Pilgrim Hosts may be able to offer cheaper options off-piste in Trépail.

The Verezenay Lighthouse - le Phare de Verzenay - was constructed in 1909 by Joseph Goulet to bring publicity to his champagne brand. In addition to the lighthouse there was a theatre, restaurant and dancing. Sadly WW II destroyed all but the tower which has been restored as an ecomuseum dedicated to the wine industry.

(0.0) From the entrance to the Cathédral take rue Rockefeller[Pass the Médiathèque on the left]**(0.1)** At the crossroads, turn left and continue on rue Chanzy and rue Gambetta through numerous intersections **(1.2)** Continue straight ahead on rue Gambetta[Pass the city of Reims administration buildings on your right]**(1.6)** At the crossroads, turn right[Rue Saint Julien]**(1.6)** Bear right into the grounds of the **Basilica of Saint Remi**[Continue

stage 20   Reims to Verzenay

with the basilica on your right]**(1.8)**Cross the road in front of the basilica entrance and follow the pedestrian zone between the shops[Esplanade Flechambault]**(2.1)**Continue ahead over the canal bridge, turn right and right again to rejoin the canal-side path[Keep the canal on your immediate left] **(7.4)**Continue straight ahead on the grassy track[Pass the restaurant - Saint Léonard - on your right] **(11.3)**Beside the lock, continue straight ahead under the road bridge**(11.8)**Beside the boat dock in **Sillery**, turn right**(11.9)**At the T-junction, turn left on rue du Canada[Large stone house directly in front] **(12.0)**Turn right onto rue de Mailly, direction Mailly - Champagne, D308[Cross the motorway and the railway track, GR°654] **(14.1)**At the crossroads in **Le Puits**, turn left[Yellow GR°145 sign - Verzenay 2km] **(15.7)**At the top of the hill, turn sharp right on the tarmac track[Yellow sign - Verzenay]**(15.8)**Turn left onto gravel track, uphill between vines[Pass le Moulin de Verzenay on your left] **(16.8)**Cross straight over the road and continue on the track up the hill**(16.8)**At the next crossroads, turn left[Calvaire]**(17.0)**At the crossroads continue straight ahead into the woods[Village of Verzenay on left]**(17.5)**Fork left after leaving the woods, downhill[Avenue de Champagne]**(17.7)**Continue straight ahead, avoid the turning to the left **(17.8)**Arrive at **Verzenay** centre[Crossroads beside the wine press]

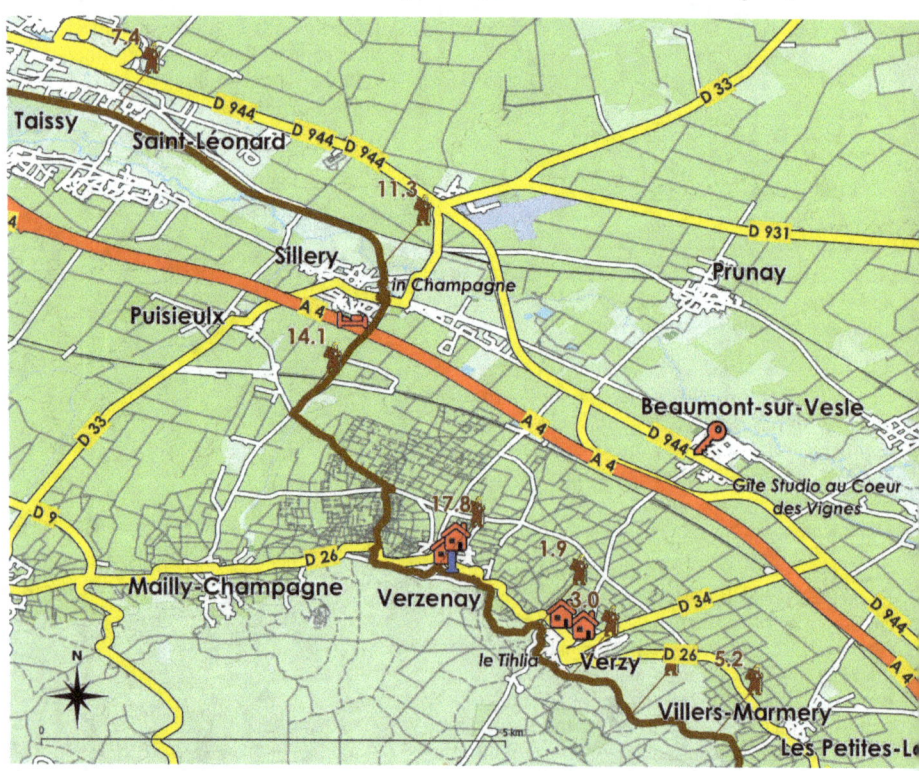

106

Reims to Verzenay — stage 20

Accommodation and Tourist Information

Beaumont-sur-Vesle

🔑 **Gîte - Studio au Coeur des Vignes**[Virginie et Sébastien],9 Rue des Vignes, 51360 Beaumont-sur-Vesle, France; Tel: www.gites.fr/gites_studio-au-coeur-des-vignes_beaumont-sur-vesle_h5253348.htm; Price:C; *Close to the Canal de la Marne à L'Aisne footpath*

Sillery

🛏 **Chambre d'Hôtes - Guest House in Champagne**[Prycille and Stéphane],22 Rue de l'Image, 51500 Sillery, France; Tel:+33(0)768020743; Email:guesthouseinchampagne@gmail.com; guesthouseinchampagne.com; Price:B; **PR**

Trépail

🏠 **Mme Jacqueminet**,17 rue Saint-Martin, 51380 Trépail, France; Tel:+33(0)3 26 57 82 29; +33(0)6 19 81 22 52; Price:D; *A very kind host*; **PR**

🏠 **M Daniel Bertrand**,6 rue des Tilleuls, 51380 Trépail, France; Tel:+33(0)3 26 57 06 40; +33(0)6 72 84 94 08; Email:danielbertrand23@orange.fr; Price:D

🏠 **B&B - Pré en Bulles**,2 rue du Stade, 51380 Trépail, France; Tel:+33(0)3 26 53 50 00; pre-en-bulles.com; Price:A

ℹ **Mairie**,Rue de la Mairie, 51380 Trépail, France; Tel:+33(0)3 26 57 05 55; Email:contact@trepail.fr; www.trepail.fr

Verzenay

🏠 **Chambre d'Hôtes - La Vigne en Rose**,2 rue Maréchal, 51360 Verzenay, France; Tel:+33(0)7 87 25 09 39; Email:la.vigne.en.rose51@gmail.com; www.la-vigne-en-rose.fr; Price:A

🏠 **Maison des Vignes**,6 rue de la Veuve Pommery, 51360 Verzenay, France; Tel:+33(0)3 26 49 48 63; +33(0)6 82 09 19 28; Email:champagnepithois-emmanuel@wanadoo.fr; maisondesvignesdeverzenay.com/; Price:A

ℹ **Mairie**,Place Carnot, 51360 Verzenay, France; Tel:+33(0)3 26 49 42 68; www.verzenay.fr

Verzy

🏠 **Chambre d'Hôtes - le Tihlia**,1 rue de Louvois, 51380 Verzy, France; Tel:+33(0)3 26 97 90 29; +33(0)6 11 23 23 38; Email:contact@letihlia.com; www.letihlia.com/chambre-hote.php; Price:B

🏠 **Chambre d'Hôtes - Champagne Alain Lallement**,19 rue Carnot, 51380 Verzy, France; Tel:+33(0)3 26 97 92 32; +33(0)3 52 74 02 04; Email:champagne.alain.lallement@club-internet.fr; champagne-alain-lallement.net; Price:A

Verzenay Lighthouse

stage 21   Verzenay to Condé-sur-Marne

Length:	23.5km
Ascent:	541m
Descent:	652m
Canterbury	488km
Col Grand Saint Bernard:	751km

La Halle - Condé sur Marne

Route: the stage from Verzenay to Condé-sur-Marne is generally off-road, temporarily leaving the champagne hill-sides for the cereal fields in the plain below.

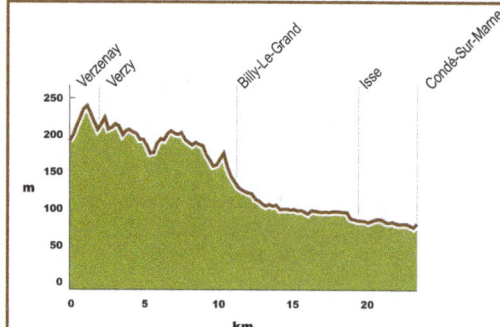

The route re-enters the Forêt de la Montagne de Reims and passes beside Verzy, but then descends to pass through open farm land to find canal-side paths for the approach to Condé-sur-Marne.

There are very few facilities, directly on the route, between Verzy and Condé.

The 58 km Canal de l'Aisne à la Marne was fully opened in 1866 and links the Canal latéral à l'Aisne at Berry-au-Bac to the Canal latéral à la Marne at Condé-sur-Marne. It was planned to be a part of a grand canal scheme that would circumnavigate Paris. Sadly the scheme was never completed. Today the canal largely carries grain barges and pleasure craft.

Canal de l'Aisne à la Marne Lock/Écluse - Isse   G.Garitan

Verzenay to Condé-sur-Marne   stage 21

(0.0) From the crossroads beside the wine press take the small road, rue Frédéric Bin **(0.3)** At the end of the tarmac, continue straight ahead on the gravel track **(0.5)** A little before the end of the road, turn right onto narrow track up a steep hill [White House on left] **(0.6)** Turn left onto a broad track at the top of the slope [Towards vines] **(0.7)** At the crossroads in track proceed straight ahead between vines **(1.9)** After leaving woods continue through a

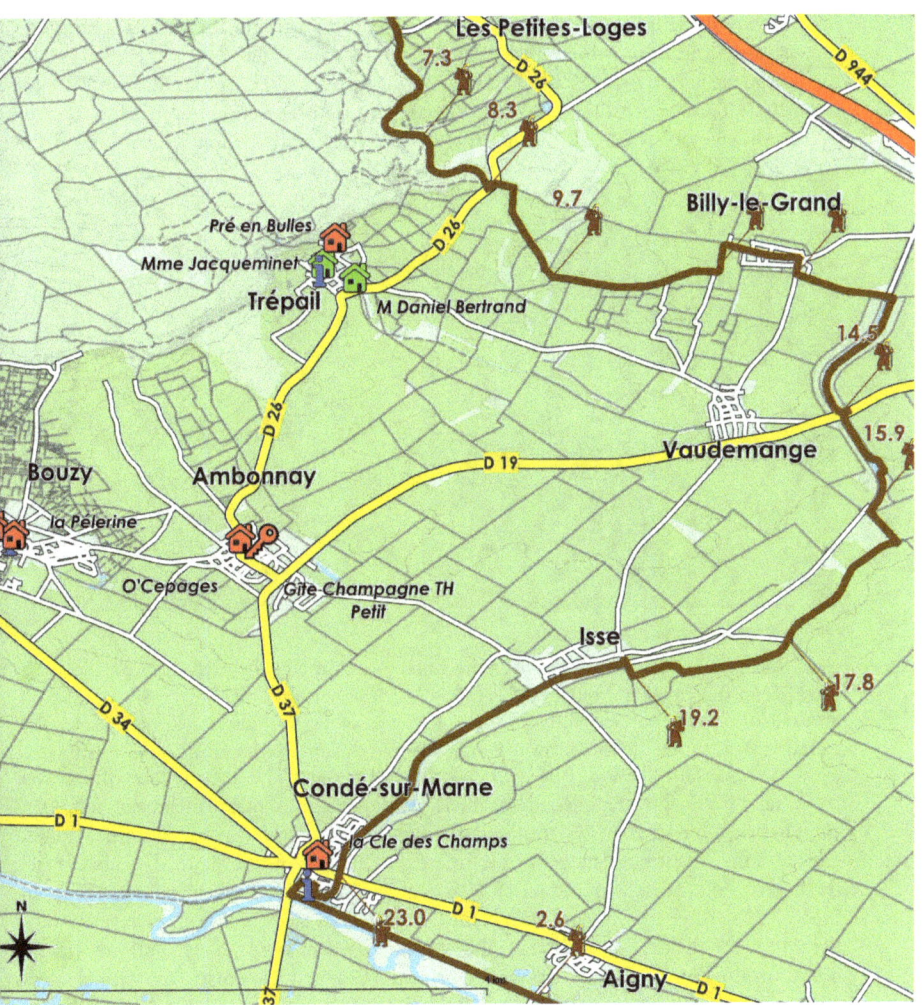

builder's yard **(2.0)** At the crossroads in **Verzy**, continue straight ahead on rue de la Croix de Mission **(2.2)** Continue straight ahead into woods [Route Forestière de CBR] **(3.0)** At the crossroads, continue straight ahead on the broad forest track **(3.4)** Continue straight ahead. Ignore the left fork **(4.2)** Continue straight ahead [Avoid the left turn - route Forestière Saint Basle] **(5.2)** At the junction, continue straight ahead [Avoid the turning to the right, route Forestière de Coutron] **(5.7)** At intersection with the road, continue straight ahead [Village of Villers-Marmery on the left] **(5.7)** At the end of the line of trees, fork

109

stage 21   Verzenay to Condé-sur-Marne

left[Towards the forest] ⁂ **(7.3)** At the crossroads in the tracks, continue straight ahead on the broad track[Continue to skirt the forest] ⁂ **(8.3)** At the T-junction with the road, turn left on the road and then immediately turn right on the track beside the trees[Yellow VF sign - Billy-le-Grand] **(8.5)** At the junction in the tracks, turn right on the gravel track[Initially parallel to the road] **(9.2)** At the crossroads in the tracks, continue straight ahead, downhill[Grass track, towards the woods] ⁂ **(9.7)** At the junction, after emerging from the woods, bear left on the broad track **(10.5)** At the junction with a tarmac road, continue straight ahead, downhill on the tarmac[Vines on your right] ⁂ **(11.0)** Bear left on the road[Keep the village to the right] **(11.3)** Bear right on the road[Enter the village of **Billy-le-Grand**] **(12.0)** At the junction beside the Mairie, turn right[Direction Vaudemange, D319] ⁂ **(12.1)** Just before reaching the sign for the exit from Billy-le-Grand, turn left on the

Forêt Domaniale de Verzy

road[Rue de la Voûte] **(13.0)** Pass over the canal and immediately turn right on the grass track[Keep the canal to your right] ⁂ **(14.5)** At the junction with the tarmac road, pass around the crash barrier and continue straight ahead on the track nearest to the canal[Bridge on the right, yellow VF sign for Condé-sur-Marne 8km] ⁂ **(15.9)** Immediately after passing the lock and with a bridge on your right, turn left on the gravel track[Yellow VF sign - Condé-sur-Marne, 7 km] **(16.3)** As the main track bears left, turn right between the trees ⁂ **(17.8)** At the crossroads with the tarmac road, continue straight ahead on the grass track[Hedgerow on the left] **(18.8)** At the next crossroads with a gravel track, turn right[Track will bear left] ⁂ **(19.2)** At the T-junction, turn right[Cross the canal bridge] **(19.5)** After crossing the bridge, turn sharp left and then right on the tarmac track beside the canal[Canal on your left, village of **Isse** on your right] **(20.1)** Continue straight ahead on the canal-side path[Under the bridge] ⁂ **(23.0)** At the crossroads with a major road, after passing the lock, continue straight ahead remaining beside the canal.[Condé-sur-Marne] **(23.3)** Beside the port, turn right and then right again on rue du Port[Pass the silos on your left] **(23.5)** Arrive at **Condé-sur-Marne** centre in place Alexandre Batilliot[Beside the Mairie]

Verzenay to Condé-sur-Marne — stage 21

Accommodation and Tourist Information

Ambonnay
🏠 **Chambre d'Hôtes - O'Cepages**, 1 rue Saint-Vincent, 51150 Ambonnay, France; Tel:+33 6 01 13 68 50; Email:chambres.ocepages@gmail.com; web.facebook.com/people/OCepages/100057350533838; Price:A

🗝️ **Gîte - Champagne TH Petit**, 11 rue Colbert, 51150 Ambonnay, France; Tel:+33(0)9 74 56 59 41; +33(0)6 83 17 53 46; www.champagnethpetit.com; Price:B

Bouzy
🏠 **Chambre d'Hôtes - la Pélerine**, 13 rue Gambetta, 51150 Bouzy, France; Tel:+33(0)3 26 52 90 19; Email:rosay.francois@neuf.fr; pelerine.fr; Price:B

🏠 **Chambre d'Hôtes - les Barbontines**, 1 place André Tritant, 51150 Bouzy, France; Tel:+33(0)3 26 53 97 58; +33(0)3 26 51 70 49; Email:contact@lesbarbotines.com ; www.lesbarbotines.com ; Price:A

ℹ️ **Mairie**, 12 rue Pasteur, 51150 Bouzy, France; Tel:+33(0)3 26 57 70 70; Email:mairie@bouzyenchampagne.com; www.bouzyenchampagne.com

Condé-sur-Marne
🏠 **Chambre d'Hôtes - la Cle des Champs**[Denis Wolter], 2 rue Albert Barre, 51150 Condé-sur-Marne, France; Tel:+33(0)3 26 68 94 75; +33(0)6 85 66 53 64; Email:denis.wolter@orange.fr; web.facebook.com/people/La-Cle-des-Champs/100054282139675; Price:B

ℹ️ **Mairie**, Place Alexandre Batilliot, 51150 Condé-sur-Marne, France; Tel:+33(0)3 26 67 98 77; www.conde-sur-marne.fr

Jâlons
🏠 **Chambre d'Hôtes - Sawan**, 11 rue de la Mairie, 51150 Jâlons, France; Tel:+33(0)6 78 04 24 18; Email:sawan.jalons@gmail.com; www.gite-sawan.fr; Price:A

Tournesol - close to Trépai

stage 22 — Condé-sur-Marne to Châlons-en-Champagne

Length:	18.7km
Ascent:	169m
Descent:	163m
Canterbury	511km
Col Grand Saint Bernard:	728km

Cathédrale Saint-Etienne - Châlons-en-Champagne

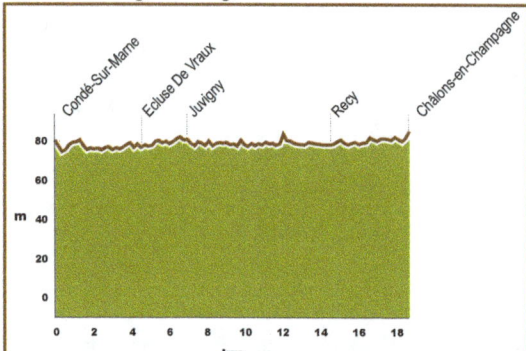

Route: the gentle stage from Condé-sur-Marne to Châlons-en-Champagne follows the tow-path of the Canal Latéral à la Marne. The GR®145/654 merge with the GR®14 from Condé-sur-Marne to near Vitry-en-Perthois. The town of Châlons-en-Champagne was formerly known as Châlons-sur-Marne and this name still appears as this on older signs.

There are small shops and a café/bar in Vraux. Châlons-en-Champagne has a full range of facilities.

Châlons-en-Champagne has preserved much evidence of its past, as shown by its timber-framed facades and its religious buildings. It is the capital (préfecture) of the Marne department and has long been a major economic hub, having a strategic location on the river Marne. Châlons is often referred to as Little Venice, and there has always been an artistic energy to the town.

It owes its name to the Gallic people of Châlons who settled to the northeast of the present city. By 20 BC the Romans had established a road network throughout ancient Gaul, including the Via Agrippa, the main route connecting Milan to Boulogne-sur-Mer, crossing the Marne at Châlons. From the 9th century, Châlons became a prosperous market town trading agricultural produce with neighbouring regions.

Outside the narrow Gallo-Roman walls, a square was created called the Place du Marché au Blé (the Corn Market), which is known today as the Place de la République.

During the 18th Century the city was extended, with the ramparts being replaced by boulevards forming the shape of the town that you see today. Construction included seventeen religious institutions and some outstanding architectural masterpieces. The Cathedral of Saint-Etienne includes parts of the Romanesque building created in the 12th century. It was mainly rebuilt in Gothic style and two additional structures (in Baroque style) were added in the 17th Century.

Condé-sur-Marne to Châlons-en-Champagne stage 22

(0.0)From place Alexandre Batilliot, take rue du 8 Mai[Pass the church on your right](0.1)At the T-junction, turn left[Large arch doorway on your left](0.2)At the crossroads with impasse de Silo , continue straight ahead over the bridge(0.3)After crossing the bridge, immediately turn left and continue on the canal-side track[Between the canal and the river la Marne] (2.6)At the road junction, continue straight ahead on the canal-side track[Bridge on the left] (4.6)At the next road junction, turn left on the road and cross the bridge[Lock - **Ecluse de Vraux** - on the right of the bridge](5.4)Just before reaching the next bridge, turn right on the track[Juvigny 2km, yellow VF sign] (5.9)At the crossroads with a gravel track, continue straight ahead[Bridge on the left](6.8)At the T-junction with a gravel track, turn left over the bridge (7.0)At the T-junction with the busy road, turn right on the D1[Enter **Juvigny**](7.1)At the crossroads, turn right on the narrow ruelle St Martin[Towards house n° 4](7.3)Continue straight ahead on the grassy track[Cross the field](7.6)At the T-junction with the road, turn right over the bridge[Yellow VF sign - Châlons 11km](7.7) Turn left onto the track shortly before crossing a second bridge[Between trees] (8.8)With a road to the left, continue straight ahead on the track(9.6)At the T-junction, turn left onto a wider gravel road [Towards a copse of trees] (9.8)At the crossroads, turn right (12.0)

Châlons-en-Champagne - Little Venice

stage 22 — Condé-sur-Marne to Châlons-en-Champagne

At the junction with a broader track, bear right on the broad track through the woods[Pass under the motorway] **(12.4)** At the junction immediately after the motorway, continue straight ahead on the broad gravel track**(12.9)** At the junction in the tracks, continue straight ahead towards the church[Trees on your right] 🚶 **(13.5)** The track joins a road, continue ahead and then turn right over 2 bridges and then turn left beside the canal[Church on the left] 🚶 **(14.6)** At the crossroads with a gravel track, proceed straight ahead on the concrete track with the bridge on your left[Village of **Recy** to your left] 🚶

Cathédrale Saint-Etienne - Rosette

Condé-sur-Marne to Châlons-en-Champagne stage 22

(16.0) With a bridge and tarmac road on the left, continue straight ahead on the concrete track[Canal on your left]**(16.1)**Take the right fork on the gravel track 🚶 **(17.7)**At the junction with a tarmac road, continue straight ahead[Pass rue de l' Association Foncière on your right]**(17.9)**Take the right fork beside house n°25**(18.2)**At the T-junction at the end of rue des Frères Navlet, turn left[Keep the river and railway on your right]**(18.7)**Arrive at **Châlons-en-Champagne (LXIX)**.   Note:- to gain access to the town centre turn left[Crossroads with rue Jean Jaurès, beside la Marne river bridge]

Accommodation and Tourist Information

Châlons-en-Champagne

🏠 **Auberge de Jeunesse**,4 avenue du Général Patton, 51000 Châlons-en-Champagne, France; Tel:+33(0)3 26 26 46 28; Email:ajchalons@orange.fr; www.hifrance.org/auberge-de-jeunesse/chalons-en-champagne.html; Price:C; *Open May to October*

🛏 **Presbytère - Notre Dame**,3 place Notre Dame, 51000 Châlons-en-Champagne, France; Tel:+33(0)7 68 72 40 51; Email:paroisse@paroisse-cc.fr; chalons.catholique.fr/stetienne/; Price:D

🛏 **Hotel - d'Angleterre**,19 place Monseigneur Tissier, 51000 Châlons-en-Champagne, France; Tel:+33(0)3 26 68 21 51; Email:info@hotel-dangleterre.fr; www.hotel-dangleterre.fr; Price:A

🛏 **Hôtel - de la Cité**,12 rue de la Charrière, 51000 Châlons-en-Champagne, France; Tel:+33(0)3 26 64 31 20; +33(0)3 26 70 96 22; Email:contact@hotel-de-la-cite.com; www.hotel-de-la-cite.com; Price:B; *In addition to standard rooms simple double rooms for pilgrims are available st reduced* priceemail-contact@hotel-de-la-cite.com ; **PR**

🛏 **Hôtel - le Montreal**,Avenue du Général Sarrail, 51000 Châlons-en-Champagne, France; Tel:+33(0)3 26 26 99 09; Email:hotel.le.montreal@wanadoo.fr; www.citotel.com; Price:B

🛏 **Hôtel - Pasteur**,46 rue Pasteur, 51000 Châlons-en-Champagne, France; Tel:+33(0)3 26 68 10 00; Email:contact@hotel-pasteur.fr; www.hotel-pasteur.fr; Price:A

⛺ **Gîte - La Canopée**[Pierre Vincent],11 rue des Martyrs de la Résistance, 51000 Châlons-en-Champagne, France; Tel:+33(0) 3 26 65 51 36; +33(0) 6 47 82 73 42; Email:contact@gite-canopee.com; gite-canopee.com; Price:C

⚠ **Camping de Châlons-en-Champagne**,Rue de Plaisance, 51000 Châlons-en-Champagne, France; Tel:+33(0)3 26 68 38 00; Email:camping.chalons@aquadis-loisirs.comr; www.aquadis-loisirs.com/camping-nature/camping-de-chalons-en-champagne; Price:C; *Mobile homes available*

ℹ **Office du Tourisme**,3 Quai des Arts, 51000 Châlons-en-Champagne, France; Tel:+33(0)3 26 65 17 89; Email:accueil@chalons-tourisme.com; www.chalons-tourisme.com

Fagnières

🛏 **Hôtel - Bristol**,77 avenue Pierre Semard, 51510 Fagnières, France; Tel:+33(0)3 26 68 24 63; +33(0)3 26 68 22 16; Email:contact@hotelbristol-marne.com; www.hotelbristol-marne.com; Price:B

Matougues

🛏 **Auberge - des Moissons**,8 route Nationale, 51510 Matougues, France; Tel:+33(0)3 26 70 99 17; Email:contact@auberge-des-moissons.com; www.auberge-des-moissons.com; Price:A

Saint-Martin-sur-le-Pré

🛏 **Hôtel - Première Classe Chalons en Champagne**,Avenue du 8 mai 1945, 51520 Saint-Martin-sur-le-Pré, France; Tel:+33(0)3 26 67 55 45; Email:chalonsenchampagne@premiere-classe.fr; chalons-en-champagne.premiereclasse.com; Price:B; *4 km from the centre*

stage 23 — Châlons to La-Chaussée-sur-Marne

Length:	**23.4km**
Ascent:	**256m**
Descent:	**243m**
Canterbury	**530km**
Col Grand Saint Bernard:	**709km**

Voie Romaine

Route: ahead there is a major decision on routes. The "Official Route" continues to

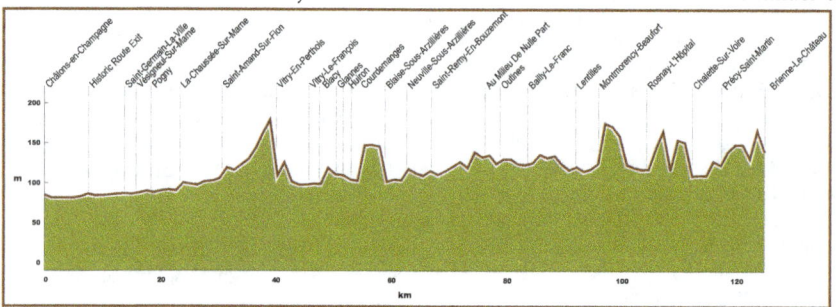

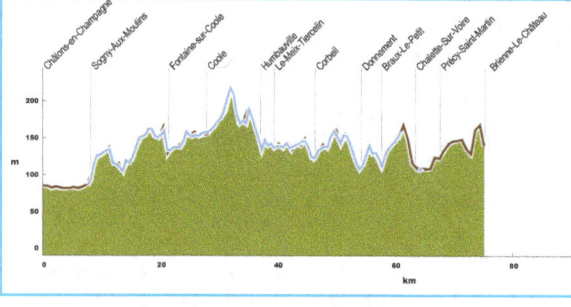

follow the chemin de St Jacques GR®145/654 via Vitry-le-François. This route is reasonably well sign-posted, but, at the time of writing, there were a number of signs missing in the exposed agricultural areas. Cyclists need to be aware that the clay surfaces of many paths beside the river can be extremely slippery in wet weather. With the exception of Vitry, accommodation choices on both the GR®145 and the Alternate Route are limited.

The GR®145 initially follows pleasant pathways beside the banks of the Marne before striking out into the open cereal fields, but adds substantially to distance (48 km) and bypasses 2 further Sigeric locations. Our preferred Alternate/Historic Route is generally off-road and with long atmospheric sections along the vestiges of a Roman road. The generally straight nature of the route makes it easy to follow but signage is minimal.

En route from Châlons to La-Chaussée-sur-Marne there are no facilities for refreshment before La-Chaussée-sur-Marne where accommodation and eating choices are also limited.

Châlons to La-Chaussée-sur-Marne   stage 23

On subsequent stages there are long stretches without grocery stores or eating places until you reach Brienne-le-Château.

The river Marne rises on the Langres plateau and with its connection to the Seine was for many years a highway for goods travelling to and from Paris. However, its strongest historic association is with the Great War when it was the line drawn by the French and British forces to halt the German invasion and subsequently launch a counter offensive. In the first battle of the Marne in September 1914 it is estimated that the French army suffered 250,000 casualties.

(0.0) From the crossroads beside bridge over la Marne on rue Jean Jaurés, take the grit pathway beside chemin du Barrage[River on your right]**(0.5)**Continue straight ahead on the pathway beside the river[GR®654 sign]**(0.8)**Continue straight ahead across the metal bridge, turn right and continue on the track[Track returns to the river-side and passes under a highway] **(2.1)**Facing an embankment, bear left on the gravel track**(2.2)**After passing between concrete blocks, turn right on an unmade path **(4.7)**A little after the river turns left and before the river turns right, turn left on the more distinct track, between

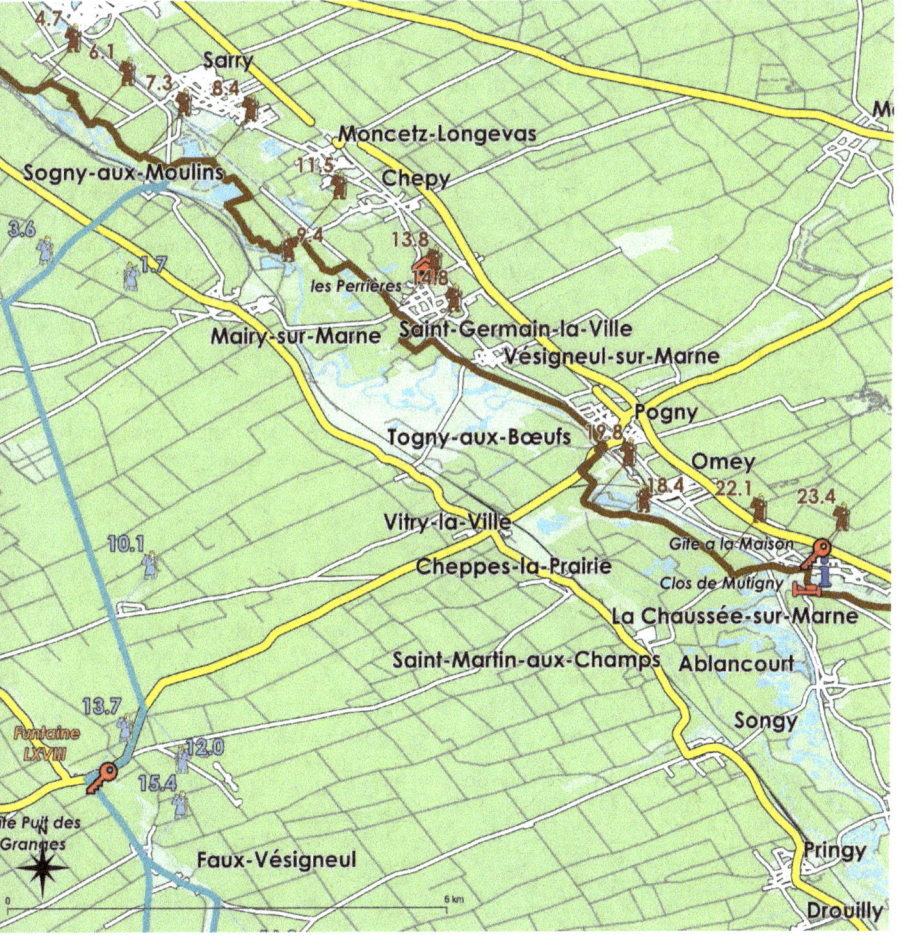

stage 23   Châlons to La-Chaussée-sur-Marne

the fields[Railway visible to the right at the junction]**(5.0)**Take the first turning to the right, towards the trees**(5.7)**Turn left on the track. Initially the woods are on your right with a field to the left 🚶 **(6.1)**Continue on the broad track[Keep the woods to your right]**(6.5)**At the junction in the tracks, continue straight ahead on the broad track with the woods on your right[Canal bridge visible on your extreme left] 🚶 **(7.3)**Turn right, keep the fields on your right, trees on your left[Church visible slightly to your right]**(7.7)**At the crossroads with the D80, cross the road with care and continue straight ahead on the gravel track. Note:- to take the shorter **Historic Route exit** right towards the church**(8.0)**Bear right on the broad track[Pass a lake on your left]**(8.1)**At the junction in the tracks, continue straight ahead beside the fence[Avoid the track to the right] 🚶 **(8.4)**At the T-junction in the tracks, turn right 🚶 **(9.4)**At the crossroads in the tracks, turn right through a gap in the trees[Pass a field on your left]**(10.4)**With the river close on your right, take the left fork through the trees on a broad track, then immediately

turn right 🚶 **(11.5)**With a canal bridge visible ahead, turn right on the broad track[Between the fields]**(12.3)**At the junction in the tracks, turn left and then turn right parallel to the canal 🚶 **(13.8)**At the crossroads with the D280, continue straight ahead on the tarmac track[Silos and village of **Saint-Germain-la-Ville** to the left of the track]**(14.6)**At the junction in the track, turn left on the well defined track[Parallel to the canal] 🚶 **(14.8)**At the T-junction in the tracks, turn left**(15.1)**At the junction in the tracks, turn right[Pass a conifer plantation on your left]**(15.5)**At the T-junction with a broad gravel track turn left and then bear right**(15.8)**At the crossroads with the D202, continue straight ahead on the tarmac track beside the canal[Village of **Vésigneul-sur-Marne** on your left] 🚶 **(18.4)**At the crossroads with the D54, turn right on the bridge over the river Marne[Village of **Pogny** on the left]**(18.5)**Immediately after crossing the bridge, turn left on the small tarmac road and then bear right**(18.8)**At the T-junction with the main road, turn left, cross the bridge and then turn left again on the track 🚶 **(19.8)**At the junction in the track, continue straight ahead with the river on your left. Note:- in wet conditions the track ahead can be very slippery[Avoid the broad track on your right] 🚶 **(22.1)**At the junction in the tracks, under the power lines, continue straight ahead towards the main road**(22.4)**At the T-junction with the D302, turn left[Pass a football field on your right]**(23.0)**After crossing the canal bridge, turn right[Rue d'El Biar] 🚶 **(23.4)**Arrive at **La-Chaussée-sur-Marne** centre[Hôtel du Midi on your left]

Accommodation and Tourist Information

La-Chaussée-sur-Marne

📍 **Gîte - a la Maison**,7 rue de Coulmier, 51240 La Chaussée-sur-Marne, France; Tel:+33(0) 674841109; Email:zami51@orange.fr; tourisme-en-champagne.com; Price:B; 3 bedrooms

🏨 **Hôtel - Clos de Mutigny**,17 avenue du Docteur Justin Jolly, 51240 La-Chaussée-sur-Marne, France; Tel:+33(0)3 26 72 94 20; Email:closdemutigny@free.fr; www.clos-de-mutigny.com; Price:A

ℹ **Mairie**,1 chemin de la Mairie, 51240 La-Chaussée-sur-Marne, France; Tel:+33(0)3 26 72 94 87; Email:lachausseesurmarne@wanadoo.fr; mairie-la-chaussee-sur-marne.fr

Saint-Germain-la-Ville

🏠 **Chambre d'Hôtes - les Perrières**[Nicole & Denis Le Saint],7 rue Châlons, 51240 Saint-Germain-la-Ville, France; Tel:+33(0)3 26 67 51 13; +33(0)6 70 35 40 32; lesperrieres.pagesperso-orange.fr; Price:B

Châlons to La-Chaussée-sur-Marne   stage 23

Historic Route via Le Meix-Tiercelin

Route: this shorter and more historically accurate route uses vestiges of the Roman road and passes the Sigeric locations of Fontaine-sur-Coole (LXVIII) and Donnement (LXVIII).

Length:	54.3km
Ascent:	710m
Descent:	632m

The substantially off-road route is shown as a single section for consistency of layout, but the journey may be broken with pilgrim friendly accommodation available in Nuisement-sur-Coole, Coole, Le-Miex-Tiercelin, Corbeil, Donnement and in the area around the southern junction with the GR®145.

There are very few facilities en route, but meals may be available with the accommodation - please enquire ahead with your host. The long straight sections of now gravelled Roman road are some of the most striking of the entire journey, but be aware that is little protection from the extremes of weather.

(0.1)Turn right beside the D80[Towards the church](0.5)At the T-junction after crossing the river bridge, turn right[Grande rue in **Sogny-aux-Moulins**](0.6)Turn left on rue d'Ecury, uphill[Direction Châlons-en-Champagne](1.7)At the crossroads with the busy D2, continue straight ahead on the track[Between open fields](3.6)At the junction with a tarmac road, turn right and then left down a gravel path, the old Roman Road[Towards the wind farm](10.1)At intersection with the road continue straight ahead on the track[D54, wind-farm on left](12.0)At the intersection with the road turn right on the road[D79 towards Fontaine-sur-Coole](13.7)At the junction in the village of **Fontaine-sur-Coole (LXVIII)** turn left[Direction Coole](15.4)Fork left. Note:- 1 km can be saved by remaining on the D4 to the crossroads in Coole[Direction Faux-Coole, D281](16.8)After passing through Faux turn right onto the gravel track[Proceed with a line of trees and a river on your right](18.7)At the junction, continue straight ahead on the main track[Keep the river to the right](20.1)At the road junction, turn right and bear left on the road[Trees on the right, open fields on the left](20.5)On the crown of the bend to the right, turn left and immediately right onto ruelle Mont Beau(21.0)At the junction with the major road turn right beside the N4[Former bar/restaurant on the right, water tower to the left](21.1)At the crossroads in **Coole** turn left onto rue de Sompuis[D4, direction Sompuis]

stage 23   Châlons to La-Chaussée-sur-Marne

(22.9) At the bend in the D4, go straight ahead on the gravel track[Roman Road] (26.6) At the crossroads with the tarmac road, continue straight ahead[Remain on the Roman Road] (26.8) Fork right after a slight bend in the track(27.0) At the crossroads in the tracks, continue straight ahead to the following T-junction, turn left and bear right to rejoin the Roman Road[Hedge on your left, large open field on right] (29.7) Continue straight ahead on the road[Water tower to the left]

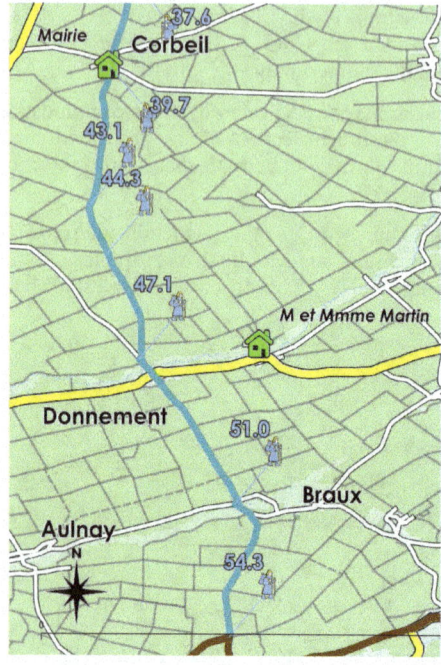

(30.3) At the junction with the D12, bear left into **Humbauville**[Voie Romaine, stone cross on right] (32.7) In the centre of le-Meix-Tiercelin continue on the D12[Direction Saint-Ouen-Domprot](33.3) Bear left onto the Voie Romaine[Metal crucifix on right] (36.1) At the crossroads, continue straight ahead on the track[Between farm buildings and towards the brow of the hill] (37.6) Proceed straight ahead at the crossroads (39.7) At the crossroads in **Corbeil**, proceed straight ahead on rue Haute des Romains[Mairie to the right beside the church] (43.1) Fork left[Pass the farm - les Ormées] (44.3) Continue straight ahead through the farm and over the hill[Small wood on the right] (47.1) At the road junction, turn left onto rue de Dampierre[Part-timbered house](47.5) At the crossroads in **Donnement (LXVII)**, continue straight ahead on rue de Braux[Direction Braux, D24] (51.0) In **Braux-le-Petit**, turn right and then left, direction Braux Centre, D5[Over a small bridge](51.3) As the road turns left, fork right onto the broad gravel track, uphill (54.3) At the crossroads in the tracks, turn right and rejoin the "Official Route"

Châlons to La-Chaussée-sur-Marne — stage 23

Accommodation and Tourist Information

Baligncourt
🏠 **M et Mmme Martin**[Odile and Didier],1 Voie Creuse, 10330 Baligncourt, France; Tel:+33(0)325921579; +33(0)624388138; Price:D

Coole
🏠 **M and Mme Dulieux**[Brigitte and Jean-Claude],1 Chemin des Puits, 51320 Coole, France; Tel: +33(0)661857145

🏠 **Mme Monique Songy**,17 rue de Chalons, 51320 Coole, France; Tel:+33(0)3 26 74 05 67; +33(0)6 48 12 91 26; Email:jpm.songy@hotmail.com; Price:D; *Highly recommended stay en famille* ; **PR**

Corbeil
🏠 **Mairie**[Béatrice and Michel Mirofle],1 rue de la Cruchière, 51320 Corbeil, France; Tel:+33(0)3 26 72 31 04; +33(0)9 60 00 13 73; Email:mairie.corbeil@orange.fr; Price:D; *2 beds in the Mairie evening meal may be possible Recommend calling Mme and M Mirofle*

Faux-Vésigneul
🔑 **Gîte - Puit des Granges**,19 Rue Montsuzon, 51320 Faux-Vésigneul, France; Tel:+33(0)6 26 64 50 78; Email:marymangeart@gmail.com; gite-mary-m.fr/gite-du-puit-des-granges; Price:A; *5 bedrooms*

Le-Meix-Tiercelin
🏠 **ESAT les Antes**,Rue du Four, 51320 Le-Meix-Tiercelin, France; Tel:+33(0)3 26 72 41 20; +33(0)3 26 72 00 59; Email:responsable-fh@lesantes.fr; lesantes.fr; Price:C; *Normally only one small room with one small bed available in a home for the rehabilitation of the disabled. It is strongly advised to call in advance as there are few options if the room is already occupied. Meals are available at reasonable cost*

ℹ **Mairie**,9 rue du Bas, 51320 Le-Meix-Tiercelin, France; Tel:+33(0)3 26 72 73 42

Nuisement-sur-Coole
🏠 **Chambre d'Hôtes - le Rondin Nature**[Régine & Patrick Picard],6 rue du Moulin, 51240 Nuisement-sur-Coole, France; Tel:+33(0)3 26 67 62 14; Email:contact@le-rondin-nature.com; www.le-rondin-nature.com; Price:B

*Église Saint-Ouen
Saint-Ouen-Domprot*

stage 24 La-Chaussée-sur-Marne to Vitry-le-François

Length:	22.5km
Ascent:	363m
Descent:	363m
Canterbury	554km
Col Grand Saint Bernard:	685km

Une Mer de Blé

Route: the stage from La-Chaussée-sur-Marne to Vitry-le-François continues beside the river Fion before taking to the rolling hills through the vast cereal fields of the region.

Take care to follow the routing instructions in the cereal fields as there are few signs and even these may have been damaged.

There is a small shop and boulangerie off-piste in Saint-Amand-sur-Fion.

Vitry-le-François offers a good range of facilities.

The original town of Vitry-le-François was largely destroyed following the invasion of Louis VII in 1142.

The present town owes its relatively modern construction (1545) and its name to King François I.

Collégiale Notre-Dame- Vitry-le-François

La-Chaussée-sur-Marne to Vitry-le-François   stage 24

(0.0) From the junction beside the Hôtel du Midi in La-Chaussée-sur-Marne centre, continue with the line of trees on your left and then turn right at the Stop sign and proceed with care beside the busy road **(0.8)** As the road bears right, take the left fork on the track [Vitry-le-François 22km, yellow VF sign] **(1.8)** At the crossroads in the tracks, continue straight ahead between the trees [Pass under the highway ahead] **(2.5)** At the junction in the tracks, continue straight ahead [Pass a plantation of beech trees on your left] **(3.6)** At the crossroads with the D81, continue straight ahead on the gravel track **(3.9)** At the crossroads with the small tarmac road, continue straight ahead on the stony track [Trees on the left of the track] **(4.2)** Take the right fork, between the fields [Parallel to the valley bottom] **(5.1)** At the T-junction in the tracks, turn left on the gravel track **(5.5)** At the junction in the tracks, turn right towards the village [Saint-Amand-sur-Fion 2km, yellow VF sign] **(6.4)** At the crossroads with the tarmac road, continue straight ahead on rue de la Liberté towards the village [Timber framed house on the right] **(7.2)** At the T-junction in **Saint-Amand-sur-Fion**, turn right and then immediately left **(7.6)** At

stage 24   La-Chaussée-sur-Marne to Vitry-le-François

the T-junction at the end of rue des Ruelles, turn right and immediately left[Pass timber framed house n° 8 on right]**(7.8)**At the T-junction at the end of rue des Hauts Prés, turn left[Towards the trees]**(8.2)**At the T-junction with the D260, turn right, uphill beside the main road**(8.4)**Fork left on the stony track[Saint-Lumier-en-Champagne 2km, yellow VF sign] **(10.0)**At the T-junction with a tarmac road, turn right and then bear left[Sports field on your right]**(10.3)**At the next T-junction, turn right**(10.7)**Immediately after passing the metal barn on your left, bear left on the gravel track **(11.5)**At the crossroads in the tracks, continue straight ahead[Pass a copse of trees on your left] **(12.7)**At the crossroads in the tracks, continue straight ahead, uphill on the gravel track[Between large fields] **(14.1)**At a junction in the tracks, continue straight ahead[Hedgerow on your right]**(14.4)** At the crossroads, turn right on the gravel track, uphill. Note:- the GR°14 continues straight ahead, while the GR°145 turns right **(15.7)**At the junction in the tracks, turn left and continue downhill between the vines, towards the large silos[Vitry-en-Perthois 2 km] **(16.0)**At the crossroads at the foot of the hill, continue straight ahead on the broad gravel track[Between the open fields]**(16.3)**At the crossroads in the tracks, turn left and quickly fork right, downhill on the narrow track[Pass chapelle Sainte Geneviève on your right] **(16.6)**Continue straight ahead beside the tarmac road[Pass house n° 4 on your left] **(16.8)**At the road junction, continue straight ahead in **Vitry-en-Perthois**[Chemin de la Chapelle]**(17.0)**Beside house n°35, fork right down the steep concrete pathway and then turn right**(17.2)**Bear right on the track**(17.3)**At the junction in tracks, turn right[Pass between the fence and the trees] **(18.0)**Continue straight ahead into the woods[Avoid the path on the left] **(19.4)**At the T-junction in the track, turn left towards the very busy main road**(19.5)**Cross the main road with great care and then turn right on the tarmac road**(20.1)** At the junction, turn left, pass the metal barrier and continue between the metal fencing **(20.5)**Turn right over the bridge and then turn left, keep the lock on your left**(20.9)**Keep to the track beside the right hand branch of the canal**(21.2)**Turn right down a steep narrow track**(21.2)**At the junction with the road, turn right[Between walled gardens]**(21.4)**At the mini-roundabout, continue straight ahead on the small path and then bear left[River on your right] **(22.5)**Arrive at **Vitry-le-François**. Note:- the town centre is to the left[Beside the Marne river bridge]

Accommodation and Tourist Information

Saint-Amand-sur-Fion

 Chambre d'Hôtes - Moulin du Ruet[Catherine and Régis],35 Rue de la Liberté, 51300 Saint-Amand-sur-Fion, France; Tel:+33 (0) 615095747; Email:lemoulinduruet@laposte.net; moulinduruet.com; Price:A; **PR**

 Chambre d'Hôtes - Les Deux Cour ,5 Petite rue de l'Église, 51300 Saint-Amand-sur-Fion, France; Tel:+33(0)3 26 74 60 50; +33(0)6 03 02 91 43; Email:sylvain.lanfroy@wanadoo.fr; les2cours.com; Price:B

Vitry-le-François

Hôtel - Tambourin,1 Rue Auguste Choisy, 51300 Vitry-le-François, France; Tel:+33(0)3 26 72 92 92; www.hotel-tambourin.fr; Price:B

Hôtel - Eqynox,16 avenue du Perthois, 51300 Vitry-le-François, France; Tel:+33(0)3 26 62 13 13; Email:contact@eqynox-en-champagne.com; www.eqynox-en-champagne.com; Price:B; *Closed on Sunday*

Hôtel - Au Bon Séjour,2 Faubourg Léon Bourgeois, 51300 Vitry-le-François, France; Tel:+33(0)3 26 74 02 36; Email:desvigne@club-internet.fr; au-bon-sejour.fr; Price:B

 Bureau d'Information Touristique,8 Esplanade de Strasbourg, 51300 Vitry-le-François, France; Tel:+33(0)3 26 74 45 30; www.lacduder.com/vitry-le-francois

Vitry to Saint-Remy-en-Bouzemont

stage 25

Length:	21.0km
Ascent:	288m
Descent:	272m
Canterbury	576km
Col Grand Saint Bernard:	663km

The French Meseta

Route: the stage from Vitry to Saint-Remy-en-Bouzemont quickly leaves the very busy roads surrounding Vitry-le-François and continues to follow the GR®145/GR®654 - chemin de St Jacques on good farm tracks broadly parallel to la Marne river.

It is possible to break the journey in Blaise-sous-Arzillières at the pilgrim friendly Café de la Place.

Saint-Remy has very limited facilities, but does have a café/bar and small shop.

To the east of Saint-Remy lies Lac du Der - the largest (4,800 hectares) man made lake in Europe. The lake was constructed over 10 years and completed in 1974. Its purpose is to regulate the water flows in the Marne and eventually the Seine and protect Paris from potential flooding.

The lake has become a favourite green tourist destination and stopping off place for hundreds of species of migrating birds including many thousands of cranes during the winter months.

The full title of Saint-Remy is Saint-Remy-en-Bouzemont-Saint-Genest-et-Isson. Its name is a symptom of the continuing drift of the population from rural villages to the cities. As each village becomes too small to support the costs of its administration it merges with a neighbour but of course does not wish to lose its identity and so the villages become hyphenated.

(0.0) With great care follow the main road across the bridge[River Marne]**(0.3)**Just after passing the car sales lot, carefully cross the road and turn left on Vieille Route[Direction Blacy] **(1.1)**After passing under the railway bridge, take the first turning to the left on the gravel track**(1.4)**At the T-junction in the tracks, turn right[Trees on your right, field on your left]**(1.8)**With a river ford on your right, continue straight ahead over the bridge[Towards the church in **Blacy**] **(2.2)**At the crossroads with the D2, continue straight ahead[Rue de Sompuis]**(2.7)**On the edge of the village, turn left on the gravel track, uphill[Pass a radio tower] **(3.6)**At the junction in the tracks, with the radio tower on your immediate right, continue straight ahead[Towards the prominent church in Glannes] **(4.7)**At the T-junction with the road in **Glannes**, turn left beside the road**(5.0)**With a picnic area on your right, turn right on a grass track[Towards the trees]**(5.3)**At the crossroads in the tracks, turn right on the gravel track[Pass the rear of the houses on your left] **(5.8)** Cross to the far corner of the gravel area in **Huiron(5.9)**At the crossroads, turn left to follow the road uphill[Towards the water tower]**(6.0)**At the crossroads at the foot of the water tower, continue straight ahead on the D602[Rue Saint Claude] **(7.3)**At the

stage 25 — Vitry to Saint-Remy-en-Bouzemont

T-junction in front of the Mairie in **Courdemanges**, turn left**(7.9)**At the crossroads with the D2, continue straight ahead on the D14e[Direction Frignicourt]⚑**(8.8)**Turn right on the gravel track, uphill[Direction Monument Militaire de Mont-Môret]**(8.8)**At the junction at the top of the initial climb, bear left[Pass oil-well on your right]**(9.1)**Continue straight

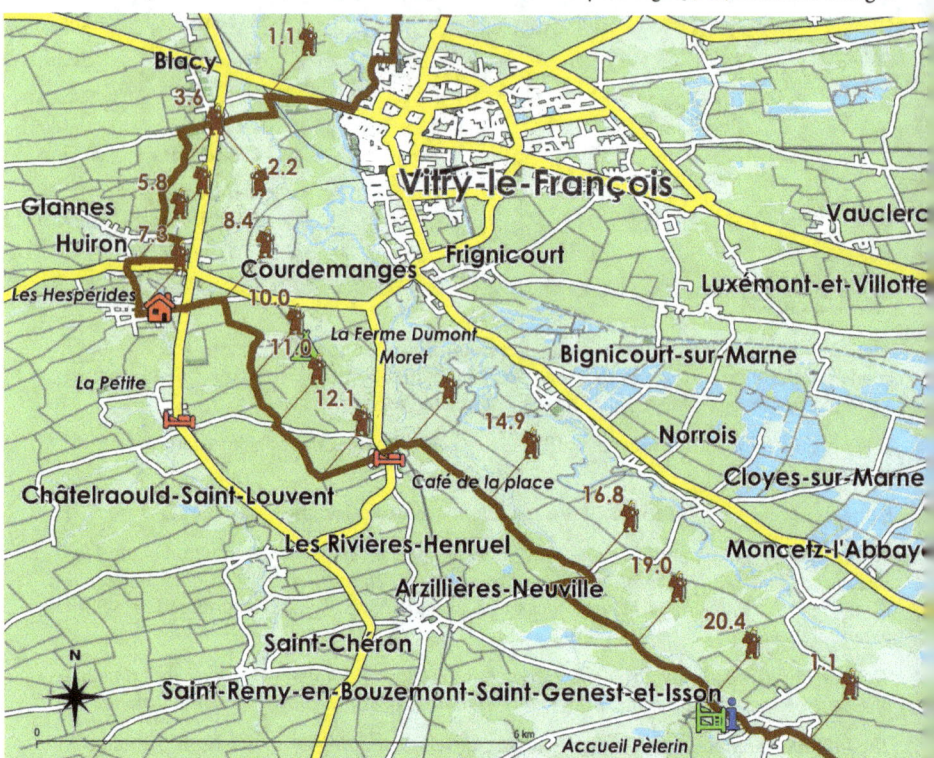

ahead on the track[Pass the monument on your left]⚑**(10.0)**At the crossroads in the tracks, continue straight ahead, towards the lone tree[Camping a la Ferme to the left]**(10.2)**At the next crossroads in the tracks, again continue straight ahead on the grass track, uphill**(10.5)**At the junction in the tracks near the top of the hill, continue straight ahead[Oil-well on the right]⚑**(11.0)**At the crossroads with a tarmac road, continue straight ahead on the gravel track[Blaise-sous-Arzillières 2 km, yellow VF sign]**(11.4)**At the junction in the track, continue straight ahead, uphill[Oil storage tank on the left]⚑**(12.1)**At the foot of the hill, turn left on the grass track**(12.8)**At the junction with the tarmac road, continue straight ahead, downhill[Chemin des Hauts Traversins]**(13.0)**At the crossroads with the D396 in **Blaise-sous-Arzillières**, continue straight ahead, on rue Basse[Pass the Café de la Place on your right]⚑**(13.4)**At the junction in the tracks, bear left[Avoid the track to the right] **(13.6)**At the next junction, turn right towards the bridge[Neuville-sous-Arzillières 3.5 km, yellow VF sign]⚑**(14.9)**Continue straight ahead on the path[Continue between the trees] **(15.5)**At the end of the plantation, turn right and then left on the gravel track⚑**(16.8)**In place Napoléon in **Neuville-sous-Arzillières**, continue straight ahead[Church on the left] **(17.0)**Bear right on the road towards Arzillières**(17.5)**Beside the picnic table and calvaire, turn left on the gravel track[Saint-Rémy-en-Bouzemont 3.5km, yellow VF sign]⚑**(19.0)**At

Vitry to Saint-Remy-en-Bouzemont   stage 25

the crossroads in the tracks, continue straight ahead on the gravel track, uphill **(20.4)** At the T-junction with the main road, turn left [Saint-Rémy-en-Bouzemont 0.5km, yellow VF sign] **(21.0)** Arrive at **Saint-Remy-en-Bouzemont** [Mairie on your right]

Rue du Pont - Saint-Remy-en-Bouzemont-Saint-Genest-et-Isson

Accommodation and Tourist Information

Arrigny
Camping de la Forêt, Presqu'Ile de Larzicourt, 51290 Arrigny, France; Tel:+33(0)3 26 72 63 17; +33(0)6 11 12 23 21; Email:laforet51@wanadoo.fr; campingdelaforet.com; Price:C; *Chalets and mobile homes available with 2 night minimum*

Blaise-Sous-Arzillières
Café - de la place, 2 rue Pont de la Noue, 51300 Blaise-Sous-Arzillières, France; Tel:+33(0)3 26 72 80 01; Price:C; *Pilgrim friendly*

Châtelraould-Saint-Louvent
La Petite Auberge, 20 Grande Rue, 51300 Châtelraould-Saint-Louvent, France; Tel:+33(0)3 26 72 01 25; hotelmania.net/hotel/chatelraould-saint-louvent/la-petite-auberge; Price:B

Courdemanges
B&B - Les Hespérides, 5 Ruelle Boury, 51300 Courdemanges, France; Tel:+33(0)3 26 74 48 81; Email:les.hesperides@orange.fr; les-hesperides51.blogspot.com; Price:A; *A cabin on stilts 2 nights minimum in high season*

La Ferme Dumont Moret, Ferme du Mont Morêt, 51300 Courdemanges, France; Tel:+33(0) 6 64 44 99 70; Email:info@ferme-mont-moret.com; www.ferme-mont-moret.com; Price:C; *Chalets and safari tents also available open April until end October*

Saint-Remy-en-Bouzemont-Saint-Genest-et-Isson
Accueil Pèlerin [Marie-Ange], Grande rue, 51290 Saint-Remy-en-Bouzemont-Saint-Genest-et-Isson, France; Tel:+33(0)6 32 27 24 24; Email:mairie.de.st.remy.en.bouzemont@wanadoo.fr; Price:D; *Kitchen available*; **PR**

Mairie, Grande rue, 51290 Saint-Remy-en-Bouzemont-Saint-Genest-et-Isson, France; Tel:+33(0)3 26 72 53 79; Email:mairie.de.st.remy.en.bouzemont@wanadoo.fr; www.saintremyenbouzemont.fr

stage 26   Saint-Remy-en-Bouzemont to Lentilles

Length:	25.0km
Ascent:	252m
Descent:	247m
Canterbury	597km
Col Grand Saint Bernard:	642km

Église Saint-Nicolas d'Outines

Route: from Saint-Remy-en-Bouzemont to Lentilles the "Official Route" - GR®145, continues to share the path with the chemin de St Jacques – GR®654.

This is an extremely exposed section with long distances between villages. You will pass the hamlet of "Au Milieu de Nulle Part" - "the middle of nowhere" which probably says it all.

The tracks are generally broad and of good quality in dry weather. However a number of signposts have fallen victim to agricultural machinery and so it is best to keep careful track of your progress in the guide book.

There is no accommodation available in the village of Lentilles with all options being significantly off-piste after Outines.

Timber framing or pan de bois is a dominant architectural feature of the area. Also known as "post-and-beam" construction, it uses heavy timbers, creating structures using squared-off and carefully fitted and joined timbers with joints secured by large wooden pegs.

It is commonplace in wooden buildings from the 19th century and earlier. The method comes from working directly with logs and trees rather than pre-cut dimensional lumber.

(0.0) From the junction in Saint-Remy-en-Bouzemont with the Mairie on your right, continue straight ahead on the D58[Towards Drosnay]**(0.5)** Just before the factory, turn left on the road[Route des Landres]**(0.7)** At the mini-roundabout, continue straight ahead[Remain on route des Landres]] **(1.1)** Continue straight ahead on the broad gravel track[Speed bump] **(3.6)** At the junction in the tracks, continue straight ahead on the main track[Lakes on the left and right] **(6.5)** At the junction immediately before the timber framed farmhouse, turn right[Lake below on your right]**(7.2)** At the junction in the tracks, continue straight ahead[Woods on your right, fence on the left] **(8.2)** At the crossroads in the tracks, follow the gravel track to the left[Pass woods on your right] **(9.2)** At the crossroads in the tracks, beside the hamlet of la Pierre, turn right towards Outines[Gîte **Au Milieu de Nulle Part** on the left at the junction] **(10.7)** At the T-junction with a road, turn right and then take the first turning to the left[Water tower on the left] **(12.0)** At the crossroads in **Outines**, turn left on the D55[Beautiful timbered church on the right]**(12.2)** Take the right fork on the small road. Note:- the route ahead has some navigation challenges. There are few signs and landmarks and often follow the less obvious tracks. Carefully follow the instructions and the distances between the waypoints[Rue du Moulin Neuf] **(14.0)** At the crossroads in the tracks, with a copse of trees on your left,

Saint-Remy-en-Bouzemont to Lentilles — stage 26

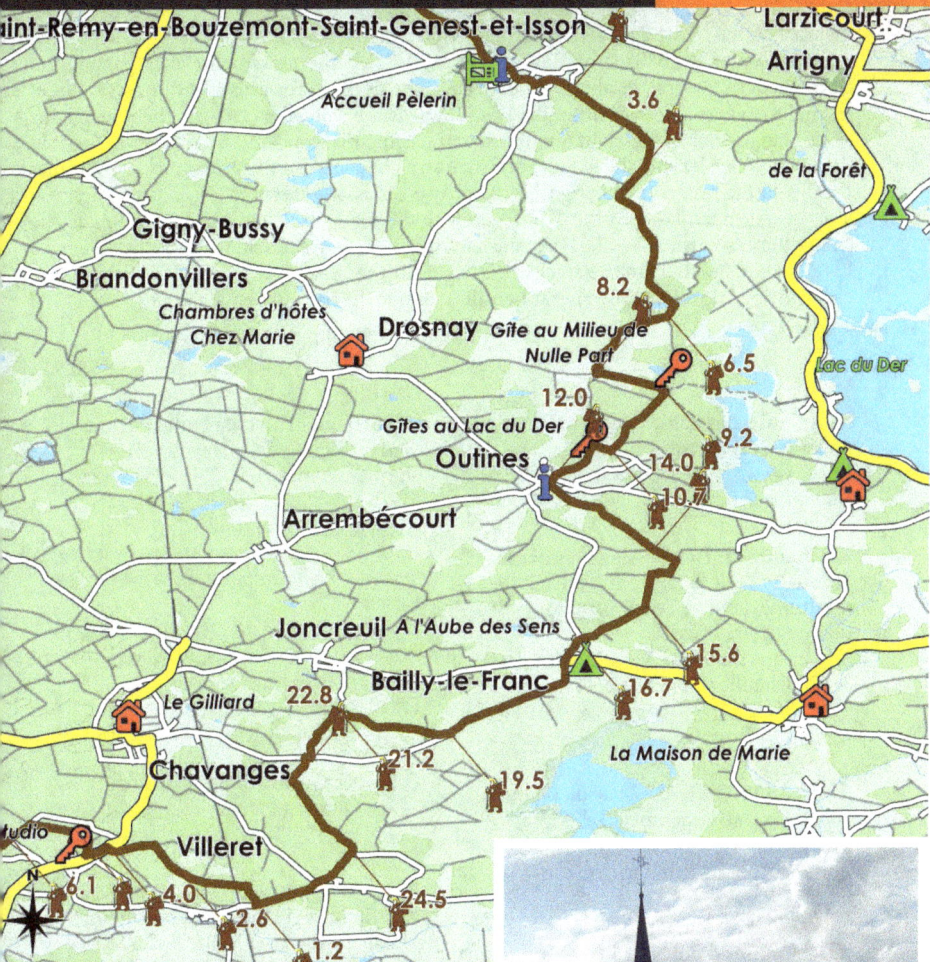

Église Saint-Nicolas d'Outines Gérard Janot

continue straight ahead on the gravel track**(14.4)**At the T-junction in the tracks, turn right on the grass track. Note:- the GR®145 and GR®14B separate at this point with the GR®14B continuing on the more definite track to the left[Pass under power lines] **(14.6)**At the foot of the hill, turn right towards the copse and then bear left between the trees and the stream[Line of white stones]**(14.9)**Bear left, cross the metal footbridge and at the crossroads in the tracks, continue straight ahead on the grass track, uphill **(15.6)**At the T-junction in the tracks, turn right on the gravel track[Towards the slender church spire]**(15.8)**At the junction in the tracks, continue straight ahead on the gravel track[Avoid

stage 26 — Saint-Remy-en-Bouzemont to Lentilles

the track to the right] (**16.7**) At the T-junction with the tarmac road road, turn left on the road and enter the village of **Bailly-le-Franc**(**17.2**) At the crossroads, after passing the church, continue straight ahead on the D56 - rue du Bois[Towards Chavanges](**17.6**) On leaving the village, bear right on the D56[Towards the woods] (**19.5**) As the road begins to bend to the right, bear right on the broad track into the woods(**19.8**) At the crossroads in the tracks, after leaving the woods, continue straight ahead on the grass track[Power lines parallel to the track on your right] (**21.2**) At the T-junction with a gravel track, beside a lone tree, turn left(**22.2**) At the T-junction with the road, turn right and then immediately left on the gravel track (**22.8**) Take the left fork on the gravel track[Towards the village] (**24.5**) At the junction in the tracks bear right on the broad gravel track[Farm buildings close on your right] (**25.0**) Arrive at **Lentilles**[Beside the half timbered church]

Accommodation and Tourist Information

Bailly-le-Franc

A l'Aube des Sens, 7 Rue Qui Boue, 10330 Bailly-le-Franc, France; Tel:+33 (0) 6 19 20 81 65; www.alaubedessens.com; Price:A; *Glamping in domes*

Châtillon-sur-Broué

Chambre d'Hôtes - Alaguyauder le Studio, 3 rue de la Loge, 51290 Châtillon-sur-Broué, France; Tel:+33(0)6 51 04 58 65; booking.com; Price:A

Le Clos du Vieux Moulin, 33 rue Lac, 51290 Châtillon-sur-Broué, France; Tel:+33(0)3 26 41 30 43; www.leclosduvieux-moulin.fr; Price:C

Chavanges

B&B - Le Gilliard, 12 rue du Gilliard, 10330 Chavanges, France; Tel:+33(0)3 25 92 11 21; www.chambres-hotes.fr/chambres-hotes_chambres-d-hotes-le-gilliard_chavanges_h854398_en.htm; Price:B

Drosnay

Chambres d'hôtes - Chez Marie, 1 rue du Haut Jard, 51290 Drosnay, France; Tel:+33(0)684273356; Email:sweety668@hotmail.fr; booking.com; Price:A; *Dinner possible*; **PR**

Montmorency-Beaufort

Apartment - Le Studio[Emilie Rougette], 27 rue Principale, 10330 Montmorency-Beaufort, France; Tel:+33 (0)9 81 11 99 89; Email:emilie.collombar@gmail.com; www.aube-champagne.com/en/poi/le-studio; Price:A; *Price includes dinner and breakfast*; **PR**

Outines

Gîte - au Milieu de Nulle Part, La Pierre, Chemin de la Hayotte, 51290 Outines, France; Tel:+33(0)6 67 36 74 93; Email:contact@aumilieudenullepart.fr; www.au-milieu-de-nulle-part.com; Price:A; *Stay in a gipsy caravan or a tree house - 2 nights minimum during the season*

Gîtes - au Lac du Der[Mme Chatelot], 29 rue des Echalas, 51290 Outines, France; Tel:+33(0)6 83 13 01 45; Email:mtchatelot@orange.fr; www.gites-der-topnature.fr; Price:A; *Large gîtes for rent*

Mairie Outines, 4 place de l'Église, 51290 Outines, France; Tel:+33(0)3 26 72 57 60; www.outines.fr; *Can provide access to gîtes*

Rives-Dervoises

Chambre d'Hôtes - La Maison de Marie, 11 rue de la Motte, 52220 Rives-Dervoises, France; Tel:+33(0)3 25 04 62 30; +33(0)6 83 30 17 40; Email:contact@la-maison-de-marie.com; www.la-maison-de-marie.com; Price:B

Lentilles to Brienne-le-Château

stage 27

Length:	33.0km
Ascent:	468m
Descent:	445m
Canterbury	622km
Col Grand Saint Bernard:	617km

Château of Brienne-le-Château

Route: this very long and strenuous stage, from Lentilles to Brienne-le-Château, makes a wide loop around the Aérodrome de Brienne-le-Château and continues to use farm tracks over open agricultural land.

There is a brasserie slightly off-piste in the centre of Rosnay-l'Hôpital.

Accommodation options are possible after the junction with the historic route via Le Meix-Tiercelin.

Brienne-le-Château offers a good range of facilities.

Spread along the right bank of the Aube, Brienne-le-Chateau is overlooked by its imposing château. Built during the latter half of the 18th century by the cardinal of Brienne, it houses an important collection of paintings, many of them historical portraits of the 17th and 18th centuries.

The church dates from the 16th century and is best known for its impressive stained glass.

A statue of Napoleon commemorates his sojourn at Brienne from 1779 to 1784, when he was studying at the military school.

The department of Aube is named after one of the Seine's tributaries, Aube is predominantly an agricultural department, with arable land covering around a third of its surface. The northern and western parts are fairly mountainous while the south and east contain fertile woodland. It is here that some of the finest wines are produced, such as Les Riceys, Bar-sur-Aube, Bouilly and Laines-aux-Bois.

Aube has its own regional park called Foret d'Orient, a vast land of deep forests and secluded lakes. Local legend says that the knights of the crusades hid the treasure that they brought back with them in this area.

stage 27 — Lentilles to Brienne-le-Château

(0.0) From the junction beside the half timbered church in Lentilles, keep right D62[Direction Villeret]**(0.4)** Take the right fork - D2[Direction Villeret] **(1.2)** After crossing the bridge and with a railway crossing visible ahead, turn right on a gravel track[Pass a line of trees on your right]**(1.8)** Cross the railway and continue straight ahead on the grass track[Between the fields]**(2.2)** At the T-junction with the gravel track, turn right and then keep straight ahead at the next junction[Towards the woods] **(2.6)** At the junction in the tracks with the woods immediately on your left, continue straight ahead [Power lines parallel on the right]**(3.3)** At the T-junction in the tracks, turn left on the gravel track towards the village **(4.0)** At the T-junction with the D6 in **Montmorency-Beaufort**, turn left**(4.2)** In the centre of Montmorency-Beaufort, after passing house n°8, turn right on the small road uphill. Note:- 16 km may be saved by remaining on the D6 to Brienne-le-Château[Rue Haute]**(4.3)** At the top of the rise turn sharp right, steeply uphill on the grass track into the trees[Pass a conifer hedge on your left]**(4.5)** At the T-junction after the steep climb, turn right and continue straight ahead on the broad track at the next crossroads**(4.6)** At the T-junction with a gravel track, turn left**(4.9)** Take the indistinct right turn on a grass track over the brow of the hill **(5.0)** At the next junction in the tracks, turn left between the fields[Towards an isolated tree on the horizon]**(5.7)** At the crossroads in the tracks, beside the tree, turn left on the gravel track **(6.1)** At the crossroads in the tracks, continue straight ahead, uphill on the gravel track[Grass track to the right]**(6.6)** At the crossroads with a tarmac road, continue straight ahead on the gravel track[Track ahead bears left] **(7.8)** At the crossroads in the tracks, continue straight ahead[Large silo to the left]**(8.5)** At the T-

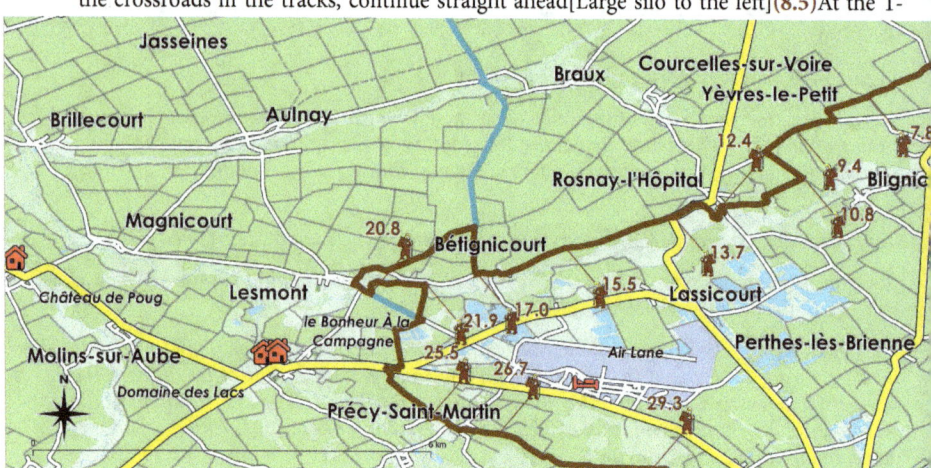

junction after a long descent, turn left[Towards the road]**(8.7)** At the T-junction with the main road, turn right **(9.4)** Continue straight ahead beside the main road[Avoid the turning to the left to les Presles]**(10.0)** With a copse of trees in the field to your right, turn left on the gravel track[Pass under the power lines] **(10.8)** At the junction in the middle of the fields, turn right[Towards the woods]**(11.4)** At the crossroads in the tracks, continue straight ahead into the woods on the broad gravel track **(12.4)** At the Stop sign in the centre of **Rosnay-l'Hôpital**, turn left[Rue Dulong]**(12.5)** Turn right on rue Saint George[Towards the church]**(13.1)** At the T-junction with the main road, cross over, turn left and continue with care beside the road **(13.7)** As the main road turns to the left, take the right fork on the small road[Chemin de Betignicourt] **(15.5)** At the crossroads in the tracks, continue straight ahead and remain on this track to the village of Betignicourt[Avoid

Lentilles to Brienne-le-Château — stage 27

the track on the left downhill into the woods] **(17.0)**Shortly before leaving Betignicourt, turn right uphill on the gravel track[Immediately after house n°14]**(17.3)**At the junction in the tracks, continue straight ahead up the hill[Avoid the turning to the left] **(18.1)**At the crossroads at the top of the hill, turn left on the broad gravel track. Note:- the Alternate Route via le-Meix-Tiercelin joins from the track ahead[Parallel to the power lines]**(19.0)**At the crossroads in the tracks, continue straight ahead on the main track[Water tower ahead] **(19.8)**At the T-junction with the D75, turn right and follow the road as it bears left[Pass an old wooden farm building on your left]**(20.4)**At the T-junction at the end of rue du Marais in **Chalette-sur-Voire**, turn left[Direction Lesmont]**(20.6)**After crossing 2 bridges, take the left fork beside the calvaire[Direction les Fontaines] **(20.8)**Turn left on the gravel track and skirt the field on your right. Note:- 1 km may be saved by remaining on the road until the track returns from the left[Pass a large barn on your left] **(21.9)**Follow the track as it turns right, away from the river[Towards a wooden cabin at the foot of the trees]**(22.6)** At the T-junction with the road, turn left and then immediately right on the gravel track[Ponds to the left of the gravel track] **(23.1)**Take the left fork, towards the main road[Ponds on your right]**(24.0)**At the T-junction with a tarmac road, turn right and with care follow the main road towards Troyes. Then take the first road on the left[Direction Précy-Saint-Martin] **(25.5)**At the T-junction, after passing a house with an aeroplane in the garden, bear left into the village of **Précy-Saint-Martin(25.9)**At the junction after passing the church, keep straight ahead on the D80[Direction Epagne]**(26.1)**Take the left fork - rue des Marronniers[Pass the Mairie on your right]**(26.4)**At the crossroads, continue straight ahead[Towards the garden centre] **(26.7)**Take the right fork, beside the water tower **(27.9)**At the junction in the tracks, bear left[Between the fields]**(28.7)**At the junction beside the woods, continue straight ahead[Avoid the 2 tracks on your right] **(29.3)**At the junction in the tracks, continue straight ahead, towards the woods[Avoid the track on

stage 27 — Lentilles to Brienne-le-Château

your left]**(29.7)**At the junction in the tracks, continue straight ahead on the main track[Parallel to the main road] **(30.3)**Join a tarmac road then bear right, downhill at the junction[Pass fruit trees on your left]**(30.5)**At the end of Voie de Précy in Saint-Léger-sous-Brienne, turn left[Towards the church]**(30.7)**Immediately after passing the church, turn right into place de la Mairie[Pass close to the churchyard walls]**(30.8)**At the crossroads, turn right on voie des Vonnes and then take the first left]**(31.3)**At the junction just before the top of the hill, continue straight ahead on the gravel track[Towards the trees] **(31.9)**At the junction in the tracks, continue straight ahead[Pass the telephone tower on your left] **(32.1)**At the crossroads in the tracks, turn left on the main track and then take the left fork[Pass a calvaire on your left]**(32.6)**At the junction in the tracks, turn right on the smaller track into the trees**(32.8)**At the T-junction with a gravel track, turn left and then immediately right on the small track, slightly uphill[Pass through the trees] **(33.0)**Arrive at **Brienne-le-Château** at a T-junction with a tarmac road Note:- the town centre is down the hill to your left. The Alternate Route for the next section will lead you to the centre and offer a more direct exit from the town[Château directly ahead]

Accommodation and Tourist Information

Brienne-le-Château
Maison Fraternelle du Pèlerin[Xavier de Zutter],96 rue de l'Ecole Militaire, 10500 Brienne-le-Château, France; Tel:+33(0)3 25 92 82 41; Email:pelerin10mfp@free.fr; Price:C; *Can also contact the tourist office or the Mairie   Open April to end October*
Hôtel - des Voyageurs,30 avenue Pasteur, 10500 Brienne-le-Château, France; Tel:+33(0)9 74 56 47 84; www.restauranthotel-voyageurs.com; Price:B
Office du Tourisme,1 rue Emile Zola, 10500 Brienne-le-Château, France; Tel:+33(0)3 25 92 82 41; Email:accueil@grandslacsdechampagne.fr; grandslacsdechampagne.fr

Lesmont
Chambre d'Hotes - le Bonheur À la Campagne,12 avenue du Général Patton, 10500 Lesmont, France; Tel:+33(0)3 25 27 22 22; +33(0)6 62 84 38 86; Email:contact@bonheur-campagne.com; www.bonheur-campagne.com; Price:A

Chambre d'Hotes - Domaine des Lacs,3 rue la Voie de Ramerupt, 10500 Lesmont, France; Tel:+33(0)3 25 92 00 70; Email:contact@domainedeslacs.com; domainedeslacs.com; *At the time of writing renovations taking place*

Pougy
Chambre d'Hôtes - Château de Poug,28 Grande Rue, 10240 Pougy, France; Tel:+33(0)3 25 37 09 41; Email:antoine.morlet@wanadoo.fr ; www.chateau-de-pougy.com; Price:B

Saint-Leger-Sous-Brienne
Hôtel - Air Lane,Zone Industrielle Aerodrome de Brienne, 10500 Saint-Leger-Sous-Brienne, France; Tel:+33(0)3 25 92 55 55; Email:air-lane@wanadoo.fr; www.hotel-air-lane.fr; Price:A

Brienne-le-Château to Dolancourt stage 28

Length:	27.6km
Ascent:	393m
Descent:	382m
Canterbury	655km
Col Grand Saint Bernard:	584km

L'Aube at Dienville

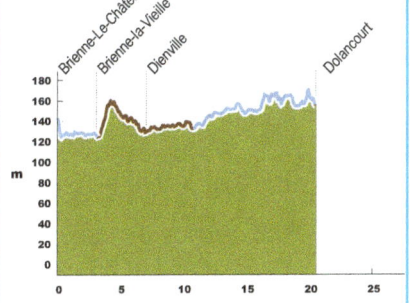

Route: the stage from Brienne-le-Château to Dolancourt begins in woodland following the valley of the Aube river, but bypassing the Sigeric location of Brienne-la-Vielle (LXVI) before making another wide loop over the rolling hills of open cereal fields. The via Francigena (GR®145) and chemin de St Jacques (GR®654) finally separate in the village of Amance.

The route can be considerably reduced by taking the Alternate Route via Jessains.

Dolancourt is dominated by the Nigloland theme park and as a result accommodation can be both expensive and fully booked in the high season.

There are opportunities to break your journey in Dienville, Amance and Jessains.

Dienville is first mentioned in 864 AD, no doubt because of its location beside the ancient via Agrippa. In 1814 it was fought over in the Battle of La Rothière where an army drawn from Russia, Prussia, Austria and some German states defeated the French Army under Napoleon. One of the few occasions that Napoleon was defeated on French soil.

(0.0) From the T-junction beside the château, proceed with the stone wall on your left[Woods on your right]**(0.5)**At the crossroads, turn left on the road and then immediately turn right on the gravel track, pass the house with the deer sculptures on your left[Château on the hill to your left]**(0.6)**After crossing the small stone bridge, bear right and follow the grass track parallel to the gravel road and rejoin the road at the end of the avenue of trees. Note:- although the "Official Route" makes its way through the trees on the right, you may

stage 28 Brienne-le-Château to Dolancourt

find the conditions better on the road **(1.1)** At the crossroads, turn left on the pathway[Into the woods] **(1.7)** At the T-junction, turn right on the grass track[Pass between 2 concrete pillars] **(1.8)** Turn left on the small track[Metal cover on the ground] **(2.1)** After crossing the gully, take the right fork **(2.3)** At the junction in the tracks between the fields, continue straight ahead on the broader track **(2.5)** Cross the railway track and continue straight ahead on the gravel track[Woods on your right] **(3.1)** At the T-junction with the road, after passing the Eco-Musée, turn right on the D11B. Note:- the Alternate Route via the town centre joins from the left[Cross the river bridge] **(3.2)** Continue straight ahead beside the road[Information panel on the right] **(3.9)** At the top of the hill with a view of the lake ahead, turn left onto the track[Enter the woods] **(4.1)** At the junction in the tracks, with apple trees on your left, turn right on the small track[Proceed between trees] **(4.2)** Briefly emerge from the woods with a view of the lake again ahead, turn left on the broad track[Re-enter the woods] **(4.4)** Take the left fork on the smaller track **(4.7)** Emerge from the woods and continue straight ahead[Trees on the left, field on the right] **(5.2)** Continue straight ahead on the track, skirting the woods[Avoid the turning to the left] **(6.2)** At the junction with a gravel track, continue straight ahead[House n° 36 on your right] **(6.4)** At the end of ruelle aux Crapauds, turn right[Towards part timbered buildings] **(6.8)** At the T-junction with the road, turn left[Cross the bridge over the river] **(6.9)** In the centre of **Dienville**, take the right fork on the D11[Pass the church on your left] **(7.4)** Take the right fork on the small

Brienne-le-Château to Dolancourt — stage 28

road, beside the walls of the château gardens[Rue du Moulin] **(7.9)**After passing the flour mill, continue straight ahead and then bear right on the gravel track[Straight track between fields]**(8.9)**At the crossroads in the tracks, just before reaching the woods, turn left[Skirt

the woods on your right] **(9.1)**Take the right fork on the grass track[Towards lone tree] **(10.1)**At the T-junction with the tarmac road, turn right **(10.6)**At the road junction, keep right on the D46. Note:- to reduce your journey by 7 km, turn left on the Alternate Route via Jessains[Towards Unienville]**(10.9)**At the road junction beside the church in **Unienville**,

Another World - Beside Unienville

turn right[Grand Rue]**(11.1)**Beside the Gîte d'Etape, turn left and then continue straight ahead on the road[Rue de la Croix]**(11.3)**As the road turns sharply to the right, turn left on the gravel track[Pass a metal barn on your right]**(11.6)**Take the right fork towards the woods **(12.4)**After crossing the canal d'amenée take the right fork**(13.4)**At the crossroads in the tracks in the woods, continue straight ahead on the broad track **(14.2)**At the junction with a gravel track, continue straight ahead**(15.1)**At the T-junction with the main road, turn left[Gîte d'Etape ahead] **(15.4)**At the junction in the centre of **Amance** continue straight ahead. Note:- the GR°654 chemin de St Jacques separates and leaves to the right[Direction Vauchonvilliers]**(15.8)**Beside the calvaire, as you begin to leave

stage 28 — Brienne-le-Château to Dolancourt

Amance, turn left and leave the main road[Pass the agricultural equipment store on your left]**(16.1)**At the junction in the tracks, continue straight ahead[Towards the woods] **(18.4)**Take the right fork, towards the houses**(18.7)**At the T-junction with the D112, turn left[Stone bench to the right of the junction]**(19.2)**At the crossroads in the centre of **Vauchonvilliers**, continue straight ahead[Rue de l'Eglise] **(19.5)**On the edge of the village take the left fork, D183[Direction Maison des Champs] **(21.4)**Just before D183 kilometre sign n°2, turn left on the track[Towards wind generators]**(21.9)**Fork right on the grassy track[Towards the woods] **(23.2)**At the crossroads in the tracks, just after passing under the power lines, turn left[Towards the farm buildings]**(23.6)**At the junction with the road in the hamlet of la Chanet, continue straight ahead[Rue Principale]**(23.8)**Turn left on the D146[Direction Bossancourt] **(24.8)**After passing the D186 kilometre sign n°1, turn right on the grassy track[Towards the woods] **(26.1)**At the T-junction with the busy D619, turn left and follow the grass track parallel to the road**(26.5)**Turn right, carefully cross the road and take the D44A[Direction Dolancourt] **(27.3)**At the T-junction, turn left on the D44[Towards Dolancourt centre]**(27.5)**At the war memorial, bear right. Note:- the Alternate Route via Jessains rejoins from the road ahead[Pass the church on your left]**(27.6)**Arrive at **Dolancourt**[Beside the church of Saint Léger]

Route via Brienne-la-Vielle (LXVI)

Route: a slightly shorter route, over level ground, visiting Brienne-le-Château centre and Brienne-la-Vielle (LXVI).**(0.0)**Turn left on the road and continue downhill[Château on your right]**(0.3)**At the T-junction at the foot of the hill, turn right[Towards the bridge]**(0.3)**Take the first turning to the left[Rue Blanchot]**(0.5)**At the T-junction, turn right and continue straight ahead at the crossroads[Towards the church] **(1.1)**At the crossroads between rue de l'Ecole Militaire and rue Maréchal Valée (D130), take the D130 direction Epagne[Low-rise apartment building on the right]**(1.2)**Turn left on rue Louis Chavance[No Through Road]**(1.5)**Take the third road on the right[Rue Léo Lagrange]**(1.7)**At the T-junction, turn left onto rue Julian Régnier[Sports ground to the right at the junction]**(2.0)**Continue straight ahead[Over railway crossing]**(2.1)**Turn right onto a gravel track immediately after the level crossing[Red and white barrier] **(2.9)**At the junction, continue straight ahead[Second red and white barrier]**(3.0)**At the T-junction turn right on rue du Vieux Moulin in **Brienne-la-Vieille (LXVI)**. Note:- town centre to the left[Furniture maker, n° 22]**(3.2)**At the road junction with the Eco-Musée on your right, continue straight ahead and rejoin the "Official Route"[Towards the river bridge]

Length:	3.2km
Ascent:	18m
Descent:	34m

Direct Route to Dolancourt via Jessains

Route: a more direct route to Dolancourt using minor roads, a disused railway and farm tracks and passing through Jessains - saving 7 km. **(0.0)**Turn left direction Jessains, D46[Pass through the hamlet of l'Autre Monde] **(1.6)**Immediately after descending from the highway bridge, turn right on the gravel track[Initially parallel to the road] **(3.5)**At the crossroads with a tarmac road, turn left[Former railway cottage on your left]**(3.9)**Bear left at the junction[Towards the village of Jessains]**(4.1)**At the T-junction in Jessains, turn right on rue de Puise[Direction Dolancourt, D46]**(4.3)**In Jessains centre, bear right[Direction Dolancourt, D46, Grand Rue] **(8.8)**At the T-junction turn right with care, direction Troyes[Very busy N19]**(9.1)**Cross the main road and turn left, direction Dolancourt, D44[Rue de la Vallée du Landon]**(9.7)**Arrive in Dolancourt, turn left onto rue de Vannage and rejoin the "Official Route" at the end of the section[Direction Jaucourt]

Length:	9.7km
Ascent:	185m
Descent:	161m

Brienne-le-Château to Dolancourt — stage 28

Accommodation and Tourist Information

Amance
🏠 **Gîte d'Etape**[Mme Nathalie Fevre],19 Grande rue, 10140 Amance, France; Tel:+33(0)3 25 41 37 36; +33(0)7 69 46 70 78; Email:commune-amance@wanadoo.fr; www.amancevilleaubois.fr; Price:C

Dienville
🏠 **Chambre d'Hotes - le Colombier**,8 avenue Jean Lanez, 10500 Dienville, France; Tel:+33(0)3 25 92 23 47; Email:lecolombier10@gmail.com ; domaine-le-colombier.fr; Price:B; *Wide range of accommodation options*

⛺ **Camping du Tertre**,Rue Fontaine du Mont, 10500 Dienville, France; Tel:+33(0)3 25 92 26 50; +33(0)6 74 59 64 72; Email:campingdutertre@gmail.com; www.campingdutertre.fr; Price:C; *Chalets also available*

⛺ **Camping le Colombier**,8 avenue Jean Lanez, 10500 Dienville, France; Tel:+33(0)3 25 92 23 47; Email:lecolombier10@gmail.com; domaine-le-colombier.fr; Price:C; *Also glamping options*

Dolancourt
🛏 **Hôtel - le Moulin du Landion**,5 rue Saint Léger, 10200 Dolancourt, France; Tel:+33(0)3 25 27 92 17; Email:contact@moulindulandion.com; moulindulandion.com; Price:A

Jessains
⛺ **Camping Municipal - Jessains**,Route de Vauchonvilliers, 10140 Jessains, France; Tel:+33(0)3 25 92 72 06; Email:mairie.jessains@orange.fr; Price:C

La-Rothière
🛏 **Auberge - de la Plaine**,13 route de la Plaine, 10500 La-Rothière, France; Tel:+33(0)3 25 92 21 79; Email:aubergedelaplaine@wanadoo.fr; www.auberge-plaine.com; Price:B

Radonvilliers
⛺ **Camping le Garillon**,10 rue des Anciens Combattants, 10500 Radonvilliers, France; Tel:+33(0)3 25 92 21 46; Email:contact@campinglegarillon.fr; www.campinglegarillon.fr; Price:C; *Mobile home available*

Unienville
🏠 **Gite d'Etape - Communal**,Rue de la Croix, 10140 Unienville, France; Tel:+33(0)6 77 69 57 41; +33 (0)3 25 92 73 05; Email:giteunienville@gmail.com; grandslacsdechampagne.fr; Price:C

The parting of the ways - Amance

stage 29 — Dolancourt to Clairvaux

Length:	27.1km
Ascent:	855m
Descent:	818m
Canterbury	683km
Col Grand Saint Bernard:	556km

Clairvaux Abbey

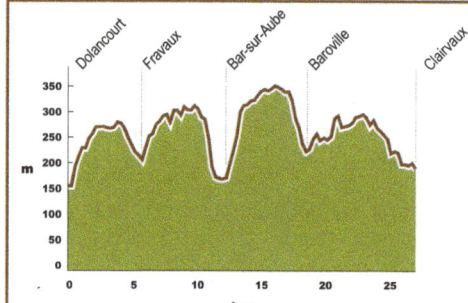

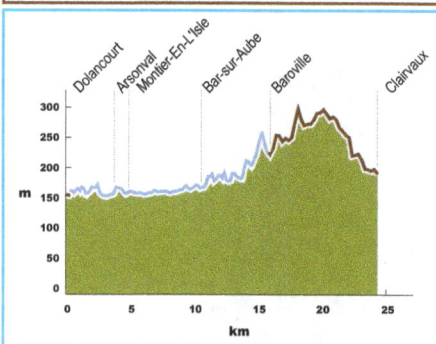

Route: this strenuous stage from Dolancourt to Clairvaux uses woodland and farm tracks which cross and recross the ridge on the western flank of the Aube valley.

The "Official Route" skirts the centre of Bar-sur-Aube where a full range of facilities can be found.

Bar-sur-Aube has useful train services to both Troyes (for Paris) and Dijon (for Switzerland and the south).

The Alternate Routes save distance and avoid the most strenuous climbs.

Over the stages between Clairvaux and Langres the accommodation options are again limited with substantial distances between them. Walkers are advised to secure accommodation in good time and carefully plan their route with due regard to their fitness and the distances involved.

The original buildings of Clairvaux Abbey, founded in 1115 by St. Bernard, are now in ruins and a high-security prison partially occupies the grounds. Nevertheless Clairvaux Abbey still remains a good example of the general layout of a Cistercian monastery. A strong wall, furnished at intervals with watchtowers and other defences, surrounded the abbey precincts. Beyond it a moat, artificially diverted from tributaries, which flow through the precincts, encircled the wall.

This water furnished the monastery with an abundant supply for irrigation, sanitation and for the use of the offices and workshops. An additional wall, running from north to south, bisected the monastery into an inner and outer ward. The inner ward housed the monastic buildings while the agricultural and other menial endeavours were conducted in the outer ward.

Dolancourt to Clairvaux   stage 29

The church itself occupied a central position with the great cloister to the south, surrounded by the chief monastic buildings. Further to the east the smaller cloister contained the infirmary, novices' lodgings and quarters for the aged monks.

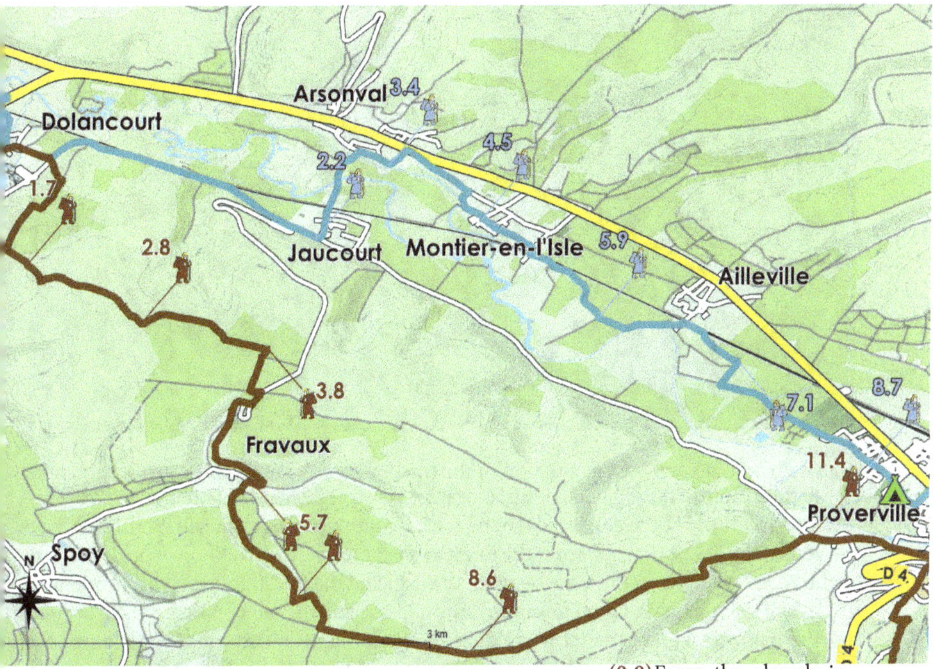

Eglise St.Pierre - Bar-sur-Aube

(0.0) From the church in Dolancourt, take the D46 [Pass the church on your left] **(0.1)** Bear right on rue de Vannage [Weir on your right] **(0.3)** At the exit from Dolancourt, turn right - direction Nigloland livraison - and immediately bear left on the forest track. Note:- the track ahead is both narrow and very steep and is not recommended for cyclists. To follow the easier and more direct Alternate Route, bear left on the road **(0.6)** At the T-junction, at the top of the very steep climb, turn right **(1.7)** At the junction in the tracks, continue straight ahead on the

stage 29 — Dolancourt to Clairvaux

Fravaux *Gérard Janot*

well defined track**(1.9)**At the junction in the track, where the main track turns right, take the first turning on the left and continue straight ahead at the next junction[Avoid the propriété privée]**(2.1)**At the crossroads in the tracks, continue straight ahead[Propriété privée on your right] **(2.8)**Emerge from the forest and bear left on the track[Open fields on your right]**(2.9)**Bear right on the track between the field and the forest[Towards the farmhouse] **(3.4)**Take the right fork, uphill towards the farmhouse and the radio mast **(3.8)**Bear right on the main track[Pass the farm buildings on your right]**(4.2)**At the T-junction in the track, turn left and then immediately right on the tarmac**(4.4)**Turn right on the grass track, steeply downhill**(4.5)**At the T-junction with the road, turn right and follow the road down-

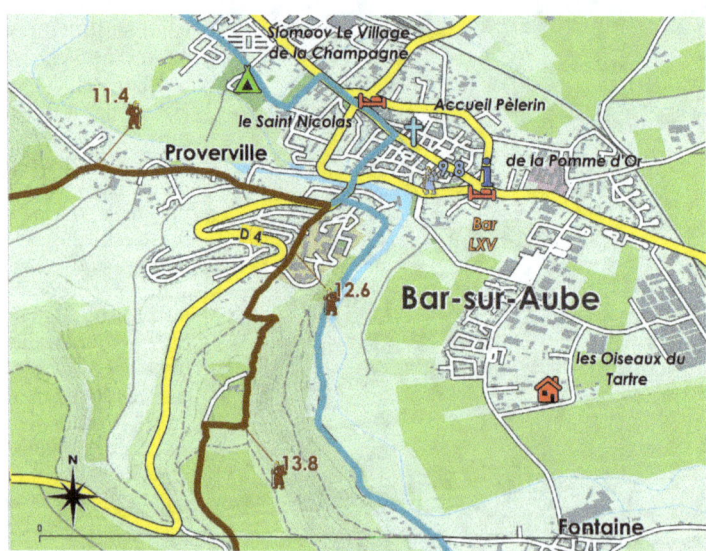

Dolancourt to Clairvaux — stage 29

hill **(5.7)** At the entry to **Fravaux**, turn left[Rue de la Fontaine]**(5.8)** At the end of the tarmac, continue straight ahead on the gravel track[Woods on your right]**(6.4)** As the main track turns left into the vines, continue straight ahead[Vines on your left, woods on your right]**(6.6)** In the woods, take the right fork **(7.1)** At the T-junction, as you leave the woods, turn left on the broad track[Towards the concrete tower]**(7.2)** Beside the tower, bear right on the stony track**(7.6)** At the crossroads in the tracks, take the second left[Downhill, between the woods] **(8.6)** At the junction in the tracks, continue straight ahead[Avoid the track to the right]**(9.0)** At the junction in the tracks, continue straight ahead in the trees, begin to descend **(11.4)** At the Stop sign, turn right on Grand Rue**(12.2)** At the T-junction, turn left**(12.3)** In **Bar-sur-Aube (LXV)** at the junction between rue Romagon and rue Pierre Brossolette, turn right. Note:- the town centre is over the river bridge on the left. The more direct route via Jaucourt arrives from the left while the less demanding valley route also leaves to the left[Up the hill]**(12.4)** As the road again turns right, continue straight ahead on the gravel track[Via Francigena panel on your left] **(12.6)** Take the left fork**(12.8)** At the road junction, continue straight ahead[Lycée on your left]**(12.9)** At the fork in the track continue straight ahead[Uphill]**(13.0)** At the entrance to the woods, turn left on the unmade track[Keep the metal fencing on your right]**(13.2)** At the junction at the end of the metal fencing, turn right[Uphill]**(13.5)** On reaching an open grass area beside a timber framed house, bear left across the grass[Keep the metal fence on your left] **(13.8)** At the end of the grassed area turn right[Pass between the wooden barriers, keeping the woods to your left]**(13.9)** At the T-junction with the tarmac road, turn left[Farmhouse and radio tower to your right at the junction]**(14.7)** As the road bends sharply to the right, bear left onto the left-most gravel track[Signpost Bergéres] **(15.3)** Shortly after entering the woods take the left fork**(16.2)** At the crossroads in the tracks, continue straight ahead **(16.4)** At the junction in the tracks, continue straight ahead[Avoid the broad track to your right]**(16.9)** At the crossroads in the tracks turn left[VF sign, Baroville 1.5km] **(17.9)** At the junction with a broad track continue straight ahead[Downhill, between vines]**(18.0)** At the crossroads in the tracks, turn right on the tarmac[Towards the village of Baroville]**(18.4)** At the crossroads, continue straight ahead on rue de Couvignon[Towards the church]**(18.5)** At the next crossroads, turn left[Pass a metal barn on your left]**(18.7)** At the crossroads, turn right. The Aube valley route rejoins from the left[Towards the Mairie]**(18.7)** At the fork in the road in **Baroville**, bear left onto rue des Pressoirs[Direction Bayel] **(18.9)** At the crossroads, continue ahead uphill on rue de la Côte Sandrey[Coat of arms on building ahead]**(19.1)** At the edge of the village, continue straight ahead on a stony track between the vines[Towards

Clairvaux Forest

stage 29   Dolancourt to Clairvaux

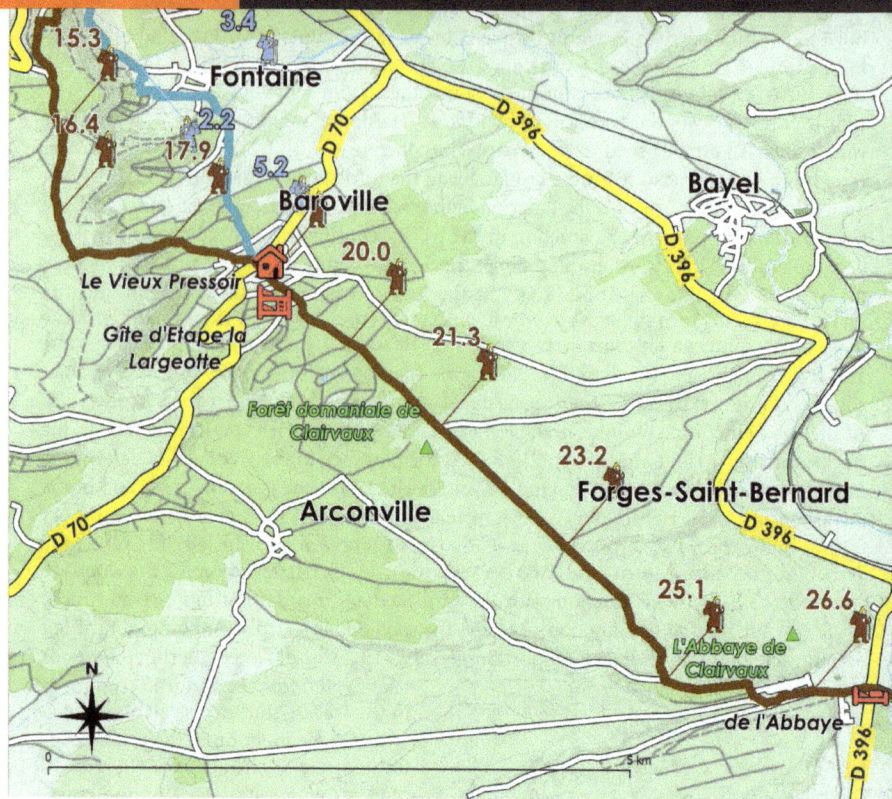

the brow of hill]**(19.3)**At the crossroads with the tarmac road go straight ahead[Wooden crucifix on the left]**(19.6)**Fork left off the concrete road onto the broad unmade road[Continue briefly between vines] **(20.0)**Continue straight ahead avoiding the track to the right[Towards the wooded ridge]**(20.2)**At the crossroads in the tracks, continue straight ahead**(20.3)**Fork left on the smaller track[Towards the gap in the woods] **(21.3)** At the junction with the broad track in the woods continue straight ahead on the forest road[Sign Sommière des Moines] **(23.2)**At the crossroads with a very broad track, continue straight ahead**(23.5)**At a crossroads in the grassy track, continue straight ahead[Climb short steep hill]**(24.0)**At the junction with a broad gravel track, fork right[Pass sign Sommière de la Culbute on your left] **(25.1)**At the T-junction with the road, turn left on the road, downhill[VF sign Clairvaux 1.5km] **(26.6)**At the T-junction beside the abbey entrance, turn left keeping the abbey wall on you left[Bar to the right of the junction]**(27.1)** Arrive at **Clairvaux** at the crossroads with D396[Abbey grounds on the left, hotel on the right]

Dolancourt to Clairvaux
stage 29
L'Aube Valley

Route: a slightly shorter and substantially less strenuous route remaining close by l'Aube and passing through Jaucourt and Montier-en-l'Isle using minor roads and riverside tracks. (0.0)Bear left and remain on the D46[Woodland to the right] (2.2)In **Jaucourt**, turn left towards Arsonval, D113[Grande Rue, cross the railway](3.1)Turn right onto rue du Désert[After crossing the second river bridge] (3.4) In **Arsonval**, bear left on the road[Uphill towards main road](3.6)At the T-junction, turn sharp right direction Bar-sur-Aube. Take the minor road to the right of the D619[Exit Arsonval sign](4.2)Turn right on the small road[Rue de l'Abreuvoir] (4.5)In the centre of **Montier-en-l'Isle**, continue straight ahead on rue de l'Isle[Church on your right](5.0)At the end of the street turn right on rue du Prieuré[Cross the railway](5.0)Immediately after crossing the railway, turn left on the gravel track[Pass an orchard on the right] (5.9)Fork left into an open field[Towards a line of trees](6.1)Bear left on the track[Keep the river to your right](6.5)Turn left onto a larger gravel track and then right before the railway crossing[Parallel and close to the railway] (7.1)Fork right into trees[Railway behind](7.3)Turn left[After crossing a concrete bridge] (8.7)Continue straight ahead direction Centre Ville[Through a housing estate](9.2)Turn left down an avenue of trees, rue du Jars[Salle de Spectacle on your right](9.4)At the T-junction turn right[Avenue du Général de Léclerc] (9.8)In **Bar-sur-Aube (LXV)** centre, turn right on rue d'Aube[Beside the Mairie and tourist office](10.1)At the crossroads beside the river, continue straight ahead over the bridge[Direction Proverville](10.2)At the junction beside the car park, continue straight ahead[Rue Pierre Brossolette](10.3)Rejoin the the "Official Route" [Junction with rue Romagon]

Length:	10.3km
Ascent:	218m
Descent:	213m

La petite église de Clairvaux

stage 29 — Dolancourt to Clairvaux

L'Aube Valley to Baroville

Route: for cyclists and for those wishing to avoid the initial steep climb of les Côtes d'Aube. The Alternate Route generally follows very minor roads in the river valley before returning to the champagne vineyards on the hillsides and reduces your total distance by 1.2 km.

Length:	5.2km
Ascent:	269m
Descent:	214m

(0.0) Turn right onto rue Gaston Bachelard[Direction Cité Scolaire G. Bachelard] (2.2) Fork right on impasse Buffery, the road becomes a track after leaving the houses[Junction after distinctive house with sloping roof on the right](2.5) Turn left on the track[Downhill] (2.6) At the junction, turn right and then bear left[Pass a tennis court on your left](2.7) At the junction with the tarmac road, turn left and then take the right fork[Pass the modern bungalows on your right](3.1) At the next fork in the road, bear right on rue Saint Antoine[Conifer hedge on your right] (3.4) Continue straight ahead and bear gently to the right on road[Ignoring blue and white sign to the right](3.5) Shortly after passing a metal crucifix on your left, take the left fork[Narrower track between the trees](3.8) At the junction, continue straight ahead on the tarmac[Towards the woods] (5.2) At the crossroads in Baroville, continue straight ahead to rejoin the "Official Route"[Towards the church]

Accommodation and Tourist Information

Bar-sur-Aube

Accueil Pèlerin, 4Bis rue Saint-Pierre, 10200 Bar-sur-Aube, France; Tel:+33(0)3 25 27 06 34; Price:C; *Contact the Office du Tourisme for reservations*

Chambre d'Hôtes - les Oiseaux du Tartre, Rue de l'Europe, 10200 Bar-sur-Aube, France; Tel:+33(0)630620120; Email:catminh10@hotmail.fr; catminh10.wixsite.com/oiseaux-du-tartre; Price:B

Hôtel - le Saint Nicolas, 2 rue du Général de Gaulle, 10200 Bar-sur-Aube, France; Tel:+33(0)3 25 27 08 65; www.lesaintnicolas.com; Price:A

Hôtel - de la Pomme d'Or, 79 Faubourg Belfort, 10200 Bar-sur-Aube, France; Tel:+33(0)9 70 35 19 09; www.hoteldelapommedor.com; Price:B

Slomoov - Le Village de la Champagne, 11 rue des Varennes, 10200 Bar-sur-Aube, France; Tel:+33 (0)3 85 53 76 60; Email:resa@slowmoov.fr; slowmoov.com; Price:B; *Accommodation in quirky chalets and gipsy caravans;* **PR**

Office du Tourisme, 4 Boulevard du 14 Juillet, 10200 Bar-sur-Aube, France; Tel:+33(0)3 25 27 24 25; Email:contact@tourisme-cotedesbar.com; www.tourisme-cotedesbar.com

Baroville

Gîte d'Etape - la Largeotte[Michel Urbain], 4 rue de la Côté Sandrey, 10200 Baroville, France; Tel:+33(0)3 25 27 00 36; +33(0)6 74 04 41 82; Email:champagne.urbain@wanadoo.fr; www.champagne-urbain.fr ; Price:C; *Open all year except for the grape picking season*

Chambre d'Hôtes - Le Vieux Pressoir[Michel Urbain], 4 rue de la Côté Sandrey, 10200 Baroville, France; Tel:+33(0)3 25 27 00 36; +33(0)6 74 04 41 82; Email:champagne.urbain@wanadoo.fr; www.champagne-urbain.fr ; Price:B

Clairvaux-sur-Aube

Hôtel - de l'Abbaye, 19 route de Dijon, 10310 Clairvaux-sur-Aube, France; Tel:+33(0)3 25 27 80 12; Email:hrabbaye-clairvaux@orange.fr; www.hotel-restaurant-abbaye.fr; Price:B

Longchamp-sur-Aujon

Gîte - Chez Jo, 10 rue Piverotte, 10310 Longchamp-sur-Aujon, France; Tel:+33(0)3 25 27 37 60; +33(0)6 28 37 93 66; Email:mauger.georges@orange.fr; www.gitechezjo.com; Price:C

Clairvaux to Châteauvillain

stage 30

Length:	23.8km
Ascent:	670m
Descent:	622m
Canterbury	710km
Col Grand Saint Bernard:	529km

Châteauvillain   *Patrice Thomas*

Route: the generally off-road stage from Clairvaux to Châteauvillain initially zig-zags in woodland on the hills above the Aujon valley and temporarily shares the path of the GR® 703 – Sentier Historique de Jeanne d'Arc. The route then crosses the valley to climb the parallel ridge top before descending to the small town of Châteauvillain.

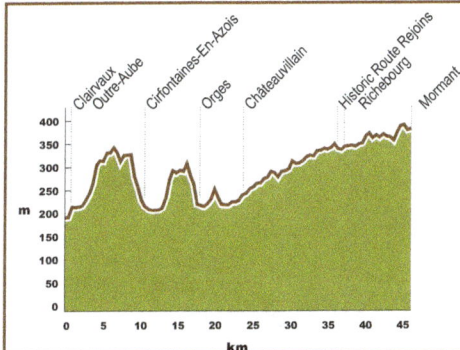

The "Official Route" bypasses Blessonville (LXIV). A local group of via Francigena enthusiasts have signposted this historic alternative and offer accommodation in their homes.

Châteauvillain is a small town with a limited accommodation but a reasonable range of other facilities.

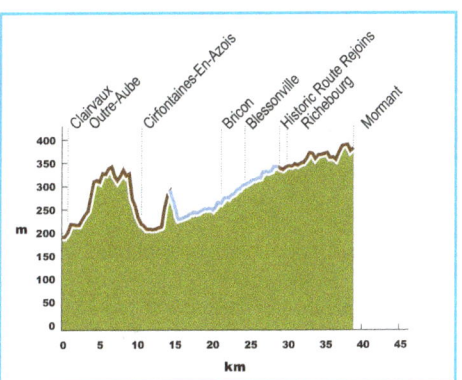

The Parc aux Daims was created by the Duke of Vitry in 1655 and comprises 272 hectares of woodland to the south-east of Châteauvillain.

Deer park - Châteauvillain

stage 30 Clairvaux to Châteauvillain

(0.0) From the crossroads beside the Hôtel de l'Abbaye in Clairvaux take the D12[Direction Longchamp-sur-Aujon]**(0.8)**After leaving **Outre-Aube**, where the road turns sharp left, continue straight ahead on the gravel track[Pass lone birch tree on your left]**(0.9)**Continue straight ahead up the hill, avoiding the turning to the right**(1.0)**Slightly before the top of the hill turn right on the smaller track. Note:- pay special attention as this turning is easily missed. Bikers and others wishing to avoid the possibly muddy forest tracks ahead can remain on the track to Longchamp-sur-Aujon where they should turn right and follow the D12 to Cirfontaines-en-Azois[Between fields towards the wooded valley] **(2.5)**Towards the end of the meadow, bear left on the track[Line of trees and the end of the meadow on your right]**(3.0)**At the crossroads in the track continue straight ahead**(3.5)**At the crossroads in the track with a small foot bridge on your right, turn left[Pass a sign for the Sentier Historique de Jeanne d'Arc on your right] **(4.4)**Turn right to leave the main track and follow the path up a small bank. Note:- this path may be easily overlooked**(4.4)**At the top of the bank, turn right[Back tracking on the main track]**(4.9)**In the clearing, turn sharp left and follow the broad gravel road**(5.0)**In the next clearing, bear right[Avoid the stony track on the left] **(5.6)**Remain on the broad track as it bends to the right**(6.0)**Bear left remaining on the broad gravel track **(6.9)**Continue on the broad track to the left[Avoid the wooded pathway on your right]**(6.9)**Bear right down the hill on the broad track[Ignore

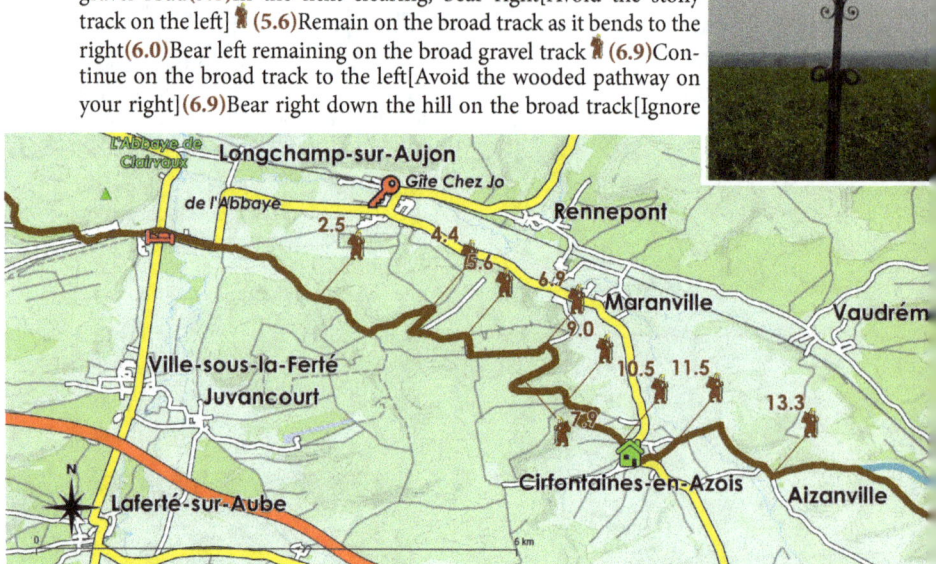

the track on the left]**(7.1)**Shortly after joining the tarmac, turn sharp right onto a wooded track **(7.9)**Continue straight ahead[Avoid the track on the right]**(8.1)**Take the right fork **(9.0)**At the crossroads in the track, continue straight ahead on the stony track**(9.1)**Continue straight ahead[Circuit des Lavoirs sign, Cirfontaine 1.5km]**(9.5)**At the crossroads, turn right on the track, keep the open field to your left[Metal barn ahead at the junction] **(9.8)**At the T-junction at the foot of the hill turn left on the grassy track **(10.5)**At the crossroads beside the farm building, continue straight ahead[Keep the farm buildings on your left]**(10.6)**At the bus stop in **Cirfontaines-en-Azois**, bear right[Pass the lavoir and Mairie on your left]**(10.7)**At the T-junction with the main road, turn right[Towards the church]**(10.9)**After passing the church in Cirfontaines-en-Azois turn left on rue de la Fon-

Clairvaux to Châteauvillain stage 30

taine aux Chênes**(11.1)**At the crossroads, continue straight ahead[Keep the Lavoir close on your right] **(11.5)**At the junction at the edge of the village bear right**(11.9)**After crossing the river, continue straight ahead beside the water mill[Sign Sainte Libère on the building on your left]**(12.1)**At the T-junction, turn right[Circuit des Lavoirs, Aizanville 1km] **(13.3)**Turn left up the hill on the gravel track. Note:- 1.2km and an unnecessaru climb can be saved by remaining for 4.4 km on the quiet road until rejoining the Official Route beside the cemetery at the entrance to the village of Orges **(16.6)**At the crossroads with the tarmac road, briefly continue straight ahead on the unmade road then turn right into the

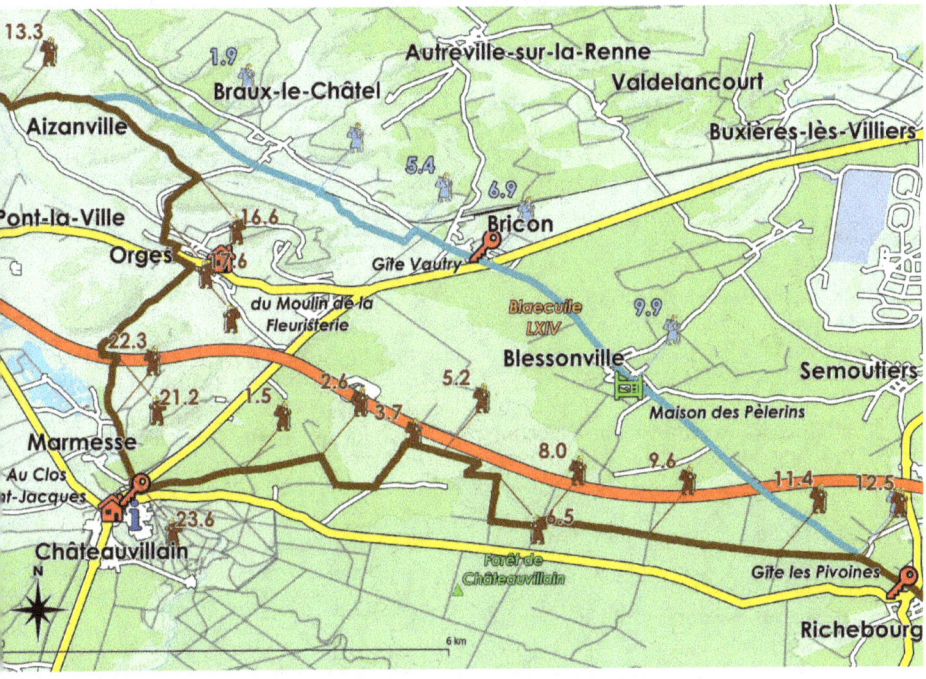

woods **(17.6)**At the T-junction with the road, turn left[Pass the cemetery on your right] **(18.1)**At the T-junction in **Orges**, turn left[Rue de la Forge]**(18.3)**Turn right on the D106, rue des Pressoirs. Note:- to visit Blessonville(LXIV), continue straight ahead on the Alternate Route[Direction Châteauvillain]**(18.4)**Continue straight ahead[Cross the river bridge] **(18.5)**At the T-junction immediately after the bridge, turn left[Direction Châteauvillain] **(18.8)**Turn right on chemin Paillot[VF sign - Châteauvillain 5.5km] **(21.2)**Bear right[Pass under the autoroute bridge] **(22.3)**At the junction bear right on the broken tarmac road[Pass stone crucifix]**(22.5)**At the T-junction with the tarmac road, turn left in the direction of "Pêche à la Truite"[Lavoir on the right of the junction] **(23.6)**Cross over railway tracks and continue straight ahead[Towards the walled gardens]**(23.8)**Arrive at **Châteauvillain** at the T-junction with the D65. Note:- for the centre of Châteauvillain bear right on rue de Penthievre[Cemetery wall ahead at the junction]

stage 30 — Clairvaux to Châteauvillain

Historic Route via Blessonville (LXIV)

Route: this more direct route follows more closely the probable historic route of Sigeric passing through the *submansione* of Blessonville (LXIV), using farm tracks and the former Roman road, now the D102 and saving 9 km. **(0.1)** Continue straight ahead on the track[Towards the woods] **(1.9)** Bear right at the junction[Keep the railway close on your left] **(3.8)** Turn right and then left on the track**(4.7)** At the T-junction, turn left and continue between the fields[Parallel to the railway] **(5.4)** At the T-junction turn left**(5.7)** At the T-junction with the road, turn right[Towards the railway crossing and the village of Bricon] **(6.9)** At the crossroads in **Bricon** continue straight ahead on the D102, direction Blessonville[Bar on the right just before the junction] **(9.9)** In **Blessonville (LXIV)** continue straight ahead on D102[Pass a church on the right, towards the motorway and the forest] **(14.4)** Continue straight ahead on the road. Note:- the "Official Route" joins from the track on the right[Pass the edge of the forest on your right]

Length:	14.4km
Ascent:	235m
Descent:	183m

Accommodation and Tourist Information

Blessonville
Maison des Pèlerins[Fabrice Noirot],41bis rue Principale, 52120 Blessonville, France; Tel:+33(0)6 22 78 90 95 ; Email:fmusrp@orange.fr; Price:C

Bricon
Gîte - Vautry[Christophe Vaudremont],3 rue du Maréchal Leclerc, 52120 Bricon, France; Tel:+33(0)3 25 03 62 66; +33(0)7 89 53 83 29; Email:c.vaudremont@laposte.net; Price:B; *Special price for pilgrims with credentials*

Châteauvillain
Chambre d'Hôtes - Au Clos Saint-Jacques [Jean-Louis and Nadine Depont],45 rue Saint-Jacques, 52120 Châteauvillain, France; Tel:+33(0)6 48 52 11 41; +33(0)3 25 32 21 18; Email:nadinedepont@wanadoo.fr; www.tourisme-arc-chateauvillain.com; Price:A

Appartment - Les Castels Lodges[Pauline Mailley],27 Rue de Penthièvre, 52120 Châteauvillain, France; Tel:+33 (0) 611618732; Email:castels.lodges@gmail.com; lescastelslodges.com; Price:B; *Room only*

Office de Tourisme des Trois Forêts,4 route de Châtillon, 52120 Châteauvillain, France; Tel:+33(0)3 25 02 52 17; +33(0)6 70 14 17 38; Email:tourisme.ot3f@orange.fr; www.tourisme-arc-chateauvillain.com

Cirfontaines-en-Azois
Alain and Myriam Marcillet,Grande rue, 52370 Cirfontaines-en-Azois, France; Tel:+33(0)6 76 20 67 55

Orges
Chambre d'Hôtes - du Moulin de la Fleuristerie,4 Chemin de la Fleuristerie, 52120 Orges, France; Tel:+33(0)6 22 10 89 48; Email:accueil@moulindelafleuristerie.fr; moulindelafleuristerie.fr; Price:B; *Breakfast and dinner available at additional cost*

Châteauvillain to Mormant

stage 31

Length:	22.4km
Ascent:	349m
Descent:	207m
Canterbury	734km
Col Grand Saint Bernard:	505km

Sanglier - Wild Boar

Route: the GR®145 from Châteauvillain to Mormant continues on minor roads and isolated forest tracks over generally level ground.

The woods are a popular with hunters and home to deer and wild boar. Hunting may take place on any day. It is advisable not to deviate from the tracks and if possible wear something bright.

There is only one choice for accommodation directly in Mormant all others are significantly beyond or well off-piste.

Dating from the beginning of the 12th century, the Abbaye de Mormant also served as a hospital of the Knights Templar providing shelter and care for pilgrims travelling the old Roman road between Reims and Langres.

Abbaye de Mormant

stage 31   Châteauvillain to Mormant

(0.0) Cross the main road and take the smaller road with the cemetery on your right. Note:- cyclists and others that may wish to avoid the forest tracks and reduce their distance by 3km, can turn right at this point towards the centre of Châteauvillain and then turn left on the D107 to rejoin the "Official Route" in Richebourgh. The D107 is normally a very quiet road[VF sign Richebourg 13.5km] **(1.5)** At the crossroads with the track, continue straight ahead[Pass the farm buildings across the field on your right] **(2.6)** At the T-junction, turn right on the grassy track[Woodland on your left as you proceed]**(3.2)** At the next T-junction, turn left on the grassy track towards the woods **(3.7)** At the crossroads with the tarmac road, turn left on the gravel track into the woods[VF sign Richebourg 9.5km]**(3.9)** Continue straight ahead[Red and white metal barriers]**(4.7)** At top of the rise turn sharp right **(5.2)** At the crossroads in the forest continue straight ahead**(5.8)** At the T-junction in the woods, with the sound of the autoroute to your left, turn right**(6.0)** At a crossroads in the forest briefly continue straight ahead and then turn left **(6.5)** At the crossroads in the track, turn right[Keep the metal deer fencing on your right]**(6.8)** In the clearing at the end of the fencing, continue straight ahead on the partially gravelled track**(7.3)** At the junction with the broader track, turn left **(8.0)** At the T-junction, turn left on the main track**(8.1)** Bear right on the main track[Pass the sign "Route Foestière François d'Orléans"]**(8.5)** At the junction in the tracks, continue straight ahead[Avoid the turning to the left] **(9.6)** At the crossroads in the tracks, continue straight ahead **(11.4)** At the junction in the tracks at the end of the long straight track, bear slightly left[Avoid the broad track signed "Route Forestière de la Maison Renaud" and the wooded track to the left] **(12.5)** Emerge from the forest at the T-junction with a minor road, turn right. Note:- the **Historic Route rejoins** from the left[VF sign Richebourg 1km, Chambre d'Hôtes ahead on the left]**(13.5)** At the crossroads with the D10 in **Richebourg**, continue on the D102, direction Leffonds[Rue de la Levée de César] **(13.9)** At the crossroads at the exit from Richebourg, continue straight

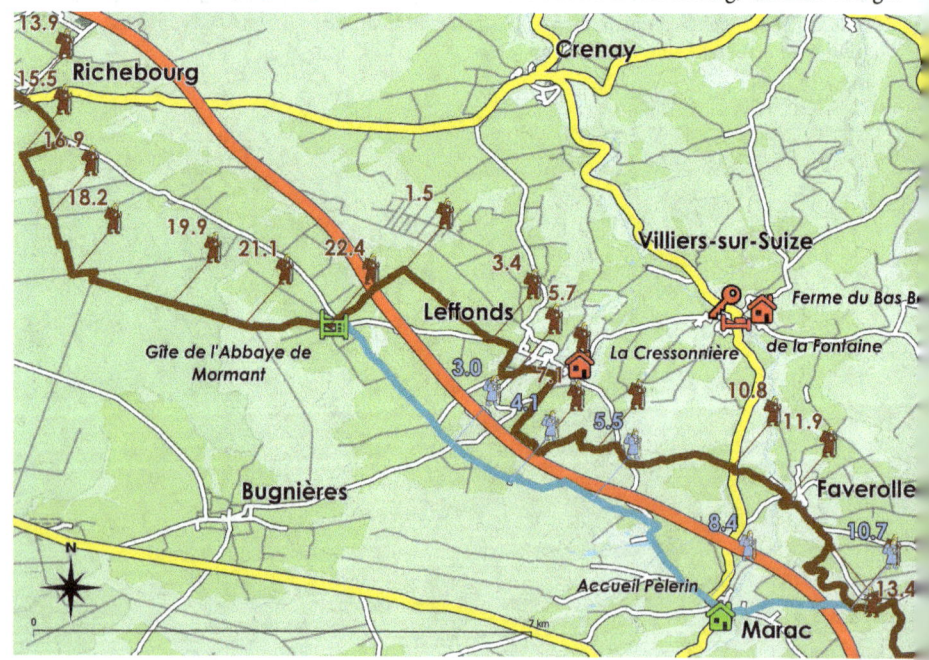

Châteauvillain to Mormant — stage 31

ahead[D102, direction Leffonds]**(14.8)**Turn right onto the tarmac track. Note:- to reduce the distance by 2 km and avoid further forest tracks, remain on the road to the end of the section beside the hamlet of Mormant[VF sign Mormant 8 km] **(15.5)**At the junction in the middle of the fields with the Richebourg church visible to the right, turn left on the grass track towards the forest**(16.1)**At the T-junction immediately before entering the woods turn left and immediately right. Note:- at the time of writing there is an electrified fence at the entry to the woods, with an insulated wire gate - proceed with care**(16.2)**After entering the forest turn left and then right on the well defined track**(16.5)**At a crossroads with a broad track, continue straight ahead and then slightly to the right on the narrower track **(16.9)**At a T-junction with a broad track in a grassy area, turn left**(17.0)**At the end of the grassy area, turn right on the narrow track**(17.5)**At the T-junction in the tracks, turn left**(17.6)**Turn right on the track **(18.2)**At a T-junction with a gravelled road, turn left on the road**(18.5)**Turn right[Route Forestière du Long-Boyau]**(18.7)**At the junction in the track, turn left on the broad track **(19.9)**As the main track bends to the right (Route Forestière de Champ Corot) continue straight ahead on the grassy track**(20.0)**At the junction in the tracks, continue straight ahead on the small grass track[Downhill]**(20.8)**Continue straight ahead at crossroads in the tracks **(21.1)**At the crossroads in the track, continue straight ahead**(21.2)**At the junction with a broad gravel track, continue straight ahead**(21.9)** On emerging from the woods, continue straight ahead towards the hamlet[Large open field on left] **(22.4)**Continue straight ahead on the tarmac road into the hamlet of Mormant and the remaining abbey buildings[VF sign - Leffonds 4.5km]**(22.4)**Arrive at **Mormant**[Beside ancient Abbaye de Mormant]

Accommodation and Tourist Information

Leffonds

Gîte de l'Abbaye de Mormant[Mme Annick Michelot],12 rue de l'Abbaye, 52210 Leffonds, France; Tel:+33(0)3 25 31 21 41; +33(0)6 79 01 33 53; Email:a.michelot52@yahoo.fr; www.meubles-tourisme-abbaye.com; Price:C; *In the hamlet of Mormant 2km before reaching Leffonds beside the end of stage and vestiges of the abbey*

Chambre d'Hôtes - La Cressonnière,21 rue de la Cressonnière, 52210 Leffonds, France; Tel:+33(0)3 25 01 29 45; +33(0)6 75 32 72 43; Email:dominique.begny@gmail.com; Price:A; *Dinner possible can sleep in a gypsy caravan*

Marac

Accueil Pèlerin[Elisabeth Garnier],1 rue de Champagne, 52260 Marac, France; Tel:+33(0)3 25 87 36 46; +33(0)6 76 91 15 20 ; Email:elisabeth.garnier0157@orange.fr; Price:B; *Price includes dinner*

Richebourg

Gîte - les Pivoines[Alain Barret],1 Impasse Grand Cour, 52120 Richebourg, France; Tel:+33(0)3 25 31 03 74; Email:alainbarret52@orange.fr;www.bienvenue-hautemarne.fr; Price:B

Villiers-sur-Suize

Chambres d'Hôtes - Ferme du Bas Bois[Eric and Roselyne Gruot],15 rue Théodore Régnier, 52210 Villiers-sur-Suize, France; Tel:+33(0)3 25 31 11 80; +33(0)6 80 30 16 11; Email:fermebasbois@wanadoo.fr; rando.forets-parcnational.fr/service/2834-Ferme-du-bas-bois; Price:B

Auberge - de la Fontaine,2 place de la Fontaine, 52210 Villiers-sur-Suize, France; Tel:+33(0)3 25 31 22 22; www.aubergedelafontaine.fr; Price:B

Gîte - de la Vallée de la Suize,1 rue du Pont, 52210 Villiers-sur-Suize, France; Tel:+33(0)3 25 31 22 22; Email:emilie.minne@laposte.net; web.facebook.com/Le-gite-de-la-Vallée-de-la-Suize-111632734078932; Price:B

stage 32 — Mormant to Langres

Length:	34.9km
Ascent:	909m
Descent:	816m
Canterbury	756km
Col Grand Saint Bernard:	483km

Langres

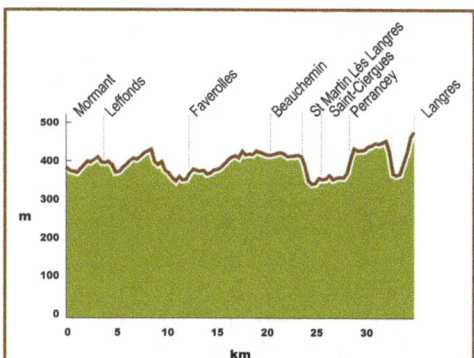

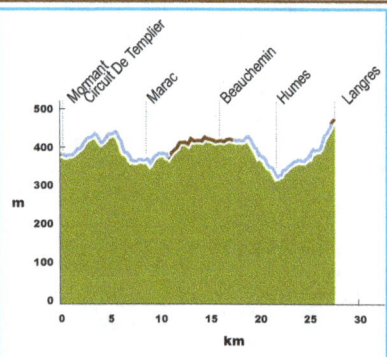

Route: the long and strenuous stage from Mormant to Langres continues on a mix of woodland and farm tracks and minor roads. Langres is an ancient hilltop town reached by a stiff climb over the final few kilometres. Two Alternate Routes offer the possibility of reducing distance by 6 km overall while a third Alternate allows you pass by the modern day Humes (LXIII) and also reduce distance, but will require several kilometres beside a busy road.

Accommodation in Langres can be surprisingly expensive while L'Abri du Pèlerin is small and may be occupied. Gite d'Etape - Sainte Anne is off-piste and 2 km prior to the town centre, but offers a warm welcome. It is advisable to secure your accommodation in advance and plan your day accordingly. There is a bar/restaurant in Saint-Ciergues, but no other facilities on the route before the outskirts of Langres.

Denis Diderot, born in Langres in 1713 and was the most prominent French Encyclopedist. He was educated by the Jesuits and, refusing to enter one of the learned professions, was turned adrift by his father and went to Paris, where he lived from hand to mouth for a time. His **Pensees Philosophiques,** in which he attacked both atheism and the received Christianity, was burned by order of the Parliament. In the circle of the leaders of the Enlightenment, he became well-known for his **Letters on the Blind**, which supported Locke's theory of knowledge.

Mormant to Langres — stage 32

(0.1) Go straight ahead on rue de l'Abbaye[Pass the arched stone building on your right] **(0.1)** At the T-junction, turn right[D102] **(0.2)** Continue straight ahead on the gravel track. Note:- the shorter Alternate Route initially follows the road to the right **(1.5)** At the T-junction, turn right on the main track[Towards the radio tower] **(2.0)** At the junction in the tracks, continue straight ahead on the main track[Towards the radio tower] **(2.3)** Avoid the track to your left and remain on the main track as it passes the radio tower **(3.4)** At the T-junction with the road, turn left[Sign Leffonds Cente – 2km] **(3.8)** Shortly after passing the sign for the entry to **Leffonds**, turn right on a gravel track. Note:- unfortunately Leffonds offers neither shops nor eating places["Circuit des Templiers", pass an orchard on your left] **(4.4)** At the T-junction with the small tarmac road, turn left **(4.5)** At the T-junction with a tarmac road, turn left["Circuit des Templiers"] **(4.7)** With house n° 22 on your left, turn right onto the gravel track **(5.0)** At the T-junction with the small tarmac road, turn right towards the church **(5.3)** At the T-junction at the top of the hill, beside the church, turn right["Circuit des Templiers"] **(5.7)** Shortly after passing a stone crucifix on your left, leave the tarmac road and bear left on the gravel track[Etang de Chênot – 6.5km] **(6.5)** At the junction in the tracks, continue straight ahead **(7.1)** At the crossroads in the woods, continue straight ahead on the narrow track **(7.2)** At the T-junction with a broader track, turn left **(7.9)** At the crossroads in the tracks, continue straight ahead **(8.0)** Turn sharp right["Etang de Chênot"] **(8.5)** At the T-junction in the track turn left and keep left at the next junction **(8.8)** At the T-junction with a tarmac road, turn right **(9.3)** Turn left and leave the tarmac road["Circuit de Mausolée", direction Faverolles] **(10.8)** At the T-junction with

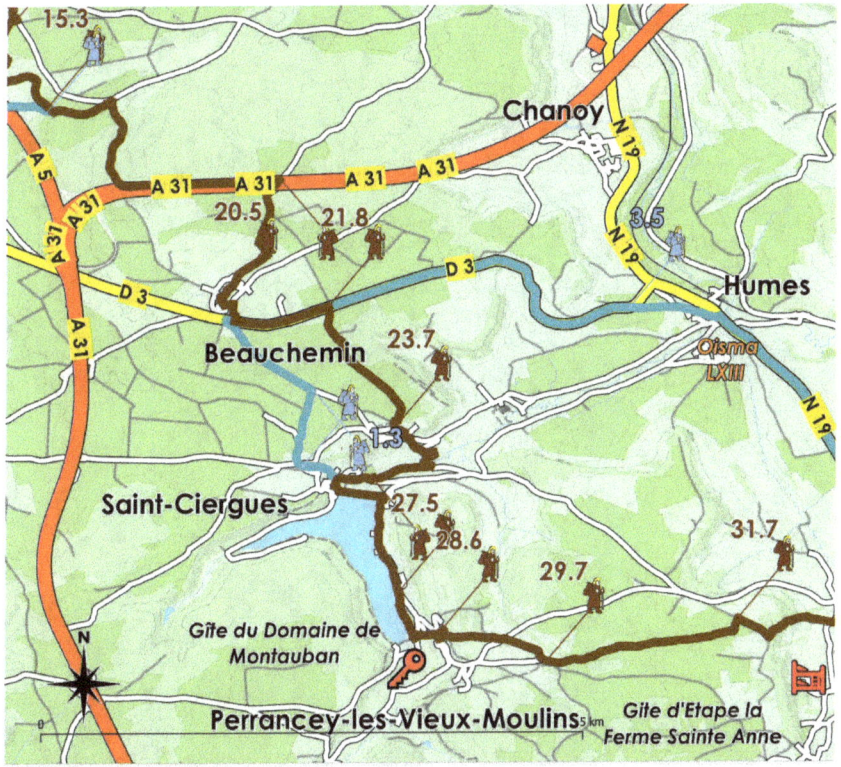

155

stage 32 — Mormant to Langres

the tarmac road, turn right and then immediately left[Direction Faverolles]**(11.8)**At the road junction, continue straight ahead towards Faverolles["Mausolée Gallo-Romain"] **(11.9)**After crossing the river bridge, bear right on the road**(12.7)**Immediately in front of the Mairie in **Faverolles**, bear right remaining on the road[Direction Beauchemin]**(12.5)** At the road junction, bear right[Towards Beauchemin - 7 km]**(12.9)**Take the right fork on chemin de Beauchemin **(13.4)**Turn right off the tarmac road onto the farm track. Note:- to reduce distance by approximately 1.5km and avoid more woodland tracks, you can continue straight ahead on the small road to rejoin the "Official Route" at the crossroads**(13.7)** Take the left fork, downhill, into a glade and between trees**(13.9)**At the T-junction in the tracks with a field ahead, turn left and remain in the woods **(15.3)**At the T-junction with the road, turn left on the road. Note:- the Alternate Route via Marac joins from the right[Beside rock outcrop]**(16.0)**At the crossroads, turn right[Direction Beauchemin] **(18.6)**At the T-junction, turn right and cross the bridge over the autoroute, direction Beachemin[VF sign Beauchemin - 2km] **(20.5)**Beside the war memorial in **Beauchemin**, take the left fork and then take the next left between the houses**(20.6)**At the T-junction, turn right[Pass a large barn on your left]**(20.9)**At the T-junction, turn left and continue with care beside the D3. Note:- the direct route to Saint-Ciergues follows the minor road to the right leading directly to the Réservoir de la Mouche[Direction Humes] **(21.8)**Turn right onto a stone and grass track, towards the silos and water tower. Note:- to pass beside Humes (LXIII) remain on the road and follow the Alternate Route to Langres[VF Sign St

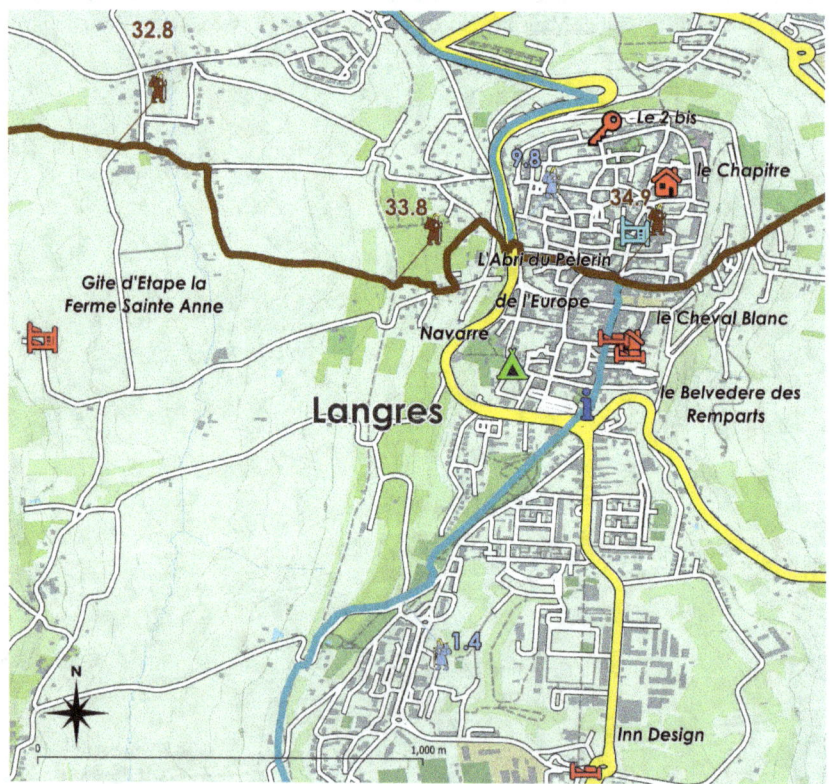

Mormant to Langres stage 32

A durable waymark

Martin lès Langres - 2 km] **(23.7)** At the T-junction in **St Martin lès Langres**, turn left["Circuit du Val de Mouche"]**(23.8)** Just after passing the church, turn sharp right down the hill[Magnificent view of the barrage]**(23.9)** At the T-junction with a road, beside the stone crucifix, turn left and then immediately right**(24.1)** At the T-junction with the road, turn right down the hill**(24.6)** At the bottom of the hill, after passing through Moulin de St Martin, turn right on the gravel track **(25.2)** At the T-junction with the small road, turn right[Cross over the bridge]**(25.5)** At the T-junction turn left, towards the Auberge de Lac. Note:- the Alternate Route joins from the right[Running water opposite the junction]**(25.6)** Just before reaching the Auberge in **Saint-Ciergues**, turn left downhill on the small road[Large stone at the entrance to the road]**(25.7)** At the T-junction with the road at the foot of the hill, turn left[Cross the barrage]**(26.1)** At the end of the barrage, turn right on the path beside the road[D286, direction Langres] **(27.5)** Bear right away from the road on the gravel path beside the lake[Toilet block ahead]**(28.1)** At the T-junction in the tracks, turn left[Metal barrier]**(28.2)** At the crossroads with the main road, continue straight ahead up the hill[Pass No-Entry sign, VF sign Perrancey 0.5 km]**(28.4)** At the T-junction in the centre of **Perrancey**, turn right and immediately left on the small road up the hill[Pass a church on your right] **(28.5)** Shortly after joining a grassy track, turn sharp right[Between a stone wall and the rear of the house]**(28.6)** At the end of the grassy area, bear left on the grass track up the hill**(29.1)** At the T-junction in the tracks, turn right towards the road**(29.2)** At the junction with road, cross over and continue straight ahead on the gravel track **(29.7)** At the junction with the tarmac road, turn left and continue on the gravel track **(31.7)** At the T-junction with a gravel track, turn right["Circuit de la Croisée de Voie Romain"]**(32.1)** Turn left onto the grass track[GR° sign, Langres - 2km]**(32.5)** Take the right fork downhill between the trees**(32.6)** At the junction in the tracks, turn right[Downhill] **(32.8)** At the T-junction with the road, turn left. Note:- turn right for Gite d'Etape - Sainte Anne["Circuit de la Croisée de Voie Romain"]**(32.9)** Beside the church in Brevoines, bear right on the road[Rue du Chanoine Roussel]**(33.1)** Turn right on chemin du Murot **(33.8)** Turn left and pass through the tunnel under the disused railway**(33.9)** At the T-junction in the track, turn right up the grassy slope[GR° sign, Langres Centre 1.1km]**(34.0)** At the T-junction on the grass track, turn right**(34.0)** At the T-junction with the tarmac road, turn left up the hill**(34.1)** Turn left[GR° sign Brevoines]**(34.3)** At the T-junction, turn right**(34.4)** At the T-junction with rue Louis Massotte, cross over and take the uphill path with the metal handrails**(34.5)** At the T-junction with a tarmac path, turn left towards the main road**(34.5)** At the T-junction with the main road, turn initially left and take the pedestrian crossing, then turn right and left to enter the town through the archway - Porte Neuve**(34.6)** Continue straight ahead on rue Boulière. Note:- the GR°145 will turn right to climb the steps and follow the walls around the town[Pass house n° 21 on your right]**(34.7)** Take the right fork on rue Jean Roussat[Pass Hôtel de la Poste on your right] **(34.9)** Arrive at **Langres** centre[Place Diderot]

stage 32 — Mormant to Langres

Direct Route via Marac

Route: initially follows traces of the Roman road, passing through woodland before joining minor roads to enter Marac and cross the A5 autoroute, saving 4.5 km. (0.0) Bear right on the road[D102] (0.1) As the road bends to the left, continue straight ahead on the **Circuit de Templier**, direction Bugniéres. Note:- a woodland section ahead may be difficult for cyclists in wet conditions. The section can be avoided by remaining on the D102 (3.0) At

Length:	10.7km
Ascent:	171m
Descent:	175m

the crossroads continue straight ahead on the Ancienne Voie Romaine[Remain parallel to motorway] (4.1) At the T-junction, turn left and bear right[Into the woods] (4.3) Turn right and then left[Onto a grassy track] (4.6) Take the left fork (5.0) At the T-junction in the track, turn right[Straight track, parallel to the Autoroute] (5.5) At the crossroads, continue straight ahead (5.7) At the T-junction, bear left onto a gravel track (6.5) At the T-junction turn right onto a minor road. Note:- cyclists taking the D102 rejoin from left[Autoroute visible to the left at the junction] (8.4) At the road junction, continue straight ahead[Enter **Marac**, D102] (8.8) At the T-junction in Marac turn left on rue des Charmes[Direction Langres, D102] (9.1) Take the left fork[D155, direction Rolampont] (10.7) As the road passes through the woods, after crossing the autoroute bridge, continue straight ahead on the road. Note:- the "Official Route" rejoins from the left[Rock outcrop in the woods to the left]

L'Abri du Pèlerin - Langres

Direct Route to Saint-Ciergues

Route: a minor road leading directly to Saint-Ciergues and the Réservoir de la Mouche saving 2 km. (0.0) Turn right and immediately left[Direction Saint Ciergues] (1.3) At the fork in the road bear right[Towards Saint Ciergues] (2.0) Continue straight ahead[Grain store on left] (2.3) At a 5 way junction

Length:	32.7km
Ascent:	14m
Descent:	61m

take the third right[Direction la Mouche, D286] (2.7) Take the left fork[Direction la Mouche, D286] (2.7) Bear right towards the Auberge du Lac on Rue du Lac. Note:- the "Official Route" joins from the left[Water trough on the right]

Beauchemin to Langres via Humes (LXIII)

Route: the D3 leads from Beauchemin to the modern Humes (LXIII) which straddles the very busy N19 leading onwards to the outskirts of Langres. The route is 3 km shorter than the GR®145, but is not recommended. (0.0) Continue straight ahead on the long straight road (3.5) At the fork in

Length:	9.8km
Ascent:	238m
Descent:	195m

the road, bear right leaving the D3[Direction Humes] (4.4) In **Humes (LXIII)** at the T-junction at the end of Grande Rue turn left[Rue de la Fontaine Saint Vinebaut] (4.4) At the intersection with the main road turn right[Cross the river bridge, N19] (8.5) At the roundabout continue uphill on the N19[Avenue de la Collinière, pass the cemetery on left] (9.0) Bear right to briefly leave the main road[Chemin des Lingons] (9.2) Return to the main road and turn right[Keep the **Langres** town walls on your left] (9.8) Turn left through the archway and rejoin the "Official Route"

Mormant to Langres — stage 32

Accommodation and Tourist Information

Langres

🏠 **Gite d'Etape - la Ferme Sainte Anne**, Faubourg de Buzon, route de Brevoines, 52200 Langres, France; Tel:+33(0)3 25 88 45 14; +33(0)6 03 08 29 77; Email:contact@gite-sainteanne.fr; www.gite-sainteanne.frr; Price:B; *Small discount if credentials are presented kitchen available*; **PR**

L'Abri du Pèlerin, 1 rue Aubert, 52200 Langres, France; Tel:+33(0)3 25 87 11 48; +33(0)6 81 49 09 85; Email:paroisselangres@gmail.com; catholangres.fr; Price:C; *2 beds open 17.00 to 19.00 credentials required*

🏠 **Chambre d'Hôtes - le Belvedere des Remparts**, 33 rue Lombard, 52200 Langres, France; Tel:+33(0)3 25 87 09 71; Email:belvederelangres@gmail.com; lebelvederedesremparts.com; Price:A

🏠 **Chambre d'Hôtes - le Chapitre**, 1 rue de la Crémaillère, 52200 Langres, France; Tel:+33(0)3 25 87 67 25 ; +33(0)6 20 71 13 28; Email:tresorerie.chapitre@yahoo.fr; www.tourisme-langres.com; Price:A

Hôtel - le Cheval Blanc, 4 rue Estre, 52200 Langres, France; Tel:+33(0)3 25 87 07 00; Email:info@hotel-langres.com; www.hotel-langres.com; Price:A

Hotel - Inn Design, Avenue du Général de Gaulle, 52200 Langres, France; Tel:+33(0)3 25 87 57 57; Email:hid.langres@gmail.com; hotel-inn-langres.fr; Price:B

Hôtel - de l'Europe, 25 rue Diderot, 52200 Langres, France; Tel:+33(0)3 25 87 10 88; hoteleuropelangres.com; Price:B

🔑 **Apartment - Le 2 bis** [Celine], 2 bis Pl. des Jacobins, 52200 Langres, France; Tel:+33(0) 6 84 94 10 15; www.airbnb.fr/rooms/543937192561859335; Price:A; *Can accommodate 6 people*; **PR**

⛺ **Camping Navarre**, 9 Boulevard Maréchal de Lattre de Tassigny, 52200 Langres, France; Tel:+33(0)3 25 87 37 92; +33(0)6 10 74 10 16; Email:contact@campingnavarre.fr; www.tourisme-langres.com/nl/CAMPING-LANGRES-01_camping-navarre; Price:C

ℹ️ **Office du Tourisme**, Square Olivier Lahalle, 52200 Langres, France; Tel:+33(0)3 25 87 67 67; Email:info@tourisme-langres.com; www.tourisme-langres.com

Perrancey-les-Vieux-Moulins

🔑 **Gîte - du Domaine de Montauban**, 3 route de Montauban, 52200 Perrancey-les-Vieux-Moulins, France; Tel:+33(0)3 25 88 12 61; +33(0)6 75 98 73 75; Email:karine.leroykl@gmail.com; web.facebook.com/domainemontauban; Price:B; *Kitchen available*

Saints-Geosmes

🏠 **Chambre d'Hôtes - Les Chambres d'Eponine**, 4 rue de la Fontaine, 52200 Saints-Geosmes, France; Tel:+33(0)3 25 88 23 40; +33(0)6 02 24 66 94; Email:petitot.christelle@gmail.com; www.langres-les-chambresdeponine.fr; Price:B; *Kitchen available*

Jum'Hotel, 2 rue du Lieutenant Didier, 52200 Saints-Geosmes, France; Tel:+33(0)3 25 87 03 36; www.jum-hotel-langres.com; Price:B

Porte des Moulins - Langres

stage 33 — Langres to Torcenay

Length:	24.4km
Ascent:	546m
Descent:	698m
Canterbury	791km
Col Grand Saint Bernard:	448km

Lac de la Liez — Clément Huvig

Route: after leaving Langres the "Official Route" from Langres to Torcenay follows pleasant canal and lakeside paths (shared with another tributary of the Chemin de St Jacques) before meandering through farmland and woods.

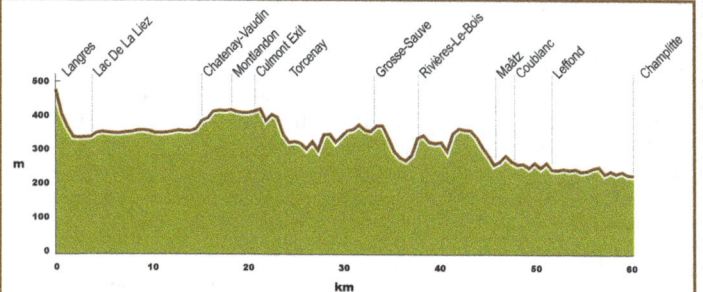

However, when considered with the following stage, the route is very long, has very limited accommodation options and beyond Torcenay the woodland tracks include difficult water crossings.

The Alternate Route via Les Archots is substantially shorter (by 13 km), but follows more, though generally minor, roads.

There is no accommodation available in Torcenay – accommodation in Chalindrey is 3 km "off-piste" and in Culmont 1.5 km. It is possible to break the journey beside the reservoir - Lac de la Liez.

In the 19th century Langres was an vital part of France's defensive system and was surrounded by a series of fortifications. Fort Cognelot at Chalindrey protected the south and the important railway junction. At its peak the fort housed 600 soldiers.

Fort Cognelot - Chalindrey

Langres to Torcenay   stage 33

(0.0) From Place Diderot take the small street downhill[Rue du Grand Cloitre] **(0.2)** Continue straight ahead downhill on the road and rejoin the GR°145[Pass through the archway in the town walls] **(0.4)** At the crossroads, after passing through the second archway, continue straight ahead **(0.9)** At the crossroads, following the road bridge, continue straight ahead[Route de Peigney] **(2.4)** Immediately after crossing the bridge over the canal, turn right on the track close beside the canal[Lac de la Lieze - 3km] **(3.3)** Just before the canal bridge, turn left onto the gravel track **(3.4)** At the T-junction in the tracks turn left on the gravel track[Pass a clump of trees on your right] **(3.9)** At the crossroads beside the end of the barrage of **Lac de la Liez**, continue straight ahead into the

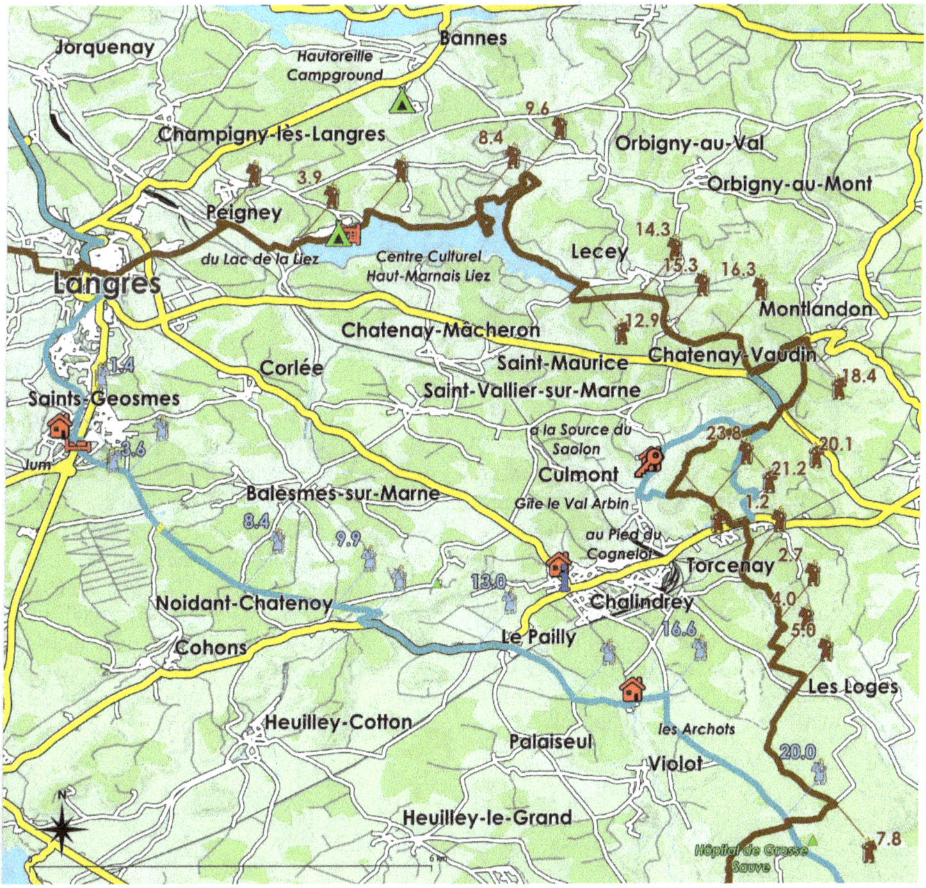

stage 33 — Langres to Torcenay

parking area and remain on the path beside the lake[Pass the hotel on your left] 🚶 **(5.2)**At the metal barrier, continue straight ahead 🚶 **(8.4)**At the crossroads, following the barrier, continue straight ahead**(8.8)**At the junction in the tracks, bear left[Keep the field on the left]**(9.2)**As the main track turns left, continue straight ahead into the trees[GR* sign, Lecey - 4km] 🚶 **(9.6)**At the junction in the tracks, bear right keeping the trees on your right[Cockle shell sign, church steeple ahead at the junction] 🚶 **(12.9)**At the crossroads with a tarmac road, turn right[Direction Chatenay-Vaudin]**(13.2)**After passing a copse of trees on your left, turn left onto a broad gravel track[Chatenay-Vaudin - 2km] 🚶 **(14.3)**At the fork in the track, take the right fork onto the smaller track[Towards metal gates]**(14.7)**At the T-junction with the road, turn right[Chatenay-Vaudin - 0.5km] 🚶 **(15.3)**Shortly after passing the church in the centre of **Chatenay-Vaudin**, take the left fork[Impasse des Vignes]**(15.6)**Keep straight ahead uphill on the tarmac[Pass an orchard on your left] 🚶 **(16.3)**At the junction in the tracks, continue straight ahead on the grass track[Avoid gravel track to the left] **(16.6)**In an open field, bear right around the edge of the field[Keep the barbed-wire fence on your left]**(17.3)**At the T-junction with the road, turn left. Note:- it is possible save 2 km, by turning right and then left proceeding with care for 900 m beside the busy N19 to the next crossroads[VF sign - Montlandon] 🚶 **(18.4)**At the junction beside the war memorial

in **Montlandon**, take the right fork and then immediately turn right[Rue du Tennis] 🚶 **(20.1)**At the crossroads with the N19, continue straight ahead, direction Torcenay, on the D307**(20.5)**Turn right on the track into the woods. Note:- a further 2km can be saved by remaining on the road to the junction beside the war memorial and then turning right to rejoin the GR*145 beside the grocery store in Torcenay. At the time of writing there were numerous fallen trees on the very muddy and sometimes overgrown path through the woods[VF sign, Torcenay - 4km] **(20.6)**Shortly after entering the woods take the left fork**(20.8)**Again take the left fork. Note:- for the accommodation in **Culmont exit** by the right fork and keep left to save 3km 🚶 **(21.2)**At the crossroads in the tracks continue straight ahead**(21.4)**Take the right fork**(21.9)**Emerge into an open field, and follow the path around the edge of the field[Keep the woods on your right]**(22.1)**At the corner of the field, turn right into the woods 🚶 **(22.5)**At the crossroads in the tracks, continue straight ahead**(23.0)**In the clearing, continue briefly ahead on the tarmac and then turn sharp left onto a track[VF sign, Torcenay - 1.5 km]**(23.1)**At the crossroads in the track, continue straight ahead and then immediately take the left fork 🚶 **(23.8)**At the T-junction in the track, turn right**(24.4)**Arrive at **Torcenay** at the T-junction with the D26. Note:- the facilities of Culmont and Chalindrey are to the right["Circuit Le Diable du Foultot"]

Langres to Torcenay

stage 33

More direct route to Hôpital de Grosse Sauve via Les Archots

Route: this more direct route leaves Langres through parkland on the famous Promenade de Blanchefontaine before joining the footpath (Voie Verte) on the disused railway track to Saint-Geosmes. The route continues on generally minor roads passing beside les Archots and the isolated B&B that has been popular with many modern day pilgrims.

Length:	20.0km
Ascent:	362m
Descent:	475m

(0.0)From place Diderot take the main street south between the shops[Small road downhill] (0.4)At the crossroads continue straight ahead. Note:- The GR®145 crosses from right to left and then continues to follow the town walls[Towards the archway](0.5)After leaving the main gate of Langres, take the pedestrian crossing keeping the roundabout on your left[Pass through the large metal gates and continue on the avenue between the trees] (1.4)Continue straight ahead downhill on the tarmac[Pass under the road bridge](1.8)At the crossroads, with the disused railway track, turn left[**Voie Verte**](2.1)At the crossroads, continue straight ahead on the Voie Verte[Water trough on the left] (3.6)At the crossroads, shortly after passing under a road bridge, continue straight ahead on the road opposite, rue Belle Vue[Towards the church in the distance](3.7)At the road junction, continue straight ahead on the tarmac path and bear right[Follow Voie Verte signs](3.9)After passing the sports hall on your left, join the road and continue straight ahead[Pass a red and white barrier](4.1)At the crossroads, turn left and leave the Voie Verte[Towards to the church] (4.1)At the mini-roundabout, continue straight ahead[Pass the cemetery on your left and church on your right](4.2)At the junction with the main road, take the pedestrian crossing and turn right[Tree lined pathway with commercial building on your left](4.4)At the road junction, turn left on the D290[Pass the hotel on the right] (5.4)At the T-junction, turn right on the D122[Towards Chalindrey](5.6)Continue straight ahead[D122, direction Noidant-Chatenoy] (8.4)At the fork in the road, keep left[Direction Chalindrey, D51] (9.9)Fork right[Direction Noidant-Chatenoy, D141] (11.1)At the T-junction turn left[Direction le Pailly, D141] (13.0) At the road junction following the entrance to **le Pailly**, continue straight ahead[Direction Chalindrey](13.4)In front of the church, turn left and then right[Direction Les-Archots, rue des Moulins] (15.1)Fork left[Direction Les-Archots](16.0)From the bridge, continue uphill on the road[Keep the **Les-Archots** B&B on your right] (16.6)At the crossroads, turn right[D136 - **Voie Romain**] (20.0) Continue straight ahead on the D136. Note:- The GR®145 joins the road from the left[Towards the Ferme de la Grosse Sauve and the former Hôpital de Grosse Sauve]

Hôpital de Grosse Sauve

stage 33 — Langres to Torcenay

Accommodation and Tourist Information

Bannes
⚠ **Hautoreille - Campground**,6 rue du Boutonnier, 52360 Bannes, France; Tel:+33(0)3 25 84 83 40; campinghautoreille.com; Price:C; *Erected tents and cabins available*

Chalindrey
🏠 **Chambre d'Hôtes - au Pied du Cognelot**,10 rue de l Hôtel de Ville, 52600 Chalindrey, France; Tel:+33(0)6 67 67 77 62 5; Email:parodi.bruno@orange.fr; www.aupiedducognelot.com; Price:B; *3km from Torcenay on the "Official Route" and 1.7 km from Pailly on the Alternate Route*

🏠 **B&B - les Archots**[M Serge Francois],2 chemin de l'Hermitte, 52600 Chalindrey, France; Tel:+33(0)3 25 88 93 64; www.tourisme-langres.com; Price:B; *On the alternate route*

ℹ **Mairie**,47 rue de Langres, 52600 Chalindrey, France; Tel:+33(0)3 25 88 50 17; www.ville-chalindrey.fr

Coublanc
Accueil Pèlerin,1 rue du Château, 52500 Coublanc, France; Tel:+33 (0) 607230325; +33 (0) 651095106; +33 (0) 621370481; Email:Mairie.Coublanc@wanadoo.fr ; Price:D; *Basic accommodation in former Mairie. 3 camp beds hot and cold water but no shower*

Culmont
🏠 **Chambre d'Hotes - a la Source du Saolon**[Varney Jean-Claude],9 rue du Haut, 52600 Culmont, France; Tel:+33(0)3 25 88 91 61; +33(0)9 65 11 08 22; Email:alasourcedusaolon@gmail.com; www.tourisme-langres.com; Price:B

🔑 **Gîte - le Val Arbin**[Samuel Bard],19 rue du Haut, 52600 Culmont, France; Tel:+33(0)3 25 88 50 34; Email:levalarbin@gmail.com; www.tourisme-langres.com; Price:C; *Equestrian holiday centre*

Langres
⚠ **Camping du Lac de la Liez**,Peigney, 52200 Langres, France; Tel:+33(0)3 25 90 27 79; Email:contact@camping-liez.fr ; www.campingliez.com; Price:C; *Chalets caravans and safari tents available*

Peigney
🏠 **Centre Culturel Haut-Marnais - Liez**,9 rue de la Plage, 52200 Peigney, France; Tel:+33(0)3 25 87 05 92; Email:cchm.liez@orange.fr; www.cchm52.fr; Price:B; *Evening meal and breakfast available*

Leaving Les Archots — Vagner Rosas

Torcenay to Champlitte

stage 34

Length:	35.8km
Ascent:	1066m
Descent:	1163m
Canterbury	815km
Col Grand Saint Bernard:	424km

Château - Champlitte

Route: this very long stage of the "Official Route", from Torcenay to Champlitte, continues on a meandering course on minor roads and often on muddy forest tracks with difficult water crossings and bypasses the Sigeric *submansione* of Grenant (LXII).

The Alternate Routes offer more direct options, saving 6.5 km and make for easier progress for all groups.

If you wish to break the journey then accommodation is available in a number of intermediate villages, although shops and cafés remain scarce.

*Champlitte is a small but very pilgrim aware town despite not lying directly on the probable Sigeric route. The tourist office has played a significant role in the rejuvenation of the route in the area and also elsewhere in France. On the Roman road close to the junction with the Les Archots route lies the **Hôpital de Grosse Sauve**. Records show that this pilgrim hospital was once in the possession of the Mormant Abbey.*

(0.0) From the junction with the D26 in Torcenay, follow the main road towards the centre of the village["Circuit Le Diable du Foultot"]**(0.2)**Turn right towards the grocery store[Direction Salle des Fetes]**(0.3)**At the crossroads, continue straight ahead[Direction Salle des Fetes]**(0.7)**Immediately after emerging from the tunnel, continue straight ahead on the tarmac road[Pass a pond on your left] **(1.2)**Continue straight ahead on the broad track, avoiding the small track to your left[Cross the bridge]**(1.5)**At the T-junction with the tarmac road, turn left downhill into the hamlet of le Foultot[Water trough on your left]**(1.7)** At the end of the tarmac, bear right and then left over the concrete bridge **(2.0)**At the T-junction at the top of the rise, turn right **(2.7)**At the T-junction at the bottom of the hill, turn left on the narrow track[Meadow on your right]**(2.9)**Continue straight ahead on the partially overgrown track[Ignore the broad track to your left]**(3.0)**Turn right on the small track. With care, cross the steep sided river ford to the left of the collapsed bridge**(3.5)**At the T-junction with the broad green fire-break, turn right on the track **(4.0)**At the start of the tarmac, turn left on the forest track**(4.5)**Take the right fork**(4.6)**At the junction in the tracks, continue straight ahead**(4.9)**At the crossroads at the top of the rise, after crossing the stream, cross the tarmac road and continue straight ahead on the forest track uphill[Chalindrey - 7 km]**(4.9)**At the crossroads in the track, continue straight ahead up the hill **(5.0)**At the T-junction with the tarmac road at the top of the hill, bear left and remain on the tarmac **(7.8)**At the T-junction in the road, turn right**(8.7)**At the T-junction with the more major road, turn left towards Grenant on the Voie Romaine, D136. Note:-

stage 34 — Torcenay to Champlitte

the Alternate Route joins from the right. Part of the 12th century pilgrim hospital of Grosse-Sauve can be seen on the left beyond the farm**(8.8)**Turn right on the small tarmac road, direction Ferme de Montficon. Note:- to visit **Grenant (LXII) exit** straight ahead on the Alternate Route [VF sign, Rivières le Bois - 4km] **(10.7)**Pass between the farm buildings and continue straight ahead on the gravel track**(11.5)**At the T-junction in the gravel tracks, turn right **(12.3)**Continue straight ahead on the tarmac road. Note:- for the more direct Alternate Route, turn left[VF sign, Rivières le Bois - 1km]**(13.2)** At the T-junction, turn right[Towards the church] **(13.4)**At the crossroads in **Rivières-le-Bois**, beside the bus stop, turn left["Circuit de Vallon de la Resaigne"]**(13.5)**In front of house n° 6, turn left direction "Aire de Jeux et de Detente"**(13.8)**Bear right onto a farm track between the fields **(14.7)**Continue straight ahead[Over the bridge]**(15.0)**At the top of the hill and behind the

church, turn sharp left onto the grass track[Pass between the well and the disused lavoir] **(15.5)**At the T-junction, turn left on rue Rente Gabrielle["Circuit de Vallon de la Resaigne", Maâtz - 6km]**(15.6)**Take the left fork, on the D122, direction Grandchamp **(15.9)**Shortly after passing the stone crucifix, bear right on the gravel track["Circuit de Vallon de la Resaigne"] **(17.3)**Take the right fork, uphill on the stony track**(18.0)**At the junction with

Torcenay to Champlitte — stage 34

the tarmac road, continue straight ahead on the tarmac[Barns on your right]**(18.2)**Take the left fork. At the end of the tarmac, beside the stone building, follow the narrow grass track **(18.9)**At the crossroads in the woods, turn left**(19.6)**Turn left**(19.6)**At the T-junction in the tracks, turn right, slightly downhill **(20.7)**At the crossroads, with a tarmac road, turn left towards the centre of Maâtz[Maâtz Centre - 0.5km]**(21.1)**At the road junction, continue straight ahead. Note:- the direct routee joins from the left[Direction Coublanc]**(21.3)**Cross the river, la Resaigne, and turn left uphill towards the church[Pass a bus shelter on your right]**(21.4)**In the centre of **Maâtz**, turn right, keeping the church on your left[Coublanc - 1.5 km (in fact 2km)]**(21.5)**At the crossroads, continue straight ahead on the D7, towards Coublanc**(21.7)**Turn left on the farm track. Note:- the "Official Route" makes a dog-leg and returns to this road. You may wish to remain on the D7 to Coublanc and save 600m [VF sign, Coublanc - 2km] **(22.3)**At the T-junction in the track, turn right towards the church in the valley[Open field on your right]**(23.2)**Return to the D7 at the T-junction in Coublanc, turn left[VF sign, Haute Saône - 3km] **(23.4)**At the crossroads in the centre of **Coublanc**, continue straight ahead[D122, direction Champlitte]**(23.6)**Bear left into place des Halles and cross the place[Pass the war memorial on your left]**(23.7)**Turn right on rue de la Barre[Pass house n° 1 on your left]**(23.7)**At the T-junction, turn left towards the No Through Road**(23.8)**Bear right over the stone foot-bridge and at the end of the bridge bear left on the road**(23.9)**At the T-junction, turn left**(24.0)**At the T-junction, turn right[Towards the farm]**(24.2)**At the end of the tarmac, continue straight ahead[Grass track between the fields and parallel to the D122] **(24.7)**At the junction with the gravel track, continue straight ahead[Woodland to the left]**(25.0)**Continue straight ahead[Across the river] **(25.7)**At the T-junction, turn right on the broad track[Towards the wooded valley] **(27.3)**At the T-junction with the tarmac road, turn right, towards the church in **Leffond(27.6)** Just after the lavoir, turn left on rue de l'Eglise follow the road and pass the church on your right**(27.8)**At the T-junction, turn left into the cul-de-sac and take the path between the houses leading to the bridge over the river**(28.0)**At the T-junction with rue de Verdu, turn

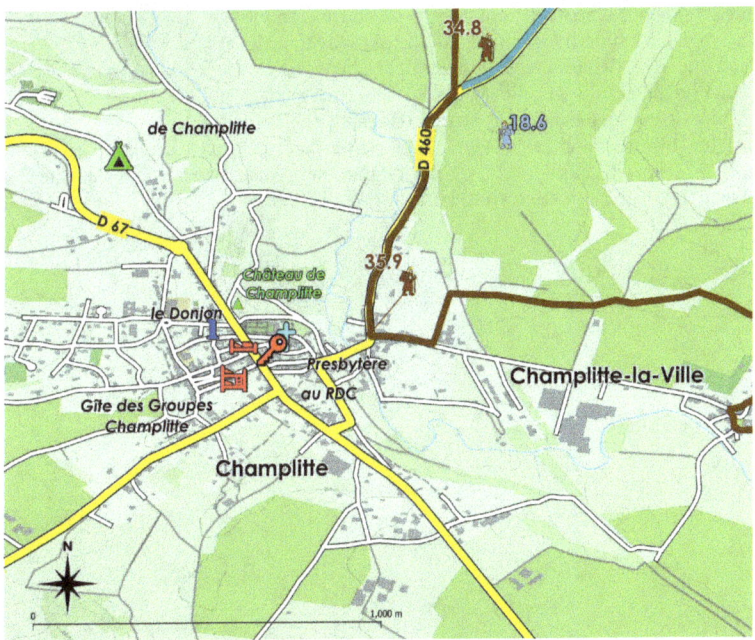

stage 34 — Torcenay to Champlitte

right and follow the road(28.2)Take the right fork with the stone cross on your left[Direction Montarlot - 4.1km] (30.5)Bear left on the track, towards the woods[Pass Moulin de la Bataille on your right] (31.9)At the T-junction with a tarmac road, turn right[A modern house directly ahead](32.5)Turn right towards the centre of Montarlot-lès-Champlitte[Cross the river bridge](32.6)At the crossroads, with the church to your left, continue straight ahead on the D222[Champlitte 3km, pilgrim sign](32.8)Turn left beside the barn (33.0) Cross the river and continue with the large farm buildings on your left (34.8)At the T-junction with the tarmac road, turn right. Note:- the alternate route via Grenant joins from the left (35.9)Arrive at **Champlitte** at the junction to Champlitte-la-Ville. Note:- continue straight ahead for accommodation and the tourist office.

From the Grosse Sauve via Grenant (LXII)

Route: follows the line of the Roman road, now sadly a route departmentale via the *submansione* of Grenant (LXII). Although the road may be busy it benefits from broad grass verges.　(0.0)Continue straight ahead on the D136[Pass the pilgrim hospital of **Grosse-Sauve** on your left] (5.7)At the T-junction, turn left[Direction Grenant, D7] (7.0)Shortly after passing the church in **Grenant (LXII)**, continue straight ahead on the small road[No Entry](7.2)At the T-junction with the route départmentale, bear right[Woods on the left, crash barrier on the right](7.5)Bear left on D17 (13.5)At the crossroads, turn right[Direction Champlitte, **D460**] (18.6)At the junction, continue straight ahead on the road to rejoin the "official route"

Length:	18.6km
Ascent:	334m
Descent:	461m

Direct Route to Maâtz

Route: by remaining on the normally quiet road through Grandchamp approximately 5 km may be saved from this long stage.(0.0)Turn left on the tarmac road(1.0)At the Stop sign at the entry to Grandchamp, continue straight ahead down the hill[Pass the metal railings on the right] (1.1)Turn right over the bridge[River la Resaigne](1.2)After crossing the bridge, turn right[Towards the church](1.3)Take the left fork, direction Champlitte[Church on the right](1.8)Keep left[Uphill] (3.6)At the T-junction in Maâtz, turn left. Note:- the GR®145 joins from the right[Direction Coublanc, towards church]

Length:	3.6km
Ascent:	50m
Descent:	56m

Torcenay to Champlitte — stage 34

Accommodation and Tourist Information

Champlitte
Gîte des Groupes - Champlitte,13 rue du Marché, 70600 Champlitte, France; Tel:+33(0)03 84 97 10 75 ; +33(0)6 84 332329; Email:gite-champlitte@orange.fr; www.gites-de-france.com/fr/bourgogne-franche-comte/haute-saone/gite-de-groupe-champlitte-70g2; Price:C; *Available to pilgrims with credentials*

Presbytère,14 rue de l'Église, 70600 Champlitte, France; Tel:+33(0)384651551; www.diocese-besancon.fr/paroisse-arcau-treychamplitte

Hôtel - le Donjon,46 rue de la République, 70600 Champlitte, France; Tel:+33(0)3 84 67 66 95; Email:hotel.du.donjon@wanadoo.fr; www.hotel-restaurant-du-donjon.com; Price:B

Apartment - au RDC[Harold Amouna],NUL9 Rue du BourgL, 70600 Champlitte, France; Tel: Booking.com; Price:B

Camping de Champlitte,Route de Leffond, 70600 Champlitte, France; Tel:+33(0)6 82 25 31 61; www.bourgognefranchecomte.com/campings/camping-de-champlitte; Price:C; *Chalets also available Open mid-April to mid October*

Office de Tourisme,2 Allée du Sainfoin, 70600 Champlitte, France; Tel:+33(0)3 84 67 67 19; www.entresaoneetsalon.fr

Grandchamp
Chambre d'Hôtes - la Vallée Verte,8 rue du Cul de Sac, 52600 Grandchamp, France; Tel:+33(0)659 814 564; +33 (0) 760 085 169; Email:contact@lavalleeverte.eu; lavalleeverte.eu; Price:A

Leffond
Accueil Pèlerin - le Moulin de la Papeterie,Route de Coublanc, 70600 Leffond, France; Tel:+33(0)3 84 67 69 09; +33(0)6 42 00 41 19; Email:marber.gautheron@gmail.com; Price:B; *Price includes evening meal*

Chambre d'Hôtes - Elle V[Valérie Lamotte],10 rue de Verdu, 70600 Leffond, France; Tel:+33(0)3 84 67 88 38; +33(0)6 65 08 95 48; Email:ellev@orange.fr; www.ellev.fr; Price:B; *Evening meal possible*

Saint-Broingt-le-Bois
Salle Seignière - Gîte de Groupe,10 rue de la Seignière, 52190 Saint-Broingt-le-Bois, France; Tel:+33(0)6 89 27 88 73; www.traiteur-du-moge.fr; Price:C

stage 35 — Champlitte to Dampierre-sur-Salon

Length:	18.6km
Ascent:	480m
Descent:	505m
Canterbury	851km
Col Grand Saint Bernard:	388km

The Mairie Lavoir - Dampierre-sur-Salon

Route: this short and generally flat stage, from Champlitte to Dampierre-sur-Salon, will follow farm tracks and minor roads to the small town of Dampierre.

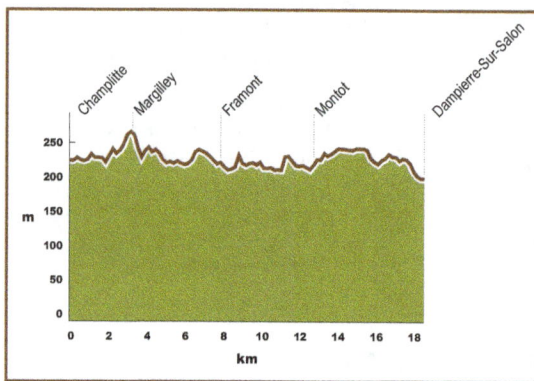

In addition to the GR®145 signs in the region to the Swiss border you will also encounter more informal via Francigena signs with yellow and white painted arrows or pilgrims. There have been a number of interpretations of the route in the area and so beware following signs leading away from the route described.

As previously, the route will make use of existing GR® paths that link and cross our trail and may also mislead.

Accommodation is once more limited in Dampierre. You may prefer to try Seveux which will also reduce the challenge of the next stage.

In the 19th century wine making was the third largest industry in Haute-Saone. Unfortunately, in 1886, the blight of phylloxera reached Champlitte and annihilated its vineyards. In a few months, 80% of the slopes that were the pride of the village for more than 400 years disappeared and subsequently the vines were abandoned for general agriculture until in 1960 when the first of the new vines was planted.

Champlitte vines

Champlitte to Dampierre-sur-Salon   stage 35

(0.0) From the junction between the D17 and D460 take the road in the direction of Champlitte-la-Ville**(0.2)** Turn left onto chemin de St Jean**(0.4)** At the end of the farm yard, turn right through the trees and continue on the track parallel to the main road **(1.5)** At the T-junction with the tarmac road, turn right to continue into Champlitte-la-Ville**(1.8)** At the T-junction, turn left and then turn left again immediately after the church[Route de Margilley] **(3.3)** In the village of **Margilley**, turn right onto the small rue de la Fontaine**(3.4)** At the T-junction, turn right onto the tarmac road and then keep left to skirt the field[Lavoir on your right]**(4.1)** At the road junction, turn right[Crucifix on your right] **(4.8)** Turn left onto the track[Between the fields]**(5.5)** Take the right fork **(7.9)** On entering the village of **Framont**, turn right[Towards the church]**(8.1)** At the T-junction beside the Mairie, turn right**(8.4)** Take the left fork, D36 [Direction Gray]**(8.7)** Immediately after passing the garden centre, take the first turning to the left on the gravel track **(10.1)** At the T-junction with a tarmac road, turn left[Pass a large commercial building on your left]**(10.3)** At the next T-junction, turn left and then bear right[Pass green metal gates on your left]**(10.5)** At the T-junction at the bottom of a small hill, turn left on the road[Walled garden on the left]**(10.6)** Just before reaching the bridge over le Salon, turn right on the gravel track[Montot - 2.6km] **(10.8)** Take the left fork, uphill towards the trees **(11.8)** At the T-junction with the road, turn left on the road[Montot 1.4km]**(11.9)** Turn right on the tarmac road[Long straight road towards the village]**(12.7)** As the road bears right, bear left on the partially gravelled track, towards the village of Montot[Conifers on your left]**(12.8)** At the junction with the road, turn left[Enter **Montot**] **(13.0)** At the Stop sign, continue straight ahead on the D171[Direction Denèvre]**(13.6)** At the junction at the exit from Montot, continue straight ahead on the D171[Pass a cemetery on your left]**(13.8)** As the D171, bends to the left, fork

stage 35 Champlitte to Dampierre-sur-Salon

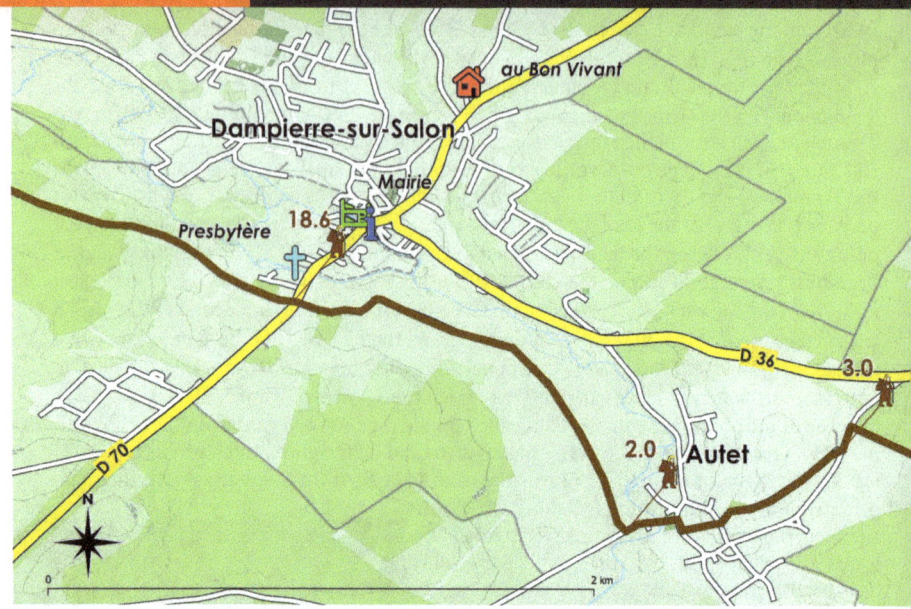

right on the small road[Pass a disused quarry on your left] **(15.0)** At the T-junction with the road, turn left**(15.9)** At the T-junction, beside the barns, turn right **(18.6)** Arrive at **Dampierre-sur-Salon**. Note:- the town centre and facilities are to the left[Crossroads with the busy D70]

Accommodation and Tourist Information

Dampierre-sur-Salon

Mairie,Place de la Mairie, 70180 Dampierre-sur-Salon, France; Tel:+33(0)384671430; Email:mairie@dampierresursalon.fr; www.dampierre-sur-salon.fr; Price:D; *4 camp beds available Reserve by phone or email when a code will be provided to a key lockbox at the Mairie. If you are unable to contact the Mairie during busioness hours then use the emergency number +33(0)786005327*

Presbytère,Rue du Presbytère, 70180 Dampierre-sur-Salon, France; Tel:+33(0)3 84 67 11 55

Chambre d'Hôtes - au Bon Vivant,22 rue des Orgevaux, 70180 Dampierre-sur-Salon, France; Tel:+33(0)3 63 65 00 55; +33(0)9 80 59 81 82; Email:christophe@desre.net; www.au-bon-vivant.fr; Price:B;
PR

Office du Tourisme des 4 Rivières,2 Bis rue Jean Mourey, 70180 Dampierre-sur-Salon, France; Tel:+33(0)3 84 67 16 94; Email:ot4rivieres@gmail.com

Dampierre-sur-Salon to Bucey-lès-Gy stage 36

Length:	34.7km
Ascent:	788m
Descent:	758m
Canterbury	870km
Col Grand Saint Bernard:	369km

Putting the Seveux lavoir to good use

Route: the "Official Route", from Dampierre-sur-Salon to Bucey-lès-Gy, makes a long wide arc to the east to regain Sigeric's route at Seveux (LX) and then continues east to avoid the busy D5. After a short stretch by the river Saône and the Seveux-Savoyeux canal the route comprises farm tracks and minor roads.

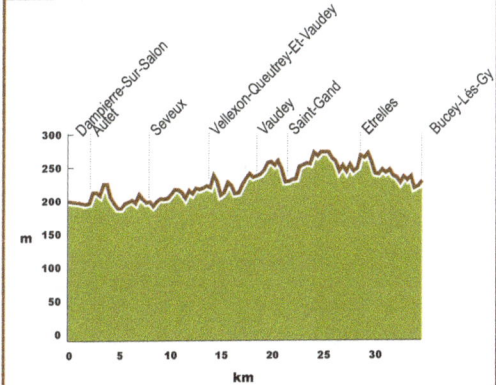

Unfortunately there are no opportunities to shorten this long stage without encountering the busy D5 road. Seveux has a shop and a struggling café, but the smaller villages en route have no other facilities for shopping or eating.

There are accommodation options off-piste but on the route there is no accommodation between Seveux and Bucey-lès-Gy.

The Saône has always been the most navigable of French rivers, with a very gentle gradient and regular flow, although subject to floods. The Roman general Vetus envisaged a canal from the Saône to the Moselle. Over the centuries canalisation, locks and tunnels (including the one from Seveux to Savoyeux) have improved navigation.

Above the Seveux-Savoyeux tunnel

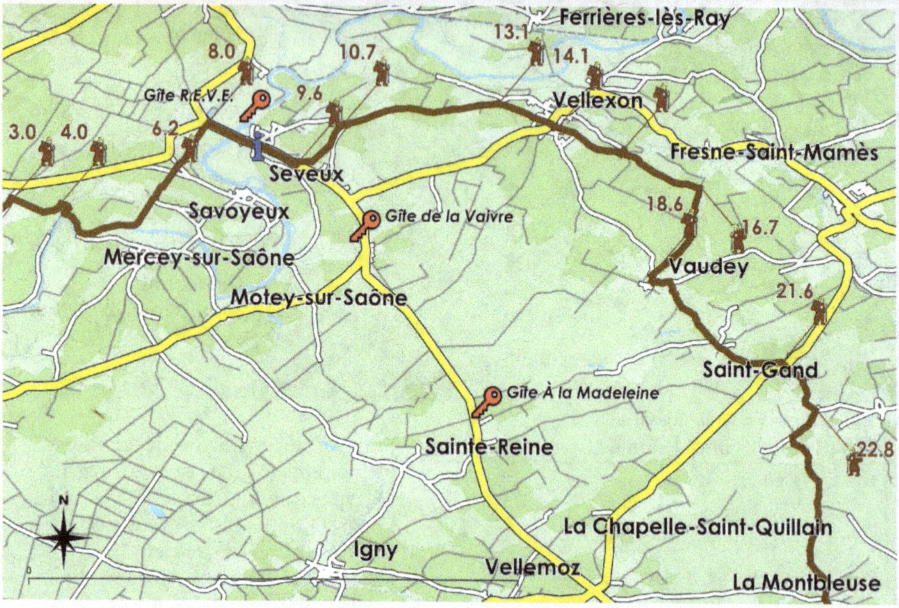

stage 36   Dampierre-sur-Salon to Bucey-lès-Gy

(0.0) From the end of the previous section, take the small road, rue de Grande Ligne to the east 🚶 **(2.0)** At the T-junction with the tarmac road, turn left [Towards the river bridge] **(2.2)** At the T-junction in **Autet**, turn right **(2.2)** Turn left on the pathway between the houses [Pass a walled garden on your right] **(2.4)** At the crossroads, continue straight ahead on rue de l'Eglise [Towards the church] 🚶 **(3.0)** At the T-junction with the more major road, turn left [Pass a large industrial building on your right] **(3.1)** Turn right on the track [Keep the car park close on your right] **(3.9)** Continue straight ahead [Avoid the bridge to your right] 🚶 **(4.0)** Bear right and then right again after passing through the tunnel under the railway [Towards the river] **(4.3)** Cross the small bridge and at the T-junction with the riverside track, turn left. Note:- to avoid the narrow bridge cyclists will need to divert through the woods and cross the stream [Cycle track beside the river] 🚶 **(6.2)** At the crossroads, continue straight ahead beside the canal [Canal enters the Seveux-Savoyeux tunnel tunnel ahead] **(6.9)** At the crossroads, continue straight ahead on the small road into the woods ["Rives de Saône" sign] 🚶 **(8.0)** At the T-junction with the main road, beside the canal bridge, turn right on the D5 towards **Seveux (LX)** [Cross the river bridge] 🚶 **(9.3)** Turn left onto rue des Corvées **(9.6)** Turn right onto the track 🚶 **(10.7)** Turn right over the bridge and immediately left 🚶 **(13.1)**

Dampierre-sur-Salon to Bucey-lès-Gy   stage 36

Take the right fork, towards the village**(13.9)**At the crossroads in the centre of **Vellexon-Queutrey-et-Vaudey**, continue straight ahead[Rue Saint-Martin] **(14.1)**Keep left and pass a large house directly on your right **(15.3)**Turn right to cross a small bridge and then turn left[Keep the woods on your left] **(16.7)**Turn right at the T-junction **(18.6)**At the T-junction in **Vaudey**, turn left onto the tarmac road and then take the next left[Rue Saint-Gand] **(19.0)**Turn right[Direction Saint-Gand] **(21.6)**At the crossroads in **Saint-Gand**, continue straight ahead[Direction la Vernotte] **(22.8)**In the hamlet of le Charme, turn right on the road[Towards the forest Bois de St-Gand] **(23.4)**Turn left and pass through the forest[Towards the hamlet of La Montbleuse] **(28.7)**In **Etrelles**, turn left and then immediately right onto ruelle de la Riotte. Bear left and left again beside the lavoir**(29.0)**Short-

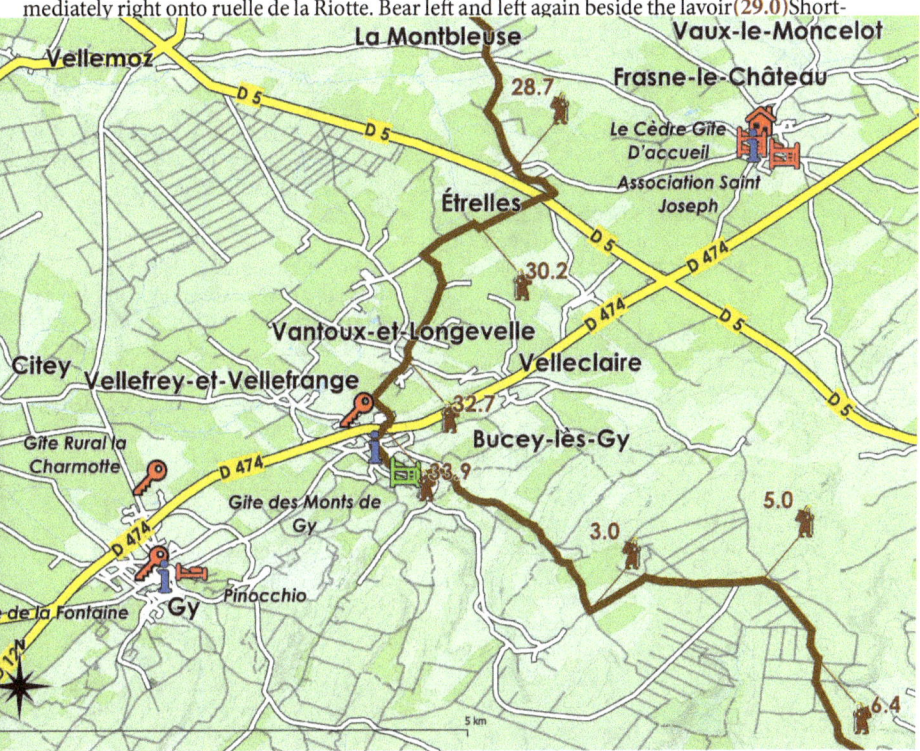

ly after passing the lavoir, bear right onto the grass track**(29.3)**Pass the church on your right, then turn right**(29.5)**Cross the main road and continue straight ahead[Pass a cemetery on your right] **(30.2)**Turn right and then left on the track**(31.0)**Turn left and continue towards the village of Vantoux-et-Longevelle **(32.7)**At the junction in the village centre, continue straight ahead[Pass the memorial on your right]**(32.9)**Take the right fork and again pass a memorial on your right**(33.4)**Turn left and continue towards the church[Pass an orchard on your right] **(33.9)**Cross the main road and continue into the village of Bucey-lès-Gy**(34.1)**In the square, turn left onto rue du Canal**(34.5)**Take the left fork[Chemin des Ecoliers]**(34.7)**Arrive at **Bucey-lés-Gy** beside the Gîte des Monts de Gy

stage 36 — Dampierre-sur-Salon to Bucey-lès-Gy

Accommodation and Tourist Information

Bucey-lès-Gy

Gîte des Monts de Gy,7 Chemin des Écoliers, 70700 Bucey-lès-Gy, France; Tel:+33(0)3 84 32 88 34; +33(0)7 82 52 94 98; Email:gite.montsdegy@gmail.com; sites.google.com/site/gitedesmontsdegy; Price:C

Gîte - Chez les Domdoms,14, rue des Estelins, 70700 Bucey-lès-Gy, France; Tel:+33(0)384329533; +33(0)641131344; Email:lesdomdoms@orange.fr; www.ot-montsdegy.com; Price:C

Mairie,3 rue du Canal, 70700 Bucey-lès-Gy, France; Tel:+33(0)3 84 32 82 78; Email:mairie-bucey-les-gy@wanadoo.fr; buceylesgy.fr

Frasne-le-Château

Association Saint Joseph,Rue Saint-Joseph, 70700 Frasne-le-Château, France; Tel:+33(0)3 84 32 48 00; Email:cep@ahs-fc.fr; www.ahs-fc.fr/etablissement.php?idM=3&idE=8

Le Cèdre - Gîte D'accueil,3 rue du Château, 70700 Frasne-le-Château, France; Tel:+33(0)3 84 32 41 68; Price:C; *Book via the Mairie*

Chambre d'Hôtes - Chateau de Frasne,1 rue de l'Eglise, 70700 Frasne-le-Château, France; Tel:+33(0)3 47 05 79 43 6; Email:info@frasnelechateau.net; frasnelechateau.net; Price:A; *Dinner available opens May15 to July 31*

Mairie - Frasne-le-Château,2 B rue du Château, 70700 Frasne-le-Château, France; Tel:+33(0)3 84 32 41 68; Email:mairie.frasne.hte.saone@wandoo.fr; frasne-le-chateau.fr

Gy

Hotel - Pinocchio,3 rue Beauregard, 70700 Gy, France; Tel:+33(0)6 72 00 25 52; Email:info@hotel-gy.fr; www.hotel-gy.fr; Price:A

Gîte Rural - la Charmotte,24route de la Chapelle-Saint-Quillain, 70700 Gy, France; Tel:+33(0)6 47 69 35 20; Email:contact@gitegy.frr; www.gitegy.fr; Price:A

Gîte - de la Fontaine[Laurent Coutout & Solène Guillet],43 Grande rue, 70700 Gy, France; Tel:+33(0)3 84 32 89 34; +33(0)6 64 32 21 10; Email:laurent.coutout@sfr.fr; www.destination70.com/dormir/meubles-et-gites/F354000209_gite-de-la-fontaine-a-gy-gy.html; Price:B

Office du Tourisme - Monts de Gy,11 Grande rue, 70700 Gy, France; Tel:+33(0)3 84 32 93 93; +33(0)7 72 39 42 55; Email:ot.montsdegy@orange.fr; www.ot-montsdegy.com

La Chapelle-Saint-Quillain

Gîte - À la Madeleine,4 rue des Lumiaux, 70700 La Chapelle-Saint-Quillain, France; Tel:+33(0)3 84 32 22 26; www.facebook.com/GitealaMadeleine; Price:B

Seveux

Gîte - de la Vaivre[Denis and Marie-Claude Coquard],5 rue de Besançon, 70130 Seveux, France; Tel:+33(0)3 84 32 99 13; +33(0)6 33 49 93 60; Email:contact@gitesdelavaivre.fr; gitesdelavaivre.fr; Price:A

Gîte - R.E.V.E.[Roger Varaut],1 rue de la Fourlotte, 70130 Seveux, France; Tel:+33(0)6 06 87 00 13; +33(0)3 84 31 21 43; Email:roger.varraut@orange.fr; gitereve.wixsite.com/gite-reve; Price:B; *Special price for pilgrims evening meal available*

Mairie,10 Grande Rue, 70130 Seveux, France; Tel:+33(0)3 84 67 10 95; mairie-seveux.fr

Bucey-lès-Gy to Besançon

stage 37

Length:	31.9km
Ascent:	812m
Descent:	795m
Canterbury	904km
Col Grand Saint Bernard:	335km

Pont Battant - Besançon

Route: the stage, from Bucey-lès-Gy to Besançon, begins on farm and woodland tracks but then continues substantially on road through the suburbs and then the centre of the city of Besançon.

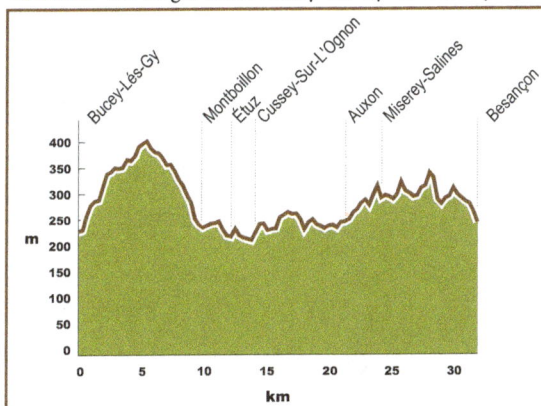

There are some surprisingly steep climbs in the suburbs but the city centre lies on floor of the river Doubs valley.

Cafés and shops can be found along the route from Cussey-sur-l'Ognon. École-Valentin offers a good choice of low cost hotels, while the city centre has a wide choice of accommodation and facilities.

Cradled in a loop of the river Doubs, at the foot of its towering citadel, the ancient city of Besançon is one of the best preserved historic cities in France. In pre-Roman times, it was the capital of an area known as Sequania.

When the area was conquered by the Romans, Julius Caesar described this naturally defensive site as the jewel in my crown.

Today Besançon is the capital of the region of Bourgogne-Franche-Comté and the department of Doubs, a thriving university town, and one of the more popular places to visit in eastern France.

The Citadel, a UNESCO World Heritage site and magnificent example of 17th-century military architecture, was designed by Vauban. It stands on a massive rock - sheer on both sides - blocking the entrance to the loop of the river Doubs. and overlooking the old centre of the city. The St. Jean Cathedral is built on the ground plan of an earlier Carolingian cathedral, with an altar at both ends. It also houses one of the great works from Fra Bartolomeo, as well as an astronomic clock. Just outside the cathedral is the Porte Noire, a Roman triumphal arch, principal vestige today of the Roman city that once stood on the site.

stage 37 Bucey-lès-Gy to Besançon

Cussey-sur-l'Ognon

(0.0) From the gîte in Bucey-lés-Gy, continue on chemin des Ecoliers and bear left up the hill **(0.2)** Turn right[Chemin de Folle] **(0.8)** Fork left[Remain on the tarmac] 🚶 **(3.0)** At the crossroads, turn left[Enter the forest] 🚶 **(5.0)** Take the right fork[Direction Montboillon] **(5.9)** Fork right onto a narrow path[Wider track on the left] 🚶 **(6.4)** Continue onto the gravel track ahead[Towards car park] **(6.7)** Continue straight ahead on the tarmac road 🚶 **(9.7)** In **Montboillon**, with the lavoir on your left, bear right and follow the grass track by the stream **(9.9)** At the road junction, turn right to cross the bridge **(9.9)** Turn left on the track[Rue de la Charriére] **(10.0)** Rejoin the road and turn left and then take the next left turn[Rue du Tremblois] 🚶 **(12.0)** Turn left at the T-junction **(12.2)** Bear right on the road[Enter **Ètuz**] **(12.8)** At the T-junction with the main road, turn right on the D3[Towards the tabac] **(12.9)** Keep left on the D3 in Ètuz towards the river bridge[Direction Cussey-sur-l'Ognon] 🚶 **(14.0)** At the junction beside the Auberge in **Cussey-sur-l'Ognon** (LX) bear left

Bucey-lès-Gy to Besançon — stage 37

onto rue de Village[Climb the hill between the Mairie and the Auberge]**(14.2)**At the junction continue straight ahead. Note:- a former version of the route turned left here and so beware conflicting signs**(14.3)**Bear left to follow the main road. Then take the next turning to the right[Shortly before the cemetery, rue d'Auxon]**(14.8)**Turn right[Rue de Sauvagney] **(15.2)**Take the left fork and follow the track[Pass close to farm buildings on your left] **(15.9)**Turn left onto a narrow grass track[Track enters the woods]**(16.1)**Turn left on the track[Towards the road] **(16.2)**Turn right on the road and then left on the track **(18.0)** Cross over the road to continue on the track[Main road to your left at the junction] **(19.5)**At the roundabout, turn right to pass under the railway and then turn right at the next roundabout**(19.9)**Bear left towards factory buildings, then turn left on the track between the trees[Perpendicular to the railway line] **(20.7)**Continue straight ahead[Chemin du Grand Bois]**(21.2)**Continue straight ahead at the roundabout in **Auxon**[Chemin de Château]**(21.6)**Turn right into the park and follow the path with the small pavilion on your immediate left**(21.7)**Exit the park and take the small road up the hill between the trees. Turn right at the top of the hill[Follow chemin de Vaux] **(22.0)**Continue straight ahead on track[Parallel to the railway track] **(23.7)**At the T-junction with the road, turn right to go down the hill[Pass a cemetery on your right]**(23.8)**Turn left onto a small path and continue straight ahead. Pass a playground on your left and turn right on the main road beside the lavoir**(24.2)**Immediately after passing the church in **Miserey-Salines**, turn left and follow rue d'Ecole **(24.8)**At the roundabout continue straight ahead**(25.5)**Pass under the highway bridge**(25.7)**Turn right on the track into the woods **(26.7)**At the T-junction, turn left on the tarmac road[Rue du Ruisseau]**(26.8)**Turn right at the roundabout[Leave École-Valentin]**(27.2)**At the next roundabout, turn left and pass the déchéterrie on your left and follow chemin des Montboucons **(28.9)**Cross the highway bridge and continue straight ahead passing a series of roundabouts on avenue des Montboucons **(31.2)**In place Maréchal Leclerc, shortly after crossing the railway bridge, turn left and then bear right through the gap in the ramparts[Pass a car park on your right]**(31.5)**Bear right, downhill, on rue des Frères Mercier[No Entry sign]**(31.9)**Arrive at **Besançon (LIX)** centre on pont Battant

The Doubs Beneath the Citadel

stage 37 — Bucey-lès-Gy to Besançon

Accommodation and Tourist Information

Besançon
🏠 **Auberge de Jeunesse - Lles Oiseaux**,48 rue des Cras, 25000 Besançon, France; Tel:+33(0)3 81 40 32 00; Email:contact@hajlesoiseaux.fr; www.fjtlesoiseaux.fr/auberge-de-jeunesse; Price:B

🏠 **Ethic Etapes Cis Besançon**,3 avenue des Montboucons, 25000 Besançon, France; Tel:+33(0)3 81 50 07 54; Email:ethicetapes@cis-besancon.fr; cis-besancon.com; Price:B

🛏 **Espace Grammont**,20 rue Mégevand, 25000 Besançon, France; Tel:+33(0)3 81 25 17 19; Email:contact@espacegrammont.fr; Price:B; *Half board*

🛏 **Escale-Jeunes**,9 rue de la Convention, 25000 Besançon, France; Tel:+33(0)3 81 81 10 18 ; Email:escalejeunes@diocese-besancon.fr; www.diocese-besancon.fr/agir-particiiper/tu-es-jeune-tourne-vers-l-avenir/escale-jeunes; Price:C

🛏 **Franciscains de Besançon - Chapelle des Buis**,89 Chemin de la Chapelle des Buis, 25000 Besançon, France; Tel:+33(0)3 81 81 33 25; Email:franciscainsdesbuis@gmail.com ; www.chapelledesbuis.org; Price:C

🏠 **Chambre d'Hôtes - le Coin des Colverts**,46 Chemin de Mazagran, 25000 Besançon, France; Tel:+33(0)3 81 52 34 78; +33(0)6 07 72 94 18; Email:lecoinddescolverts@orange.fr; lecoindescolverts.free.fr; Price:B

🏠 **Chambre d'Hôtes - le Jardin de Velotte**,31 Chemin des Journaux, 25000 Besançon, France; Tel:+33(0)3 81 50 93 55; +33(0)7 87 76 84 12; Email:lejardindevelotte@orange.fr; lejardindevelotte.free.fr; Price:B; *Reductions possible for pilgrims*

🛏 **Hôtel - au Fil de l'Eau** ,48 Chemin de la Malate, 25000 Besançon, France; Tel:+33(0)3 81 82 15 16; www.lamalate.fr; Price:A; *Change of management*

🛏 **Hôtel - Ibis Besançon Centre Ville**,21 rue Gambetta, 25000 Besançon, France; Tel:+33(0)3 81 81 02 02; Email:h1364@accor.com; all.accor.com; Price:B

🛏 **Hôtel - Mercure Parc Micaud**,3 avenue Edouard Droz, 25000 Besançon, France; Tel:+33(0)3 81 40 34 34; Email:h1220@accor.com; all.accor.com; Price:A

🛏 **Hôtel - du Nord**,8 rue Moncey, 25000 Besançon, France; Tel:+33(0)3 81 81 34 56; Email:contact@hotel-du-nord-besancon.com; www.hotel-du-nord-besancon.com; Price:B

🛏 **Hôtel - Best Western Citadelle**,13 rue Gén Lecourbe, 25000 Besançon, France; Tel:+33(0)3 81 81 33 92; www.bestwestern-citadelle.com; Price:B

ℹ **Office du Tourisme**,52 Grande rue, 25000 Besançon, France; Tel:+33(0)3 81 80 92 55; Email:info@besancon-tourisme.com; www.besancon-tourisme.com

Bonnevent-Velloreille
🔑 **Gîte - Chez Louise**,2 route de Chaux, 70700 Bonnevent-Velloreille, France; Tel:+33(0)3 84 32 45 49; Email:jcardinal@wanadoo.fr; chez-louise-bonnevent.fr; Price:A

Chalezeule
⛺ **Camping de Besançon**,12 route de Belfort, 25220 Chalezeule, France; Tel:+33(0)3 81 88 04 26; campingdebesancon.com; Price:C; *Mobile homes also available*

Cussey-sur-l'Ognon
ℹ **Mairie**,18 Grande rue, 25870 Cussey-sur-l'Ognon, France; Tel:+33(0)3 81 57 78 62; Email:mairiedecusseysurlognon@orange.fr; www.mairie-cussey.fr; *The Mairie is actively seeking accommodation options*

École-Valentin
🛏 **Hôtel - Première Classe,** 7 route d'Epinal, 25480 École-Valentin, France; Tel:+33(0)3 81 50 37 11; Email:besancon@premiereclasse.fr; www.premiereclasse.com; Price:B

Bucey-lès-Gy to Besançon — stage 37

Hôtel - Campanile Ecole Valentin, 1 rue de Châtillon, 25048 École-Valentin, France; Tel:+33(0)3 81 53 52 22; Email:besancon.valentin@campanile.fr; www.campanile.com; Price:B

Hôtel - Ibis Budget - Besançon Nord, 1 rue de la Poste, 25048 École-Valentin, France; Tel:+33(0)8 92 70 12 88; Email:h6888@accor.com; all.accor.com; Price:B

Geneuille

Hôtel - Château de la Dame Blanche, 1 Chemin de la Goulotte, 25870 Geneuille, France; Tel:+33(0)3 81 57 64 64; Email:contact@chateau-de-la-dame-blanche.fr; www.chateau-de-la-dame-blanche.fr; Price:A

Camping - les Peupliers, 18 rue des Papetiers, 25870 Geneuille, France; Tel:+33(0)6 81 16 48 33; Email:campingpeupliers@orange.fr; camping-peupliers-doubs.fr; Price:C; *Mobile homes may be available*

stage 37 — Bucey-lès-Gy to Besançon

La Porte Noire - Besançon

Besançon to Ornans

stage 38

Length:	37.6km
Ascent:	1874m
Descent:	1780m
Canterbury	936km
Col Grand Saint Bernard:	303km

The river Loue at Ornans Zairon

Route: the stage from Besançon to Ornans initially climbs very steeply to the Chapelle des Buis and the Monument de Libération. This initial section will be very challenging for heavily packed walkers and cyclists. To avoid the climb, buses are available from place St Jacques to Chapelle des Buis. Trains, which carry bikes, run regularly to Saône where the station is just 1.5 km from the closest part of the "Official Route".

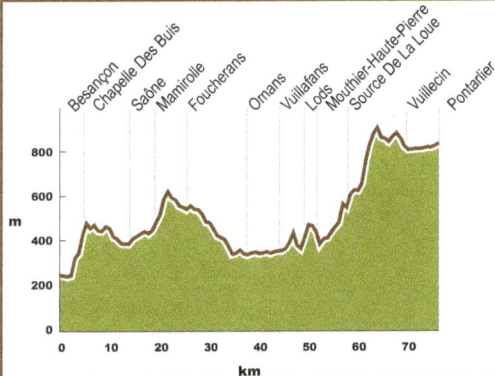

After the Monument de Libération the route proceeds through a mixture of woodland and farm tracks and minor roads. There are a number of interpretations of the route in this area. Our primary trail follows the route endorsed by the AEVF. However, you will note that it makes a very long loop to avoid the use of a minor road. Our Alternative Route will reduce the stage by 8.5 km.

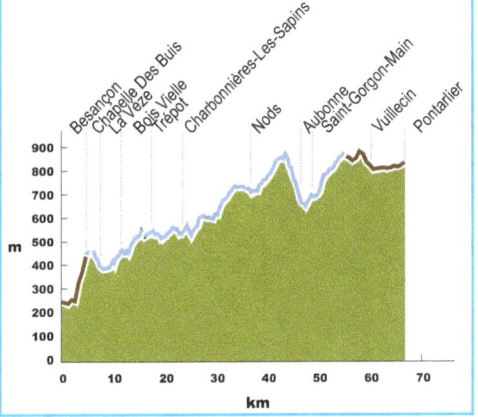

Beyond Foucherans there is a choice to follow the scenic Loue valley - the route endorsed by the AEVF - or to pass closer to the Sigeric route via the *submansione* of Nods (XVII). The Loue valley can be very busy in the holiday season and you are advised to carefully plan your itinerary and book accommodation 1 or 2 days in advance. Cyclists should be aware that at the head of the valley there is a very steep pathway that is impassable on bikes. Also note that the Gorges de Nouailles at the head of the Loue valley have suffered from land slides and subject to closure. The tourist

stage 38 — Besançon to Ornans

office in Ornans will advise on the current situation and any diversions.

Ornans, the birth place and subject of many paintings of Gustave Courbet, is an archetypal Franche-Comté town that has become the focal point of the Loue valley. Here, the river Loue is an abrupt trench with the water washing the foundations of ancient balconied houses.

When I stop being controversial, I'll stop being important, Gustave Courbet wrote to his parents in 1852.

(0.0) From Pont Battant, turn right and head south-west on quai Vauban and follow the waterside path **(2.1)** After crossing the bridge with the tunnel to your left, turn right down the ramp [Pass the lock on your right] **(2.5)** At the next bridge, continue straight ahead be-

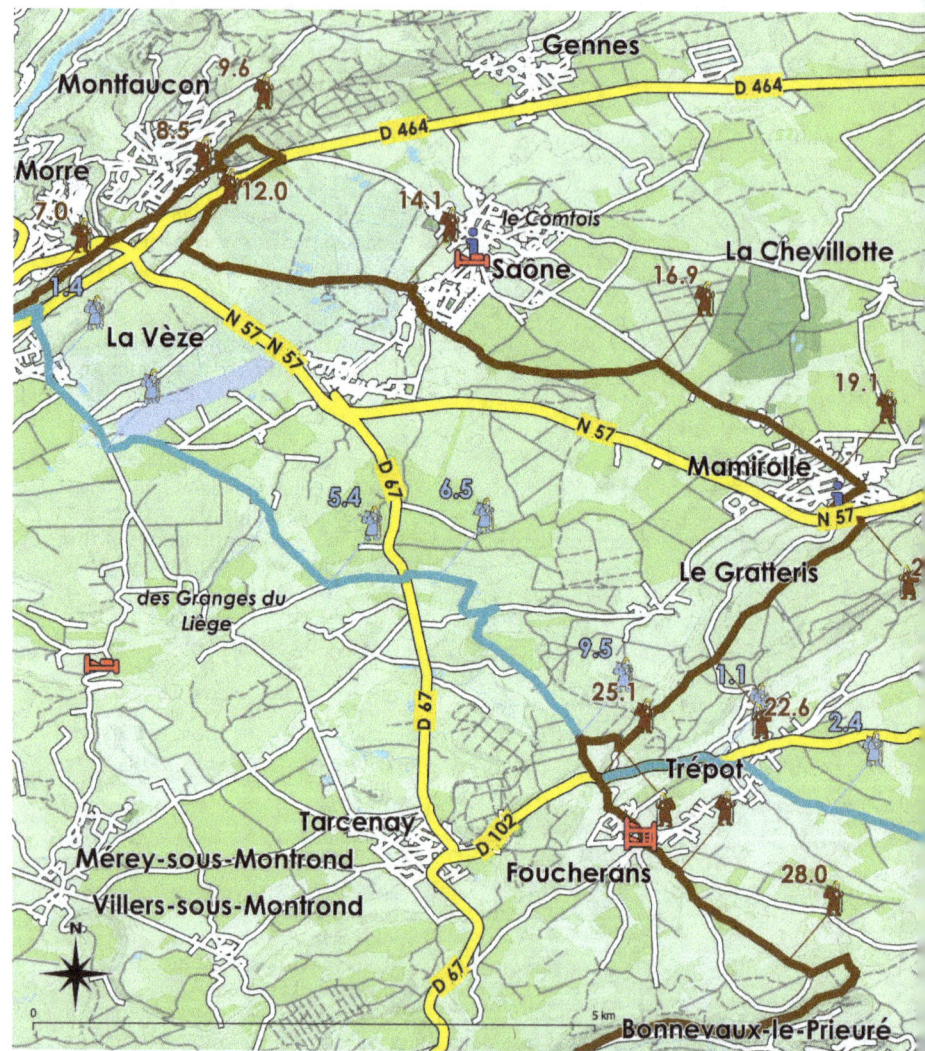

Besançon to Ornans — stage 38

Chapelle des Buis

side the river[Metal railings beside the ramp]**(2.8)**Take the pedestrian crossing, turn right and then sharp left: Note:- the "Official Route" will climb a number of steep and long flights of steps. Cyclists and those wishing an easier climb should take the less sharp turning to the left, chemin de Malpas, and follow the signs to Chapelle des Buis[No Through Road, chemin de la Petite Creuse] **(3.1)**At the T-junction with the road at the top of the steps, turn left on the road. Note:- cyclists etc. join from the right[Wooden crash barrier on the right at the junction] **(3.2)**At the crossroads, turn sharp right[Direction Chapelle des Buis]**(3.6)**Remain on the road and bear left joining chemin de la Chapelle des Buis**(3.7)**Take the right fork on the tarmac track. Note:- there are more steps ahead, to avoid these remain on the road and continue to follow the road signs for Chapelle des Buis**(3.8)** At the T-junction with a small road, cross over and climb the grassy track ahead**(4.0)**At the crossroads with a broad gravel track, continue straight ahead up the hill**(4.1)**At the crossroads with a tarmac road, continue straight ahead**(4.1)**At the crossroads with the partially gravelled track, continue straight ahead**(4.2)**At the crossroads with a tarmac road, continue straight ahead across the grass and bear right on the more major road. Note:- those taking the road route rejoin from the left[Pass house n° 44 on your right] **(4.5)**Turn sharp left remaining on the road. Ignore the path to the right[Wooden crucifix in the trees on your right]**(4.9)**Pass the **Chapelle des Buis** on your left and wonderful views over Besançon and la Citadelle and then immediately turn left. Note:- the track ahead includes a steep downhill section that could be difficult for cyclists in the wet. To avoid this remain on the D144 until the track emerges from the left[Direction Monument de la Libération]**(5.3)**With the metal bridge leading to the Monument de la Libération ahead, turn right on the stony track**(5.5)**At the T-junction with the broad track, turn right downhill **(5.6)**At the junction in the tracks, continue straight ahead[Avoid the turning to the right]**(5.7)**At the T-junction with the road, turn left. Note:- those taking the road option rejoin from the right**(6.2)**At the crossroads, continue straight ahead briefly and then bear right on the stony track into the woods[Pass beside the gate of house n° 1]**(6.4)**Take the left fork. Note:- the direct route to Foucherans leaves to the right [Parallel to the highway below] **(7.0)**At the crossroads in the tracks, continue straight ahead[Remain parallel to the main road] **(7.9)**Join the tarmac road and continue between the houses. At the junction take the second road on the right[Rue de Montfaucon] **(8.5)**At the end of the road, turn left and then take the right fork[Chemin de Rochefort]**(9.4)**At the end of the road, turn sharp left, uphill **(9.6)**Turn right onto the smaller track into woods, downhill[Beside the house, Soirée du Bois]**(10.0)**Turn right**(10.3)**On leaving the woods, bear left towards the roundabout. Take the second exit and immediately turn right on the track, below and parallel to the D464 **(12.0)**After passing the farm buildings, turn left on the track between open fields **(14.1)** At the end of the track bear left and then right at the T-junction, uphill[Enter **Saône**]**(14.4)** At the top of the hill, turn right and then left onto rue des Planchettes**(14.6)**At the crossroads, continue straight ahead and follow rue des Genévrieres **(16.9)**At the T-junction with the road, turn right and follow the road to Mamirolle **(19.1)**In the centre of **Mamirolle**, continue straight ahead through the pedestrian tunnel under the railway and then

stage 38 — Besançon to Ornans

follow rue de la Gare uphill**(19.4)**Beside the memorial, turn right[Towards the church]**(20.0)**After crossing the highway bridge, turn left onto chemin de Mont 🚶 **(20.3)** Take the first turning to the right and follow the track uphill into the woods 🚶 **(22.6)**Cross over road and continue downhill[Take the left hand small track] 🚶 **(24.0)** At the junction, turn right on the tarmac road**(24.5)**At the T-junction, turn left. Note:- the shorter alternate route joins from the right**(24.7)**Beside the Chapelle St Maximin continue straight ahead down the grassy slope**(24.8)**At the bottom of the path cross the stile and continue across the field[Towards the road and the lavoir] 🚶 **(25.1)**At the road junction, continue straight ahead on the D112e towards Foucherans. Note:- the

Chapelle Saint-Maximin - Foucherans

Besançon to Ornans
stage 38

"Official Route" follows the scenic vallée de la Loue. The route provides more options for eating and accommodation. However, while initially easy going for all groups, the route concludes with a very stiff climb through the Gorges de Nouailles to the Source de la Loue which is impassable for cyclists. Cyclists are advised to turn left and take the Alternate Route via Nods, although options are available to bypass the main obstacles these involve considerable additional distance. In the high season the Loue valley is a very popular tourist attraction with increasing traffic levels and demand for accommodation.**(25.2)** Fork right onto the stony track up the hill**(25.5)**Rejoin the road and continue uphill and enter the village of **Foucherans(25.6)**At the junction, continue straight ahead on rue de l'Eglise[Towards the church]**(26.0)**As the road forks with a stone crucifix in the centre, bear right and then turn left on rue de Bonnevaux[Pass the clock tower on your right] **(26.5)**Fork right towards the old barn**(26.9)**Take the right fork[Pass the farm, Luserole, on your left]**(26.9)**Take the left fork downhill **(28.0)**Continue straight ahead into the woods[Metal barrier]**(28.3)**At the crossroads, just before the main track bears right, turn left on the gravel track[Pass a sign board and picnic table on your right]**(28.7)**At the T-junction at the foot of a steep descent, turn right[Pass the cattle fencing on your left]**(28.9)** Take the left fork beside the cattle fencing**(29.0)**At the crossroads in the track with a concreted area ahead, turn right on the disused railway[Ornans - 7.5 km] **(32.1)**At the crossroads with a tarmac road, continue straight ahead on the old railway[Pass the wooden barriers]**(32.9)**At the crossroads with a tarmac road, continue straight ahead remaining on the old railway[Pass railway building n° 6 on your right] **(34.9)**At the next crossroads with a tarmac road, continue straight ahead remaining on the old railway[Pass the road sign for Ornans on your left]**(35.6)**Beside the roundabout, with a large trout in the centre, continue straight ahead on the footpath on the left side of the road[Direction Ornans Centre, supermarket on the left] **(36.9)**At the roundabout with the steel turbine sculpture, bear right[Direction Centre Ville]**(37.1)**At the crossroads with the D241, turn right and then turn left immediately after crossing the river**(37.6)**Arrive at **Ornans** centre[Beside the church of Saint Laurent]

Direct Route to Foucherans

Route: by passing through la Vèze on the D246 and then joining a series of farm roads and woodland tracks the stage can be reduced by 8.5 km. **(0.0)**Take the right fork**(0.5)**At the T-junction, turn right and with care take the 3rd exit from the roundabout[Direction la Vèze]**(0.8)**Take the left fork[Direction la Vèze] **(1.4)**In **la Vèze**continue straight ahead on Grande Rue[Pass the restaurant le Vèzois] **(2.5)**Turn left on the road. Note:- the signed route continues straight ahead, we prefer a more direct route[Airport runway on your left]**(3.0)**Take the right fork onto the small tarmac road, towards the woods[Chemin de Bief d'Aglans] **(5.4)**At the T-junction at the top of the hill in **Bois Vielle**, turn left on the road[Farmhouse on your left]**(6.1)**At the T-junction with the busy D67, cross the road with care and bear left on the track then bear right after 50m keeping the hedge on your left[Restaurant to the right on the main road at the junction] **(6.5)**Continue straight ahead with the woods on your immediate right[Field on your left]**(6.6)**Continue straight ahead on the path[Into the corner of the woods]**(6.8)** Take the first path to the right beside the tree with '19' painted in white. At the next junction keep straight ahead up the slope[Join the track at the top of the slope]**(7.1)**At the junction in the tracks, turn left[Towards the road]**(7.3)**At the T-junction with the road, turn left[Trees on the left and right]**(7.5)**Turn sharp right up the hill leaving the principal road["3 tonne Sauf Véhicule Agricole et Forestièr"] **(9.5)**At the junction, continue straight ahead to join the "Official Route"

Length:	9.5km
Ascent:	319m
Descent:	224m

stage 38 — Besançon to Ornans

Accommodation and Tourist Information

Foucherans
🏠 **Gîte d'Etape de Musée**,16 rue de l'Église, 25620 Foucherans, France; Tel:+33(0)6 84 27 04 67; Email:gite.etape.foucherans25@gmail.com; www.gitefoucherans25.com/; Price:C; *No shops or restaurants in the village*

Mamirolle
ℹ️ **Mairie - Mamirolle**,2 bis rue de l'École, 25620 Mamirolle, France; Tel:+33(0)3 81 55 71 50; www.mamirolle.info

Mérey-Sous-Montrond
🏠 **Auberge - des Granges du Liège**[Isabelle & Guy Laut],Les Granges du Liège, 25660 Mérey-Sous-Montrond, France; Tel:+33(0)3 81 81 88 22; Email:contact@lesgrangesduliege.fr; www.lesgrangesduliege.fr; Price:B

Ornans
🏠 **Au Sanglier Qui Fume**,1 Chemin de la Tuilerie, 25290 Ornans, France; Tel:+33(0)9 87 88 52 28; Email:sved@orange.fr; www.destinationlouelison.com/hebergement-locatif/au-sanglier-qui-fume/; Price:C; *Dinner available*

🏠 **Chambre d'Hôtes -L'Atelier du Peintre**,37 place Gustave Courbet, 25290 Ornans, France; Tel:+33(0)9 80 44 94 86; +33(0)6 33 69 64 99; Email:latelierdupeintrornans@gmail.com; www.latelierdupeintre-ornans.com; Price:A

🏠 **Chambre d'Hôtes - le Jardin de Gustave**[Marylène Rigoulot],28 rue Edouard Bastide, 25290 Ornans, France; Tel:+33(0)3 63 01 59 87; Email:info@lejardindegustave.fr; lejardindegustave.org; Price:A

🏠 **Hôtel - de la Vallée**,39 avenue du Président Wilson, 25290 Ornans, France; Tel:+33(0)3 81 62 40 43; Email:contact@hotel-ornans.fr; www.hotel-ornans.fr; Price:B

🏠 **Hôtel - la Table de Gustave**,11 rue Jacques Gervais, 25290 Ornans, France; Tel:+33(0)3 81 62 16 79; Email:reservation@latabledegustave.fr; latabledegustave.fr; Price:A

🏠 **Hôtel - de France**,51 rue Pierre Vernier, 25290 Ornans, France; Tel:+33(0)3 81 62 24 44; www.hoteldefrance-ornans.com; Price:A

⛺ **Camping la Roche d'Ully**,Allée Tour de Peilz, 25290 Ornans, France; Tel:+33(0)3 81 57 17 79; Email:contact@larochedully.com; www.camping-ornans.com; Price:C; *Tipis and bungalows also available for rent Camping open April to early October*

⛺ **Domaine le Chanet**,9 Chemin du Chanet, 25290 Ornans, France; Tel:+33(0)3 81 62 23 44; Email:campinglechanet@gmail.com; www.lechanet.com; Price:C; *Chalets and mobile homes also available*

ℹ️ **Office du Tourisme**,7 rue Pierre Vernier, 25290 Ornans, France; Tel:+33(0)3 81 62 21 50; Email:contact@destinationlouelison.com; www.destinationlouelison.com

Saône
🏠 **Hôtel - le Comtois**,4 Grande rue, 25660 Saône, France; Tel:+33(0)3 81 55 70 64; Email:brasserielesmarais@laposte.net; www.le-comtois-les-marais-saone.fr/; Price:B

ℹ️ **Mairie de Saône**,26 rue de la Mairie, 25660 Saône, France; Tel:+33(0)3 81 55 71 31; Email:contact@saone.fr; www.saone.fr

Besançon to Ornans stage 38

More Historic Route Via Nods (LVIII)

Route: following minor roads and farm and woodland tracks. The route is closer to the historic path, but unfortunately has fewer possibilities for accommodation and limited options for buying food or drinks after Trépot.

Length:	38.8km
Ascent:	1231m
Descent:	875m

(0.0)At the junction with the road turn left[Direction Trépot]
(1.1)In the centre of **Trépot** take the right fork[Pass the church on your left](1.4)At the T-junction, turn right[Pass the Depot des Pompes on your left](1.5)After passing the bar, take the left fork[White fencing on your right] (2.4)Continue straight ahead on the tarmac road and avoid the gravel track to your right[Pass wooden crucifix on your left] (2.7)Again continue straight ahead and avoid the gravel track on the right (3.8)At the crossroads with the disused railway line continue straight ahead[Sign on your left "Doubs Chemin"](4.1)Take the left fork[Blue and yellow sign](4.7)Bear slightly right on the track across the field and pass through the gap between the trees[Blue and yellow sign] (6.0)Continue straight ahead[Mont Pêle normally visible in the distance directly ahead](6.3)Bear right downhill on the tarmac[Blue and yellow sign on your left](6.5)At the T-junction with the more major road, turn left[Towards the "Dino Zoo"](6.9)Turn right and then left into the parking area for "Dino Zoo"[Blue and Yellow sign] (7.1)Bear left up the hill[No Entry sign, parking on your right](7.1)Take the left fork, uphill[Pass a stone well on your right](7.2)Beside the bus shelter on rue du Château in **Charbonnières-les-Sapins**, bear left to the T-junction and then turn right[Towards the village centre]
(7.4)Take the right fork[Rue de la Chauderotte](8.0)As the road bends to the right, take the 2nd left fork on the gravel track into the woods[Direction Pont de Fagot] (8.3)At the crossroads in the track, continue straight ahead on the small track[Blue and yellow sign](8.6)At the T-junction, turn left on the more defined track[Steeply downhill](8.8)At the T-junction with the road,

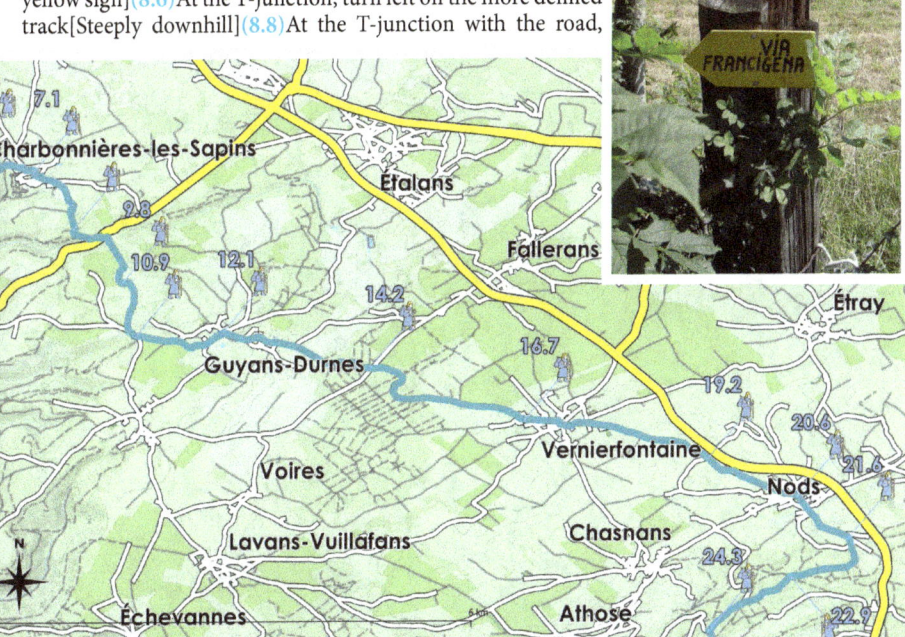

stage 38 — Besançon to Ornans

turn right[Cross the bridge]*(8.8)*Turn left into the parking space and follow the broad track, uphill[Rock outcrop on your right]*(8.9)*Take the right fork[Woods on your right, cattle fencing on your left]*(9.8)*Bear left keeping the farm buildings close on your right and follow the tarmac road away from the farm[Le Gros Champagnole]*(10.7)*At the junction, bear left *(10.9)*Take the left fork on the road[Direction Guyans-Durnes]*(11.8)* At the junction beside the church in Guyans-Durnes, continue straight ahead[D133, towards Vernierfontaine]*(12.1)*Turn right on rue de la Fruitiére[D27e, direction Vernierfontaine]*(12.4)*Take the left fork[Pass stone crucifix on your right]*(14.2)*At the crossroads in the woods, continue straight ahead[Direction Vernierfontaine - 3 km]*(16.7)*With a tree in the centre of the road junction, bear left[Pass house n° 34 on your left]*(17.1)*Turn right and then left following the signs for Nods[Pass the Fromargerie de Vernierefontaine on your left]*(17.5)*Fork right towards the Auberge and Nods[Metal

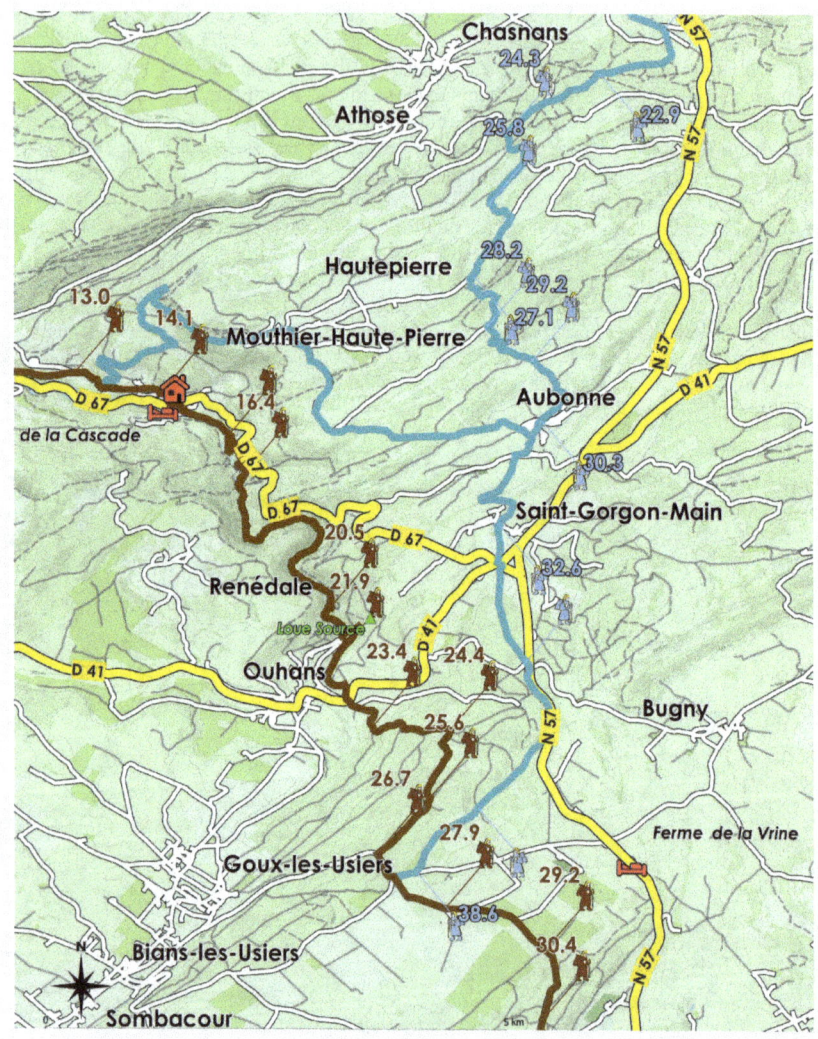

Besançon to Ornans stage 38

crucifix on your left **(19.2)** Continue straight ahead on the road[Avoid the turning on your right] **(19.7)** At the T-junction, bear right **(20.6)** At the T-junction, in the centre of **Nods (LVIII)**, keep left on the D32[Towards the church, Toutes Directions] **(20.8)** At the crossroads, continue straight ahead[Pass the pharmacy on your left and the Mairie on your right] **(21.5)** Bear right and ignore the No Entry sign **(21.6)** Fork right on chemin de la Grosse Aige[VF Historic sign] **(21.7)** Take the left fork between the trees[Forêt Communale de Nods] **(22.0)** Bear right on the road[VF sign "Sigeric"] **(22.9)** Remain on the road **(23.7)** At the road junction, bear left on the tarmac[VF sign, direction Les Fermes d'Athose] **(24.3)** At the T-junction, turn left[Direction Les Fermes d'Athose] **(25.0)** At the crossroads, turn right towards the farm - Champey **(25.8)** With farm buildings on your left and the barn on your right, bear left downhill on the gravel track[Semont - pass through metal gate] **(26.1)** At the T-junction with the road, turn right **(27.1)** After reaching a conifer plantation on your right, fork left on the gently rising track **(27.3)** Keep to the right hand side of the clearing and take the track on the far side[Track will bear left] **(27.4)** Take the right fork on the better defined track and then at the crossroads, continue straight ahead **(27.5)** Bear left **(27.7)** Emerge from the woods into a grassed area. Cross the grass and bear right with the woods close on your left **(27.9)** Join a gravel track and bear right down the hill **(28.2)** Turn left, downhill towards the woods **(28.7)** Continue on the road as it bends to the right[Avoid the track on the left] **(29.2)** Take the right fork downhill towards Aubonne **(30.3)** In **Aubonne**, bear left and then take a rapid sharp left and right turn onto rue de l'Eglise **(30.5)** Continue straight ahead on the road[Pass the church on your left] **(30.6)** At the junction bear left onto the D269 **(32.5)** In **Saint-Gorgon-Main**, bear left, right and then left again following the main road[Direction la Main, D269] **(33.2)** At the crossroads turn left and then take the first right parallel to the busy Route Nationale **(34.8)** At the tarmac crossroads continue straight ahead close to the Route Nationale **(35.1)** Enter the parking area and continue parallel to the main road **(35.4)** At the end of the parking area continue along the gravel track[Parallel to the Route Nationale] **(37.4)** At the crossroads in the tracks, continue straight ahead **(38.6)** At the T-junction with the road, turn right **(38.8)** At the junction, turn left to rejoin the Official Route"

Accommodation and Tourist Information

Athose
Gîte - l'Erable,4 route de Lavans, 25580 Athose, France; Tel:+33(0)3 81 60 03 02; +33(0)6 66 49 63 04; Email:jean-pierre.girard0@orange.fr; gitecabanedelerable.com; Price:A; *Sleeps 4*

Aubonne
Chambre d'Hôtes - la Ferme du Château,2 rue du Château, 25520 Aubonne, France; Tel:+33(0)3 81 69 90 56; www.bourgognefranchecomte.com/chambres-dhotes/chambres-dhotes-la-ferme-du-chateau; Price:B

Étalans
Chambre d'Hôtes - Hauts Doux Instants d'Evasion,13 rue Elisée Cusenier, 25580 Étalans, France; Tel:+33(0)6 86 91 38 98; Email:hautsdouxinstantsdevasion@sfr.fr; Price:B; *Pilgrim aware spa facilities available*

Hôtel - du Champ de Foire,30 rue Elisée Cusenier, 25580 Étalans, France; Tel:+33(0)3 81 59 21 01; Email:ferrand.k@laposte.net; www.hotel-restaurant-le-champdefoire.fr/; Price:B

Nods
Pierre-François Bernard,55 Grande rue, 25580 Nods, France; Tel:+33(0)3 81 60 00 32; +33(0)6 85 05 08 70; Email:bernard.qrst@wanadoo.fr; Price:D

Chambre d'Hôtes - 3 Pas Dans l'Herbe[Sophie Dimanche],1 rue du Tilleul, 25580 Nods, France; Tel:+33(0)3 81 60 06 17; +33(0)6 75 37 83 40; Email:les3pas@sfr.fr; www.3pasdanslherbe.com; Price:B

stage 39

Ornans to Pontarlier

Length:	38.8km
Ascent:	2496m
Descent:	1999m
Canterbury	974km
Col Grand Saint Bernard:	265km

Mouthier-Haute-Pierre

Route: the challenging stage from Ornans to Pontarlier continues to follow tracks and small roads on both sides of the Loue river valley. After initially continuing on the old railway, the trail will climb on the hillsides to the north and south of the river and pass through a number of villages offering tourist facilities during the holiday season.

Mouthier-Haute-Pierre is the last village before les gorges de Nouailles, and offers fantastic views over the gateway to Switzerland. The gorge has been subject to landslides in recent years and it is advisable to check its current status with the tourist office in Ornans. At the head of the gorge you will find the source of the Loue emerging from the cliff face and a restaurant offering a much needed rest stop.

Pontarlier occupies the ancient Roman station of Ariolica, in Gallia, and is located on the road from Urba (modern Orbe), to Vesontio (modern Besançon). After the Burgundian invasion in the 5th century, Pontarlier became part of the trade route from the kingdom of Burgundy to Switzerland, Germany or Lombardy. Pontarlier is briefly mentioned in Victor Hugo's, Les Misérables, when the convict Jean Valjean has to report for his parole after being released from the galleys. Today it is the gateway to a very large protected nature area, where the forest, the lakes and the green pastures are indispensable to the manufacture of the Mont d'Or cheese.

Port Saint Pierre   Rama

(0.0) From the rear of the church of Saint Laurent, turn left and then take the first turning to the right[Direction Musée Courbet]**(0.2)** At the junction beside the bridge, continue straight ahead across the square and into the narrow street[Pass Maison de Courbet on your left]**(0.8)** At the T-junction with the road, turn left on the road[Keep the river close on your left]**(0.9)** At the fork in the road, bear left towards the bridge and then bear right on the road leading away from the river[Pass the fontaine on your right] **(1.7)** Take the left fork[GR°595, Montgesoye - 3.5 km]**(2.3)** At the junction, continue straight ahead **(3.9)** Continue straight ahead under the bridge**(4.2)** At the T-junction with the road, turn left**(4.4)** At the road junction beside the river bridge, continue straight ahead with the river on your left and then bear right remaining on the road[Direction Vuillafans] **(5.8)** At the fork, keep right[Pass large stones at the entrance to the left fork]**(6.6)** Cross the bridge over the stream and continue straight ahead on the tarmac into **Vuillafans**[Modern houses on

Ornans to Pontarlier — stage 39

your left and right] (7.2)At the road junction, continue straight ahead[Rue de la Gare] (7.6)At the crossroads turn right on the road. On the crown of the first hairpin to the right, turn left on the broad gravel track and follow the track through the woods above the river (10.3)At the crossroads, bear left towards the river on the broad track(10.6)Continue straight ahead[Pass the camp site on your right](11.0)Turn left across the river bridge and then right along the main road(11.2)With a car park and small bridge on your right, take the left fork, uphill (11.7)At the crossroads, beside the fountain in **Lods**, turn right[Rue sur la Place](11.7)Beside the Point de Accueil, turn left, uphill[Rue de l'Eglise](11.8)At the junction, turn right[Rue du Château] (13.0)At the T-junction with the tarmac road, turn right downhill[Blue and yellow sign](13.6)At the junction, continue straight ahead on the road. Note:- to avoid the Gorges de Nouailles, cyclists should turn left to Hautepierre le Châtelet and follow the D269 to regain the Alternate Route via Nods at Aubonne(13.8)At the junction, continue straight ahead into Mouthier-Haute-Pierre[No-Entry sign](13.9)At the junction, bear right[Rue Robert Dame] (14.1)At the crossroads, turn left, then turn right beside the church[Rue Pavée](14.3)At the junction in **Mouthier-Haute-Pierre** follow the D67 in the direction of Pontarlier and immediately take the right fork[Rue Erenest Reye.](14.5)As the road turns left, turn right on the track towards the river(14.7)At the junction, continue straight ahead with the river on your right (15.2)At the end of the road continue on the track(15.9)At the crossroads at the top of the hill, turn right on the road downhill (16.4)Bear left through the barrier and join the forest pathway[Hydro-electric station to your right and straight ahead](16.6)At the junction in the tracks, bear right and cross the wooden bridge and continue uphill[Metal bridge to your left, Source de la Loue 1hour 20min] (20.5)Bear right and continue uphill[**Source de la Loue** to the left](21.1) In the parking area turn sharp left on the forest track[Café and restaurant "Chalet de la Loue"](21.3)Take the right fork on the small pathway, steeply uphill[Chapelle Notre Dame - 15mins](21.3)At the T-junction at the top of the steps, turn right on the narrow track (21.9)Pass through the gap between the fence posts and emerge from the woods. Continue

stage 39   Ornans to Pontarlier

straight ahead[Skirt the hill on your left surmounted by the chapel]**(22.5)**At the T-junction, with the tarmac road, turn right and continue downhill[Pass modern wooden house on your right]**(22.8)**At the crossroads continue straight ahead slightly uphill, towards the forest**(22.9)**Continue straight ahead uphill towards the woods, avoiding the fork to the left **(23.4)**Take the left fork into the woods[13% incline]**(23.8)**Bear right and then left and remain on the tarmac[Avoid gravel track to the left]**(24.1)**Bear left to continue on the tarmac[Emerge from the woods into the pastures] **(24.4)**Beside the wooden cross, take the right fork and keep right across the open field **(25.6)**At the T-junction, turn right **(26.7)**At the T-junction with the main road, turn left**(27.0)**At the double road junction, take the central road. Note:- The Alternate Route via Nods rejoins from the road ahead **(27.9)**Take the left fork and then shortly afterwards take the right fork **(29.2)**At the crossroads, continue straight ahead. Note:- a signed VF route makes a loop through the woods to the right before returning to the road, we will remain on the normally quiet road **(30.4)** At the junction, continue straight ahead on the road. Note:- the loop through the woods joins from the right **(32.3)**At the crossroads in **Vuillecin**, turn left[Pass the Mairie on your right]**(32.8)**At the T-junction, turn right[Exit the village] **(34.3)**Just before reaching the roundabout, turn left on the tarmac track[Parallel to the highway on your right]**(34.3)** Bear right on the gravel track[Take the tunnel under the highway]**(34.6)**After emerging from the tunnel, turn left beside the roundabout and continue on rue de la Fruitière**(35.1)** Cross rue de Besançon and continue on rue de Petit Saint Claude **(35.5)**At the crossroads, turn right towards the church[Rue de l'Eglise]**(35.8)**At the T-junction, turn right[Rue de laChaussée]**(36.4)**At the roundabout, bear right and follow the tarmac pathway beside the trees **(36.9)**Take the left fork to leave the old railway[Towards the sports ground]**(37.5)** Bear right to follow the river. Take the first bridge and continue with the river on your left **(38.4)**At the junction with the main road beside the second bridge, turn right**(38.8)**Arrive at **Pontarlier (LVII)**[Beside the tourist office]

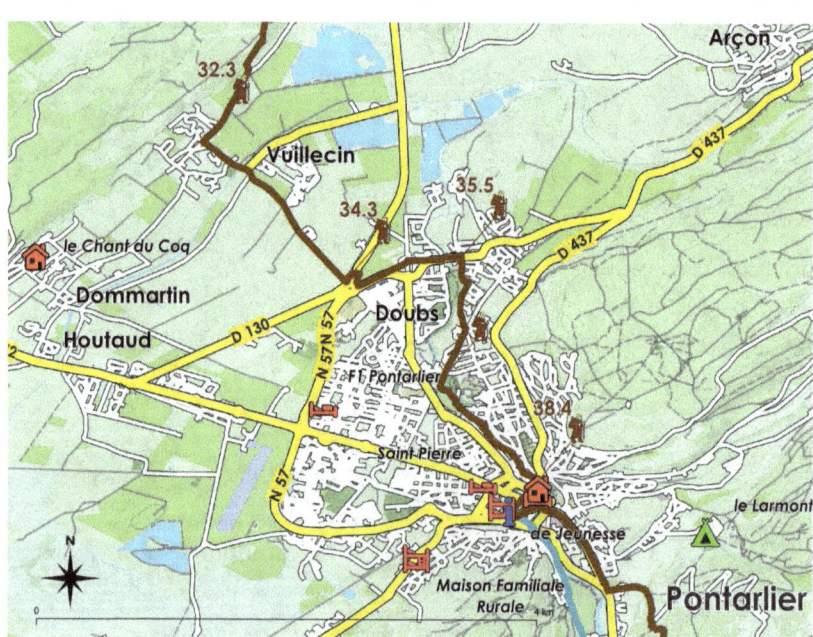

Ornans to Pontarlier stage 39

Accommodation and Tourist Information

Dommartin
🔑 **Chambre d'Hôtes - le Chant du Coq**,4 rue du Chant du Coq, 25300 Dommartin, France; Tel:+33(0)3 81 69 36 75; +33(0)6 04 09 51 92; Email:phroy25300@orange.fr ; www.le-chant-du-coq.com ; Price:B

Lods
🔑 **Chambre d'Hôtes - au Fil de l'Eau**[Annick and Christophe Moreau],4 Chemin des Forges, 25930 Lods, France; Tel:+33(0)3 81 84 09 81; +33(0)6 31 97 33 15; Email:contact@aufildelods.comr; aufildelods.com; Price:A

🏨 **Hôtel - de France**,1 place Pézard, 25930 Lods, France; Tel:+33(0)3 81 60 95 29; www.hoteldefrancelods.com; Price:B; *Open April until the end of October*

⚑ **Gîte de Groupe - La Truite d'Or**,40 route de Besançon, 25930 Lods, France; Tel:+33(0)6 76 87 58 50; +33(0)3 81 80 63 33; gitedegroupelatruitedor.fr

⛺ **Camping le Champaloux**,33 route de Besançon, 25930 Lods, France; Tel:+33(0)3 81 60 90 11; Email:mairie.lods@orange.fr; lods.fr/camping-municipal-le-champaloux; Price:C

Montgesoye
⛺ **Camping Aire Naturelle Municipale**,Route de la Grange Millet, 25111 Montgesoye, France; Tel:+33(0)3 81 62 25 81; +33(0)6 65 78 51 11; Email:montgesoyeanimationtourisme@yahoo.fr; www.destinationlouelison.com/camping/aire-naturelle-de-montgesoye/; Price:C; *Chalets available*

Mouthier-Haute-Pierre
🔑 **Chambre d'Hôtes - la Maison de Léonie**,14 route des Gorges de Nouailles, 25920 Mouthier-Haute-Pierre, France; Tel:+33(0)688244083; la-maison-de-leonie.fr; Price:B

🏨 **Hôtel - de la Cascade**,4 route Gorges de Nouailles, 25920 Mouthier-Haute-Pierre, France; Tel:+33(0)3 81 60 95 30; Email:hotellacascade@wanadoo.fr; www.hotel-lacascade.fr; Price:A; *Great views but pricey*

Pontarlier
🔑 **Maison Familiale Rurale**,20 rue des Granges, 25300 Pontarlier, France; Tel:+33(0)3 81 39 17 04; Email:mfr.pontarlier@mfr.asso.fr; www.mfr-pontarlier.com; Price:C

🔑 **Auberge de Jeunesse**,21 rue Marpaud, 25300 Pontarlier, France; Tel:+33(0)3 81 39 06 57; Email:pontarlier@hifrance.org; www.hifrance.org/auberges-de-jeunesse/pontarlier; Price:B; *Clean well organized*

🔑 **Chambre d'Hôtes - la Maison d'À Côté**,11 rue Jules Mathez, 25300 Pontarlier, France; Tel:+33(0)3 81 38 47 18; +33(0)6 87 84 09 11; www.lamaison-da-cote.fr; Price:A

🏨 **Hôtel - F1 Pontarlier**,Combe Sourchet, Zi rue Eiffel, 25300 Pontarlier, France; Tel:+33(0)8 91 70 53 58; Email:h2439@accor.com; all.accor.com; Price:C

🏨 **Hôtel - Saint Pierre**,3 place Saint-Pierre, 25300 Pontarlier, France; Tel:+33(0)3 81 46 50 80; www.hotel-st-pierre-pontarlier.fr; Price:B

⛺ **Camping le Larmont**,7 rue Edwige Feuillère, 25300 Pontarlier, France; Tel:+33(0)3 81 46 23 33; Email:contact@camping-pontarlier.fr; www.camping-pontarlier.fr; Price:C; *Chalets also available*

ℹ **Office de Tourisme**,14 bis rue de la Gare, 25300 Pontarlier, France; Tel:+33(0)3 81 46 48 33; Email:pontarlier@destination-hautdoubs.com; www.pontarlier.org

Vuillafans
🔑 **Gîte d'Etape du Pré Bailly**,Le Pré Bailly, 25840 Vuillafans, France; Tel:+33(0)3 81 60 92 36; +33(0)3 81 60 91 52; Email:Mairie.vuillafans@wanadoo.fr; www.vuillafans.fr; Price:C; *Camping also possible*

🔑 **Solange Cardeur**,1 rue Saint-Claude, 25840 Vuillafans, France; Tel:+33(0)3 81 60 91 42; +33(0)6 79 27 31 54; Email:solangecardeur@orange.fr; Price:C

⚑ **Gîte - La Tuffière**,Chemin de Montgesoye, 25840 Vuillafans, France; Tel:+33(0)3 81 60 96 76; +33(0)6 16 61 81 78; Email:latuffiere2@wanadoo.fr; www.latuffiere.com; Price:B

Vuillecin
🏨 **Ferme Hôtel de la Vrine**,RN57,, 25300 Vuillecin, France; Tel:+33(0)3 81 39 47 74; Email:ferme-hotel-de-la-vrine@wanadoo.fr; www.ferme-hotel-vrine.fr; Price:B

stage 40   Pontarlier to Jougne

Length:	22.9km
Ascent:	1021m
Descent:	871m
Canterbury	1013km
Col Grand Saint Bernard:	226km

Conifer scenic railway   *de Benutzer*

Route: for some years the modern via Francigena made a huge dog leg from Pontarlier via Sainte Croix to Yverdon-les-Bains before returning to the historic town of Orbe. It is now understood that this was an error in interpreting the name of *Antifern* from Sigeric's chronicle and in fact *Antifern* referred to the border town of Jougne(LVI). Some signposting will still lead to Sainte Croix as does the Swiss footpath 70. The newly signposted "Official Route" from Pontarlier to Jougne is higher and longer than the historic Alternative Route and climbs through woodland to above 1000m but with splendid views of Château de Joux before descending to le Val du Fort and then climbing steeply again in sometimes muddy woodland to the village of Les Fourgs. It follows a minor road through woodland, reaching 1200m, before descending to Les Hôpitaux-Neufs and merging with the historic route.

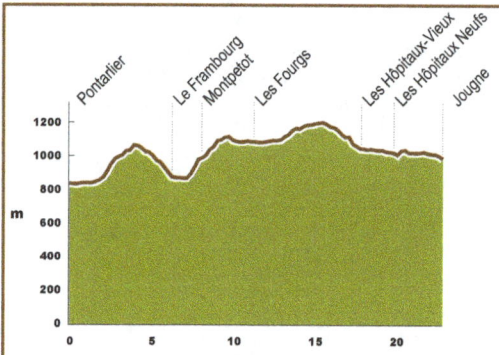

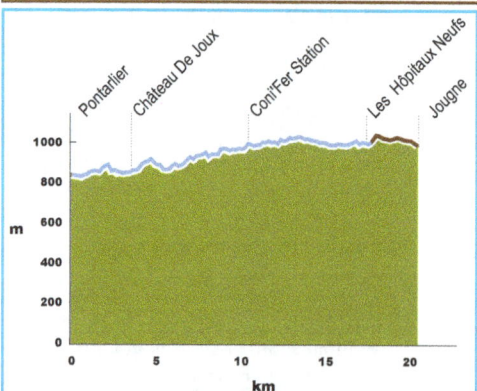

Be sure to consider weather conditions before you leave. There are opportunities to break your journey near Château de Joux and Les Hôpitaux-Neufs.

Chapelle Saint Maurice - Jougne

Pontarlier to Jougne

stage 40

In the Middle Ages, Jougne was an important toll station on the road to Italy. Of the ancient fortifications, a gate and ramparts, as well as ruins of the fort, still remain. The chapel of Saint Maurice dates from the twelfth century and has a Carolingian crypt, a vestige of a 9th century priory, where perhaps Sigeric rested.

(0.0) From the tourist office, head south-east beside the cycle track, with La Poste on your right[Rue Marpaud]**(0.1)** Turn left towards Église Saint-Bénigne**(0.2)** Pass Église Saint-Bénigne on your right and then bear left and turn right at the crossroads[Rue de la République]**(0.4)** Cross the river bridge and continue straight ahead[Faubourg Saint-Étienne] **(1.3)** At the roundabout, keep left and then take the next left on chemin du Larmont[Pass supermarket on your right]**(2.1)** On the crown of the sharp bend to the left, turn right onto the gravel track[Direction le Fort de Mahler]**(2.2)** Turn left up the hill on the gravel track **(2.4)** Turn right at the top of the steep climb**(2.5)** Continue on the main track up the hill**(2.7)** Fork right to go up a slight rise**(2.7)** Bear right remaining on the

Château de Joux

Fort du Larmont

track**(2.9)** Take the right fork[Altitude 1000m] **(3.0)** Fork left onto a narrow track**(3.1)** Take right fork**(3.1)** Turn left to follow the cliff edge, steep drop on the right[View of Château de Joux ahead]**(3.2)** Bear right and continue up the hill**(3.3)** Fork left to continue up the hill[VF cairn] **(3.9)** Continue straight ahead[Summit cairn 1062 metres]**(4.7)** Beside Fort du Larmont, bear left down the hill[View of Château de Joux] **(5.5)** Continue to zig-zag steeply downhill**(6.1)** Turn left to pass the church on your right**(6.3)** At the T-junction with the road in **le Frambourg**, turn left **(6.6)** Beside the bus stop, bear right on the path and then turn right on the road[Initially towards the woodland]**(6.9)** Turn right[Pass under the railway track]**(7.3)** Continue uphill on the path[Towards the woodland] **(8.0)** At the junction with the road, turn left and

stage 40　　　　　　　　Pontarlier to Jougne

immediately bear right[Pass through **Montpetot**](**8.3**)Continue uphill on the track between open fields and towards the woodland(**8.6**)Bear right in the woods, cross the fire break and then bear left[Keep the summit of the hill to your left] 🚶 (**9.6**)Pass Notre-Dame des Buclés, leave the woodland and cross the fields[Parallel to the main road below] 🚶 (**10.8**)Turn right on the road and continue between industrial buildings(**11.3**)At the

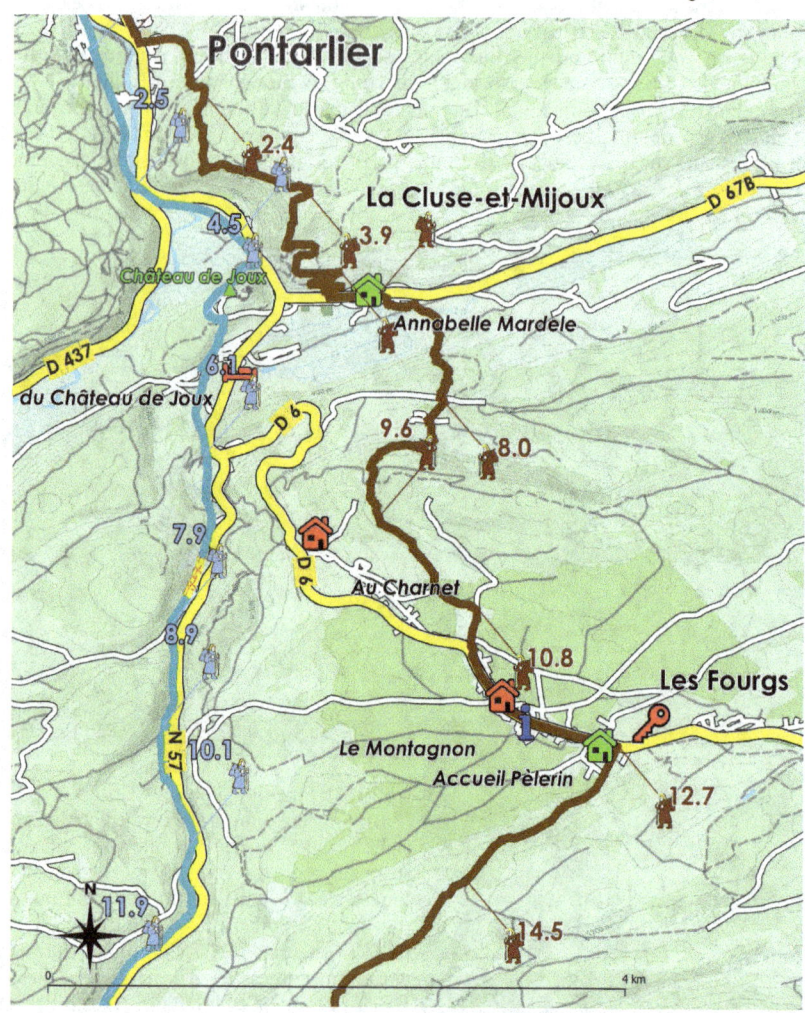

junction with the main road, D6, turn left[Pass through **Les Fourgs**] 🚶 (**12.7**)Beside the wooden bus shelter, turn right[Rue des Côtes] 🚶 (**14.5**)Keep right at the fork[Towards the farm building] 🚶 (**17.0**)At the junction continue straight ahead[Downhill](**17.9**)At the road junction, bear left[Towards the village of **Les Hôpitaux-Vieux**] 🚶 (**18.7**)At the mini-roundabout, bear slightly to your right[Pass a lavoir on your left](**19.3**)Bear left and continue through the parking area with the commercial buildings on your left[a line of trees and the main road on your right](**19.6**)At the T-junction with the main road, turn left onto the track, parallel to the main road[Pass under the highway bridge] 🚶 (**19.8**)Continue

198

Pontarlier to Jougne

stage 40

straight ahead beside the main road[Towards the entry to **Les Hôpitaux Neufs**]**(20.1)** Immediately before a parking area on your right, turn left uphill on the track. Note:- the alternate route joins from ahead[Vehicle No Entry sign]**(20.5)** At the T-junction with a small road, turn right on the road **(20.9)**As the road turns sharply to the right, continue straight ahead on the track through the trees**(21.4)**Enter the parking area and then turn left to take the tunnel under the highway[Wooden sign for Jougne]**(21.5)**At the top of the rise, bear right towards the traffic island and then turn left beside the main road[Direction Jougne]**(21.9)** Opposite the supermarket car park, take the second left[Rue de Faubourg] **(22.5)**Take the right fork, downhill[Pass Chalet Saonoin on your right and the lavoir on your left] **(22.7)**Take the left

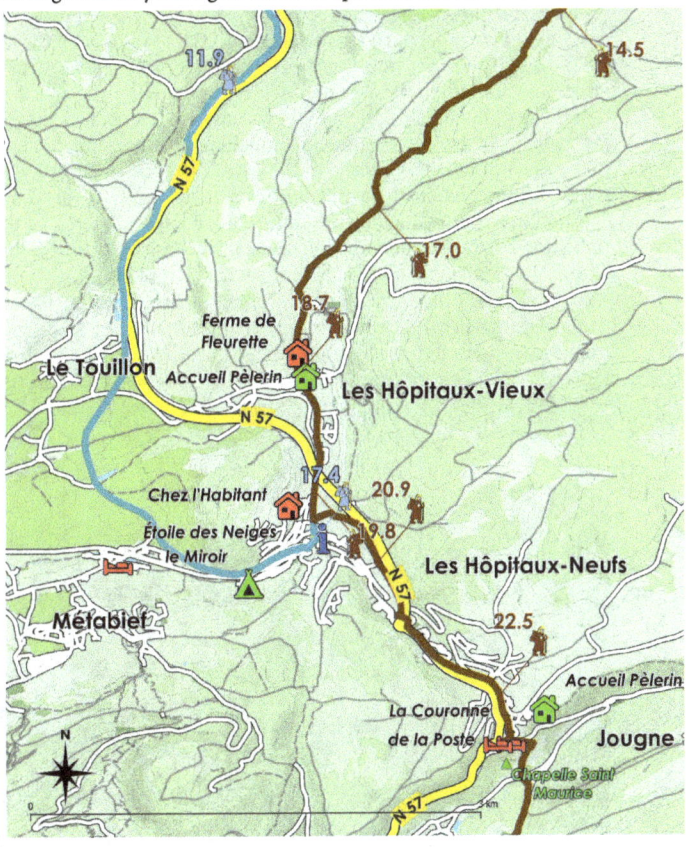

fork on rue de l'Eglise[Pass through the archway towards the church]**(22.9)**Arrive at **Jougne (LVI)** centre[Beside the church]

Historic Route to Les-Hôpitaux-Neufs

Route: the alternate route follows close to the former Roman road that was probably the route taken by Sigeric via Antifern - Jougne. The route makes use of the disused railway and then a track beside the ConiFer tourist railway for much of the distance to Jougne (LVI). **(0.0)**At the Stop sign, continue straight ahead. The "Official Route" turns left towards the church.**(0.2)**At the end of the road, turn right and cross the main road beside the traffic lights, climb the steps and turn left on rue le Fauconnière[Beside parking area]**(0.3)**At the end of the parking area pass through the green metal barrier and continue on the tarmac path[River on your left] **(1.0)**With great care pass through the gate and cross the railway track[Pass through a second gate]**(1.1)**Bear left on the grass track[Railway line close on your left]**(1.3)**At the T-junction with the gravel track, continue straight ahead[Close to the railway]**(1.5)**At the T-junction beside the railway bridge, turn right uphill[Direction le Pont des Rosiers]**(1.6)**

Length:	17.7km
Ascent:	1173m
Descent:	1003m

stage 40   Pontarlier to Jougne

Take the left fork[Narrow track close to the railway] (2.5)At the T-junction with the main road, turn left, cross the river bridge and immediately turn right on the pathway[Blue and yellow signs, direction Fort de Joux] (3.5)At the T-junction with a road and with a level crossing on your left, turn right[Remain on the road passing the **Château de Joux** on your left] (4.5)Bear right into the parking area[Sign "P1"](4.6)Bear left, keeping the picnic tables on your left, to the T-junction with the road. Turn right towards the brow of the hill, then turn right again on the path between the trees. Note:- the path is extremely difficult for cyclists. To avoid the obstacles - remain on the road and descend to the main road, cross the road with care and proceed to the right. Take the right turn, direction Oye et Pallet and rejoin the route where the path emerges from the right[Steeply descending path](5.1)At the T-junction with the road, turn right(5.2)Turn left and then take the second turning on the right, towards 2 wooden sheds[Direction le Hameau du Moulin](5.3)Continue straight ahead[Disused railway track] (6.1)At the T-junction with the tarmac road, continue straight ahead on the narrow path and climb the embankment back onto the old railway(6.5) At the T-junction with a broader track, continue straight ahead on the broad track into the trees[House with 3 garages on the left](6.6)In the clearing, continue straight ahead on the railway track[Weir on your left](6.8)At the junction take the right fork, avoid the path

Les Hôpitaux Neufs

directly ahead beside the ponds[Sawmill on your left at the junction] (7.9)At the crossroads with the tarmac road, continue straight ahead on the old railway[Former railway building on your right] (8.9)At the junction with the road, again continue straight ahead on the old railway[Pond on your left](9.5)At the crossroads, continue straight ahead and mount the embankment to rejoin the old railway[The crossroads leads to the main road on the left and into the woods on the right] (10.1)At the crossroads with a tarmac road, turn right on the tarmac[Former railway building on your left at the junction](10.4)Fork left on the gravel track[Pass beside the **Coni'Fer station** andbar](10.8)Continue straight ahead on the track beside the scenic railway[Pass the Fontaine Ronde below on your left](11.0)At the junction, continue straight ahead[Beside the railway] (11.9)Remain by the railway to the terminus in les Hôpitaux Neufs[Pass bridge on your left] (17.4)In **les Hôpitaux Neufs** exit the train station and turn left on route de la Poste[Towards the church](17.5)At the T-junction turn left[Keep the church to your left](17.7)Immediately after passing a parking area on your left, turn right to take the track uphill towards the trees and rejoin the "Official Route"[No Entry for vehicles]

Pontarlier to Jougne

stage 40

Accommodation and Tourist Information

Jougne
🏠 **Accueil Pèlerin**,6 rue de la Loge, 25370 Jougne, France; Tel:+33(0)6 35 90 88 48; Email:paget.daniele@orange.fr; Price:C

🛏 **Hôtel - de la Poste**,9 route des Alpes, 25370 Jougne, France; Tel:+33(0)3 81 49 27 24; hotelrestaurantdelapostele1900.business.site; Price:B; *Good pizza*

🛏 **Hôtel - La Couronne**,6 rue de l'Église, 25370 Jougne, France; Tel:+33(0)3 81 49 10 50; Email:lacouronnejougne@free.fr; couronne-hotel-jougne.fr; Price:A

La-Cluse-et-Mijoux
🏠 **Annabelle Mardele**,1 les Fourneaux, 25300 La-Cluse-et-Mijoux, France; Tel:+33(0)6 25 01 91 00; Email:annabelle.mardele@gmail.com; Price:C

🛏 **Auberge - du Château de Joux - Hotel**,127 au Frambourg, 25300 La-Cluse-et-Mijoux, France; Tel:+33(0)3 81 69 40 41; Email:aubergeduchateaudejoux@gmail.com; aubergeduchateaujoux.wixsite.com/aubergechateaujoux; Price:A

Les-Fourgs
🏠 **Accueil Pèlerin**[Jean-Claude Tissot],78 Grande rue, 25300 Les-Fourgs, France; Tel:+33(0)7 85 29 94 00; +33(0)3 81 69 50 54; ++33(0)785 290 000; Email:tiss25@hotmail.com; Price:C

🏠 **Chambre d'Hôtes - Au Charnet**,8 rue des Bucles, 25300 Les-Fourgs, France; Tel:+33(0)6 71 60 27 50; +33(0) 3 81 69 45 71; www.aucharnet.com; Price:A

🏠 **Chambre d'Hôtes - Le Montagnon**[Josiane et Philippe Aymonier],20 Grande rue, 25300 Les-Fourgs, France; Tel:+33(0)3 81 69 44 03; www.lemontagnon.com; Price:B

🔑 **Gîte de Groupe - La Randonnée**,102 Grande rue, 25300 Les-Fourgs, France; Tel:+33(0)6 51 47 97 43; Email:gite.larandonnee25@gmail.com; gitelarandonnee.wixsite.com/gitelesfourgs; *Can accommodate 14*

ℹ **Office de Tourisme des Fourgs**,36 Grande rue, 25300 Les-Fourgs, France; Tel:+33(0)3 81 69 44 91; Email:lesfourgs@destination-hautdoubs.com; www.les-fourgs.com

Les-Hôpitaux-Neufs
🏠 **Chambre d'Hôtes - Chez l'Habitant**,5 rue Bellevue, 25370 Les-Hôpitaux-Neufs, France; Tel:+33(0)6 17 12 07 60; Email:xb.chambresdhotes@gmail.com; www.airbnb.com/rooms/40081778; Price:B

⛺ **Camping le Miroir**,25 route de la Poste, 25370 Les-Hôpitaux-Neufs, France; Tel:+33(0)3 81 49 10 64; accueil@camping-lemiroir.com; camping-lemiroir.com; Price:C; *Chalets also available*

ℹ **Mairie**,1 place de la Mairie, 25370 Les-Hôpitaux-Neufs, France; Tel:+33(0)3 81 49 13 34; www.cclmhd.fr

Les-Hôpitaux-Vieux
🏠 **Accueil Pèlerin**,1 Chemin des Coudrettes, 25370 Les-Hôpitaux-Vieux, France; Tel:+33(0) 7 70 99 35 56; +33(0) 3 81 49 00 29; Email:francoisecordereix@hotmail.fr

🏠 **Chambre d'Hôtes - Ferme de Fleurette**,14 rue des Agettes, 25370 Les-Hôpitaux-Vieux, France; Tel:+33(0)6 33 25 34 01; gite-metabief-doubs.fr; Price:B

Métabief
🛏 **Hôtel - Étoile des Neiges**,4 rue du Village, 25370 Métabief, France; Tel:+33(0)3 81 49 11 21; Email:contact@hoteletoiledesneiges.fr; www.hoteletoiledesneiges.fr; Price:A

Pilgrim food - Vacherin Mont d'Or

stage 41 — Jougne to Orbe

Length:	19.3km
Ascent:	1076m
Descent:	1583m
Canterbury	1036km
Col Grand Saint Bernard:	203km

Mosaic from the Roman villa - Orbe

Route: the stage from Jougne to Orbe will initially pass beside the Chapelle St-Maurice with its 9th century crypt and then briefly climb to follow the tarmac rue Julius Caesar to enter Switzerland (no border formalities at the time of writing). The route will leave the road in Ballaigues, where you can find shops and a café and then follow the paths in the gorge beside the river Orbe.

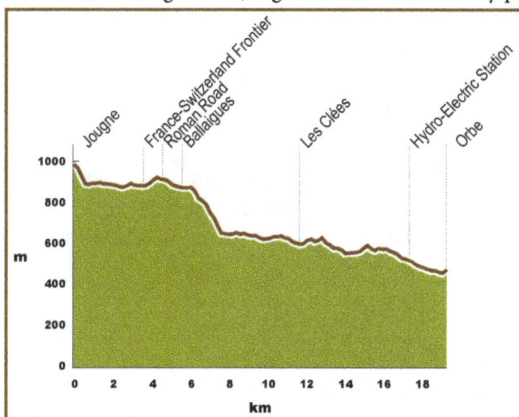

In Switzerland our primary route will follow Swiss regional hiking trail 70. However, the trail was designed and way-marked when the via Francigena was falsely thought to pass via Saint-Croix and Yverdons and so we will not join it until we approach the outskirts of Orbe. The route followed by footpath 70 to Lausanne does not appear to have any direct linkage to the ancient via Francigena and follows a curious dog leg, exacerbated by the hairpin loop through Orbe. An Alternative Route from Orbe will follow a more direct track and is probably closer to that followed by Sigeric. However, footpath 70 does allow a visit to the Cluniac Romainmôtier Priory.

Commercial accommodation in Switzerland will in general be more expensive than in France. However, there are a number of Pilgrim Hosts who provide a lower cost option. Orbe offers a good range of facilities and access to the Swiss rail network.

During the Roman era, Orbe was known as Urba. By the Middle Ages, Orbe sat on the road over the Jougne Pass, and at the crossroads of two major transportation routes. One stretched from the Jura Mountains to the Alps, while the other ran from the Rhine River to the Rhone River. The municipality grew up on both sides of the Orbe and at some point during the Middle Ages, a bridge was built across the river, which joined the two settlements. Around the end of the 11th century, Romainmôtier Abbey acquired some land in the town, on which they built a hospital and this later expanded into the nearby Notre-Dame chapel. The entire old town of Orbe is part of the Inventory of Swiss Heritage Sites

Jougne to Orbe   stage 41

(0.0) From the church in Jougne, proceed downhill[Towards the war memorial]**(0.1)** In front of the war memorial, turn left and downhill, in the direction of la Ferrière[Pass the post office on your right]**(0.2)** Fork right onto the second of the two tracks steeply downhill[The track just to the right of the sign for rock falls]**(0.6)** Pass the Chapelle St-Maurice with its 9th century crypt, on your left and cross the road ahead**(0.8)** At the T-junction with the tarmac road, bear right onto the road 🚶 **(2.6)** Continue straight ahead[Rue Jules César]**(3.3)** At the end of the tarmac, continue straight ahead on the gravel track[Pass a gîte on your left]**(3.6)** Continue straight ahead across the **France-Switzerland frontier**[Sentier Jougnena Table 6 – 15 mins.] 🚶 **(4.1)** At the junction, continue straight ahead[Cycle Route 6]**(4.6)** Shortly after passing the left turn for Le Friand, continue straight ahead. Note:- to walk on the vestiges of the **Roman road** take the left fork onto a grass track and follow the Alternate Route[Gravel parking area on the left] 🚶 **(5.2)** At the T-junction, turn left[Towards the village of Ballaigues]**(5.4)** Beside the pedestrian crossing, bear right and follow the smaller tarmac road[Below and parallel to the main road]**(5.6)** Rejoin the main road and continue into the centre of **Ballaigues**. Note:- the route via the Roman road joins from the left ahead[Pedestrian route 5 crosses the "Official Route"]**(6.1)** Shortly after passing the water fountain on your left, take the path to the right[Cross the fields and pass under the highway] 🚶 **(6.6)** After passing under the highway, fork right into the woods**(6.9)** Cross the broad

track and continue straight ahead, steeply downhill**(7.1)** Again cross the broad track and continue ahead into the gorge of the river Orbe**(7.5)** At the T-junction turn left and cross the river. Continue on the path with the river on your left 🚶 **(11.7)** On reaching the village of **Les Clées**, bear right and continue on the road, with the bridge on your left**(12.3)** As the road bears right, take the track to the left[Woods on your left and an open field on your right] 🚶 **(12.7)** Re-enter the woods and continue with the river on your left 🚶 **(14.4)** At the junction, continue straight ahead keeping the river on your left**(14.9)** Recross the river and turn right at the T-junction 🚶 **(15.9)** At the crossroads, turn right downhill**(16.0)** Take the

203

stage 41 — Jougne to Orbe

left fork**(16.1)**In the parking area, bear left[Pipeline on the right]**(16.3)**At the T-junction with the road, turn right and continue downhill**(16.7)**Take the right fork **(17.1)**After passing under the electricity line, turn right on the road[Towards the hydro-electric station]**(17.4)**Bear left with the **Hydro-Electric station** on your right**(17.6)**On the crown of the first hairpin to the right, continue straight ahead on the track[Keep the river on your right] **(18.3)**Bear right and cross the river and immediately turn left on the road**(18.6)**At the T-junction, turn left[Tourisme Pédestre sign]**(18.9)**Bear right on the tarmac[Pass football pitch on the left]**(19.1)**Turn left over the river bridge[Orbe Gare 10 min.]**(19.2)**After crossing the bridge, continue up the hill on the tarmac**(19.3)**Arrive at **Orbe (LV)** with the railway station on your right

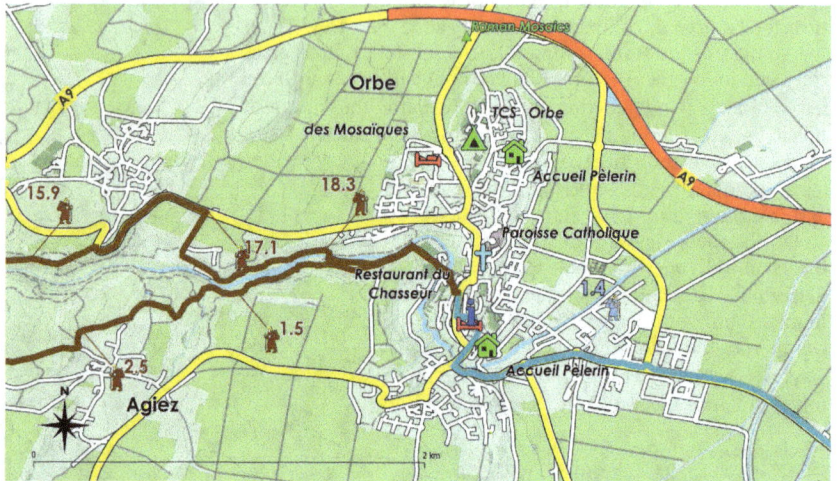

Roman Road

Route: this short diversion allows you experience a visible section of Roman road. The route may be muddy in wet conditions but you should be able to find the grooves made by the passage of carts over the last 2 millennia. **(0.0)**Bear left on the grass track into the woods[Tourisme Pédestre sign]**(0.2)**At the crossroads in the track, continue straight ahead[Sentier de la Jougnena]**(0.3)**Take the right fork, then bear left avoiding the second right fork[Sentier de la Jougnena, pass vestiges of the Roman road]**(0.5)**At the T-junction at the end of the track, turn left[Sentier de la Jougnena]**(0.8)**At the T-junction turn right[Commercial building on your right] **(1.2)**At the T-junction in **Ballaigues**, turn left and rejoin the "Official Route"[Pass the bus stop on your left, Grande Rue]

Length:	1.2km
Ascent:	31m
Descent:	71m

Jougne to Orbe — stage 41

Accommodation and Tourist Information

Ballaigues

🛏 **Hôtel Restaurant - Croix d'Or**, Place du Château 2, 1338 Ballaigues, Switzerland; Tel:+41(0)21 565 69 70; Email:croixdor@netplus.ch; lacroixdor.ch; Price:A

Lignerolle

🏠 **B&B - Chez Epicure**, Rue du Collège 2, 1357 Lignerolle, Switzerland; Tel: +41(0)79 653 53 52; Email:contact@chezepicure.ch; chezepicure.ch; Price:A; **PR**

Orbe

✝ **Paroisse Catholique**, Chemin de la Dame 1, 1350 Orbe, Switzerland; Tel:+41(0)24 441 32 90; +41(0)79 595 20 63; Email:paroisse.orbe@cath-vd.ch; Price:D; *No unaccompanied women*

🏠 **Accueil Pèlerin** [Carole Zimmermann], Chemin de la Magnenette 45, 1350 Orbe, Switzerland; Tel: +41(0)24 441 19 79; +41(0)79 258 13 22; Price:C; *Not Saturday or Tuesday nights*

🏠 **Accueil Pèlerin** [Julie Boly], Rue Pierre Viret 11, 1350 Orbe, Switzerland; Tel: +41(0)79 959 49 47; Price:D; *Saurday to Monday only*

🛏 **Hôtel Restaurant - du Chasseur**, Rue Sainte-Claire 2, 1350 Orbe, Switzerland; Tel: +41(0)24 441 67 80; Email:info@hotel-au-chasseur.com; www.hotel-au-chasseur.com; Price:A

🛏 **Hôtel - des Mosaïques**, Chemin du Suchet 14, 1350 Orbe, Switzerland; Tel: +41(0)24 441 62 61; Email:info@hoteldesmosaiques.ch; www.hoteldesmosaiques.ch; Price:A

⚠ **TCS Camping Orbe**, Route du Signal 9, 1350 Orbe, Switzerland; Tel:+41(0)24 441 38 57; Email:camping.orbe@tcs.ch; www.campingtcs.ch; Price:C; *Pods and chalets also available*

ℹ **Office du Tourisme**, Grand-rue 1, 1350 Orbe, Switzerland; Tel:+41(0)24 442 92 37; +41 (0)24 423 61 01; www.yverdonlesbains-region.ch

Vallorbe

🏠 **Auberge Pour Tous**, Rue du Simplon 11, 1337 Vallorbe, Switzerland; Tel:+41(0)21 843 13 49; +41(0)78 898 86 72; www.aubergepourtous.ch; Price:B

⚠ **Camping de Vallorbe**, Rue des Fontaines 8, 1337 Vallorbe, Switzerland; Tel:+41(0)21 843 23 09; +41 (0)79 952 64 40; Email:camping@sports-loisirs-vallorbe.ch; sports-loisirs-vallorbe.ch; Price:C; *Caravans and tents can also be rented*

*Swiss Regional Hiking Trail - 70
The modern via Francigena*

stage 42 — Orbe to Cossonay

Length:	25.9km
Ascent:	1019m
Descent:	922m
Canterbury	1055km
Col Grand Saint Bernard:	184km

Romainmôtier Abbey   Arnaud Gaillard

Route: the stage from Orbe to Cossonay will follow regional hiking trail 70 and initially

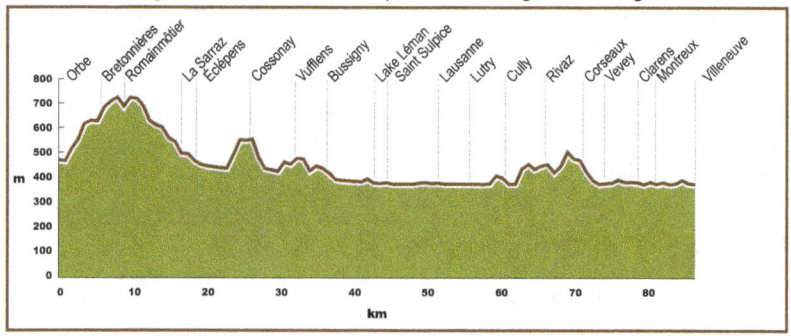

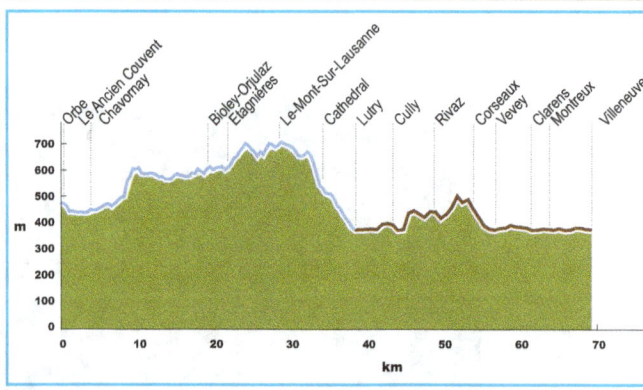

back-track on the opposite bank of the Orbe river climbing through the Bois des Chênes to Romainmôtier before making a woodland loop to La Sarraz where the terrain flattens and the path continues across farmland and on a pleasant path beside a stretch of La Venoge river. Most villages and small towns have both shops and cafés. Unfortunately there is a limited choice of accommodation in Cossonay.

The direct route to Lausanne will reduce your journey by 17 km and follows more closely the route of Sigeric

Orbe to Cossonay stage 42

The first monastery at Romainmôtier was built in the fifth century by Romanus of Condata and rebuilt in the seventh century by Duke Chramnelenus. In the tenth century the monastery and its lands were given to the Cluny Abbey when the present church was built by Abbot Odilo of Cluny. The monastery reached the height of its powers in the fourteenth and fifteenth century but began its decline in the sixteenth. The church is one of the oldest Romanesque buildings remaining in Switzerland and houses an early form of the pulpit from the eighth century, fourteenth century frescoes and the fifteenth century choir chairs. The thirteenth century Prior's house is located next to the Abbey. The house with its magnificent halls, large fireplaces, coffered ceilings and wall paintings has been fully restored.

(0.0) From the junction beside the Orbe railway station retrace you steps across the river bridge and between the football fields**(0.7)** Take the left fork and continue with the river on your right[Pass the chalet on your right] **(1.5)** Keep right up the hill[Pipeline crosses the river on your right]**(1.6)** Turn left and begin the climb out of the gorge[Footbridge on your right]**(2.1)** At the crossroads continue straight ahead on the stony track[Balade Viticole des

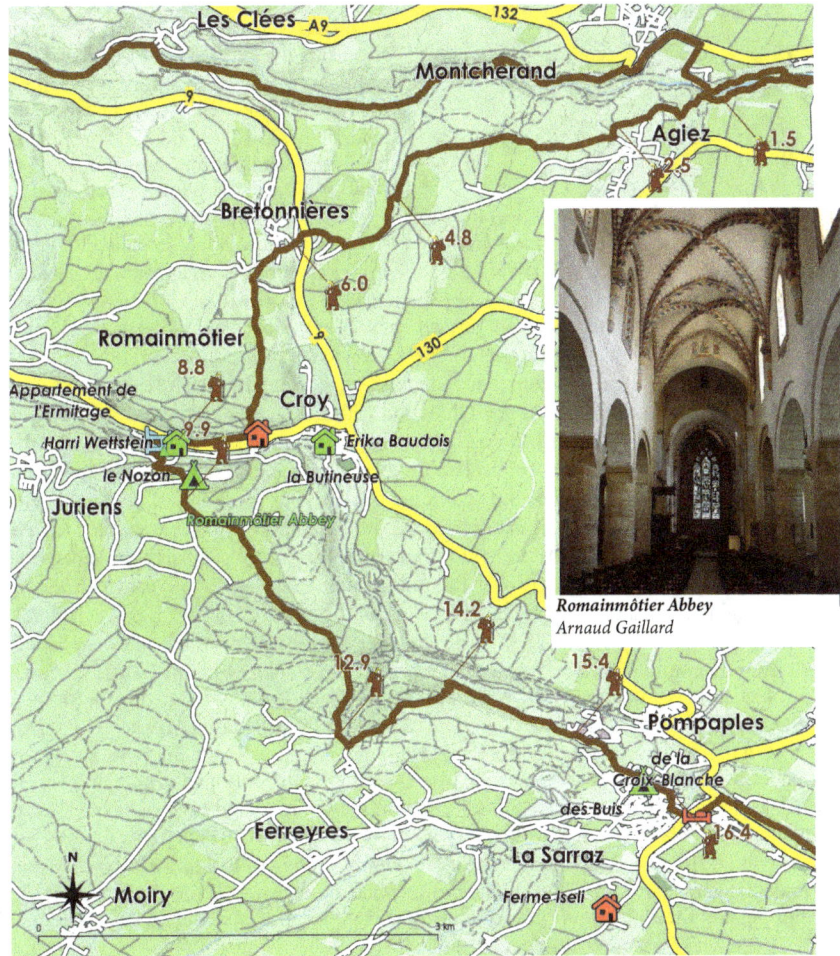

Romainmôtier Abbey
Arnaud Gaillard

stage 42 — Orbe to Cossonay

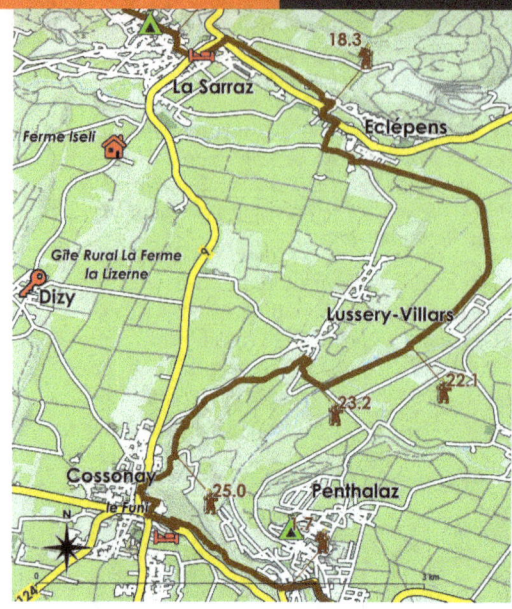

Côtes-de-l'Orbe]**(2.3)**Shortly before reaching the houses, fork right into the woods**(2.5)**At the junction, bear left on the tarmac road[Pass farmhouse on your left]**(2.7)**Turn sharp right on the narrow path into the woods**(3.3)**At the road junction, turn right and then left **(4.8)**In the clearing turn sharp right and then bear left and pass the house on your right side**(4.8)**At the road junction, turn left**(5.3)**Bear right at the T-junction with the larger road**(5.5)**Turn right on the narrow path into the woods**(5.7)**At the T-junction, turn right on the road and pass under the highway and railway bridges[Enter **Bretonnières**] **(6.0)**At the crossroads, continue straight ahead up the hill[Pass the lavoir on your right]**(6.2)**At the T-junction, turn left and then take the left fork between the fields[Direction Place de Tir] **(8.8)**At the road junction in **Romainmôtier**, cross the road and take the second road on your right, downhill[Towards the abbey, low wall on the left]**(9.3)**On the crown of the sharp right hand bend, after passing the abbey and leaving Romainmôtier, fork left and then turn left again at the end of the car park**(9.5)**At the junction with the larger road, turn left and bear right between the fields **(9.9)**Take the left fork[Follow the line of trees] **(12.9)**At the T-junction with the tarmac road, turn left, pass a car park on your left and take the track on your left[Direction La Sarraz]**(13.5)**At the crossroads in the tracks beside the refuge, turn left **(14.2)**At the T-junction following the steep descent, turn right[Keep the river - le Nozon - on your left] **(15.4)**At the T-junction with the tarmac road, turn right[Pass the hospital car park on your right]**(15.6)**After passing the car park take the right fork and then bear left on the track into the woods**(16.2)**In the car park, bear right and take the tarmac pathway at the car park exit[Pass the swimming pool on your left] **(16.4)**Turn right on the road and pass the church on your left**(16.6)**At the T-junction in **La Sarraz**, turn left[Pass the supermarket on your right]**(16.8)**At the end of the road, turn right and immediately left on rue des Terreaux**(17.1)**Cross over the railway and take the narrow path between the houses and then turn right up the hill[Chemin de Mormont]**(17.3)**Fork right on the gravel track[Chemin des Vignes] **(18.3)**Turn right over the the railway track and then take the exit from the roundabout, towards the church**(18.6)**In **Éclépens** with the water fountain on your left, turn right and then turn left at the crossroads and continue with the river - la Venoge - on your left [Les Trois Noyers] **(22.1)**After passing an industrial area on your left, turn left and then right over the river bridge and continue beside the river**(22.9)**At the junction with the main road, turn right over the bridge and continue straight ahead on the track as the road bears to the left **(23.2)**Rejoin the road and turn right into Lussery and then immediately turn left and left again to follow Chemin de Plan to the town of Cossonay **(25.0)**At the T-junction, turn right[Chemin des Linardes]**(25.5)**At the crossroads beside the garage in Cossany turn left and then left again[Towards the clock tower]**(25.8)**After passing the clock tower immediately turn right towards the church[Rue du Temple] **(25.9)**Arrive at **Cossonay** beside the church

Orbe to Cossonay — stage 42

Accommodation and Tourist Information

Cossonay-Ville
Hôtel - le Funi[Michel & Marianne Tanniger],Avenue du Funiculaire 11, 1304 Cossonay-Ville, Switzerland; Tel:+41(0)21 863 63 40; Email:info@lefuni.ch; www.lefuni.ch; Price:A

Croy
Erika Baudois,Chemin de la Foule 8, 1322 Croy, Switzerland; Tel:+41(0)24 453 13 62; Price:B

B&B - la Butineuse[Madame Catherine],Le Pont de l'Etang 7, 1322 Croy, Switzerland; Tel:+41(0)76 519 78 78; booking.juratroislacs.ch; Price:A

Dizy
Gîte Rural - La Ferme la Lizerne[Francois-Philippe de Venoge],Rue du Village 16, 1304 Dizy, Switzerland; Tel: +41(0)78 949 45 05; Email:sdevenoge@gmx.ch; www.fermelalizerne.ch; Price:B; *Dormitory and private rooms good food. Woofers welcome*; **PR**

La-Sarraz
B&B - Ferme Iseli,Route de Dizy 1, 1315 La-Sarraz, Switzerland; Tel:+41(0)21 866 66 01; +41(0)79 157 21 04; Email:reservation@ferme-iseli.ch; www.ferme-iseli.ch; Price:A

Hôtel - de la Croix-Blanche,Grand rue, 1315 La-Sarraz, Switzerland; Tel:+41(0)21 866 71 54; Email:croixblanche@bluemail.ch; www.hotelcroixblanche.ch; Price:A

Camping des Buis,Route de la Piscine 20a, 1315 La-Sarraz, Switzerland; Tel:+41(0)21 565 13 15; Email:admin@piscinedelavenoge.ch; piscinedelavenoge.ch; Price:C; *Cabins and pods also available*

Penthalaz
Camping de Penthalaz,Chemin de la Piscine 5, 1305 Penthalaz, Switzerland; Tel:+41(0)79 202 24 61; piscine.penthalaz.ch; Price:C

Romainmôtier-Envy
Appartement de l'Ermitage,Rue du Bourg 9, 1323 Romainmôtier-Envy, Switzerland; Tel: +41(0)79 535 88 04; Email:ermitage.romainmotier@gmail.com; Price:B

Harri Wettstein,Rue du Bourg 12, 1323 Romainmôtier-Envy, Switzerland; Tel:+41(0)21 802 44 18; +41(0)76 349 83 71; Price:C; *No meals*

Camping - le Nozon,Route du Signal 2, 1323 Romainmôtier-Envy, Switzerland; Tel:+41(0)24 453 13 70; Email:domstreit@bluewin.ch; www.camping-romainmotier.ch; Price:C

Direct Route to Lausanne

Length:	38.4km
Ascent:	1071m
Descent:	1174m

Route: the direct route saves 17 km over the "Official Route" with the opportunity to find accommodation at several points. After leaving Orbe the route follows a combination of tourist footpaths and cycling routes to le-Mont-sur-Lausanne on the hills overlooking lake Geneva and then follows a tributary of the chemin St Jacques into the city of Lausanne, passing beside the Cathedral of Notre Dame of Lausanne and rejoining the "Official Route" on the lake shore.

(0.0)From the junction beside the railway station climb the ramp, turn right on the road(0.2)Beside the Casino turn left[Rue de la Poste](0.2)At the T-junction, turn left and immediately right[Narrow street](0.3)In place du Marché, beside the restaurant du Chasseur, bear right on rue Centrale[No Entry sign](0.4)Take the right fork, direction Cossonay on rue du Grand Pont[Pass **le Ancien Couvent des Clarisses**](0.5)At the crossroads, continue straight ahead[Cross the river bridge](0.7)After crossing the bridge turn left[Route de Saint-Éloi, direction Chavornay](1.4)At the roundabout, turn right direction Chavornay and join cycle track on the left side of road[Pass the Nestlé factory on left](3.9)On the entry to **Chavornay** turn right to cross over the main road following the cycle path and pass in front of the hotel and railway station[Industrial buildings to the right](4.5)Turn left[Under the railway bridge](4.6)Fork left on the larger road[Rue du

stage 42　　　　　　　　Orbe to Cossonay

Château](4.7)At the junction, turn right[Rue du Château](4.8)At the T-junction with the major road, turn right[Boulangerie ahead at the junction](5.2)Bear left onto rue de Collège[Café on your left](5.3)On the apex of the bend to the left, turn right[Tourisme Pédestre sign](5.7)Take the right fork, the tarmac gives way to an unmade road (6.3)At the junction, after passing under the motorway, turn right down the hill(6.4)Turn left, just in front of a large white house, pass through the courtyard and continue with the woods to the right (8.2)Fork left[Tourisme Pédestre sign](8.2)Turn left up the hill [Tourisme Pédestre sign](8.6)Turn right at the top of the steep hill[Tourisme Pédestre sign](9.1)Fork right up the hill[Tourisme Pédestre sign](9.4)Cross the concrete road and continue on the track[Towards the tower](9.7)Turn right at the crossroads in the track[Tourisme Pédestre sign](9.9)Turn left direction Etagnières[Tourisme Pédestre sign](10.1)

The track emerges onto a concrete road, turn right down the hill[Tourisme Pédestre sign](10.3)Bear left down the hill beside "Golf du domaine du Brésil"[Tourisme Pédestre sign](11.1)At the T-junction, turn right down the hill[Sign for the golf club](11.3)Turn left just after passing the house - Goumens-le-Jux[Tourisme Pédestre sign](11.7)Bear right at

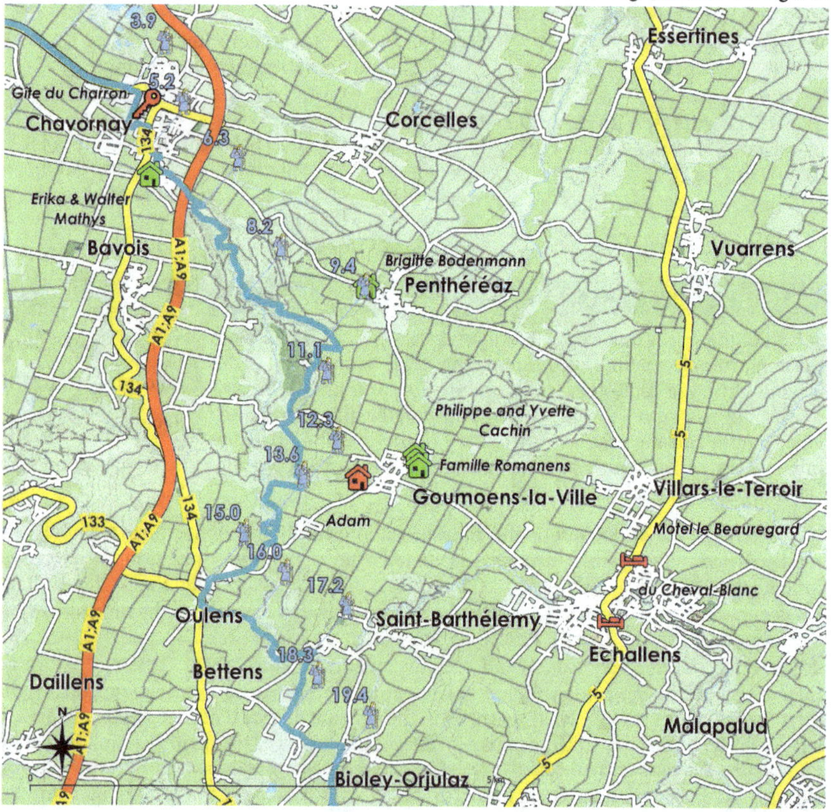

Orbe to Cossonay stage 42

the fork ⚶(12.3)Turn right direction Etagniérs[Tourisme Pédestre sign](13.0)Turn left onto Chemin du Talent, slightly uphill and towards the church spire(13.2)Fork right onto the concrete road[Tourisme Pédestre sign](13.3)Bear right between trees[Tourisme Pédestre sign] ⚶(13.6)The track emerges onto a concrete road, turn left[Pass a water treatment plant on right](14.6)At the crossroads, continue straight ahead on route d'Eclagnens[Towards Oulens-sous-Echallens] ⚶(15.0)Bear left into village[Route du Centre](15.3)At the T-junction, turn left[Direction Echallens](15.4)Turn left on the gravel track, towards the woods[Junction opposite "Antiques"] ⚶(16.0)Turn right in front of woods[Keep the trees on left](16.3)Take the left fork, towards the river [Tourisme Pédestre sign](16.5)After crossing the river, turn right keeping the farm buildings on your left[Tourisme Pédestre sign] ⚶(17.2)At the T-junction with the more major road turn right and immediately bear left beside the trees[Tourisme Pédestre sign] ⚶(18.3)At the T-junction, turn left direction Bioley-Orjulaz[Large factory at the bottom of the hill on left](18.9)At the junction, continue straight ahead[Direction Assens](19.1)At the crossroads, just before reaching the village of **Bioley-Orjulaz**, turn right onto Cycle Route n° 22[Direction Lausanne] ⚶(19.4)At the crossroads, continue straight ahead following the Cycle Route[Towards the woods](20.0)Fork left and then bear right on chemin de la Forêt[Avoid the gravel track beside the woods to the left] ⚶(21.7)Bear right [Into **Etagnières**](22.0)Continue straight ahead towards the village centre[Cycle Route n° 22, direction Lausanne](22.2)At the T-junction with the main road, turn right and immediately left, Cycle Route n° 22[Junction opposite the railway station] ⚶(24.4)Pass through Morrens and bear right on Chemin de la Mèbre[Cycle Route n° 22, direction Lausanne] ⚶(28.5)At the T-junction, in **le-Mont-sur-Lausanne** turn left[Leave Cycle Route n° 22](28.6)At the roundabout, turn right [Direction Lausanne] (29.1)Beside Hôtel Central on place de Coppoz, continue straight ahead on the left side of the road and join the pathway in the park that separates the 2 roads. Note:- if you wish to reach the wider facilities of Lausanne, then bus n° 8 will take you from the bus stop near the roundabout to the centre of the city[Towards the

stage 42   Orbe to Cossonay

church steeple, keep the line of trees on your left](29.3)Pass the church on your left and continue straight ahead[Between two lines of trees] (29.6)At the end of the avenue of trees, return to the pavement on the right of the road and continue straight ahead[Open grassed area to your right](29.8)At the crossroads, beside the Auberge Communale le Mont, turn left and then bear left[Chemin du Pré-d'Ogue, pass No Through Road sign on your right](29.8)Take the right fork, downhill[Chemin du Vallon](30.0)At the end of the tarmac road, continue straight ahead and follow the track across the field[Two garages on your right](30.4)At the T-junction with road, cross the road and turn right[Pass a parking area close on your left](30.5)At the end of the parking area, go down the 3 steps and turn left to enter the fenced area around the sawmill. Curiously the path passes between the mill buildings.[Pass the yellow tower and adjacent wooden building, close on your right, yellow diamond on the wooden building] (30.8)Fork right downhill on the gravel track[St Jacques route n° 4](31.0)Turn right, down the hill on the wooden steps[Direction lac de Sauvabelin](31.1)Turn right over the wooden foot-bridge and then immediately left[Keep the stream close on your left](31.3)Beside the highway bridge, turn right[Enter parking Vivarium](31.4)Turn sharp right and climb the concrete steps. Note:- to avoid the steps, remain on the road to the T-junction with the main road and then turn right into the woods on the broad track to the crossroads with the "Official Route" where you should turn left[Under the highway bridge, beside the Buvette](31.5)At the top of the steps, bear left then right[Keep the highway on your right](31.6)Shortly before reaching the bridge over the highway, turn left into the woods[Tourisme Pédestre](31.8)At the crossroads with the tarmac track, continue straight ahead (31.9)At the junction with the main road, cross over and turn left and then bear right on chemin des Celtes[Towards parking area](32.1)Beside the bus stop for Lac de Sauvabelin, keep right on the road[Towards the Auberge du Lac de Sauvabelin](32.2)At the end of the buildings on the right, take the

Tour de Sauvabelin - Sauvabelin forest, Lausanne

middle of the three paths[Towards la Tour](32.3)With la Tour directly ahead, take the left fork[Pass the tower on your right](32.5)At the T-junction after passing the tower, turn left on the tarmac[Views of lake Geneva through the trees](32.6)At the crossroads, turn right(32.7)At the T-junction with the car park directly ahead, turn left(32.8)At the T-junction with the road, take the pedestrian crossing and turn right[Beside the old funicular station] (32.8)At the end of the funicular station, bear left diagonally across the car park and take the footpath[Pass the house with the red and white shutters on your right] (33.0)At the viewpoint over the entire length of the lake, bear right and then turn left[Follow the yellow footpath sign](33.1)At the T-junction, turn left and then left again[Follow the n° 4 footpath sign](33.2)Turn left on the track, following the n° 4 sign[Modern low rise office building on your right] (33.2)At the T-junction in the tracks, turn right[Grass on your right, trees on your left](33.5)At the foot of the track,

Orbe to Cossonay stage 42

bear left around the circle and then turn left following the Tourisme Pédestre sign[Pass Fondation de l'Hermitage on your right](33.6)As the pathway starts to turn sharply to the right, turn left through the trees[Tourisme Pédestre sign](33.7)At the crossroads in the tracks, continue straight ahead downhill(33.9)At the T-junction with the main road, rue de la Barre, turn left[Towards the mini-roundabout](33.9)At the mini-roundabout, continue straight ahead, then bear left in the direction of the cathedral[Pass Château Saint-Marie on your right] (34.0)Cross the place du Château and then bear left into rue de Cité Derrier[Initially towards the Préfecture](34.2)At the junction with rue Charles-Vuilermet, bear left[Under the archway](34.2)At the junction with place de la Cathédrale, continue straight ahead and skirt the cathedral[**Cathedral** walls on the right](34.3)From the side entrance to the cathedral, bear left and downhill[Pass MUDAC - Musée de Design et d'Arts Appliqués Contemporains on the right](34.4)At the T-junction, turn left[Pass between the stone pillars and cross the road bridge](34.5)At the traffic lights, continue straight ahead, direction Vevey[Beside the metro station](34.7)At the traffic lights continue straight ahead[Pass Parc de Mon-Repos on the left] (35.1)Shortly after passing the steps on the left, bear right at the traffic lights[Avenue du Léman](35.4)Bear left on Avenue du Léman[Direction Vevey, pass a park on the right](36.1)At the roundabout, continue straight ahead on Avenue du Léman[Enter Pully and pass a further roundabout] (37.0)At the major crossroads, continue straight ahead[Towards the lake](37.3)At the roundabout, after passing under the railway, continue straight ahead[Trees in the centre of the road] (37.6)At the traffic lights, after passing the arched railway bridge on the left, turn right[Chemin de la Damatajre](37.9)At the traffic lights, turn left[Direction Vevey Montreux, Cycle Route n° 7] (38.4)At the entry to **Lutry**, continue towards the marina. Note:- the "Official Route" merges from the right

stage 42 — Orbe to Cossonay

Accommodation and Tourist Information

Chavornay
🏠 **Erika & Walter Mathys**,Chemin du Vieux Moulin 10, 1373 Chavornay, Switzerland; Tel:+41(0)24 441 49 89; Email:ew.mathys@bluewin.ch; Price:B

🗝 ⌂**Gîte - du Charron**[Yvan et Tania Benoît],Grand'rue 69, 1373 Chavornay, Switzerland; Tel:+41(0)24 441 09 43; Email:site@hotes.ch; www.hotes.ch; Price:B

Chéseaux-sur-Lausanne
🛏**Pub & Hôtel - Le Galion**,Route de Genève 1, 1033 Chéseaux-sur-Lausanne, Switzerland; Tel:+41(0)21 703 17 17; +41(0) 79 864 54 83; Email:info@galions.ch; www.galion.ch; Price:A

Cugy VD
🛏**Motel - des Pins**,Route de Bottens 4, 1053 Cugy VD, Switzerland; Tel:+41(0) 21 731 35 68; www.echallens-tourisme.ch; Price:A

Echallens
🛏**Auberge - du Cheval-Blanc**,Route de Lausanne 11, 1040 Echallens, Switzerland; Tel:+41(0)21 881 12 96; www.cheval-blancechallens.ch; Price:A

Goumoens-la-Ville
🏠 **Famille Romanens**,Chemin des Oches 3, 1376 Goumoens-la-Ville, Switzerland; Tel:+41(0)21 881 35 17; Price:B

🏠 **Philippe and Yvette Cachin**,Chemin de la Louye 2, 1376 Goumoens-la-Ville, Switzerland; Tel:+41(0)21 881 27 81; Email:y.cachin@bluewin.ch; Price:B

🏠 **B&B - Adam**[Yoko & Michel Adam],Route d'Eclagnens 14, 1376 Goumoens-la-Ville, Switzerland; Tel:+41(0)76 411 37 76; +41(0)21 881 57 48; Email:adam-beef@romandie.ch; bnb-yoko-et-michel-adam-bed-breakfast.vaudhotels.com; Price:B

Lausanne
✝ **Cure Saint.Amédée**,Route du Pavement 97, 1018 Lausanne, Switzerland; Tel:+41(0)21 647 22 32; Email:paroisse.lausanne.stamedee@cath-vd.ch; www.cath-vd.ch/cvd_parish/st-amedee; Price:C

Penthéréaz
🏠 **Brigitte Bodenmann**,Chemin du Bois-Désert, 1375 Penthéréaz, Switzerland; Tel:+41(0)21 881 51 80; +41(0)79 466 80 88; Email:brigitt.bodenmann@gmail.com; Price:C; *Sleep in a dormitory or on the straw*

Villars-le-Terroir
🛏**Motel - le Beauregard**,Route d'Yverdon, 1040 Villars-le-Terroir, Switzerland; Tel:+41(0)21 881 19 17; Email:kopa-motos@bluewin.ch; www.echallens-tourisme.ch; Price:A

Cossonay to Lausanne

stage 43

Length:	25.6km
Ascent:	587m
Descent:	769m
Canterbury	1081km
Col Grand Saint Bernard:	158km

Lausanne Cathedral of Notre Dame

Route: the stage from Cossonay to Lausanne continues on a mixture of generally quiet roads and farm and woodland tracks to the suburbs of Lausanne. A parkland path leads to the shores of lake Geneva to join the network of paths that will lead eastwards along the north shore.

The lake is served by a steamer network that might offer a pleasant alternative for those pilgrims with tired feet.

Lausanne is a large city with good access to all forms of public transport. It is a perfect place to take a break and enjoy the pleasant lake-shore walks.

There has been a settlement on the hill of Lausanne since at least the Stone Age, but most histories of the city trace its origin to the Roman camp Lausanna, which occupied a position just down the hill towards the lake, in what is now the village of Vidy.

Relocated to a more defensible hilltop in the Middle Ages, Lausanne's increasing wealth and importance were largely derived from its placement on the primary north-south routes between Italy and the north sea. Today, the town is built on three hills, surrounded by vineyard-covered slopes, with Lake Geneva at its feet.

It also is part of the Swiss Riviera that stretches to Montreux and the eastern end of the lake, an area that has been a second home to writers, artists and musicians for over 150 years, starting with the Shelleys and Lord Byron, (Frankenstein is rumoured to have been written here). Other famous residents included Ernest Hemingway and Charlie Chaplin who lived in Vevey from the mid 1930s.

Notre Dame de Lausanne is regarded as Switzerland's most impressive piece of early Gothic architecture, it was built in several stages, with the first builder beginning construction work in 1170, using Roman materials.

stage 43   Cossonay to Lausanne

(0.0) From beside the church in Cossonay continue south on rue de Temple **(0.1)** At the roundabout take the second exit[Route de Lausanne] **(0.3)** At the end of the wall turn sharp left into the woods and then turn right and continue beside the funicular **(1.7)** At the roundabout next to the Coop take the bridge over the railway and turn right at the next roundabout[Direction Lausanne] **(2.2)** Turn right beside the garage and then right at the T-junction[Towards the football field] **(2.9)** Beside the sports field car park, bear left into the trees **(3.3)** At the road junction, turn right[Continue with the open field on your left and

then take the next right turn] **(5.1)** At the T-junction turn left and take the bridge over the highway **(6.1)** At the T-junction in **Vufflens**, turn right[Grand Rue] **(6.8)** After leaving the town and passing an orchard on your right, turn right[Chemin des Bois] **(8.3)** Under the power lines, take the left fork **(9.0)** At the T-junction turn left[Chemin du Refuge] **(9.4)** Immediately after passing the tarmac car park on your left, turn right[Towards the allotments, chemin de Gravernay] **(10.5)** At the T-junction in **Bussigny**, turn left **(10.7)** Bear right on rue de la Gare, and at the station take the underpass before turning right and left to continue on chemin du Vallon **(11.4)** Bear right under the highway and then turn left. Keep the factory on your right and follow the river[Chemin de la Chocolatière] **(12.6)** Beside the small river bridge, turn left, pass under the major highway and continue to follow the river **(15.4)** Bear left and leave the river and pass the equestrian centre on your right **(16.0)** At the T-junction with the main road, turn right and right again at the crossroads, then take the track to the left leading back to the river **(16.3)** Cross the road and take the bridge over the river. Then turn left and follow the river to the lake shore **(17.0)** Turn left over the river bridge and follow the **Lake Léman (Geneva)** shore paths **(18.8)** At the T-junction with the road, turn right and follow avenue du Léman. Note:- lake steamers depart from the jetty[Pass the church of **Saint Sulpice** on your right.] **(19.9)** Im-

Cossonay to Lausanne — stage 43

Lake Steamer - La Suisse *Sergey Ashmarin*

mediately before the parking area on your left, turn right and then left to return to the lake shore path. Remain as close to the lake as possible to the end of the stage 🚶 **(25.6)** Arrive at **Lausanne (LIV)** place du Port

stage 43 — Cossonay to Lausanne

King David and Prophets Lausanne Cathedral

Cossonay to Lausanne — stage 43

Accommodation and Tourist Information

Echandens
Hôtel Pont de la Venoge, Chemin du Tennis 4, 1026 Echandens, Switzerland; Tel:+41(0)21 701 50 55; Email:info@pontdelavenoge.ch; pontdelavenoge.ch; Price:A

Lausanne-Bussigny
Hôtel - Ibis Budget, Rue de l'Industrie 67, 1030 Lausanne-Bussigny, Switzerland; Tel:+41(0)21 706 53 53; Email:h7599@accor.com; all.accor.com; Price:A

Lausanne
Auberge de Jeunesse Jeunotel, Chemin du Bois-de-Vaux 36, 1007 Lausanne, Switzerland; Tel:+41(0)21 626 02 22; Email:lausanne@youthhostel.ch; www.youthhostel.ch/lausanne; Price:A

B&B - Ada-Logements, Avenue de Tivoli 60, 1007 Lausanne, Switzerland; Tel:+41(0)21 625 71 34; Email:ada-logements@bluewin.ch; www.kobo.ch/ada-logements; Price:A

Hôtel - Swiss Chocolate by Fassbind, Rue Marterey 15, 1005 Lausanne, Switzerland; Tel:+41(0)21 601 80 00; Email:scl@byf.ch; byfassbind.com; Price:A

Hôtel - Bellerive, Avenue de Cour 99, 1007 Lausanne, Switzerland; Tel:+41(0)21 614 90 00; Email:info@hotelbellerive.ch; hotelbellerive.ch; Price:A

Hôtel - du Marché, Rue Pré-du-Marché 42, 1004 Lausanne, Switzerland; Tel:+41(0)21 647 99 00; Email:info@hoteldumarche-lausanne.ch; www.hoteldumarche-lausanne.ch; Price:B

Camping de Vidy, Chemin du Camping 3, 1007 Lausanne, Switzerland; Tel:+41(0)21 622 50 00; Email:info@clv.ch; www.campinglausannevidy.ch; Price:C; *Bungalows also available*

Lausanne Tourisme, Avenue de Rhodanie 2, 1001 Lausanne, Switzerland; Tel:+41(0)21 613 73 73; Email:info@lausanne-tourisme.ch; www.lausanne-tourisme.ch

Prilly
B&B - Deillon, Route des Flumeaux 10, 1008 Prilly, Switzerland; Tel:+41(0)21 625 76 80; +41(0)76 735 35 00; Email:deillon@2wire.ch; www.bnb-prilly.ch; Price:A

Saint-Sulpice
Hotel - Starling, Route Cantonale 31, 1025 Saint-Sulpice, Switzerland; Tel:+41(0)21 694 85 85; Email:contact@shlausanne.ch; starling-hotel-lausanne.com; Price:A

Offices of the International Olympic Committee - Lausanne

stage 44 — Lausanne to Villeneuve

Length:	35.0km
Ascent:	1915m
Descent:	1919m
Canterbury	1106km
Col Grand Saint Bernard:	133km

Vineyards - Epesses   Hansueli Krapf

Route: this beautiful stage from Lausanne to Villeneuve, offers great views of the lake and the Alps beyond and combines easy walking along more lake-side paths with some stiff climbs into the hillside vineyards.

Steamers are available from Lausanne to a number of ports along the route.

The lake-shore is a popular destination in the summer months and so accommodation can be in short supply, but there are ample stopping places for food and drink along the entire stage.

Vevey marks the half-way point of the "Official Route" from Canterbury to Rome.

A settlement existed at Vevey as early as the 2nd millennium BC.

Under Rome, the city's situation on the north east shore of Lake Geneva and at the fork in the Roman road from Italy over the Simplon Pass, made it an important settlement. It was known as Viviscus or Vibiscum and mentioned for the first time by the ancient Greek astronomer and philosopher Ptolemy, who gave it the name Ouikos.

The Reformation made the region around Montreux and Vevey an attractive haven for Huguenots from Italy, who brought their artisanal skills and set up workshops and businesses. In 1798, Napoleon liberated the region from the Bernese and in the 19th century, the tourist industry became a major commercial outlet, which continues today.

Château de Chillon, Switzerland's most visited historical building was originally owned by the House of Savoy. The Castle houses several medieval frescoes and Gothic dungeons, the latter of which were the subject of a poem penned by Lord Byron: **The Prisoner of Chillon**. The poet directly references the château in the line: "There are seven pillars of Gothic mould/ In Chillon's dungeons deep and old…"

The Montreux Jazz festival has a world famous reputation for its diverse and renowned musical performances. Although it was initially a jazz-only festival, it has since broadened its musical horizons.

Lausanne to Villeneuve stage 44

(0.0) From place du port, continue east along the lake shore (4.3) Bear right through the car park towards the boat dock and follow the lake-side [keep the lake immediately on your right] **(6.5)** Turn left and then right to follow the main road [Route de Lausanne] **(7.0)** Beside the Villettes railway station, cross the road, descend the ramp, pass under the railway and bear right, parallel to the railway and into the vineyards [Direction Villette Bourg] **(9.1)** On reaching the **Cully** railway station, bear right on the small road [Close to the railway, Café la Gare on the left] **(9.2)** Turn right and take the road under the railway and

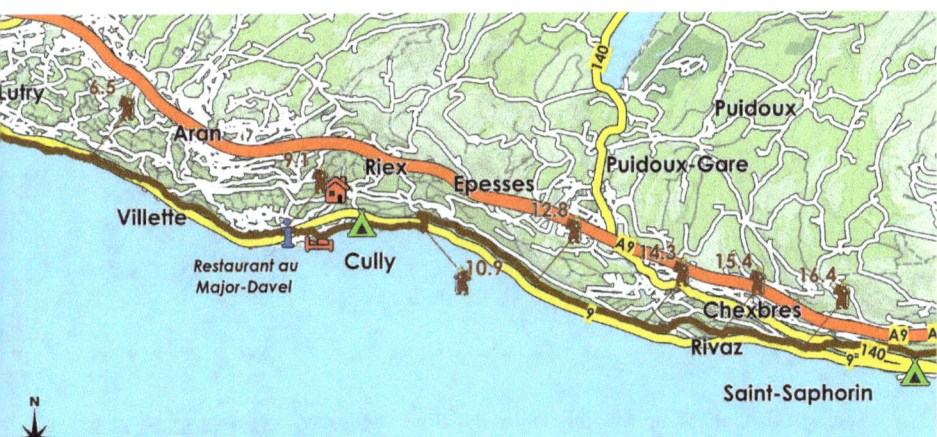

then immediately turn left on rue du Temple [Pass the church on your left side] **(9.5)** At the T-junction, turn right towards the steamer jetty and then left to continue on the lake shore **(10.9)** As the river enters the lake, turn left and climb to steps [Pass under the railway and highway] **(11.1)** Turn sharp right in the hamlet [Chemin du Calamin, parallel to lake-shore] **(11.8)** At the junction, continue straight ahead **(12.8)** At the next junction, again continue straight ahead [Winery on the right at the junction] **(14.3)** At the crossroads, turn right, downhill on the tarmac road [Viewpoint on the right at the junction] **(14.6)** On the outskirts of the village of **Rivaz** turn right and right again [Cross the bridge] **(14.7)** Turn left on rue du Collége [Beside the covered water trough] **(14.7)** Turn left on route des Bons Voisins [House with large clock ahead] **(14.8)** Turn right on chemin des Paleyres [Continue in the vineyards parallel to the lake-shore] **(15.4)** At the crossroads, continue straight ahead, chemin de la Vigne-a-Gilles [Château on the lake-side below] **(16.2)** At the T-junction, turn right [Towards the village] **(16.4)** In front of the bell tower in Saint-Saphorin bear left up the hill [Sentier des Rondes] **(16.6)** At the crossroads con-

The Fork of Vevey

stage 44 — Lausanne to Villeneuve

tinue straight ahead up the hill[Sentier des Rondes]**(16.7)**At the junction, bear left up the hill**(16.7)**At the T-junction with the road turn right and then bear left uphill on the narrow road[Keep the wall close on the left]]**(17.0)**At the fork bear left on chemin du Burignon[Under the railway]**(17.3)**On the bend to the right bear right on the lower road[Parallel to the railway, Chemin de Chavonchin] **(18.1)**At the fork, bear right on chemin des Combes**(18.3)**At the junction, keep left[Chemin des Combes] **(19.2)**On the crown of the bend to the right, turn sharp left[Chemin du Grand Pin]**(19.4)**At the crossroads, turn sharp right and go downhill on chemin des Rochettes[Towards Corseaux]**(19.6)**At the T-junction in **Corseaux**, turn left on rue du Village[Vinicole Corseaux]**(19.7)**At the junction, bear right downhill[Rue du Village, boulangerie on the left]**(19.7)**At the T-junction, turn left[Hotel on the left] **(20.3)**At the traffic lights continue straight ahead and then take the first turning to the right - chemin de Meruz[Direction Corsier Village]**(20.9)**At the T-junction, turn left under the railway bridges[Funicular station on the right] **(21.1)**At the roundabout continue straight ahead on avenue Nestlé[Direction Vielle Ville]**(21.3)** Turn right on avenue de Savoie[Beside the Nestlé

Charlie Chaplin - Vevey Quays

Lausanne to Villeneuve — stage 44

offices] **(21.4)** Turn left and proceed along the lake-shore[Quai Ernest Ansermet] **(22.6)** From the Grande Place in **Vevey (LIII)**, continue straight ahead along the lake-shore[Boat dock on the right] **(24.1)** Beside the marina, in la-Tour-de-Peilz, bear left on rue du Port and then turn right at the T-junction **(24.2)** At the end of the road, turn left and then right on Grand Rue **(27.1)** In **Clarens**, turn right on chemin de Ile de Salagonto and return to lake-side and then turn left[Follow quai de Clarens] **(29.5)** Beside the Tourist Office in **Montreux** continue straight ahead[Quai de la Rouvenaz] **(34.4)** On entry to Villeneuve, bear right to remain close to the water[Leaving Cycle Route n° 1] **(35.0)** Arrive at **Villeneuve**[Beside the steamer jetty]

Château de Chillon - Montreux

stage 44 — Lausanne to Villeneuve

Accommodation and Tourist Information

Chardonne
⛺ **Camping de la Pichette**,Chemin de la Paix 37, 1803 Chardonne, Switzerland; Tel:+41(0)21 925 35 07; Email:camping.pichette@vevey.ch; www.vevey.ch/vivre-vevey/economie-et-tourisme/camping-de-la-pichette; Price:C; *Open April to end September*

Corseaux
🏠 **Villa Clairval**,Sentier de Priolaz 2, 1802 Corseaux, Switzerland; Tel:+ 41(0)79 898 26 37; Email:tcholia@yahoo.fr; Price:D; *1 room subject to availability*

Cully
🏠 **B&B - le Vigny**,Chemin du Vigny 10, 1096 Cully, Switzerland; Tel:+41(0)21 799 38 12; +41(0)79 764 69 24; bnb.ch/en/le-vigny-17; Price:A; *Lower cost options if sleeping in the cabin or henhouse*

🛏 **Hôtel Restaurant - au Major-Davel**,Place d'Armes 8, 1096 Cully, Switzerland; Tel:+41(0)21 552 19 50; Email:info@major-davel.ch; www.major-davel.ch; Price:A

⛺ **Camping de Moratel**,Route de Moratel 2 , 1096 Cully, Switzerland; Tel:+41(0)21 799 19 14; Email:camping.moratel@bluewin.ch; spbmc.ch; Price:C

ℹ **Office du Tourisme**,Rue de la Gare 10, 1096 Cully, Switzerland; Tel:+41(0)84 886 84 84; Email:info@montreuxriviera.com; www.montreuxriviera.com

La-Tour-de-Peilz
⛺ **Camping de la Maladaire**,Route de Saint-Maurice 310, 1814 La-Tour-de-Peilz, Switzerland; Tel:+41(0)21 944 54 54; Email:camping.lamaladaire@gmail.com; www.lamaladaire.com; Price:C

Montreux
🏠 **Auberge de Jeunesse Montreux-Territet**,Passage de l'Auberge 8, 1820 Montreux, Switzerland; Tel:+41(0)21 963 49 34; Email:montreux@youthhostel.ch; www.youthhostel.ch/montreux; Price:A

✝ **Paroisse du Sacré-Coeur de Montreux**,Avenue des Planches 27, 1820 Montreux, Switzerland; Tel:+41(0)21 963 37 08; Email:paroisse.montreux@cath-vd.ch; www.cath-vd.ch/cvd_parish/montreux

ℹ **Tourist Information Point**,Grand-rue 45, 1820 Montreux, Switzerland; Tel:+41(0)84 886 84 84; Email:info@montreuxriviera.com; www.montreuxriviera.com

Noville
⛺ **Camping - les Grangettes**,Route des Grangettes, 1845 Noville, Switzerland; Tel:+41(0)21 960 15 03; Email:noville@treyvaud.com; www.myvaud.ch/en/P16573/camping-les-grangettes; Price:C; *Mobile home and Pod available*

Vevey
🏠 **Vevey House Hostel**,Place du Marché 5, 1800 Vevey, Switzerland; Tel:+41(0)21 922 35 32; Email:info@veveyhouse.com; www.veveyhouse.com; Price:B

✝ **Paroisse de Notre Dame**,Rue des Chenevières 10, 1800 Vevey, Switzerland; Tel:+41(0)21 944 14 14; Email:paroisse.vevey.notre-dame@cath-vd.ch; www.cath-vd.ch/paroisses/vevey-notre-dame

🏠 **B&B - Arquebusiers**[Jean-Pierre & Elisabeth Narbel],Chemin des Arquebusiers 20, 1800 Vevey, Switzerland; Tel:+41(0)21 921 52 10; +41(0)79 643 00 34; Email:enarbel@vtxnet.ch; www.bnb.ch; Price:B

ℹ **Office du Tourisme**,Grande place 29, 1800 Vevey, Switzerland; Tel:+41(0)84 886 84 84; Email:info@montreuxriviera.com; www.montreux-vevey.com

Villeneuve
🛏 **Hotel - du Quai**,Rue du Quai 4, 1844 Villeneuve, Switzerland; Tel:+41(0)21 966 17 17; Email:info@hotel-duquai.ch; www.hotel-duquai.ch; Price:A

⛺ **Camping des Horizons Bleus**,Rue du Quai 11, 1844 Villeneuve, Switzerland; Tel:+41(0)21 960 15 47; camping-club-vaudois.ch; Price:C; *Mobile homes available*

ℹ **Tourist Information Point**,Place de la Gare 5, 1844 Villeneuve, Switzerland; Tel:+41(0)84 886 84 84; Email:info@montreuxriviera.com; www.montreuxriviera.com

Villeneuve to Saint-Maurice — stage 45

Length:	30.7km
Ascent:	1489m
Descent:	1423m
Canterbury	1141km
Col Grand Saint Bernard:	98km

Château d'Aigle   Emmanuelle Adjoa Bessi

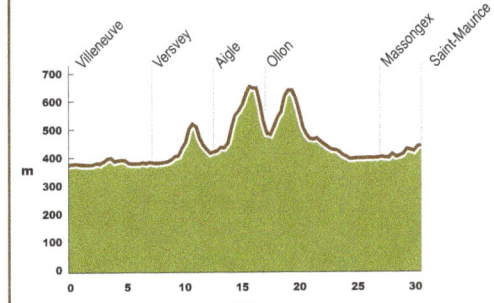

Route: the stage from Villeneuve to Saint-Maurice initially follows tracks and minor roads on the valley floor, passing through the modern village of Versvey (LII) - it is unlikely that this would have been the location of the Sigeric submansione as the current village lies in the historic flood plain of the Rhône. There is, however, evidence of Roman occupation on the hillsides on both flanks of the valley. In 1978 and 1980, 2 of the oldest Roman milestones in Switzerland were discovered on the hillsides close to Versvey.

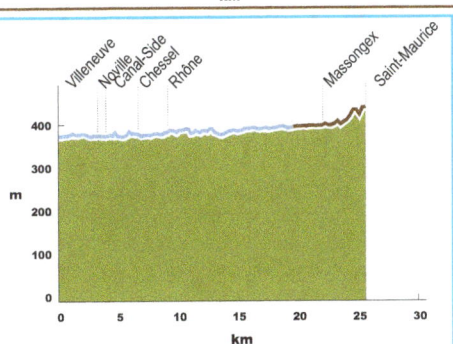

After Versvey, route 70 once more climbs into the vineyards before passing through Aigle and then climbing and descending on the wooded hillside roads and finally crossing the Rhône.

The Rhône valley direct route, although bypassing, Versvey saves 5 km and avoids the strenuous hillside climbs.

There is the opportunity to break the journey at Aigle, Olon and Massongex.

Saint-Maurice is best known for its Abbaye de Saint-Maurice d'Agaune. Situated against a cliff in a picturesque section of the Simplon Pass, between Geneva and northern Italy. The abbey is renowned for its connection to stories of the martyrdom of the Theban Legions. Built on the ruins of a 1st Century B.C. Roman shrine to the god Mercury in the Roman staging-post of Agaunum, the Basilica of St. Maurice of Agaunum became the centre of a monastery under the patronage of King Sigismund of Burgundy, the first ruler in his dynasty to convert from Arian to Trinitarian Christianity. After being a point of contention and serial ownership over the centuries, Pope Gregory XVI finally gave the abbey its title of See of Bethlehem in Perpetuity, in 1840. The

stage 45 — Villeneuve to Saint-Maurice

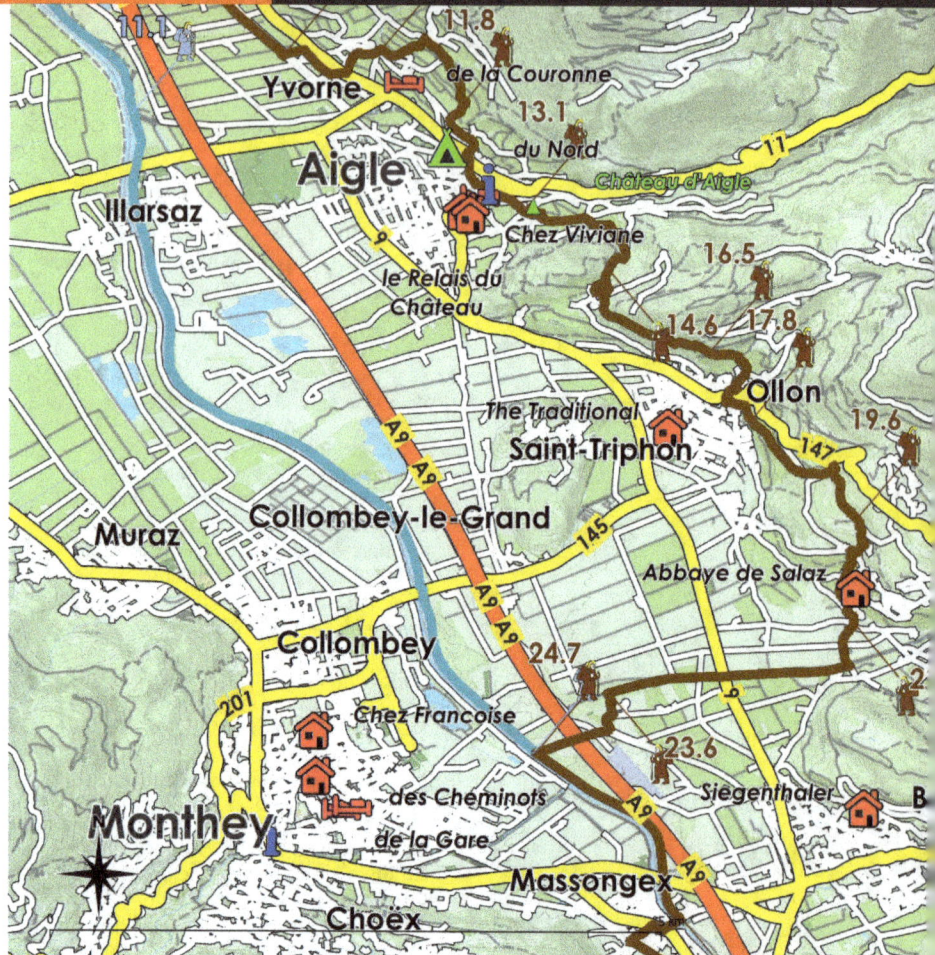

abbey has been built and rebuilt over a period of at least fifteen centuries. Excavations on the site have revealed a baptistry dating back to the 4th and 5th centuries, a series of four main churches built over one another dating from the 5th to the 11th century, and crypts built between the 4th and 8th century. The current church was first built in the 17th century, but the tower is 11th century.

(0.0) Beside the steamer jetty, turn left [Towards the Villeneuve railway station] **(0.1)** Take the subway under the railway tracks and then turn right on route d'Arvel **(0.4)** At the roundabout, continue straight ahead and then turn right on route de Champfleuri and continue parallel to the railway 🚶 **(1.8)** At the traffic lights, turn left and immediately right onto the tarmac track [Continue with the canal on your right] **(2.6)** Turn right over the canal bridge and then bear left remaining beside the canal [Towards the water purification plant] 🚶 **(3.8)** After passing the water plant, bear right and then briefly left on the road, then follow the tarmac track [Continue parallel to the canal] **(4.8)** In the village of Roche, bear right [Pass a small rest area on the left] 🚶 **(5.0)** At the T-junction, turn left and then take the first right [Towards the railway] **(5.2)** Take the subway under the railway and immediately turn

Villeneuve to Saint-Maurice — stage 45

left[Continue with the railway close on your left] **(6.8)** On reaching the village, turn right and immediately left**(7.2)** At the crossroads, in **Versvey** (LII), turn left and then right to continue with the railway close on your left **(8.9)** Turn left over the bridge and then take the first turning to the right[Between industrial buildings]**(9.4)** At the second crossroads, turn left. Cross the main road and continue straight ahead[Pass a cemetery on your right] **(10.0)** Turn right and pass behind the restaurant. Then take the first turning to the left and continue to climb through the vineyards**(10.5)** At the crossroads in Vers-Morey, turn sharp right. Keep right as the road more gently descends through the vineyards. **(11.5)** Take the left fork up the small road[Embankment on your left]**(11.8)** At the junction, bear right between the walls**(12.0)** At the complex junction, continue straight ahead and then bear left over the bridge**(12.1)** Bear right towards the centre of Aigle following rue de Bourg**(12.3)** At the end of the pedestrian zone, turn left**(12.4)** Arrive at Aigle centre[Place du Marché] **(0.0)** From place de Marché take Avenue du Cloitre and pass the church on your left in the old town of Aigle[Between vineyards] **(0.4)** After passing the church bear left, right and left again to pass the Château on your left[Follow signs for Château Musées]**(1.0)** Take the right fork and then keep left broadly parallel to the railway[Direction Verchiez] **(1.9)** Cross the railway tracks

227

stage 45 — Villeneuve to Saint-Maurice

The Rhône bridge at Massongex

and continue with the railway on your right**(2.1)**Just before the bridge under the railway, turn sharp left, uphill on the tarmac and recross the railway. Following the track along the hillside through the woods **(3.5)**Descend through the vineyards on chemin des Morretes[Pass "Sam Sufi" on your right] **(4.1)**Beside the water fountain in **Ollon**, bear left and then right[Chemin du Bornel Dessus]**(4.3)**At the crossroads with the clock tower on your right, continue straight ahead and then turn left and follow chemin de la Roche **(4.7)**Take the left fork up the hill**(5.5)**Briefly bear right on the tarmac road and then continue straight ahead on the track into the woods as the road turns sharply to the right **(6.4)** Continue straight ahead, downhill, on the tarmac[Beside the farm]**(6.8)**Turn right[Ruelle du Four a Pains]**(6.9)**At the crossroads, turn left**(6.9)** Immediately before the car park, turn sharp right and then sharp left and continue on the grass track through the vines**(7.2)**At the road junction, bear left and then right, downhill[Ruelle des Fontaines] **(7.8)**Take the right fork[Direction Bex]**(8.3)** Immediately after crossing the bridge over the waterway, turn right on the track and continue with the waterway close on your right **(10.3)**Before reaching the railway, turn left through the woods and pass beside the equestrian centre. Bear right to take the bridges under the railway and over the highway **(11.4)**On reaching the banks of the Rhône turn left and follow the track. Note:- the Alternate Route joins from the right **(13.8)**Turn right and cross the pedestrian bridge, at the main road junction in **Massongex**, turn right and then left on route de la Gare[Direction la Poste]**(14.3)**Cross the railway tracks and immediately turn left[Continue with the railway close on your left] **(16.5)**Turn left, under the railway and then turn right on the main road[Towards the Château de Saint Maurice]**(17.0)**On entering Saint Maurice fork left[Grand Rue]**(17.2)**Arrive at Saint-Maurice (LI) centre, beside the Abbaye de Saint Maurice[Town Hall to your left]

Château de Saint-Maurice

Villeneuve to Saint-Maurice — stage 45

The Rhône Valley Direct Route

Route: follows pleasant pathways on the side of le Grand Canal and then on the banks of the Rhône. The Alternate Route will rejoin route 70 before reaching Saint Maurice.

Length:	19.7km
Ascent:	439m
Descent:	417m

The route will reduce your total journey by 5 km and avoid 600m of climbing and descending. If you elect to take this route and continue to Saint Maurice, your stage from Villeneuve is a little under 26 km.

(0.0)From the jetty, continue straight ahead[Direction Noville](0.6)Turn right and leave the main road immediately after crossing the bridge over the waterway[Towards the lake, Cycle Route n°7](0.7)Turn left to follow the Tourisme Pédestre sign[Keep the lake to the right](2.1)Proceed straight ahead on route des Saviez[Equestrian centre on the right](3.0)At the T-junction, at the entry to Noville, turn left[Chemin du Battoir](3.2)At the crossroads in the centre of **Noville** bear right on the more major road[Rue des Anciennes Postes](3.3)Take the right fork on the road[Direction Evian](3.3)Turn right on chemin des Bousses[House, la Belette, on the left](3.4)At the T-junction turn right remaining on chemin des Bousses[Tourisme Pédestre sign](3.6)At the junction bear left[Tourisme Pédestre sign](4.0)Join the **canal-side** path and turn left[Keep the canal on your right](5.5)As the tarmac becomes an unmade track, go straight ahead remaining beside the canal (6.6)At the junction with the main road, cross over to continue on the track beside the Grand Canal[**Chessel** is to the right where drinking water can be obtained](7.8)Bear right over canal bridge and turn left to continue on the canal-side path[Now, keep canal on your left](9.1)Turn right and pass through the trees towards the river, then turn left to follow the path beside the **Rhône**. Note:- those wishing to visit the named Sigeric village of Versvey (LII) should take the canal bridge and continue straight ahead for 1200 metres. There is some controversy over whether this low lying modern village is an appropriate interpretation of the name Burbulei from Sigeric's chronicle. The village is to the left. Rejoin the route by retracing your steps to this point[Shortly before the next bridge](11.1)Continue straight ahead over the bridge[Tourisme Pédestre signs to Aigle Centre](19.7)Continue straight ahead beside the river. Note:- Swiss Route 70 joins from the left

Accommodation and Tourist Information

Aigle

B&B - Chez Viviane,Route d'Ollon 17, 1860 Aigle, Switzerland; Tel: +41(0)78 803 04 37; Email:viviane.mottier@hotmail.com; www.airbnb.co.za/rooms/23368515; Price:B

B&B - le Relais du Château,Chemin de Rochebord 20, 1860 Aigle, Switzerland; Tel:+41(0)24 466 63 31; Email:info@bnb.aigle.ch; bnb-aigle.ch; Price:A

Hôtel - du Nord,Rue Colomb 2, 1860 Aigle, Switzerland; Tel:+41(0)24 468 10 55; Email:info@hoteldunord.ch; www.hoteldunord.ch; Price:A

Camping de la Piscine,Avenue des Glariers, 1860 Aigle, Switzerland; Tel:+41(0)24 466 26 60; Email:campingdelapiscine@bluewin.ch; www.campingdelapiscine.ch; Price:C; *Pre-erected tents available*

Aigle Tourisme,Place du Marché 2, 1860 Aigle, Switzerland; Tel:+41(0)24 466 30 00; Email:info@aigle-tourisme.ch; www.alpesvaudoises.ch/en/stories/aigle

Bex

Sœurs de Saint Maurice - La Pelouse,Route de Chiètres 27, 1880 Bex, Switzerland; Tel:+41(0) 24 463 04 50; Email:accueil@lapelouse.ch; www.lapelouse.ch/; Price:B

B&B - Siegenthaler[Rosemarie & Fritz Siegenthaler],Avenue de la Gare 22, 1880 Bex, Switzerland; Tel:+41(0)24 463 27 81; Email:f.siegenthaler@theswissmail.ch; bnb.ch; Price:A

stage 45   Villeneuve to Saint-Maurice

Les Evouettes
⚠ **Camping des Ravers**, Route des Ravers 25, 1897 Les Evouettes, Switzerland; Tel:+41(0)24 481 65 03; camping.ch; Price:C; *Open April to October*

Monthey
🏠 **Chambre d'Hôtes - Chez Francoise**, Chemin D'arche 47, 1870 Monthey, Switzerland; Tel: +41(0)79 256 71 87; Email:froll2104@gmail.com; www.monthey-tourisme.ch; Price:B; *Excludes breakfast*

🏠 **Chambre d'Hôtes - Chez Laurence**, Avenue de la Gare 57, 1870 Monthey, Switzerland; Tel:+41(0)24 472 28 83; +41(0)79 376 17 66; Email:lvm@netplus.ch; www.montheytourisme.ch; Price:B; *Excludes breakfast*

🛏 **Hôtel - des Cheminots**, Rue du Closillon 1, 1870 Monthey, Switzerland; Tel: +41(0)24 471 22 08; Email:info@hoteldescheminots.com; www.hoteldescheminots.com; Price:A

🛏 **Hôtel - de la Gare**, Avenue de la Gare 60, 1870 Monthey, Switzerland; Tel:+41(0)24 471 93 93; Email:info@hotelgaremonthey.com; www.hotelgaremonthey.com; Price:A

ℹ **Office du Tourisme**, Place Centrale 3, 1870 Monthey, Switzerland; Tel:+41(0)24 475 79 63; Email:tourisme@monthey.ch; www.monthey-tourisme.ch

Ollon
🏠 **Chambre d'Hôtes - Abbaye de Salaz**, Route de l'Abbaye 15, 1867 Ollon, Switzerland; Tel:+41(0)24 499 10 48; +41(0)79 586 38 32; Email:vin@abbaye-de-salaz.ch; www.abbaye-de-salaz.ch; Price:B; *Former abbey of Saint Maurice*

🏠 **B&B - The Traditional**[Mme Pauline Weber], Chemin du Collège 25, 1867 Ollon, Switzerland; Tel:+41(0)24 499 19 55; +41(0)79 848 83 16; Email:pweber273@gmail.com; www.ollon.ch/N380/hebergement-restauration.html; Price:A

Saint-Maurice
🛏 **Hôtellerie Foyer Franciscain**, Antoine de Quartery 1, 1890 Saint-Maurice, Switzerland; Tel:+41(0)24 486 11 11; www.hotellerie-franciscaine.ch; Price:A

🛏 **Abbaye de Saint-Maurice**, Avenue d'Agaune 15, 1890 Saint-Maurice, Switzerland; Tel:+41(0)24 486 04 04; Email:pelerinage@stmaurice.ch; www.abbaye-stmaurice.ch; Price:A

🛏 **Hôtel - la Dent-du-Midi**, Avenue du Simplon 1, 1890 Saint-Maurice, Switzerland; Tel:+41(0)24 485 12 09; Email:dentdumidi@torrente.ch; hotel-restaurant-dent-du-midi.ch; Price:A

ℹ **Office de Tourisme**, Place de la Gare 2, 1890 Saint-Maurice, Switzerland; Tel:+41(0)24 485 40 40; Email:info@saint-maurice.ch; www.saint-maurice.ch

Vouvry
🛏 **Hôtel - Edirol**, Rue de la Praise 32, 1896 Vouvry, Switzerland; Tel:+41(0)24 481 14 16; Email:info@hotel-edirol.ch; www.hotel-edirol.ch; Price:A

Yvorne
🛏 **Auberge - de la Couronne**, Les Maisons Neuves 38, 1853 Yvorne, Switzerland; Tel:+41(0)24 466 94 22; Email:contact@aubergedelacouronne.ch; aubergedelacouronne.ch; Price:A

The Rhône footpath and cycle track

Saint-Maurice to Martigny

stage 46

Length:	17.6km
Ascent:	1061m
Descent:	1025m
Canterbury	1172km
Col Grand Saint Bernard:	67km

Amphitheatre - Martigny

Route: the stage from Saint-Maurice to Martigny follows the western side of the Rhône valley on a mix of woodland tracks and quiet roads.

After crossing the ridge in the Bois Noir the track remains flat to Martigny at the foot of the Grand Saint Bernard Pass.

There are café/bars in Evionnaz, La Balmaz and Vernayaz.

Martigny offers a full range of facilities and transport connections to Aosta.

The Gaulish name of the settlement in the 1st century BC was either Octodurus or Octodurum. Octodurus was conquered by the Roman Republic in 57 BC, in order to protect the strategically important pass of Poeninus (now known as the Great St. Bernard Pass). A restored Roman amphitheatre, temples, citizen living quarters, and thermal baths can be still be seen in Martigny today.

An episcopal See was established in Martigny in the 4th century, making the Roman Catholic Diocese of Sion the oldest bishopric in what is now Switzerland. There are no records of the town during the early medieval period, but in the Middle Ages, it took Martin of Tours as its patron saint, and became known by the German name of Martinach. The church of Martigny, presumably at the site of the ancient cathedral, was consecrated to St. Mary in 1177, and to Notre-Dame-des-Champs in 1420. Martigny was placed under the protection of the House of Savoy in 1351 and its citizens were granted a degree of autonomy, but in the 1840s, Martigny was the stage of a confrontation between the liberal-radical Young Switzerland and the conservative Old Switzerland movements, culminating in the Battle at the Trient of 21 May 1844. As a result, the town was split into the independent municipalities of Martigny-Ville, Charrat, Martigny-Bourg and Martigny-Combe, but this was reversed in the 20th century to become the unified community we find today.

Martigny is surrounded by vineyards and orchards, because the climate is ideal for growing strawberries, apricots, grapes and asparagus.

stage 46   Saint-Maurice to Martigny

(0.0) From the abbey take place du Parvis and then turn right beside the town hall[Grand Rue] **(0.4)** At the end of the road, turn right on avenue de la Gare and continue past the railway station keeping the railway tracks on your right **(1.0)** At the T-junction, turn right and cross the railway bridge. Then take the second turning on the left**(1.7)** At the crossroads following the bridge over the waterway, bear right[Direction Vérolliez] **(2.0)** Immediately before reaching the car park in Vérolliez, turn left on the tarmac and pass behind the Maison de la Famille. Bear left and keep the woods to your right. **(2.5)** Turn left between the fields and turn right when you reach the road**(2.7)** Turn left and pass the industrial

Cascade de Pisse-Vache

buildings on your left[Direction Les Emonets] **(3.9)** At the end of the road, turn left and then right to follow the track through the woods[Direction Evionnaz]**(4.5)** Continue straight ahead[Take the footbridge over the gorge] **(5.0)** At the T-junction with the road, turn left[Direction Evionnaz]**(5.4)** Turn right to proceed parallel to the motorway**(5.9)** At the crossroads go straight ahead[Downhill] **(6.0)** Bear right and continue down the main

Saint-Maurice to Martigny — stage 46

street of **Evionnaz**[Church on right]**(6.4)**At the T-junction turn left[Cycle Route n°1]**(6.4)**Turn right onto a small road, towards the hill-side[Direction Martigny] **(8.6)**Turn right at the crossroads on the entry to **La Balmaz**, stay close to the mountain-side on your right[Direction Martigny]**(9.0)**Turn right onto the main road beside the railway track[Cycle track towards rocky outcrop]**(9.6)**Take the right fork and pass through the village of Miéville before returning to the main road **(10.0)**Immediately after passing the power plant, turn right on the road and follow the track at the foot of the cliff[Towards the waterfall - Cascade de Pisse-Vache]**(10.6)**Bear left to cross the railway track. The track bears right and recrosses the railway **(11.2)**Turn left, cross the bridge and then turn right[Towards the hydro-station] **(12.3)**At the T-junction with the main road in **Vernayaz**, turn right towards Martigny[Pass the Victoria bar]**(12.9)**Just before the garage, turn right onto the track and continue between the orchards and the foot of the cliffs **(13.7)**At the T-junction, turn right and then left **(16.1)**After passing the hydro-station, go straight ahead on the road towards Martigny[Rue de la Bâtiaz]**(16.5)**As the road turns left, bear right on the tarmac track[Continue at the foot of the cliffs] **(16.7)**At the T-junction, turn right and enter Martigny over the river bridge[Tower high on the hilltop to the right]**(17.0)**After crossing the bridge, turn right and then left on rue de la Dranse **(17.2)**Bear right towards the school and diagonally cross the park**(17.5)**Exit the park and bear left[Rue du Manoir]**(17.6)**Arrive at **Martigny** centre in place Centrale[Tourist office to the left on rue de la Gare]

Forêt du Bois-Noir

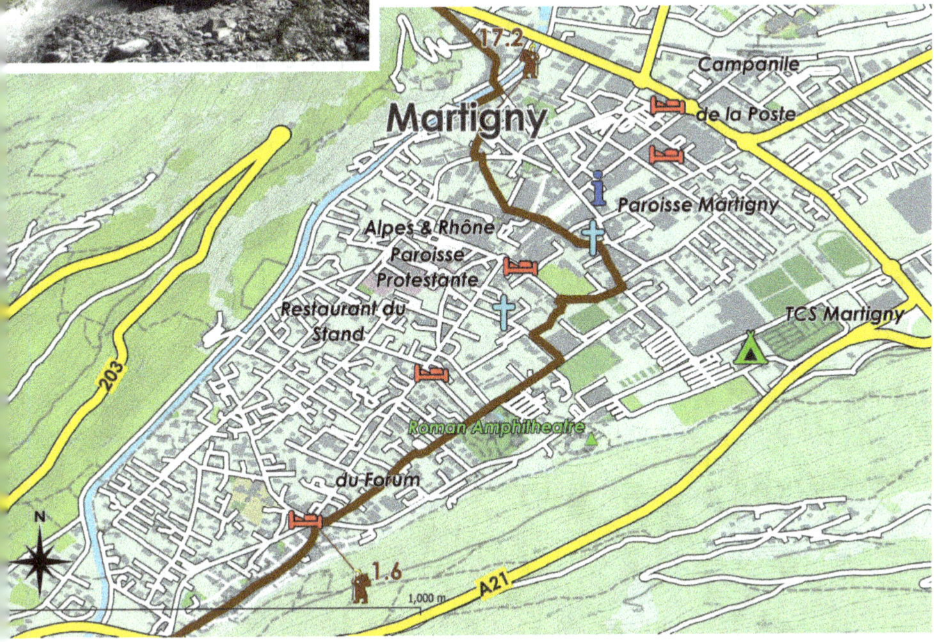

stage 46

Saint-Maurice to Martigny

Accommodation and Tourist Information

La-Balmaz-Evionnaz
🏠 **Restaurant and B&B - le Pernollet**,Rue des Échelles 52, 1902 La-Balmaz-Evionnaz, Switzerland; Tel:+41(0)24 485 32 00; Email:infoproprive@gmail.com; cafe-pernollet.ch; Price:A

Martigny
✝ **Paroisse Martigny**,Rue de l'Hôtel-de-Ville 5, 1920 Martigny, Switzerland; Tel:+41(0)27 722 22 82; Email:secretariat@paroissemartigny.ch; www.paroissemartigny.ch; Price:D

✝ **Paroisse Protestante**,Rue d'Oche 3a, 1920 Martigny, Switzerland; Tel:+41(0)27 722 33 52; +41(0)78 654 26 48; Email:paroissep@bluewin.ch; coudedurhone.erev.ch; Price:D

🛏 **Hotel Restaurant - du Stand**,Avenue du Grand-Saint-Bernard 41, 1920 Martigny, Switzerland; Tel:+41(0)27 722 15 06; Email:mail@hoteldustand.ch; www.hoteldustand.ch; Price:B

🛏 **Hôtel - du Forum**,Avenue du Grand-Saint-Bernard 72, 1920 Martigny, Switzerland; Tel:+41(0)27 722 18 41; Email:info@hotel-forum.ch; www.hotel-forum.ch; Price:A

🛏 **Hôtel - de la Poste**,Rue de la Poste 8, 1920 Martigny, Switzerland; Tel:+41(0)27 722 14 44; Email:info@hoteldelapostemartigny.ch; hoteldelapostemartigny.ch; Price:A

🛏 **Hôtel - Campanile**,Rue du Leman 15, 1920 Martigny, Switzerland; Tel:+41(0)27 722 27 01; Email:martigny@campanile.com; martigny.campanile.com; Price:A

🛏 **Hôtel - Alpes & Rhône**,Avenue du Grand-Saint-Bernard 11, 1920 Martigny, Switzerland; Tel:+41(0)27 722 17 17; Email:info@alpes-rhone.ch; www.alpes-rhone.ch; Price:A; *Can arrange baggage transfer from St Maurice and to Orsières with advanced notice*

⛺ **Camping TCS - Martigny**,Rue du Levant 68, 1920 Martigny, Switzerland; Tel:+41(0)27 722 45 44; Email:camping.martigny@tcs.ch; www.campingtcs.ch; Price:C; *Pods and 3 dormitories available*

ℹ **Office de Tourisme**,Avenue de la Gare 6, 1920 Martigny, Switzerland; Tel:+41(0)27 720 49 49; Email:info@martigny.com; www.martigny.com

Saint-Maurice
🛏 **Motel - Hôtel Garni Inter-Alp**,Route Cantonale 3, 1890 Saint-Maurice, Switzerland; Tel:+41(0)24 485 37 47; Email:info@interalp.ch; www.interalp.ch; Price:A

⛺ **Camping du Bois-Noir**,Route Cantonale 7, 1890 Saint-Maurice, Switzerland; Tel:+41(0)27 767 12 52; +41(0)79 321 99 21; Email:info@camping-duboisnoir.ch; www.campingduboisnoir.ch; Price:C; *Open April 1 to October 30 mobile homes also available*

Vernayaz
🛏 **Hotel Restaurant - de la Gare**,Rue de la Gare 1, 1904 Vernayaz, Switzerland; Tel:+41 27 764 11 76; Email:alicemoreira1970@gmail.com; www.hotelvernayaz.ch; Price:B

Cow fighting held each autumn in the Martignyy amphitheatre

Christof Berger

Martigny to Orsières

stage 47

Length:	20.7km
Ascent:	1670m
Descent:	1258m
Canterbury	1190km
Col Grand Saint Bernard:	49km

The lower Grand Saint Bernard Paul Usburg

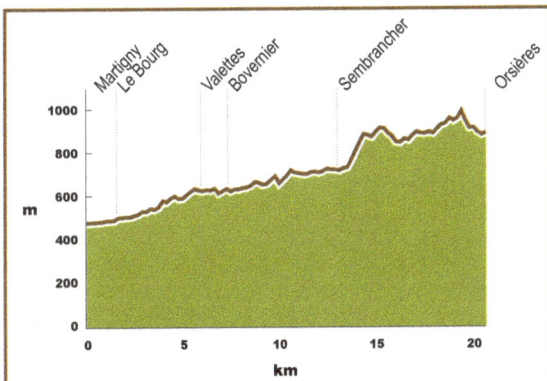

Route: the road over the Grand Saint Bernard Pass is normally cleared of snow and the road barriers (beyond the tunnel entrance to the south of Bourg-Saint-Pierre) opened between early June and late September each year. However, the weather in the high Alps is unpredictable and so it is vital to verify conditions before your ascent. In the event that the pass is closed, there is a bus from Martigny, via Sembrancher, Orsières, Bourg St Pierre and the road tunnel to Etroubles and Aosta. At the time of writing the service has just resumed following a period of suspension - www.tmrsa.ch. A train service is available from Martigny to Bovernier, Sembrancher and Orsières or via Brig and Milan to Aosta.

While the trail is long to the summit it is also progressive offering few difficulties in good weather. The route follows often narrow paths on the wooded hillsides but remains roughly parallel to the summit road, offering a number of "outs" if weather conditions deteriorate.

You can break the stage from Martigny to Orsières at Sembrancher which has both cafés and shops.

At an altitude of 900 metres, Orsières is home to a number of architectural treasures, the undisputable jewel in the crown being the church and its bell tower. Dedicated to Saint Nicolas, it was built in 1895 on the site of two known former churches: the first built between 1177 and 1296, the second consecrated in 1497. Orsiéres is also known for the medicinal and aromatic plants grown on its surrounding slopes, and used to make herbal teas, or in the manufacture of beauty and healthcare products.

stage 47 — Martigny to Orsières

(0.0) From place Centrale, head south-east on rue de l'Hôtel-de-Ville and rue de Octodure **(0.3)** Turn right towards the sports ground [Keep the football field as close as possible on your left and skirt the ice-hockey stadium - Forum d'Octodure. At the junction with rue du Forum, turn right] **(1.6)** At the roundabout, take the exit to **le Bourg (2.1)** At the roundabout, continue straight ahead direction Grand St Bernard [Church to the right just before roundabout] **(2.4)** Just before river bridge, turn left direction Orsières [Pass a picnic area on the right and the railway on the left] **(2.5)** Pass through the car park and turn left [Take the flight of steps] **(3.4)** Cross the railway and turn right **(3.8)** Turn left after passing under the railway **(3.9)** Turn sharp right to go up a flight of steps **(4.4)** Take left fork **(4.7)** Take the right fork and descend towards the river. Take the bridge over the river and pass under the rail-

La Dranse

way before climbing through the woods towards the main road **(5.3)** On the south side of the main road, at the end of the small road - le Borgeaud, take the foot bridge and immediately turn right [Pass the petrol station on your left] **(5.5)** Bear left and right to skirt the ENI office building and continue on the straight road ahead [Rue de l'Oléoduc] **(6.0)** At the crossroads in **Valettes**, turn left and then right on the elevated road [Rue Principale] **(6.5)** Take the lower road and pass under the highway and the railway [Continue beside the Bovernier railway station] **(7.1)** Turn right to go under the road bridge [Pédestre sign, rue Principale] **(7.3)** At the crossroads, continue straight ahead [Rue de l'Eglise] **(7.4)** Beside the church in **Bovernier**, turn left and then right **(7.7)** At the junction with main road turn right [Marbrerie on right] **(8.0)** Just before the main

236

Martigny to Orsières   stage 47

road bends to the right, bear right on the small tarmac road[No Through Road]**(8.3)**Turn right onto a grass track[Route du Cleusuit] **(10.3)**Continue on the grass track **(12.6)** Turn left over a railway bridge and then bear right on rue de la Gravenne**(13.1)**Turn right at the crossroads in the centre of **Sembrancher** on rue Amédée IV**(13.2)**At the T-junction, turn right direction Grand St Bernard**(13.4)**Turn left and then right and right again to pass under the railway **(13.6)**Turn left and climb the hill on the part made road. Bear right towards the hairpin on the larger road**(13.8)**Beside the hairpin bend take the higher of the tracks to the right[Railway station below on the right]**(14.5)**Bear left on the partially made road **(14.9)**At the road junction, take the smaller road to the right**(15.3)**In place de Village in La Garde, take the left and lower fork[Farm below] **(16.7)**Take the right fork: Note:- for La Catogne Gîte and Restaurant, take the left fork to Douay[Follow the power lines] **(18.0)**At the T-junction with the recycling centre on your right, turn right and skirt the recycling centre, keeping it to your left**(18.2)**At the junction with a broader road and with the entrance to the recycling centre to your left, turn right and follow the road uphill**(18.3)**Turn sharp left on the tarmac road[Towards the trees]**(18.6)**At the junction in the tracks turn right and pass under the power lines **(19.1)**Take the right fork into the trees**(19.7)**At the junction, after crossing the gorge, turn left on the broad track and descend towards Orsières **(20.3)**Carefully cross the railway tracks and continue on the road as it bears left**(20.5)**At the junction with Route du Saint Bernard, cross the parking area and take the narrow Ruille du Betty between apartment buildings to your right[Pass water trough on your left]**(20.5)**Return to Route du Saint Bernard and bear right across the river bridge[Towards the Church]**(20.7)**Arrive at **Orsières (L)** beside the church[Place de l' Eglise]

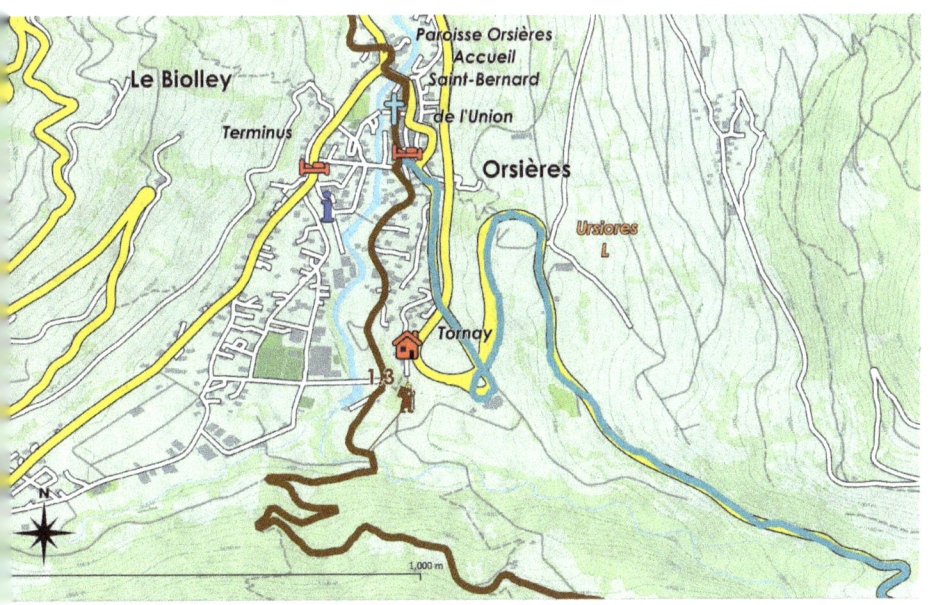

237

stage 47 — Martigny to Orsières

Accommodation and Tourist Information

Orsières

Paroisse Orsières - Accueil Saint-Bernard, Place de l'Eglise 1, 1937 Orsières, Switzerland; Tel:+41(0)27 783 11 44; Email:secretariat@paroisses-entremont.ch; www.paroisses-entremont.ch/via-francigena; Price:C

B&B - Tornay [Marie-Claude Tornay], Route de Seneire 16, 1937 Orsières, Switzerland; Tel:+41(0)27 783 10 12; +41(0)79 259 19 25; +41(0)79 582 70 35; Email:mtornay@drasnet.ch; www.bnb.ch; Price:A

Hôtel - de l'Union, Rue de la Commune, 1937 Orsières, Switzerland; Tel:+41(0)27 783 11 38; Email:chezjo@st-bernard.ch; www.chezjo.ch; Price:A

Hôtel - Terminus, Route de la Gare 25, 1937 Orsières, Switzerland; Tel:+41(0)27 552 11 00; Email:info@terminus-orsieres.ch; terminus-orsieres.ch; Price:A; *Dormitory beds also available*

Gîte and Restaurant - Le Catogne, La Douay 12, 1937 Orsières, Switzerland; Tel:+41(0)27 783 12 30; Email:le.catogne@outlook.com; www.giteserge.ch; Price:A; *Close to La Douay railway station*

Office du Tourisme, Route de la Gare 34, 1937 Orsières, Switzerland; Tel:+41(0)27 775 23 81; Email:info@saint-bernard.ch; www.saint-bernard.ch

Sembrancher

Gîte - les 3 Collines, Route de la Garde 5, 1933 Sembrancher, Switzerland; Tel: +41(0)79 657 20 97; +41(0)78 744 62 07; Email:les3collines@gmail.com; giteles3collines.ch; Price:B

Orsières

Orsières to Col-Grand-St-Bernard

stage 48

Length:	27.4km
Ascent:	3302m
Descent:	1712m
Canterbury	1210km
Col Grand Saint Bernard:	29km

Approaching the summit

Route: from Orsières to Col-Grand-St-Bernard footpath 70 is generally off-road making a steady, but continuous climb with short steeper sections.

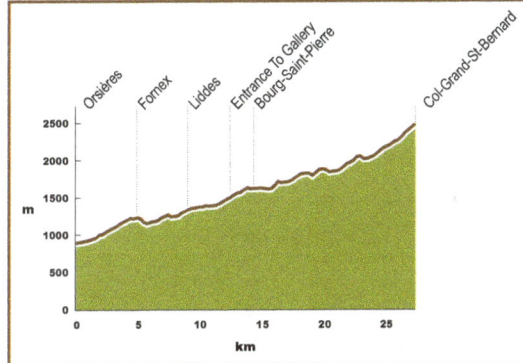

The route passes through the intermediate villages of Liddes and Bourg-Saint-Pierre where food and lodging are possible.

It is essential to verify the weather conditions on the pass before leaving Orsières and if possible en route. Public transport or the Alternate Route using the main road should be considered if there is significant snow or low cloud.

Options are available to divert from route 70 to the main road in the event of bad weather during the climb.

The hospice is open all year, but if you are tempted to make the crossing when the road is closed ensure that you have appropriate equipment. Snow-shoes can be hired in Orsières.

Cyclists are recommended to use the Alternate Road Route as there are a number of barriers that will be difficult to cross and narrow sections of trail. However, cyclists must be aware that the road is used by heavy trucks and passes through often poorly lit galleries. Great care is needed and it is suggested that a very early start is made to avoid as much traffic as possible. That said, the climb is a popular weekend outing for cyclists from both sides of the border.

The Great St Bernard Pass is the most ancient route through the Western Alps, crossing at 2,473 metres and one of the highest of the Alpine frontier passes. Named after Saint Bernard of Menthon, who founded a hospice at its summit in the 11th century, the Great-St-Bernard Pass has been in use since the Bronze Age, with tribes and armies tramping their way to and fro for millennia since. In 390 BC, a Gaulish army crossed to defeat Rome and from the earliest times ordinary people used the pass to trade goods between northern Europe and Italy.

Hannibal's famous crossing of the Alps in 217 BC is indelibly associated with the Great-St-Bernard Pass, though there's little actual evidence of it actually having taken place.

stage 48   Orsières to Col-Grand-St-Bernard

(0.0)Leave the southern facade of the church on the narrow ruelle de lÉglise[Between apartment buildings with the river parallel on your right](0.2)At the road junction turn right and then left before reaching the river bridge. Note:- to take the road route turn

Bourg St.Bernard	1 h 10	Barrage de Toules 1730 m
La Pierre	1 h 30	
Col du Gd.St.Bernard	3 h	
La Letta	30 min	
Col du Névé de la Rousse	4 h	
Ferret	6 h 30	

left[Keep the river to your right](0.7)Stay on the tarmac road and bear right(1.0)Fork left[Weir on the right] (1.3)Turn right to cross over the bridge[RP1993 on bridge](1.3)

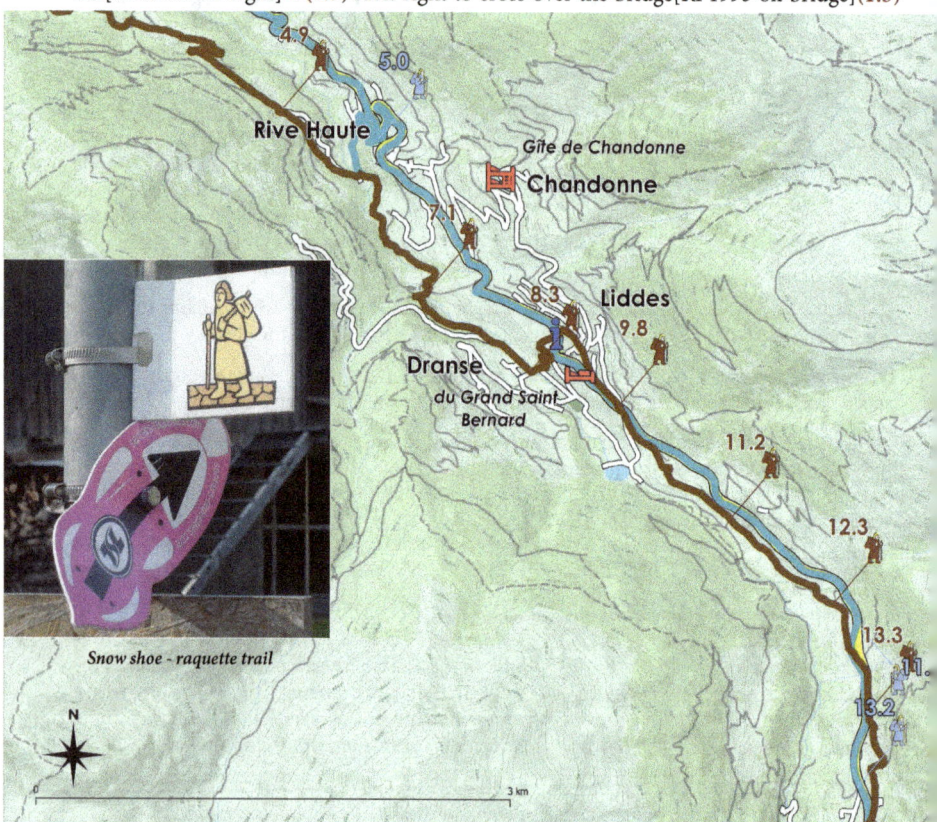

Snow shoe - raquette trail

Orsières to Col-Grand-St-Bernard stage 48

Bear right uphill**(1.6)**Bear left uphill 🚶 **(4.9)**At the fork above Fornex bear right. Note:- cyclists may prefer to bear left on the roadway for an easy descent to the river crossing[Towards village]**(4.9)**Take the right fork[Pass between the houses in **Fornex**]**(5.2)**Bear left down the hill towards the woods on a narrow track**(5.7)**As the track emerges onto the road turn right[Towards the river]**(5.7)**Cross the bridge, turn right direction Liddes. Note:- the track ahead is extremely difficult for cyclists who should turn left and climb the hill to join the on-road route[Follow narrowing path with the river on the right] 🚶 **(7.1)**The narrow track intersects with broad track, turn right to cross river and then turn left on the track through woods**(8.0)**At the junction with broad track turn left[Towards the village of Drance] 🚶 **(8.3)**At the T-junction in Drance turn left and then on the apex of the right hand bend take the path between the farm buildings steeply uphill[Cross the river]**(8.7)**At the T-junction with the road, turn left**(9.0)**At the junction with the main road, cross the road, bear left across the parking area and then bear right through the narrow road between the buildings**(9.0)**At the T-junction, turn right and pass through the centre of **Liddes** 🚶 **(9.8)**At the junction with the main road, cross over and take the small road. Then immediately take the left fork[Direction Palasuit]**(10.6)**After passing the farm of Palasuit on your right, cross the river and continue on the grass track across the fields 🚶 **(11.2)**At the junction with the par-

tially made road, continue straight ahead[Parallel to power lines] 🚶 **(12.3)**Take the right fork, keep the main road on your left and the power lines on your right**(12.7)**Cross the main road and continue on the track with the main road to your right[Towards the avalanche gallery] 🚶 **(13.3)**At the end of the avalanche gallery, pass on the left side of the car park and continue on the grass track[Pass the large farm buildings on your right]**(13.8)**At the T-junction with the broad track, turn right[Pass behind the hotel] 🚶 **(14.4)**Pass under the roadway and continue straight ahead into **Bourg-Saint-Pierre (LXIX)(15.0)**Beside the church bear right, cross the river bridge and immediately take the grass track to the right 🚶 **(15.8)**At the junction with the broad track, turn left[Direction Lac des Toules]**(16.6)**Bear left down the hill 🚶 **(16.9)**Continue straight ahead with the river on the left**(17.2)**Pass the house on your right and then pass through a small wicket gate onto a narrow grass track**(17.8)**Approaching the face of the dam, turn right onto the gravel track 🚶 **(18.2)**Fork left with the reservoir on the left 🚶 **(19.2)**Continue straight ahead on the small track down-

stage 48   Orsières to Col-Grand-St-Bernard

The Col road

hill towards the water[Avoid the track up the hill] 🚶 **(21.6)**Continue straight ahead, direction Col St Bernard. Note:- ahead the route is often blocked by cattle fencing. Cyclists can turn left here over the wooden bridge to regain the on-road route at the upper end of the avalanche gallery**(22.4)**Continue straight ahead[Direction Col St Bernard] 🚶 **(22.9)**Bear left[Towards farm buildings]**(23.0)**Turn left beside the farm buildings[Towards the road] **(23.7)**Turn sharp left towards the road**(23.8)**Turn sharp right onto a path running parallel to the road 🚶 **(24.5)**Cross over the road and continue straight ahead. Note:- even in summer there is often snow and ice on the pathway ahead. If in doubt turn right to follow the road to the summit[Tunnel air vent to the right] 🚶 **(27.4)**Arrive at **Col-Grand-St-Bernard** summit[Hospice to the left]

Orsières to Col-Grand-St-Bernard — stage 48

Road Route to the Summit

Route: the main road passes through enclosed galleries and should be approached with great care. An early start should be considered to minimise the amount of traffic that you will encounter. Traffic conditions normally improve above the tunnel entrance. The road route may be preferred by cyclists, and walkers in difficult weather conditions and has the advantage of easy access to more points of shelter.

Length:	27.3km
Ascent:	3450m
Descent:	1866m

(0.0)Turn left and then keep right to join the main exit road towards the col Grand-Saint-Bernard[Rue de Grand-Saint-Bernard](0.5)Continue straight ahead and continue climbing[Under the road bridges] (5.0)On the crown of the bend to the left, just after passing Fontaine-Dessous, continue straight ahead. Note:- walkers and cyclists join here from the "Official Route"[Road joins from the right] (11.8)Continue straight ahead. Note:- at the **entrance to gallery**, cyclists continue straight ahead, walkers can bear right onto a small track and then bear left crossing over the gallery and rejoining the road beyond the gallery end (13.2)For the summit cyclists will need to continue straight ahead on the road. Note:- to visit Bourg Saint Pierre or to avoid the 4km gallery ahead bear right into the town and join the "Official Route" leading to the barrage (14.5)Continue straight ahead[Entry to avalanche gallery] (20.2)Bear right to leave gallery[Before the tunnel entrance] (22.8)The "Official Route" crosses from the right, continue straight ahead[Towards tunnel air vent] (27.3)Rejoin the "Official Route" at the summit of the Col-Grand-Saint-Bernard[Hospice to the left]

Looking back on Switzerland

stage 48 — Orsières to Col-Grand-St-Bernard

Accommodation and Tourist Information

Bourg-Saint-Pierre

🏠 **Maison Saint-Pierre**[Damien Bernard], 1946 Bourg-Saint-Pierre, Switzerland; Tel: +41(0)79 225 53 06; +41(0)78 814 69 95; Email:alain.michellod@gsbernard.net; www.maisonstpierre.ch; Price:C; *Reduced price with credentials*; **PR**

🛏 **Hospice du Grand-Saint-Bernard**,Situated on the Col summit, 1946 Bourg-Saint-Pierre, Switzerland; Tel:+41(0)27 787 12 36; Email:hospice@gsbernard.com; www.gsbernard.com; Price:B; *Price includes dinner*

✝ **Paroisse**,Rue de l'Eglise, 1946 Bourg-Saint-Pierre, Switzerland; Tel:+41(0)27 783 11 44; www.paroisses-entremont.ch; Price:D

🛏 **Auberge - de l'Hospice**,Situated on the Col summit, 1946 Bourg-St-Pierre, Switzerland; Tel:+41(0)27 787 11 53; Email:info@aubergehospice.ch; www.aubergehospice.ch; Price:A; *Closed for the winter*

🛏 **Hôtel - Restaurant du Crêt**,Route du Gd-Saint-Bernard 33, 1946 Bourg-Saint-Pierre, Switzerland; Tel:+41(0)27 787 11 43; Email:reception@hotel-du-cret.ch; hotel-du-cret.ch; Price:B; *There is also a dormitory*

🛏 **Auberge - les Charmettes**[Gilbert Tornare-Delasoie], 1946 Bourg-Saint-Pierre, Switzerland; Tel:+41(0)27 787 11 50; Email:info@les-charmettes.ch; www.les-charmettes.ch; Price:A; *Price group B in dormitory*

🛏 **Hôtel - au Bivouac-de-Napoléon**,Route du Grand-Saint-Bernard, 1946 Bourg-Saint-Pierre, Switzerland; Tel:+41(0)27 787 11 62; Email:nfo@bivouac.ch; www.bivouac.ch; Price:A

🛏 **Hostel - Petit Vélan**,Rue du Bourg 26, 1946 Bourg-Saint-Pierre, Switzerland; Tel:+41(0)766344193; Email:petitvelan@frilingue.ch; petit-velan.frilingue.ch; Price:A

⛺ **Camping du Grand-Saint-Bernard**, 1946 Bourg-Saint-Pierre, Switzerland; Tel: +41(0)79 370 98 22; Email:reservation@campinggrand-st-bernard.ch; web.facebook.com/CasaDonAngeloCarioni; Price:C; **PR**

Liddes

🏠 **Gîte de Chandonne**,1 rue de la Chapelle, 1945 Liddes, Switzerland; Tel:+41(0)79 302 80 47; Email:gitechaandonne@gmail.com; chandonne.ch; Price:B

🛏 **Hôtel - du Grand Saint Bernard**,Rue du fond de Ville 1, 1945 Liddes, Switzerland; Tel:+41(0)27 783 13 02; Email:info@hotel-gd-st-bernard.ch; www.hotel-gd-st-bernard.ch; Price:A

ℹ **Office de Tourisme - Liddes and Bourg-Saint-Pierre**,Route du Grand-Saint-Bernard, 1945 Liddes, Switzerland; Tel:+41(0)27 775 23 82; Email:liddes@saint-bernard.ch; www.saint-bernard.ch

Saint-Rhémy-en-Bosses

🛏 **Casa Don Angelo Carioni**,Strada Statale 27 del Gran San Bernardo km 30, 11010 Saint-Rhémy-en-Bosses, Switzerland; Tel: +39 3356 012847; Email:alberto.dassisti@gmail.com; www.prodomoimpresasociale.it; Price:C

🛏 **Hotel - Italia**,Grand-Saint-Bernard Pass 2, 11010 Saint-Rhémy-en-Bosses, Switzerland; Tel: +39 0165 780908; +39 0165 74825; +39 3287 896978; Email:info@gransanbernardo.it; www.gransanbernardo.it; Price:A

and now..Italy

Route Comparisons
The Direct Route
The Official Route

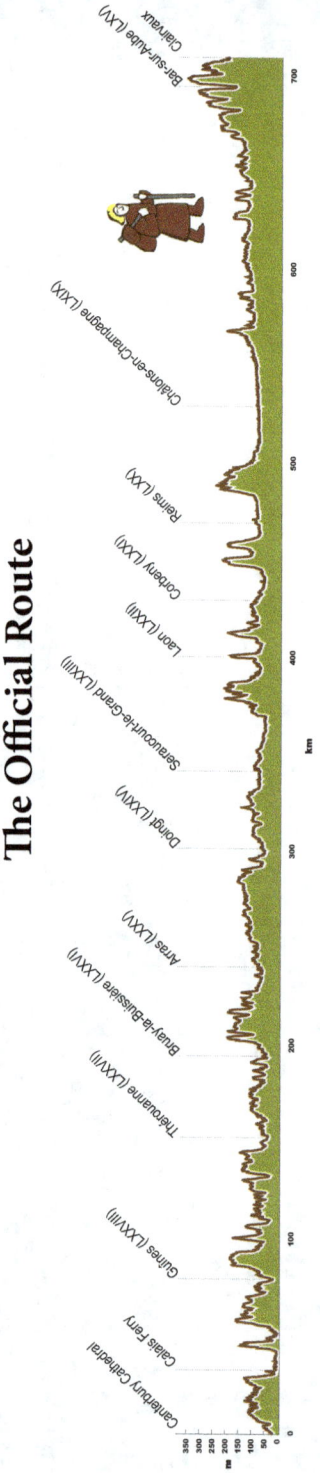

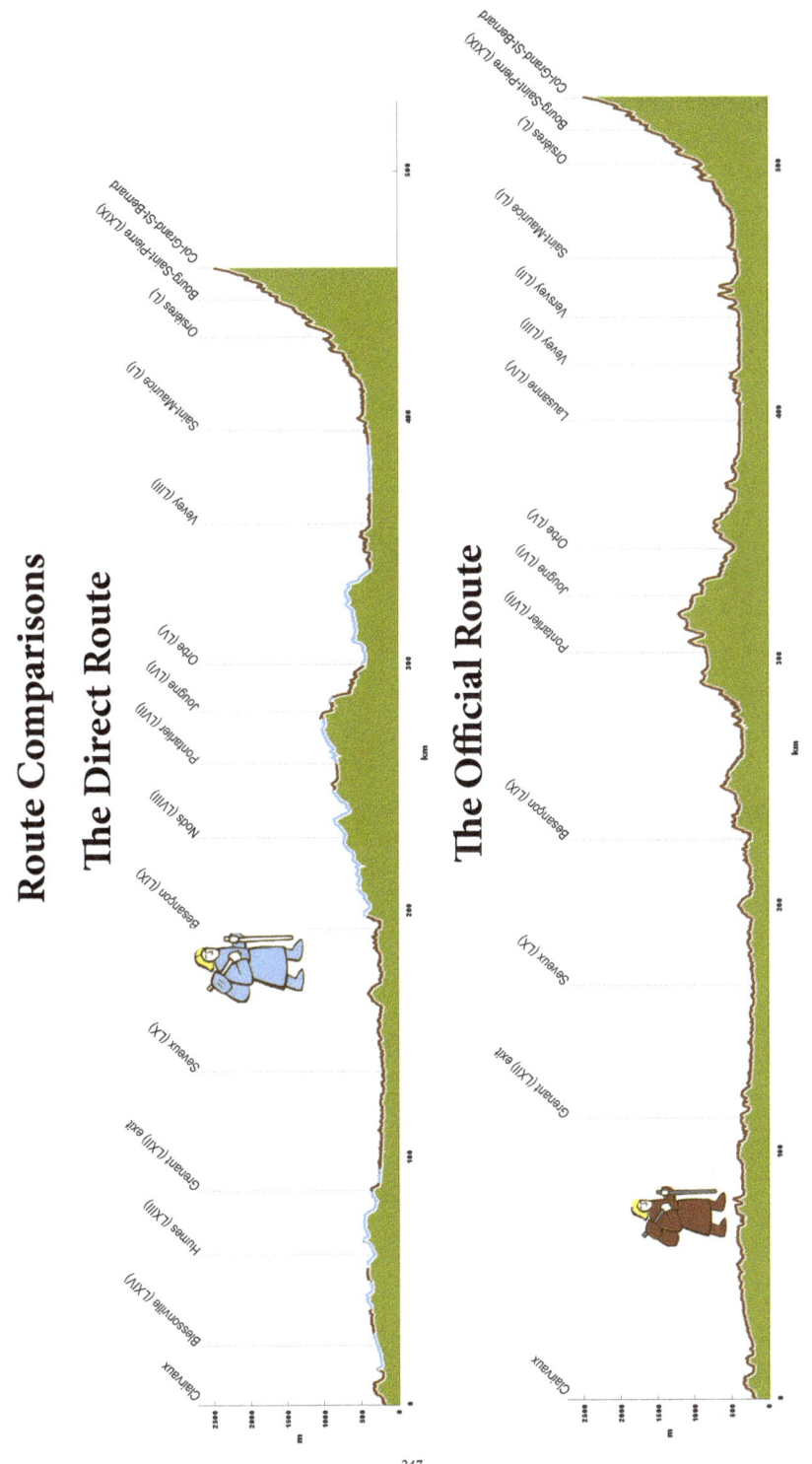

www.ingramcontent.com/pod-product-compliance
Lightning Source LLC
LaVergne TN
LVHW020137080526
838202LV00048B/3958